FIRE PUNCH

3

STORY AND ART BY
TATSUKI FUJIMOTO

CHARACTERS

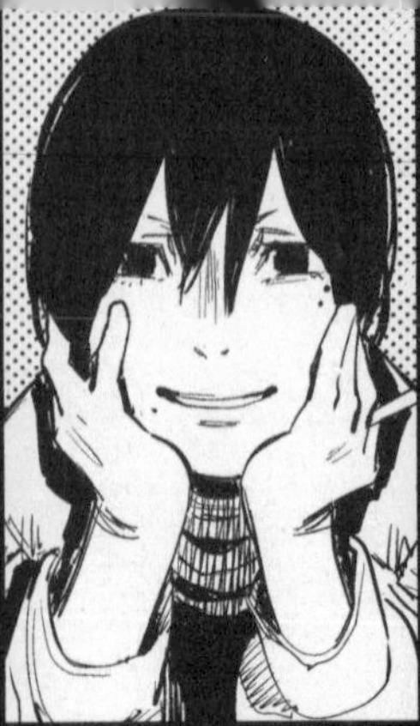

TOGATA

A mysterious girl who is trying to film a movie starring Agni.

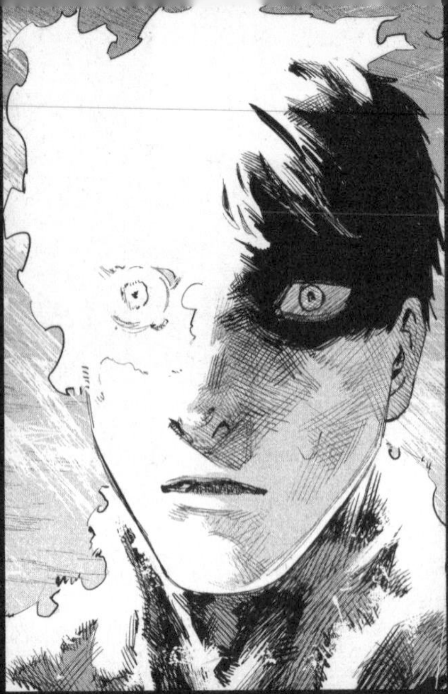

AGNI

A Blessed with the power of regeneration, his little sister is killed by Doma, who engulfs Agni in flames that will never extinguish.

JUDAH

A soldier of Behemdorg who is a Blessed with the power of regeneration.

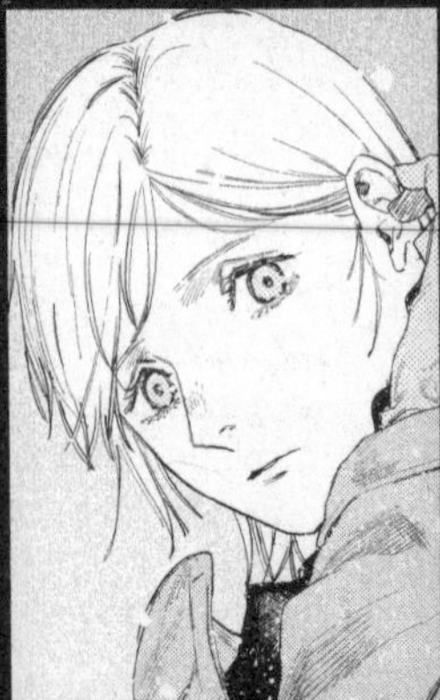

NENETO

A girl taken to Behemdorg with Sun.

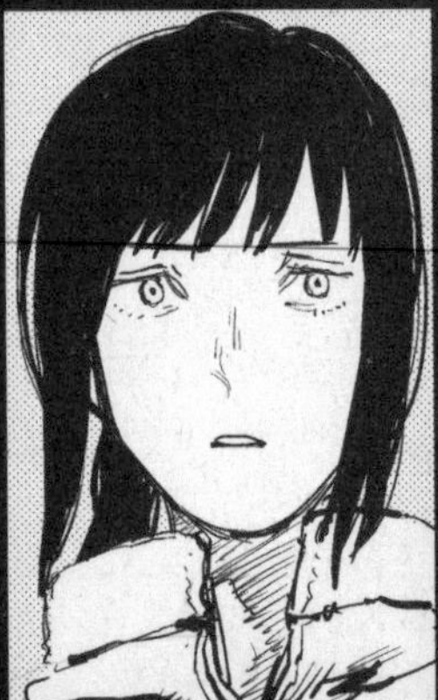

DAIDA

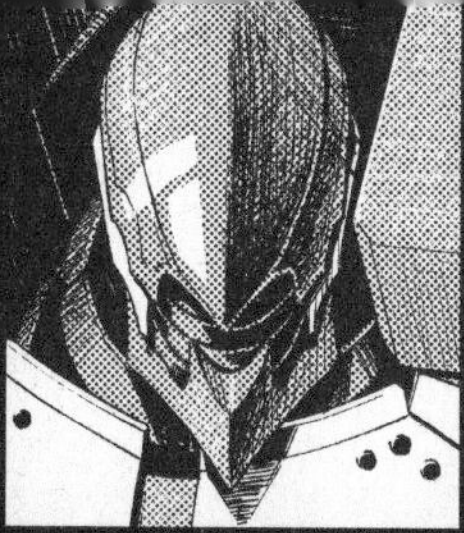

An inmate on Behemdorg's death row who is a Blessed with the ability to increase his muscular strength.

FUGAITAI

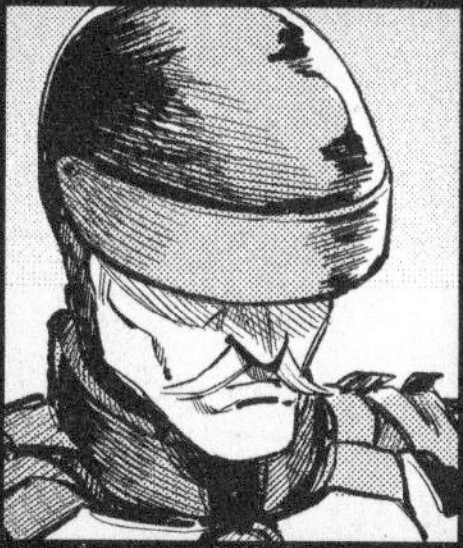

An inmate on Behemdorg's death row who is a Blessed with the ability to manipulate all iron within his field of vision.

KALOU

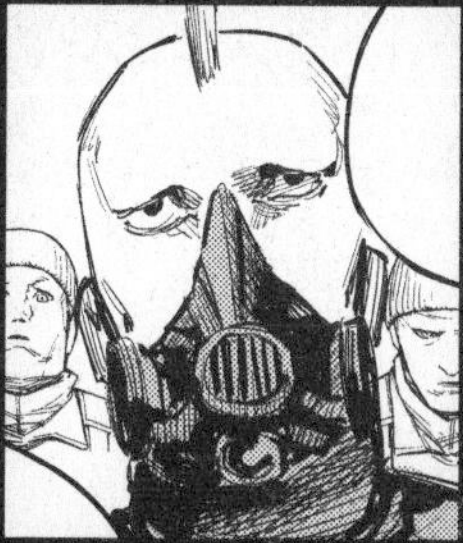

An inmate on Behemdorg's death row who is a Blessed with the ability to manipulate the wind in order to fly.

JACK

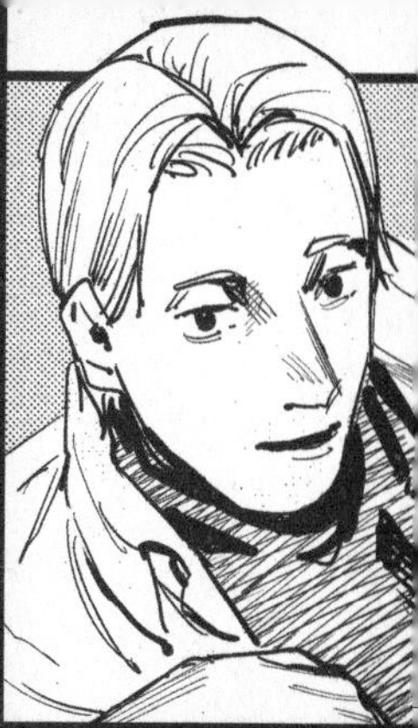

A soldier of Behemdorg who is a Blessed with the power to heal wounds.

SUN

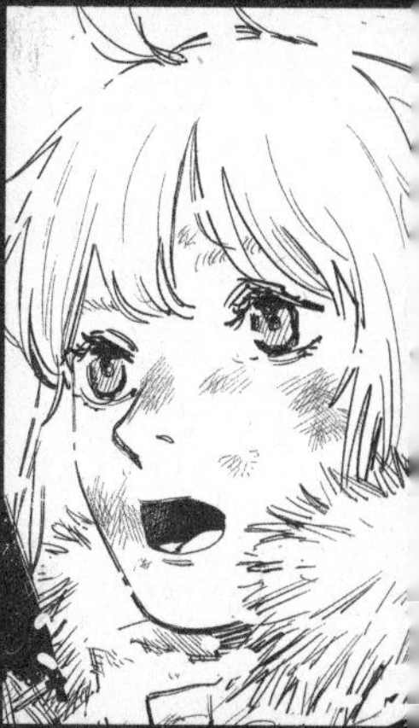

A Blessed with the power of electricity. Agni saves his life.

STORY

Humans who possess unique powers are called Blessed, and two such Blessed, Agni and Luna, live in a world frozen over by the Ice Witch. One day, Agni and Luna's village is attacked by a Behemdorg soldier named Doma, who's a Blessed whose flames won't extinguish until they've completely consumed their fuel. Luna loses her life, but Agni survives, suffering a living hell of trying to master the art of controlling the flames that endlessly consume him. He seeks revenge on Doma, but when the two are reunited, Agni is beheaded and his severed head is taken to be thrown into the sea. During the train ride there, Togata appears and, intent on documenting Agni's life on film, she wipes out the soldiers and frees his head. Free to regenerate, Agni reluctantly takes on the role of Togata's protagonist and vengeful hero. However, the day before Agni's vengeance is to be taken, Togata visits Behemdorg with a secret plan to kill Angi! She meets Doma and is so disenchanted with him that she selects a crew of violent Blessed to act as Doma's

FIRE PUNCH

STORY AND ART BY
TATSUKI FUJIMOTO

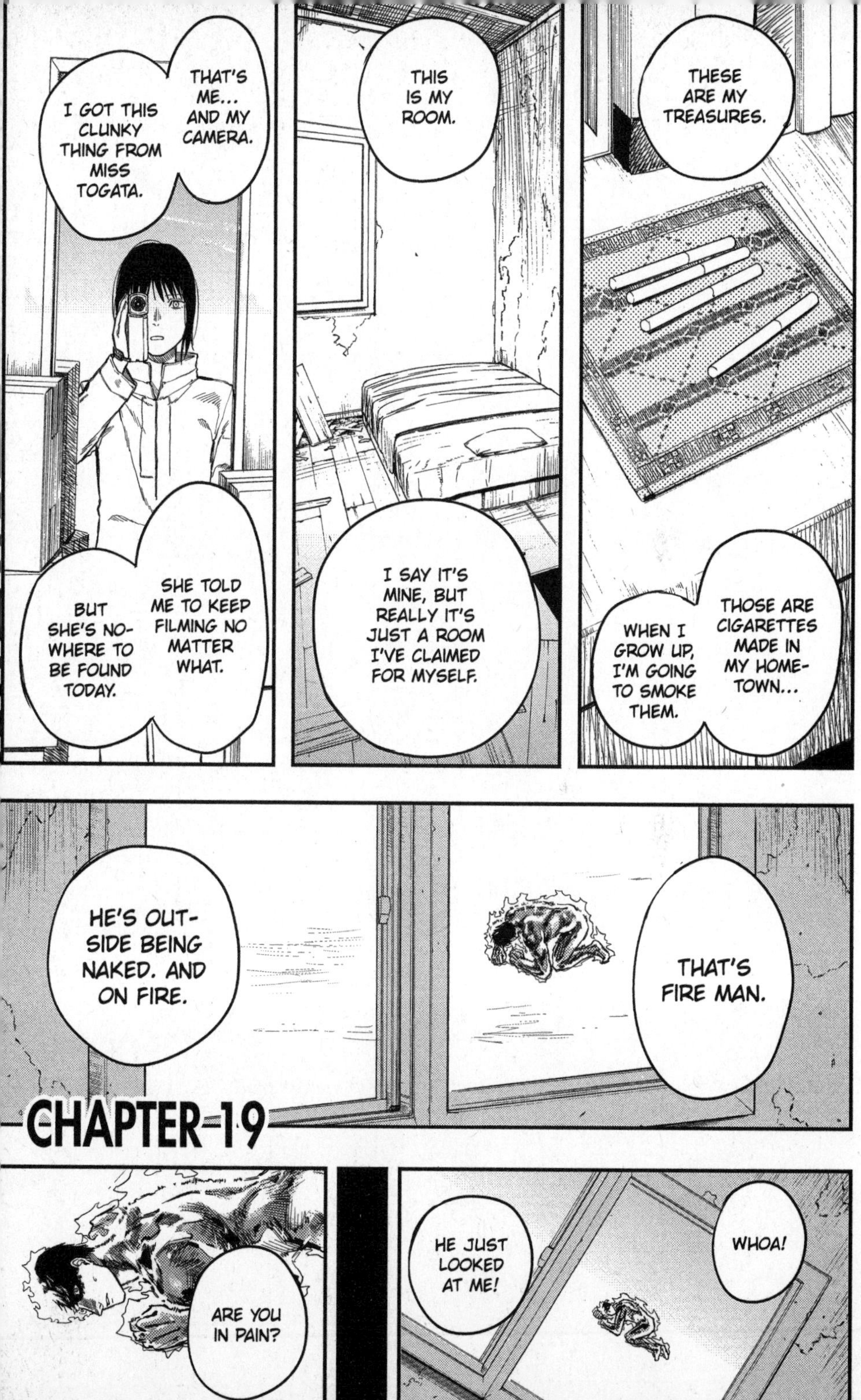
THESE ARE MY TREASURES.
THOSE ARE CIGARETTES MADE IN MY HOME-TOWN...
WHEN I GROW UP, I'M GOING TO SMOKE THEM.
THIS IS MY ROOM.
I SAY IT'S MINE, BUT REALLY IT'S JUST A ROOM I'VE CLAIMED FOR MYSELF.
THAT'S ME... AND MY CAMERA.
I GOT THIS CLUNKY THING FROM MISS TOGATA.
SHE TOLD ME TO KEEP FILMING NO MATTER WHAT.
BUT SHE'S NO-WHERE TO BE FOUND TODAY.
THAT'S FIRE MAN.
HE'S OUT-SIDE BEING NAKED. AND ON FIRE.
CHAPTER-19
WHOA!
HE JUST LOOKED AT ME!
ARE YOU IN PAIN?

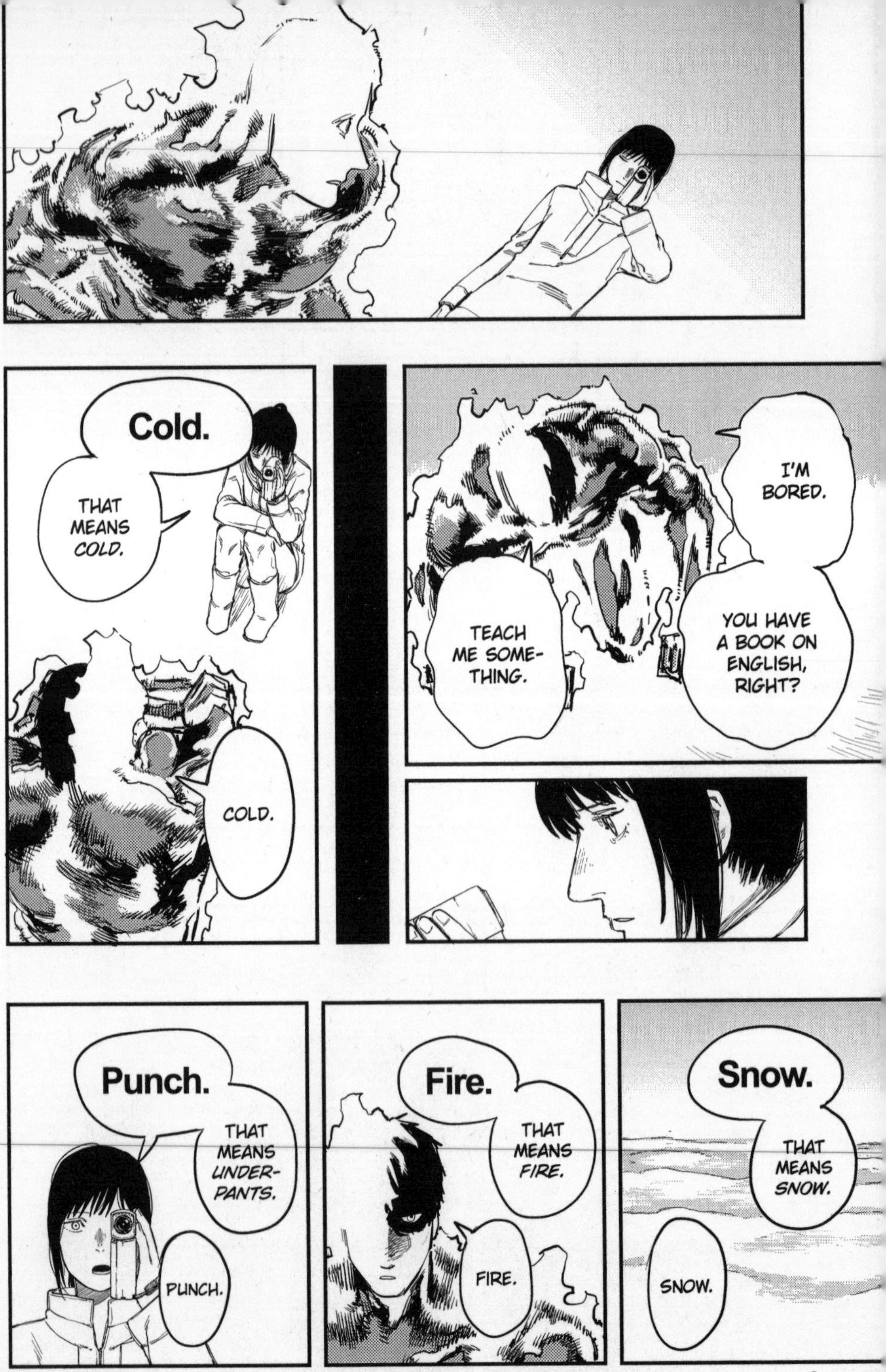
I'M BORED.
YOU HAVE A BOOK ON ENGLISH, RIGHT?
TEACH ME SOME-THING.
Cold.
THAT MEANS COLD.
COLD.
Snow.
THAT MEANS SNOW.
SNOW.
Fire.
THAT MEANS FIRE.
FIRE.
Punch.
THAT MEANS UNDER-PANTS.
PUNCH.

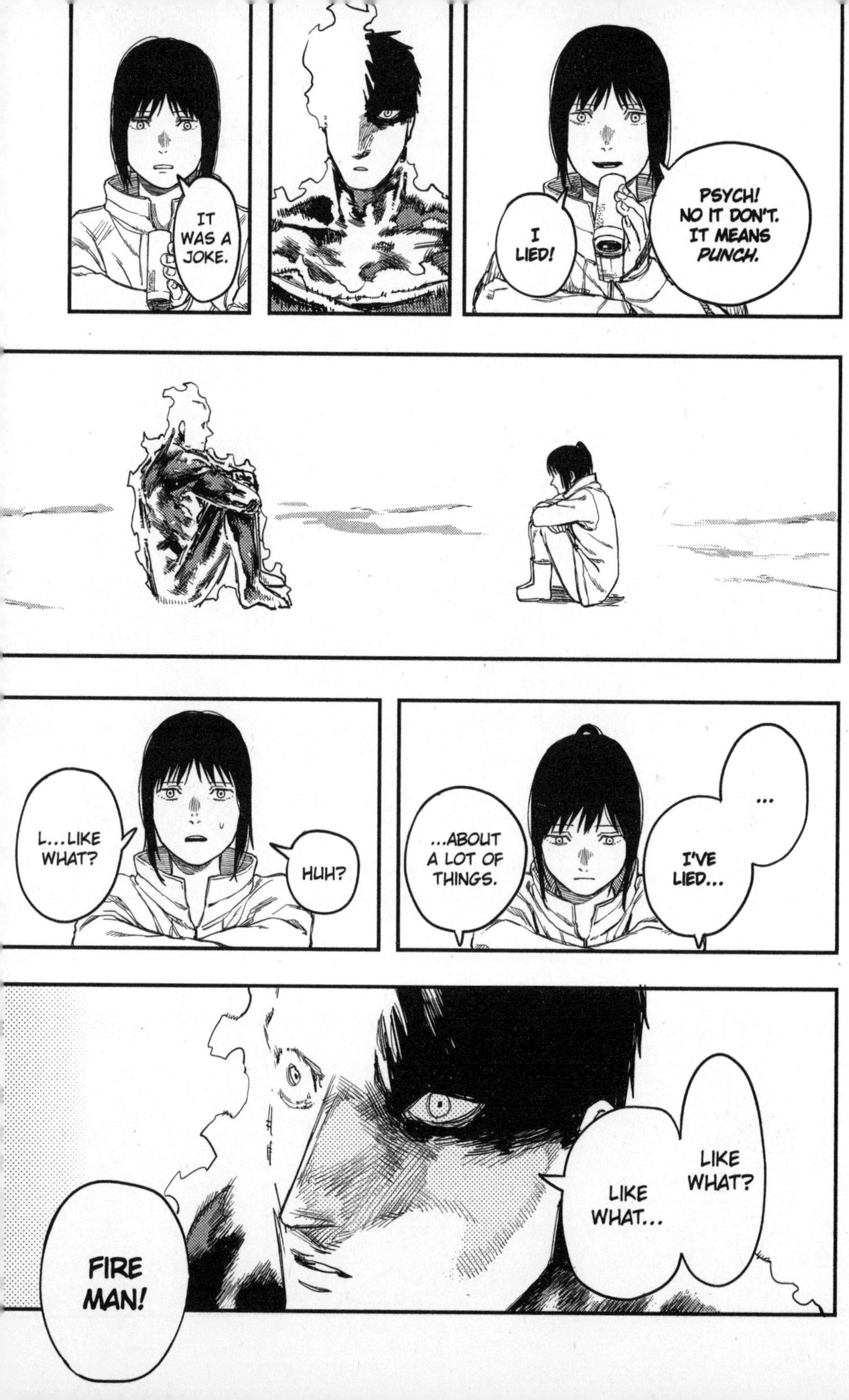
PSYCH! NO IT DON'T. IT MEANS *PUNCH.*
I LIED!
IT WAS A JOKE.
...
I'VE LIED...
...ABOUT A LOT OF THINGS.
HUH?
L...LIKE WHAT?
LIKE WHAT?
LIKE WHAT...
FIRE MAN!

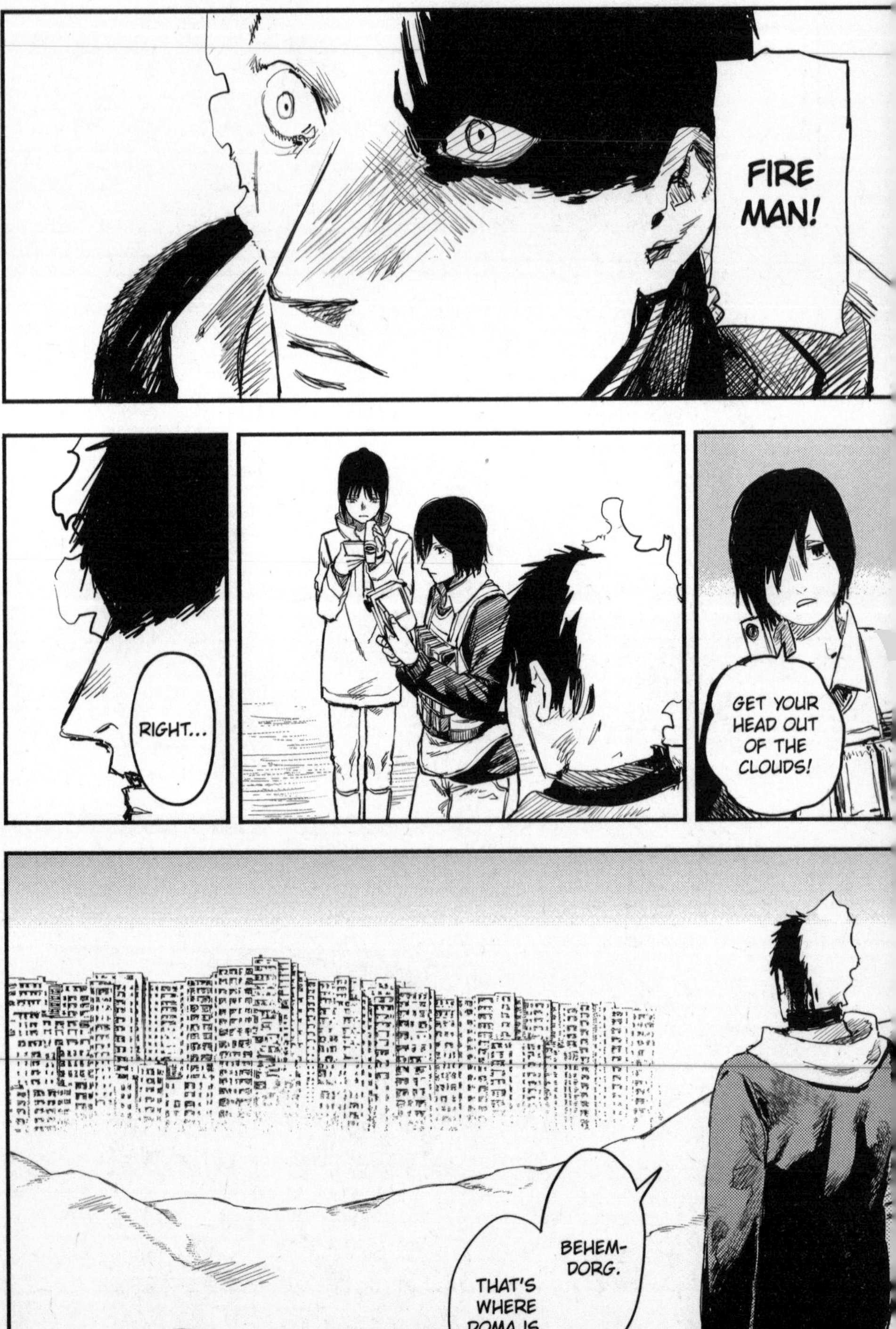
FIRE MAN!
GET YOUR HEAD OUT OF THE CLOUDS!
RIGHT...
BEHEM-DORG.
THAT'S WHERE DOMA IS.

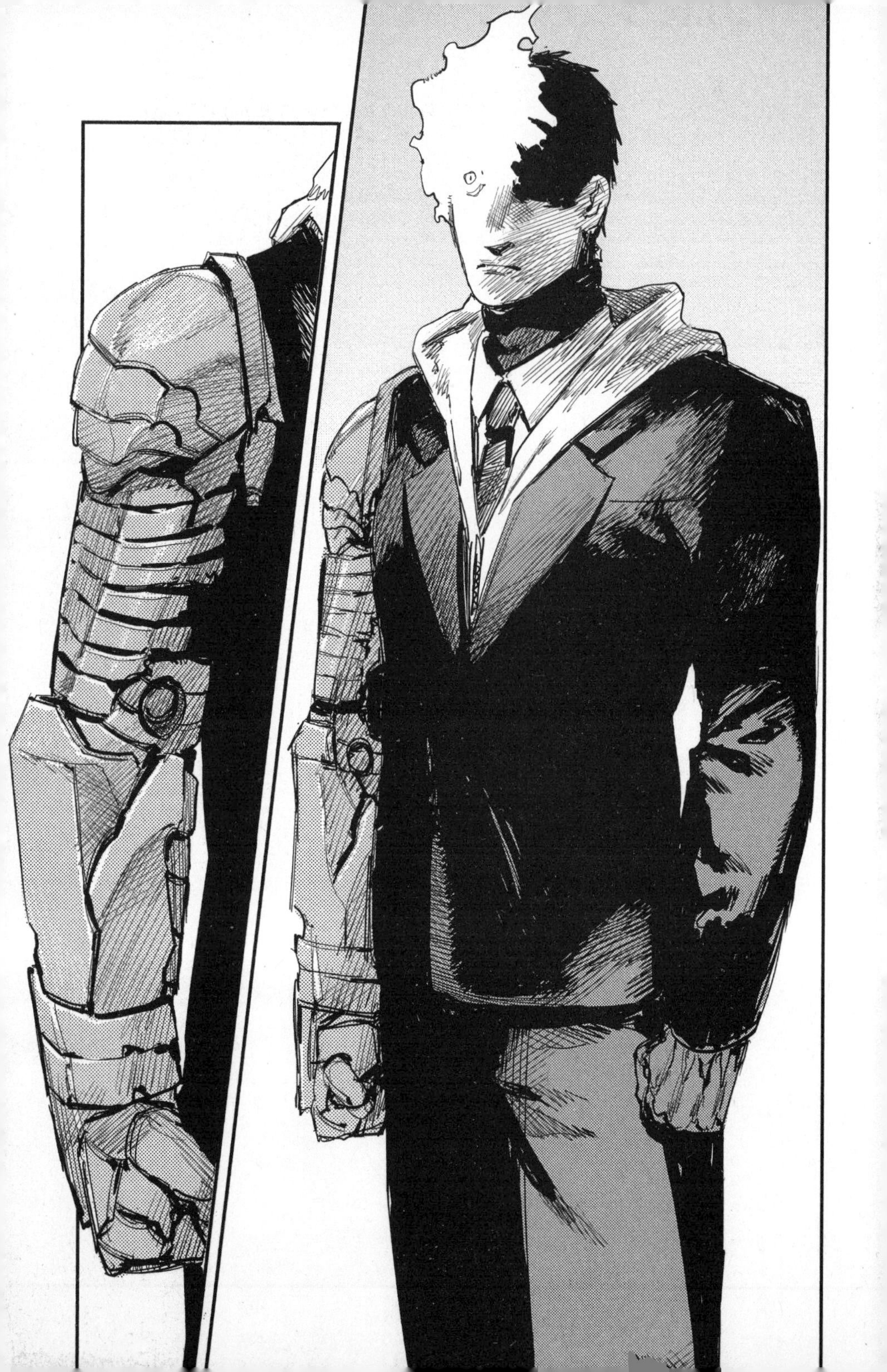

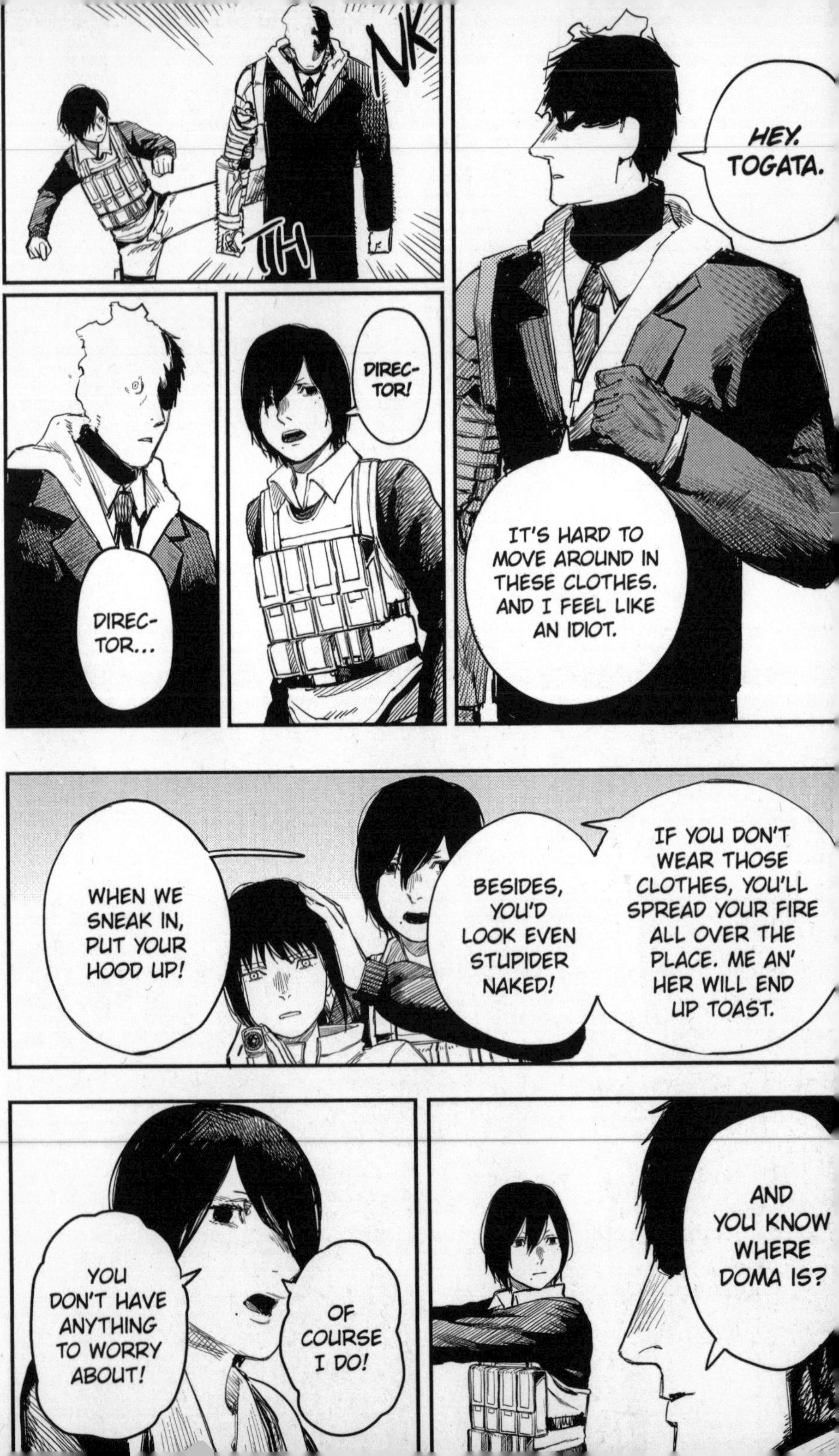
HEY. TOGATA.
IT'S HARD TO MOVE AROUND IN THESE CLOTHES. AND I FEEL LIKE AN IDIOT.
NK
TH
DIREC-TOR!
DIREC-TOR...
IF YOU DON'T WEAR THOSE CLOTHES, YOU'LL SPREAD YOUR FIRE ALL OVER THE PLACE. ME AN' HER WILL END UP TOAST.
BESIDES, YOU'D LOOK EVEN STUPIDER NAKED!
WHEN WE SNEAK IN, PUT YOUR HOOD UP!
AND YOU KNOW WHERE DOMA IS?
OF COURSE I DO!
YOU DON'T HAVE ANYTHING TO WORRY ABOUT!

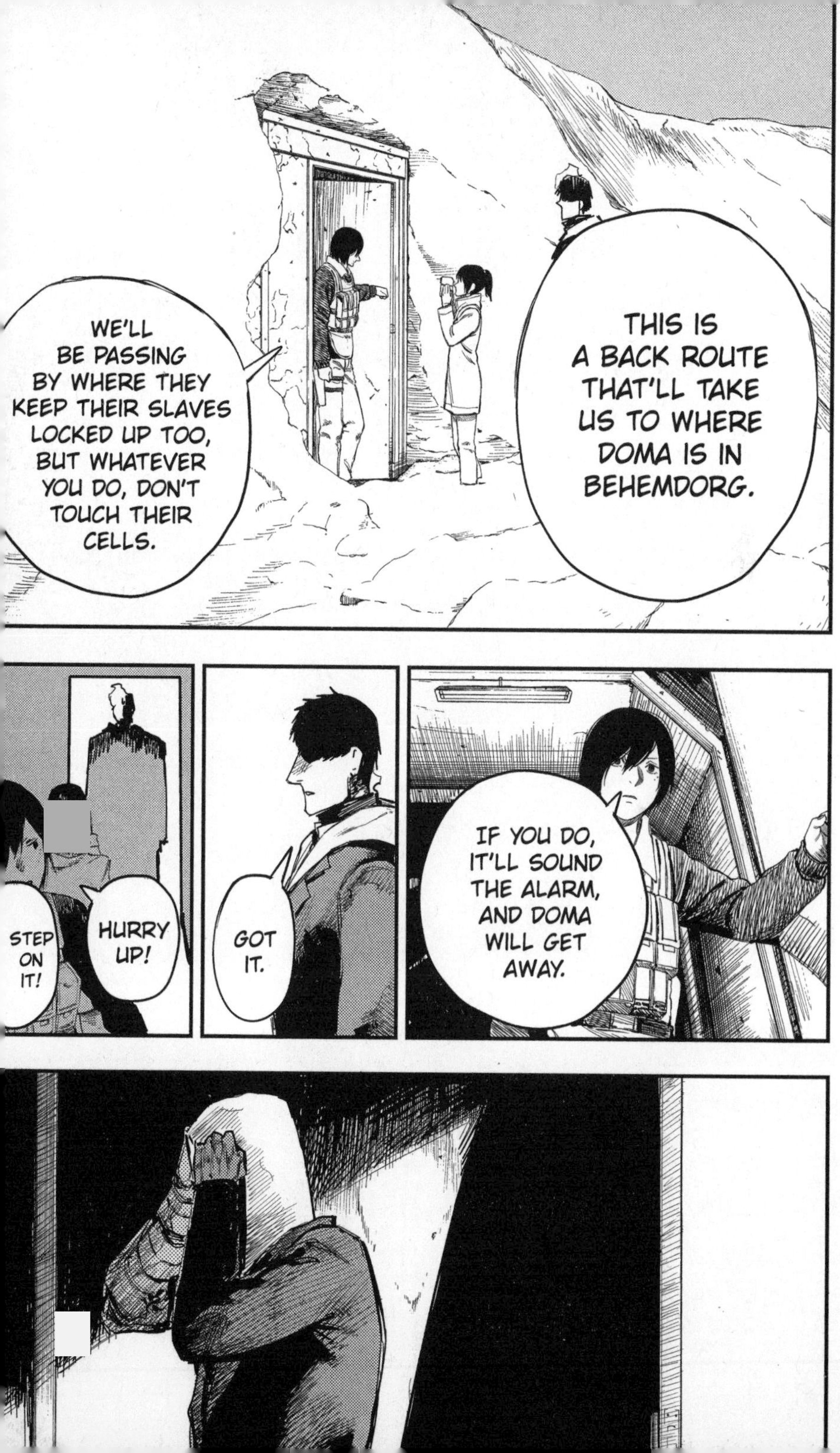
THIS IS A BACK ROUTE THAT'LL TAKE US TO WHERE DOMA IS IN BEHEMDORG.
WE'LL BE PASSING BY WHERE THEY KEEP THEIR SLAVES LOCKED UP TOO, BUT WHATEVER YOU DO, DON'T TOUCH THEIR CELLS.
IF YOU DO, IT'LL SOUND THE ALARM, AND DOMA WILL GET AWAY.
GOT IT.
HURRY UP!
STEP ON IT!

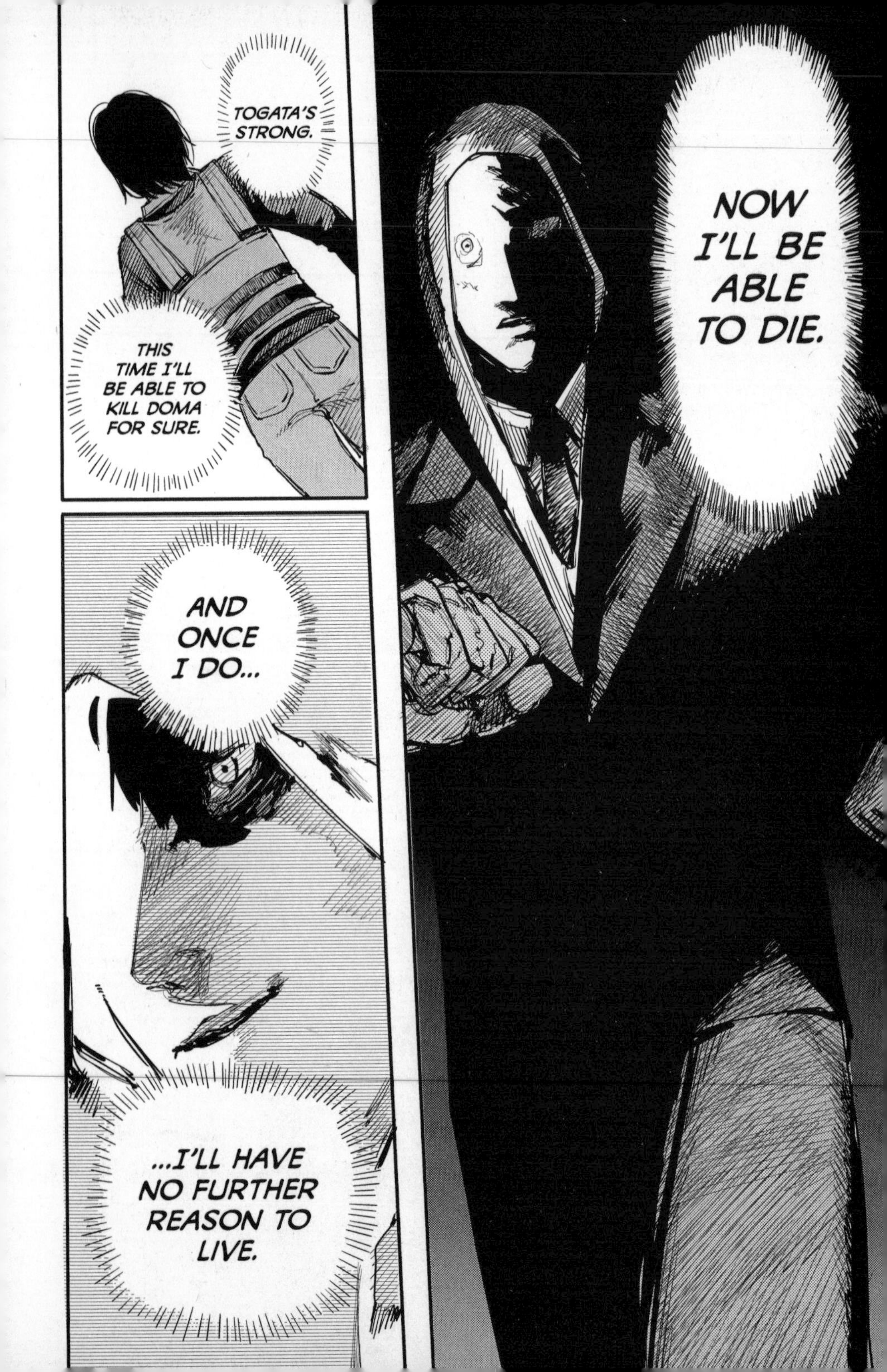
NOW I'LL BE ABLE TO DIE.
TOGATA'S STRONG.
THIS TIME I'LL BE ABLE TO KILL DOMA FOR SURE.
AND ONCE I DO...
...I'LL HAVE NO FURTHER REASON TO LIVE.

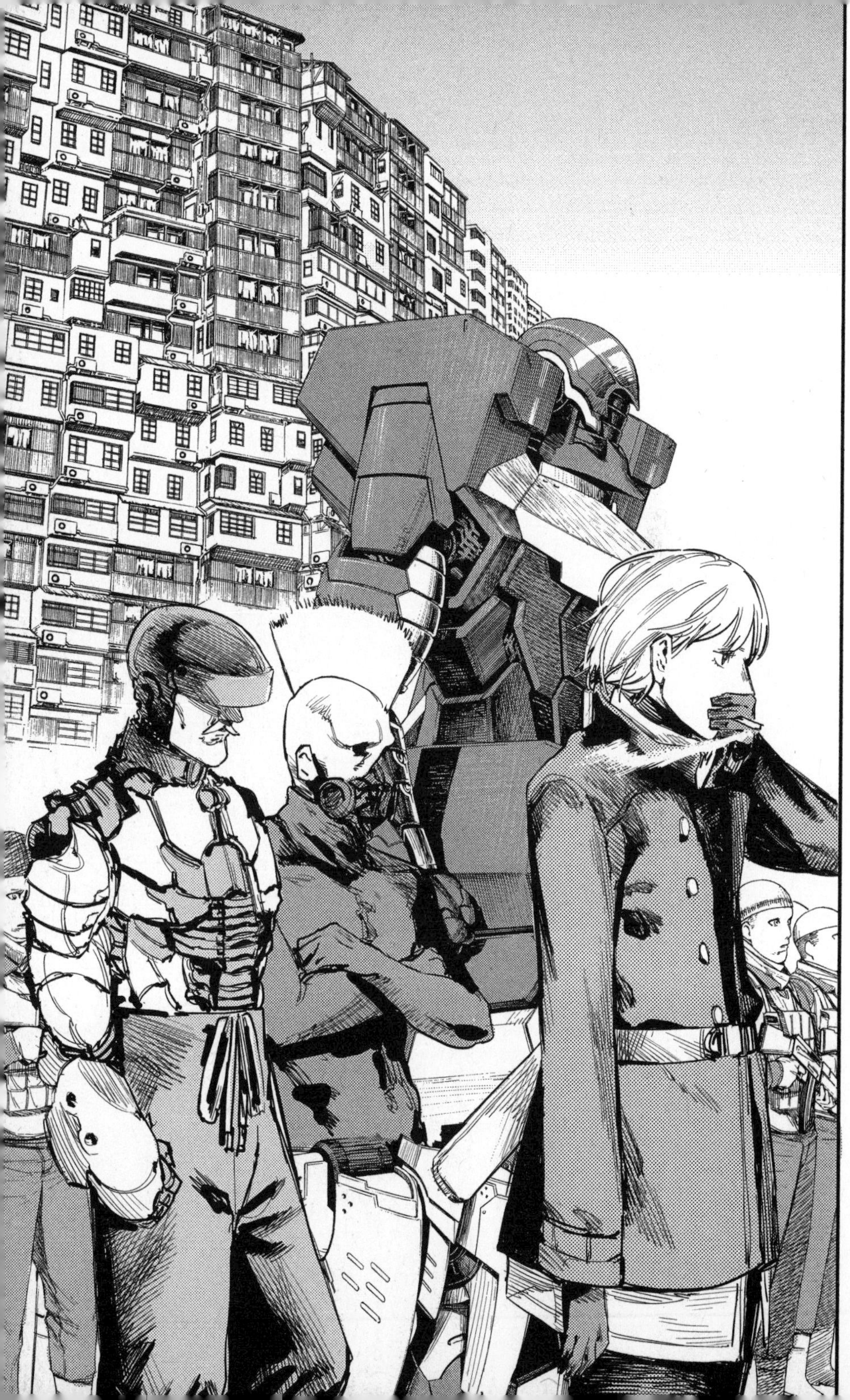

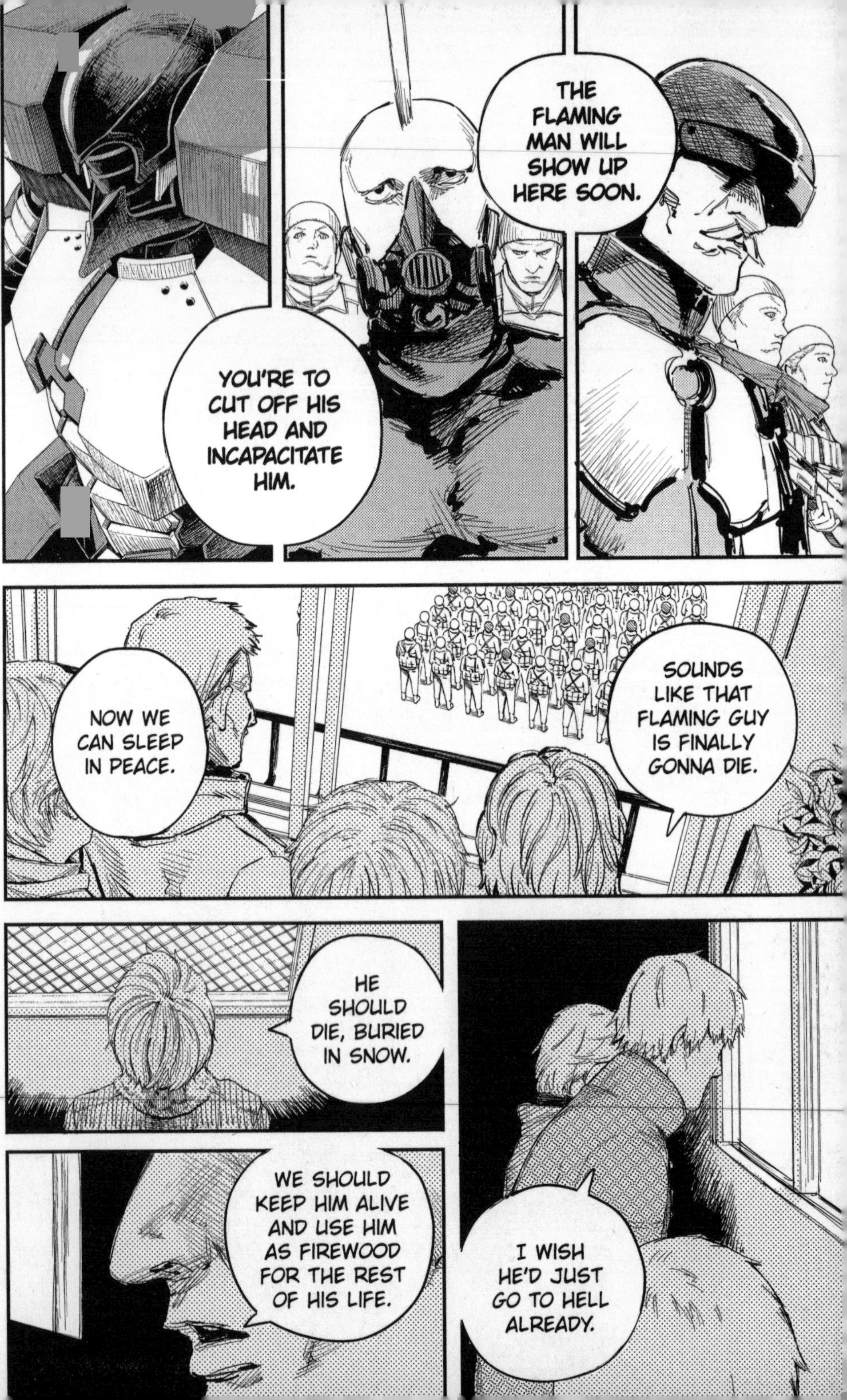
THE FLAMING MAN WILL SHOW UP HERE SOON.
YOU'RE TO CUT OFF HIS HEAD AND INCAPACITATE HIM.
SOUNDS LIKE THAT FLAMING GUY IS FINALLY GONNA DIE.
NOW WE CAN SLEEP IN PEACE.
I WISH HE'D JUST GO TO HELL ALREADY.
HE SHOULD DIE, BURIED IN SNOW.
WE SHOULD KEEP HIM ALIVE AND USE HIM AS FIREWOOD FOR THE REST OF HIS LIFE.

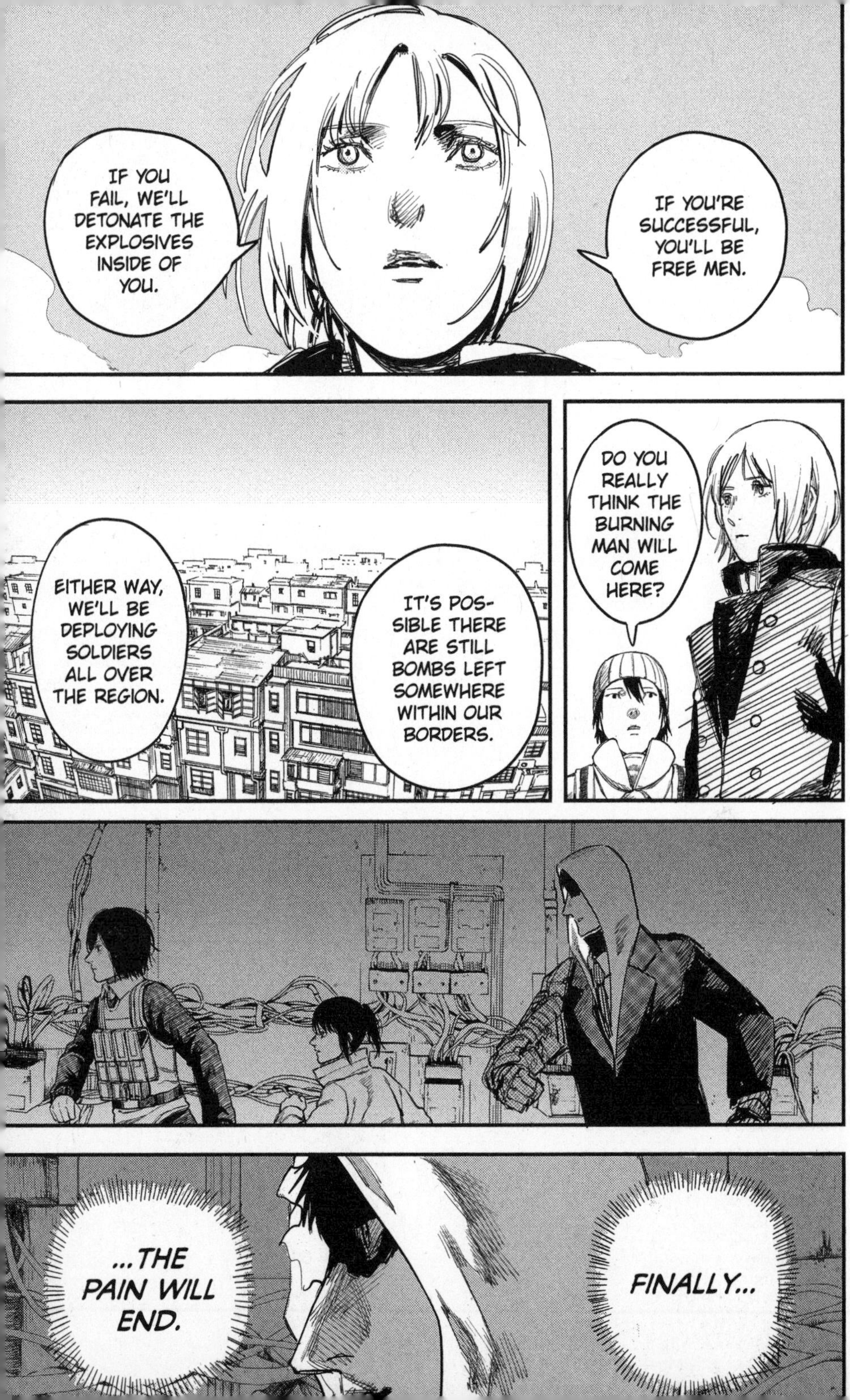
IF YOU'RE SUCCESSFUL, YOU'LL BE FREE MEN.
IF YOU FAIL, WE'LL DETONATE THE EXPLOSIVES INSIDE OF YOU.
DO YOU REALLY THINK THE BURNING MAN WILL COME HERE?
IT'S POS-SIBLE THERE ARE STILL BOMBS LEFT SOMEWHERE WITHIN OUR BORDERS.
EITHER WAY, WE'LL BE DEPLOYING SOLDIERS ALL OVER THE REGION.
FINALLY...
...THE PAIN WILL END.

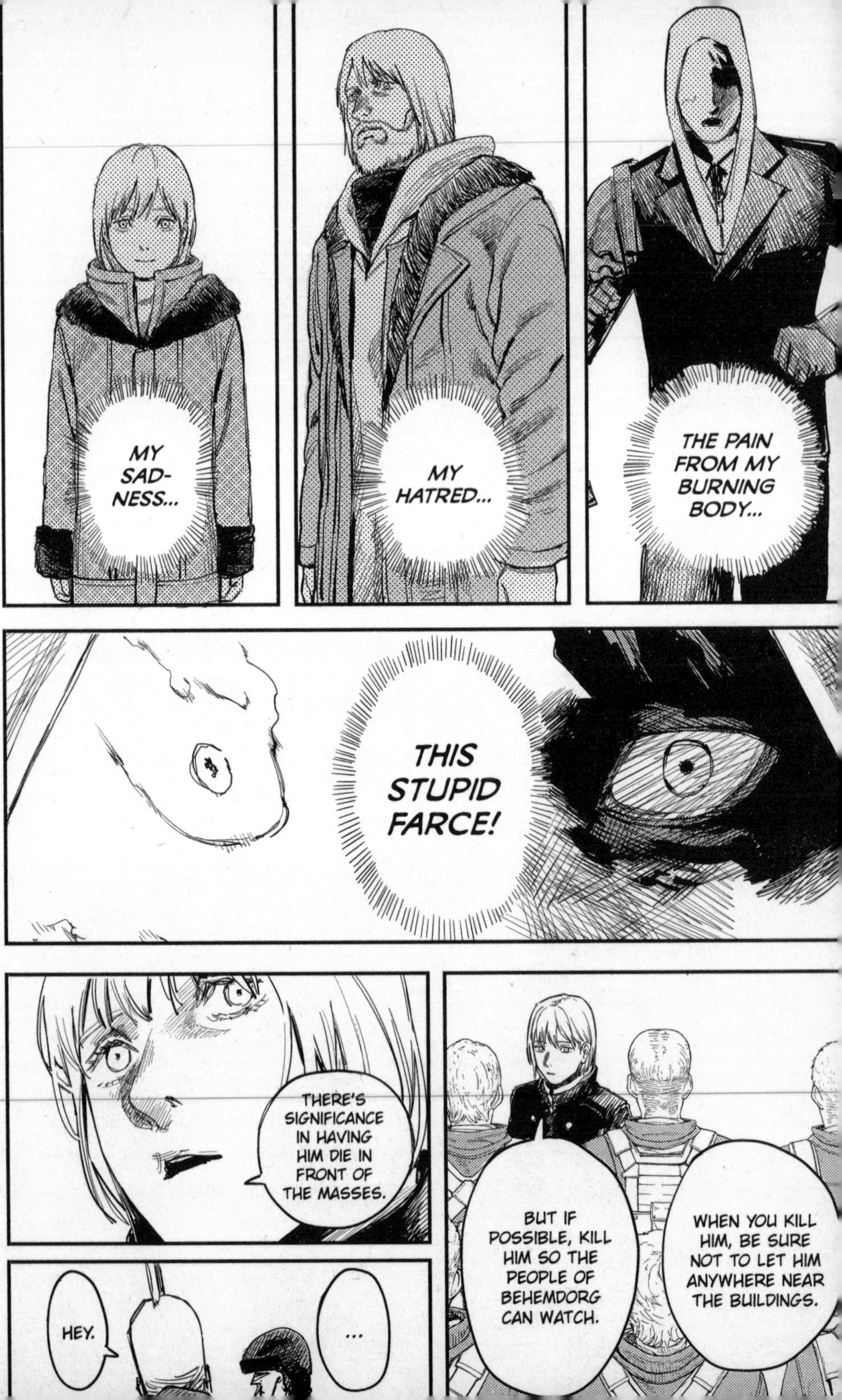
THE PAIN FROM MY BURNING BODY...
MY HATRED...
MY SAD-NESS...
THIS STUPID FARCE!
WHEN YOU KILL HIM, BE SURE NOT TO LET HIM ANYWHERE NEAR THE BUILDINGS.
BUT IF POSSIBLE, KILL HIM SO THE PEOPLE OF BEHEMDORG CAN WATCH.
THERE'S SIGNIFICANCE IN HAVING HIM DIE IN FRONT OF THE MASSES.
...
HEY.

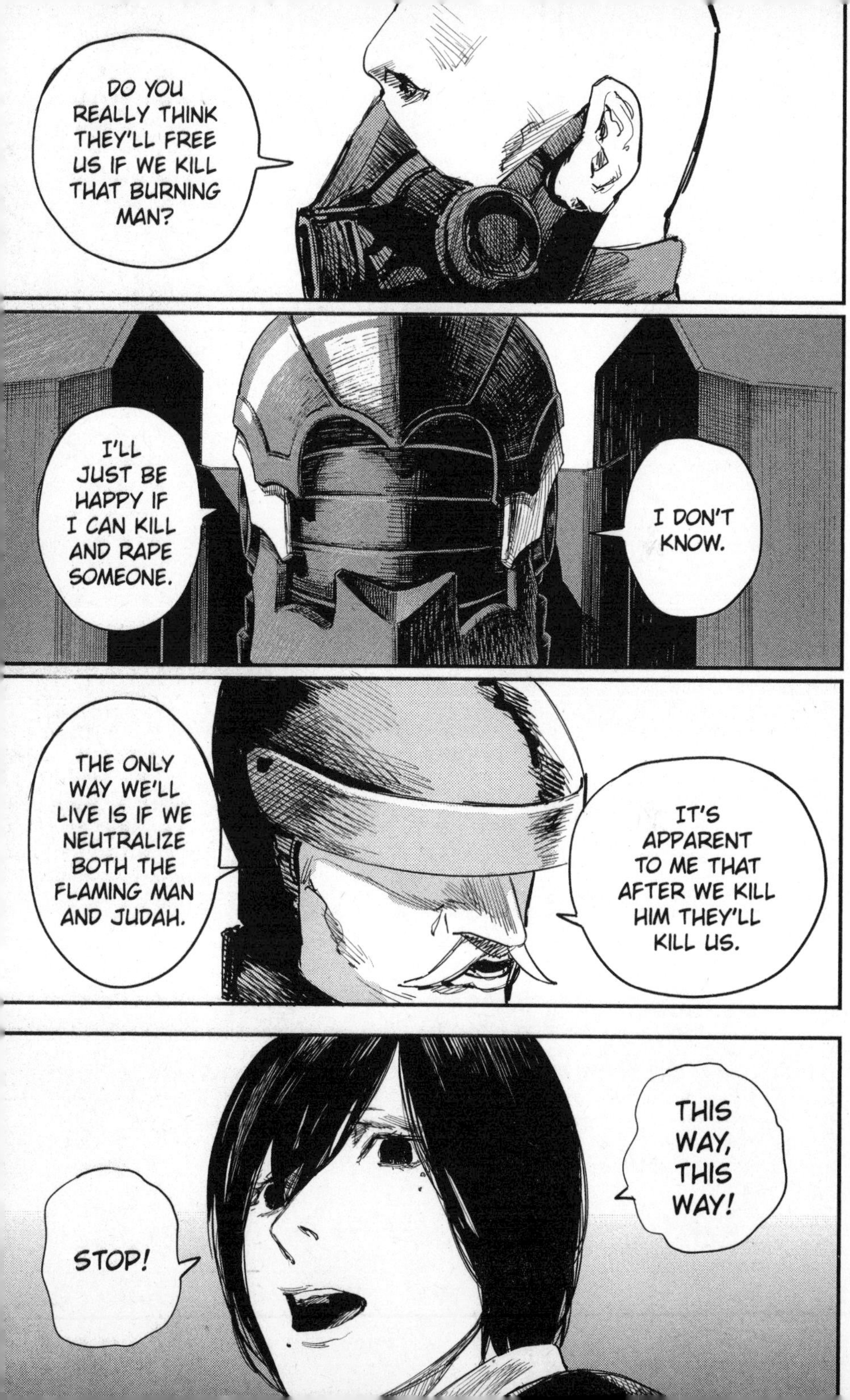
DO YOU REALLY THINK THEY'LL FREE US IF WE KILL THAT BURNING MAN?
I DON'T KNOW.
I'LL JUST BE HAPPY IF I CAN KILL AND RAPE SOMEONE.
IT'S APPARENT TO ME THAT AFTER WE KILL HIM THEY'LL KILL US.
THE ONLY WAY WE'LL LIVE IS IF WE NEUTRALIZE BOTH THE FLAMING MAN AND JUDAH.
THIS WAY, THIS WAY!
STOP!

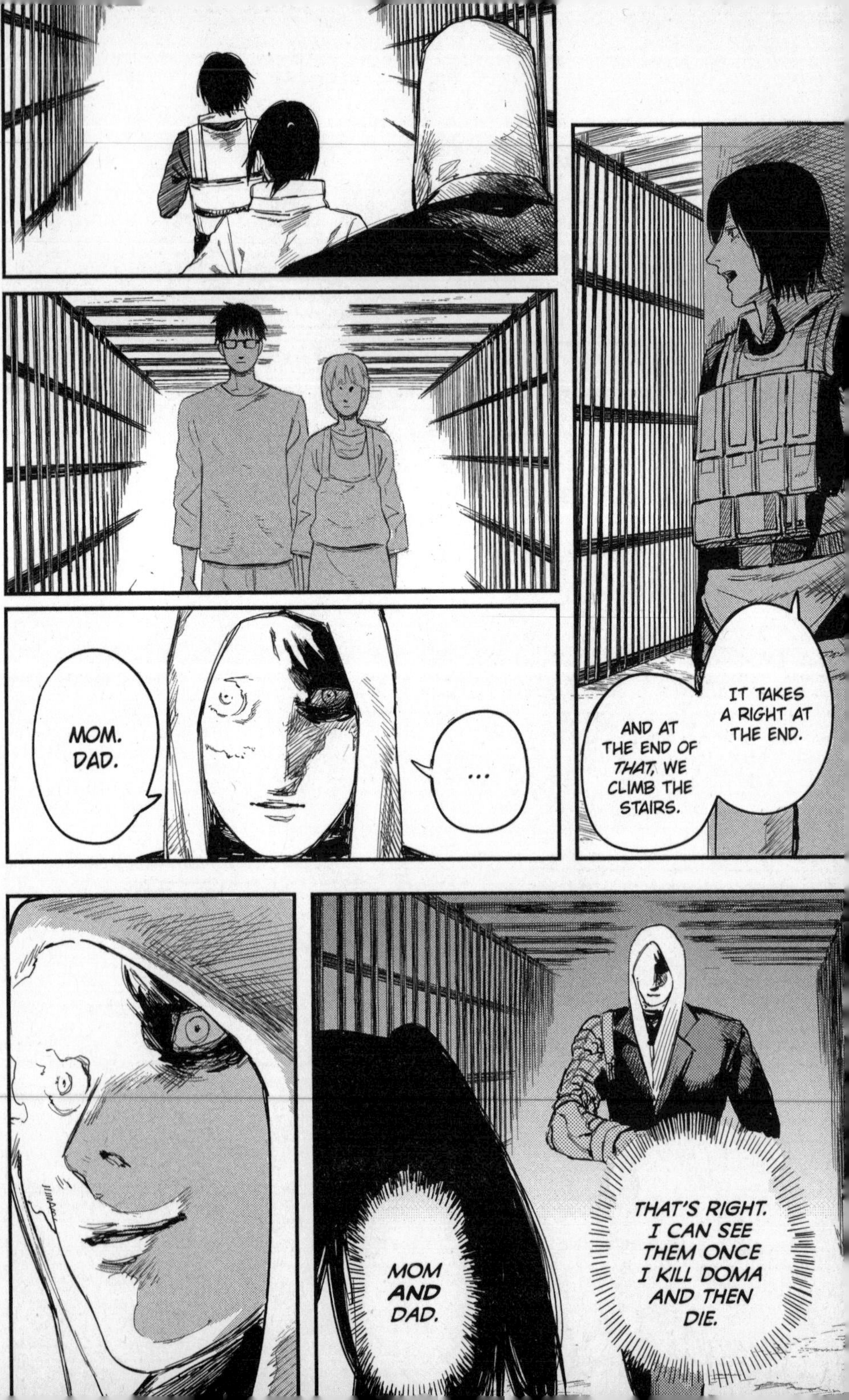
IT TAKES A RIGHT AT THE END.
AND AT THE END OF *THAT,* WE CLIMB THE STAIRS.
...
MOM. DAD.
THAT'S RIGHT. I CAN SEE THEM ONCE I KILL DOMA AND THEN DIE.
*MOM **AND** DAD.*

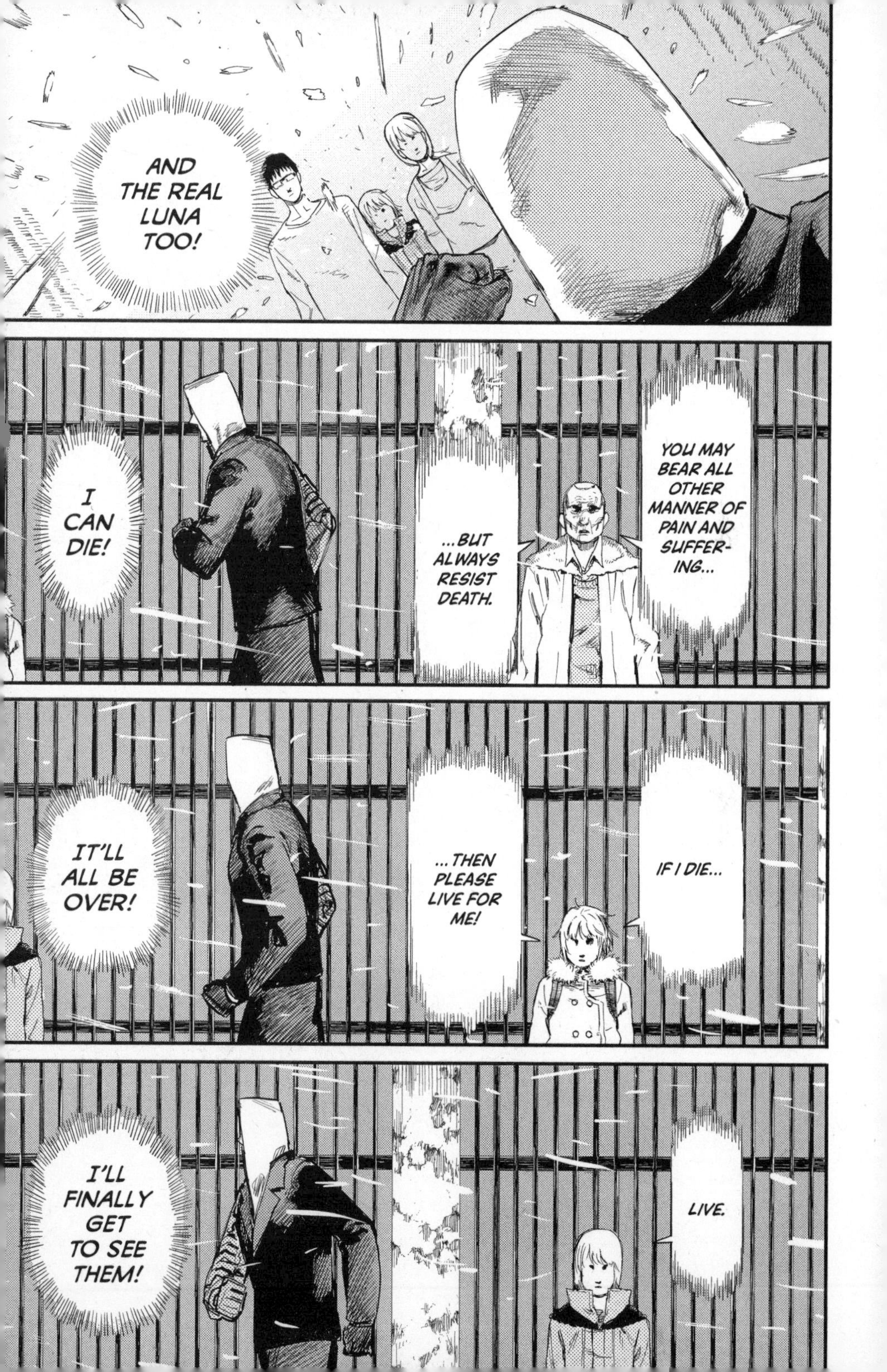
AND THE REAL LUNA TOO!
YOU MAY BEAR ALL OTHER MANNER OF PAIN AND SUFFERING...
...BUT ALWAYS RESIST DEATH.
I CAN DIE!
IF I DIE...
...THEN PLEASE LIVE FOR ME!
IT'LL ALL BE OVER!
LIVE.
I'LL FINALLY GET TO SEE THEM!

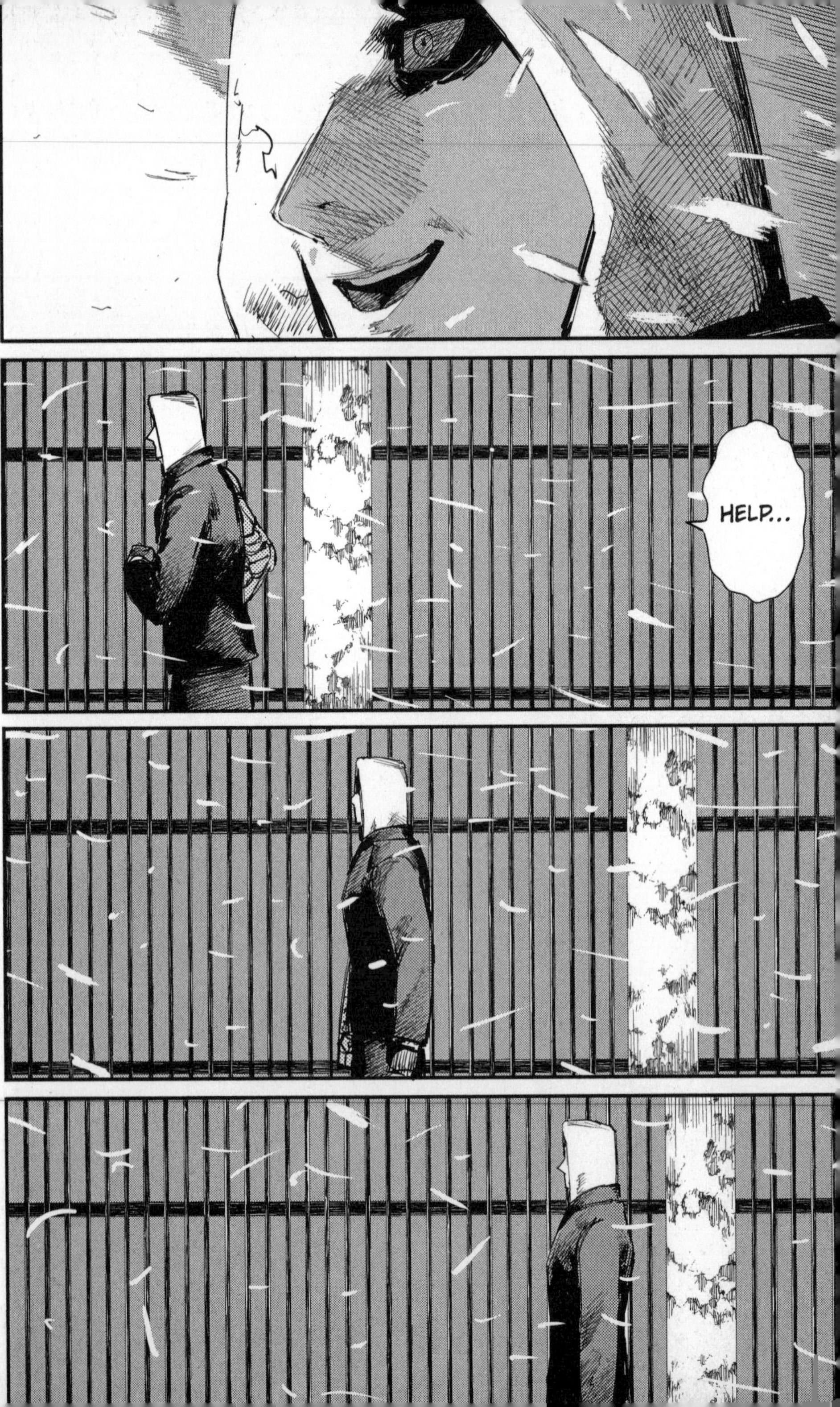
HELP...

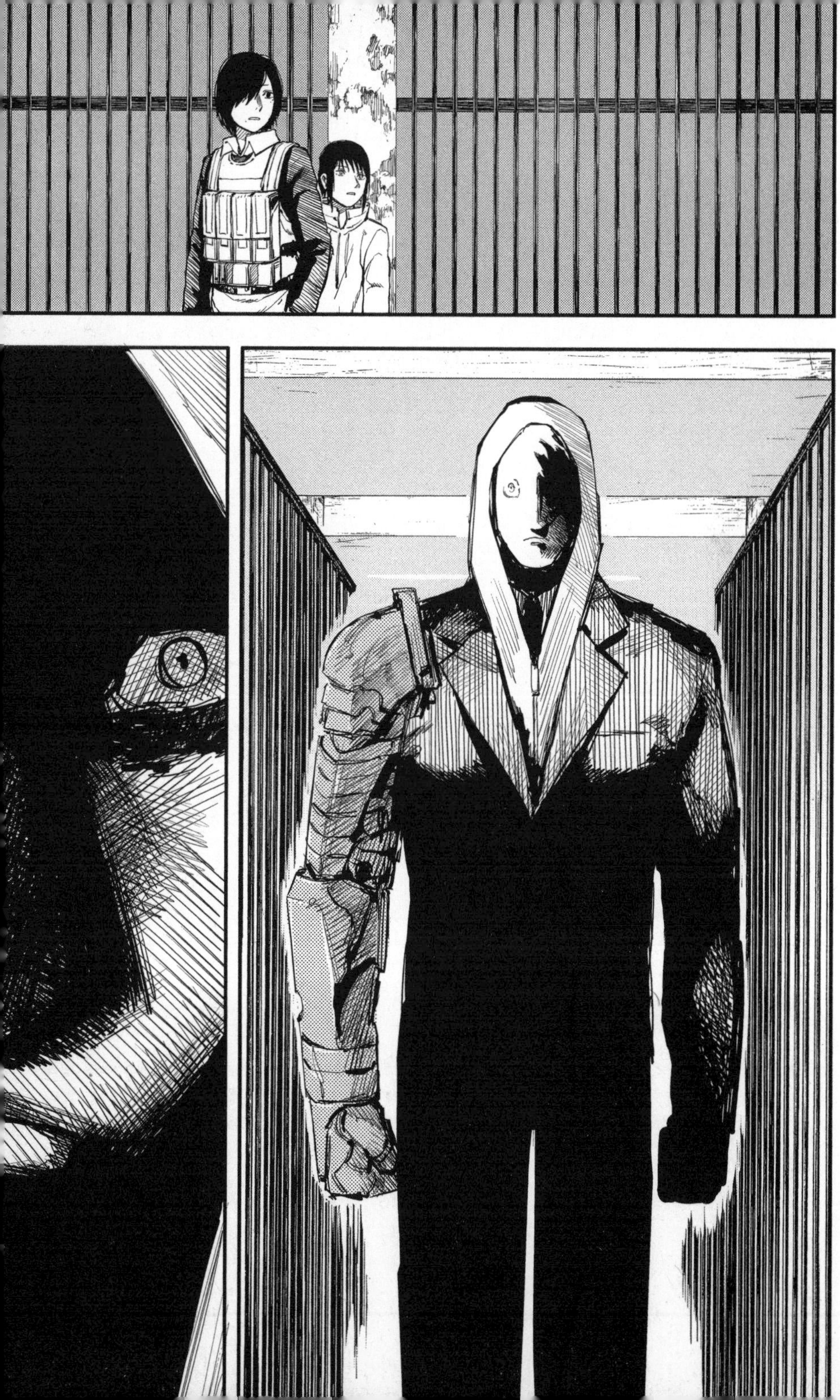

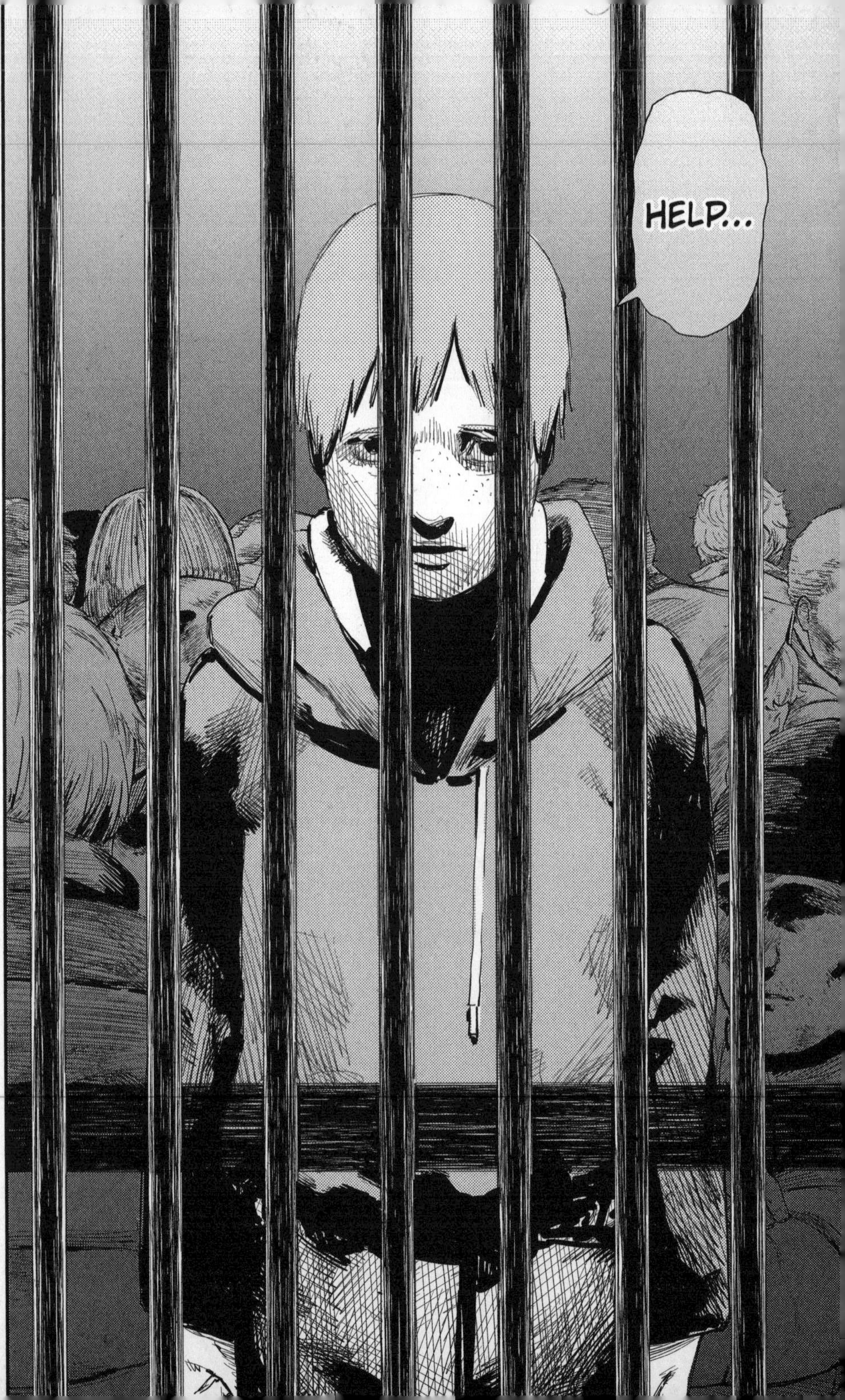
HELP...

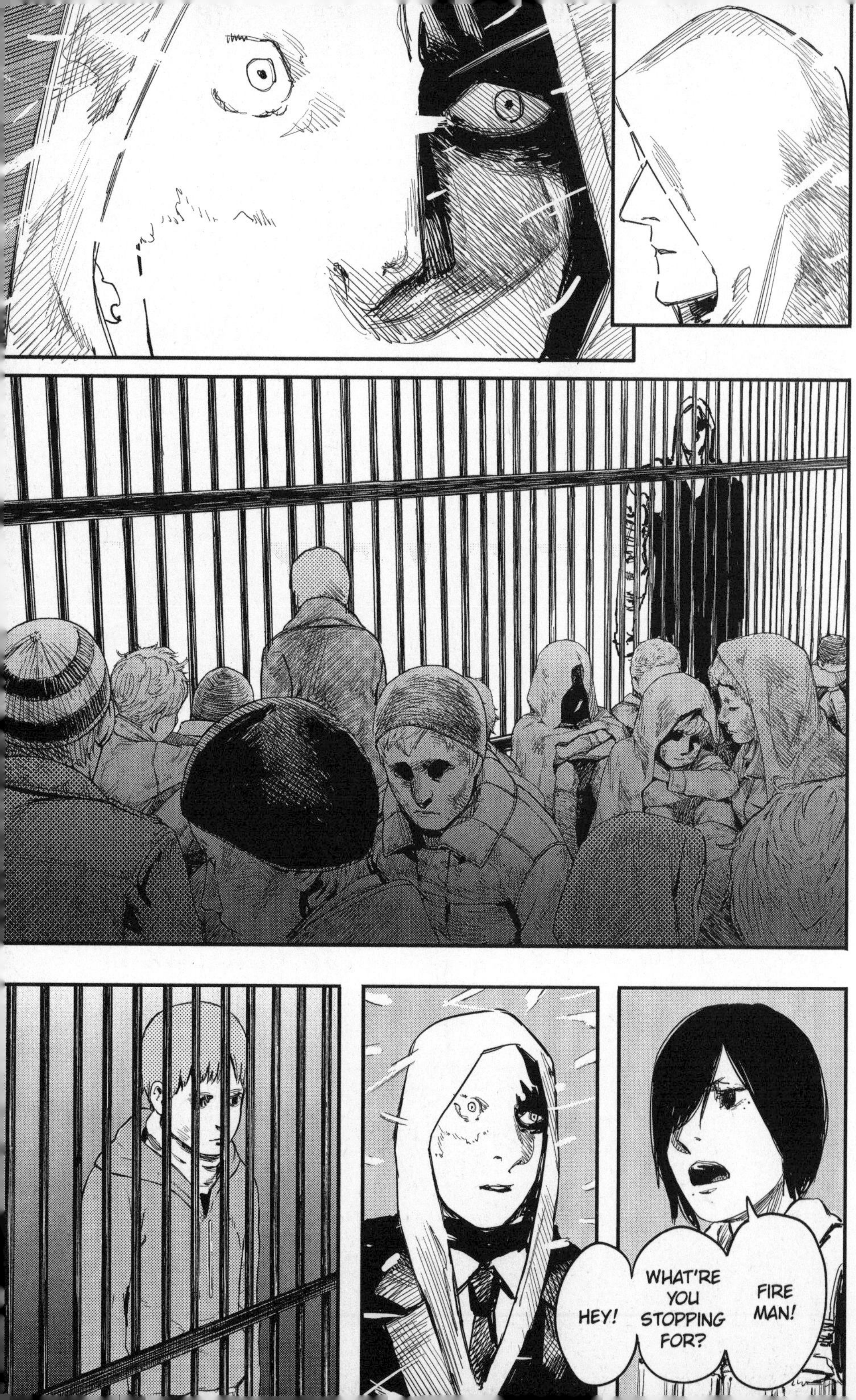
FIRE MAN!
WHAT'RE YOU STOPPING FOR?
HEY!

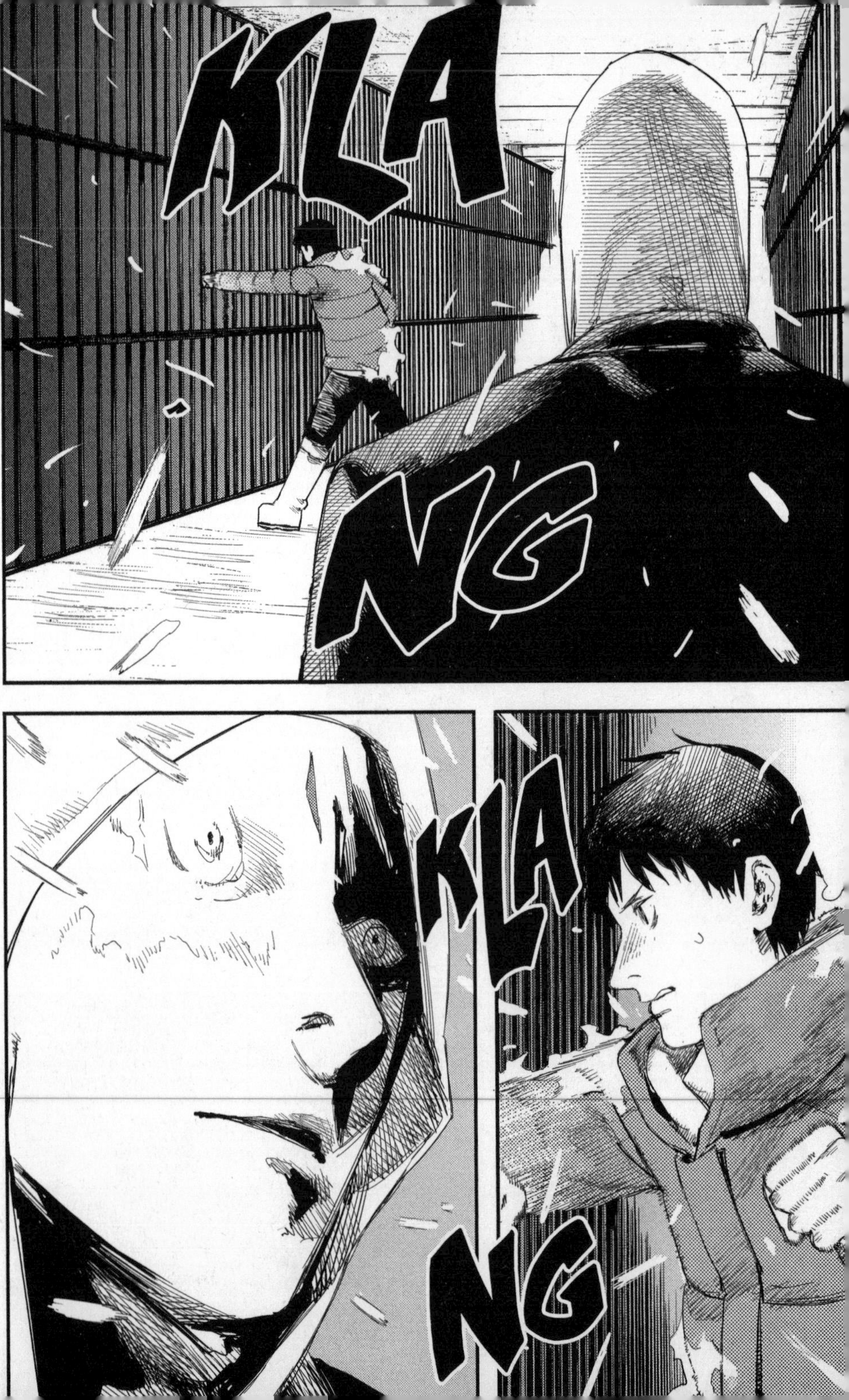
KLA
NG
KLA
NG

CHAPTER 20

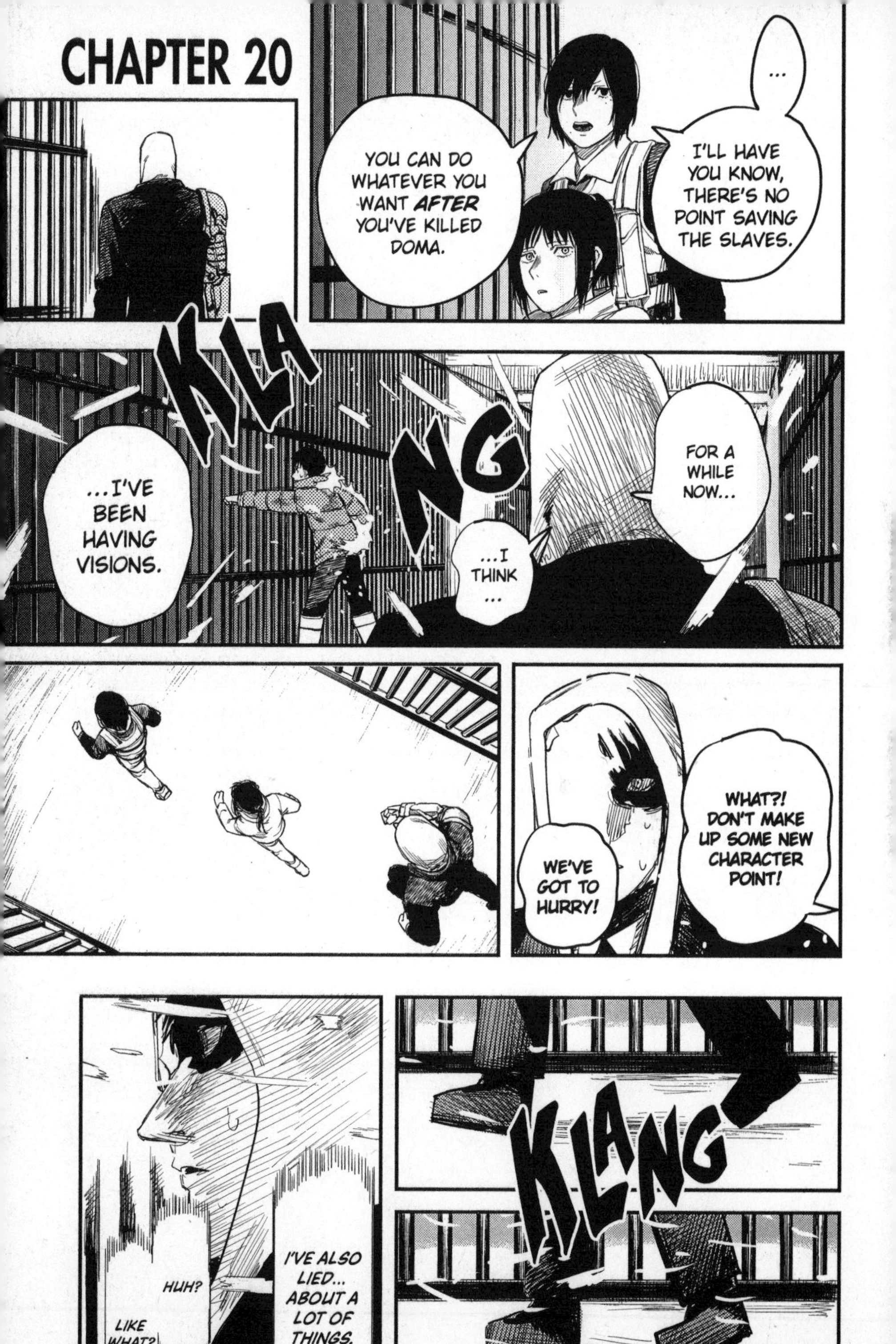
...
I'LL HAVE YOU KNOW, THERE'S NO POINT SAVING THE SLAVES.
YOU CAN DO WHATEVER YOU WANT *AFTER* YOU'VE KILLED DOMA.
FOR A WHILE NOW...
...I THINK...
KLANG
...I'VE BEEN HAVING VISIONS.
WHAT?! DON'T MAKE UP SOME NEW CHARACTER POINT!
WE'VE GOT TO HURRY!
KLANG
I'VE ALSO LIED... ABOUT A LOT OF THINGS.
HUH?
LIKE WHAT?

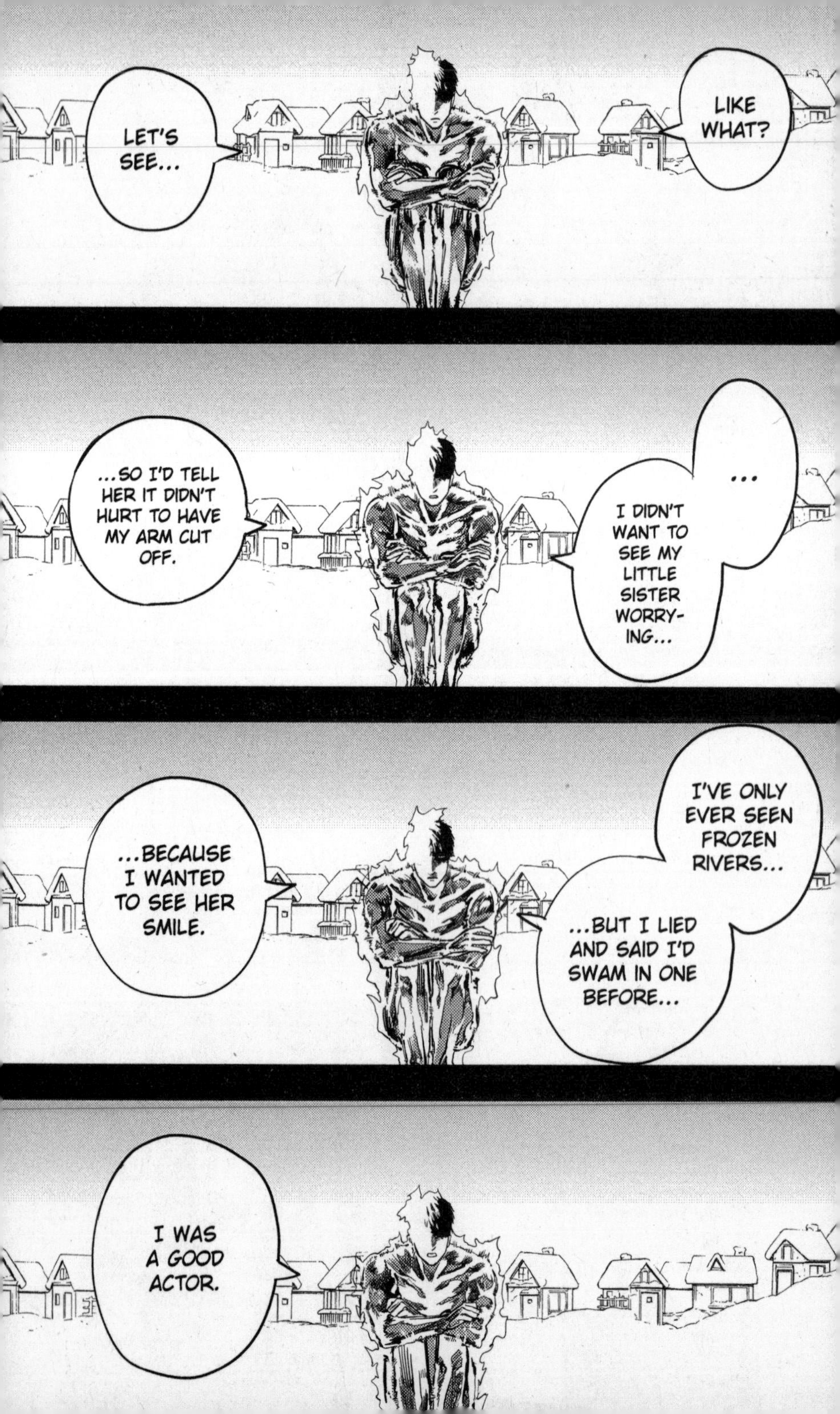
LIKE WHAT?
LET'S SEE...
...
I DIDN'T WANT TO SEE MY LITTLE SISTER WORRYING...
...SO I'D TELL HER IT DIDN'T HURT TO HAVE MY ARM CUT OFF.
I'VE ONLY EVER SEEN FROZEN RIVERS...
...BUT I LIED AND SAID I'D SWAM IN ONE BEFORE...
...BECAUSE I WANTED TO SEE HER SMILE.
I WAS A GOOD ACTOR.

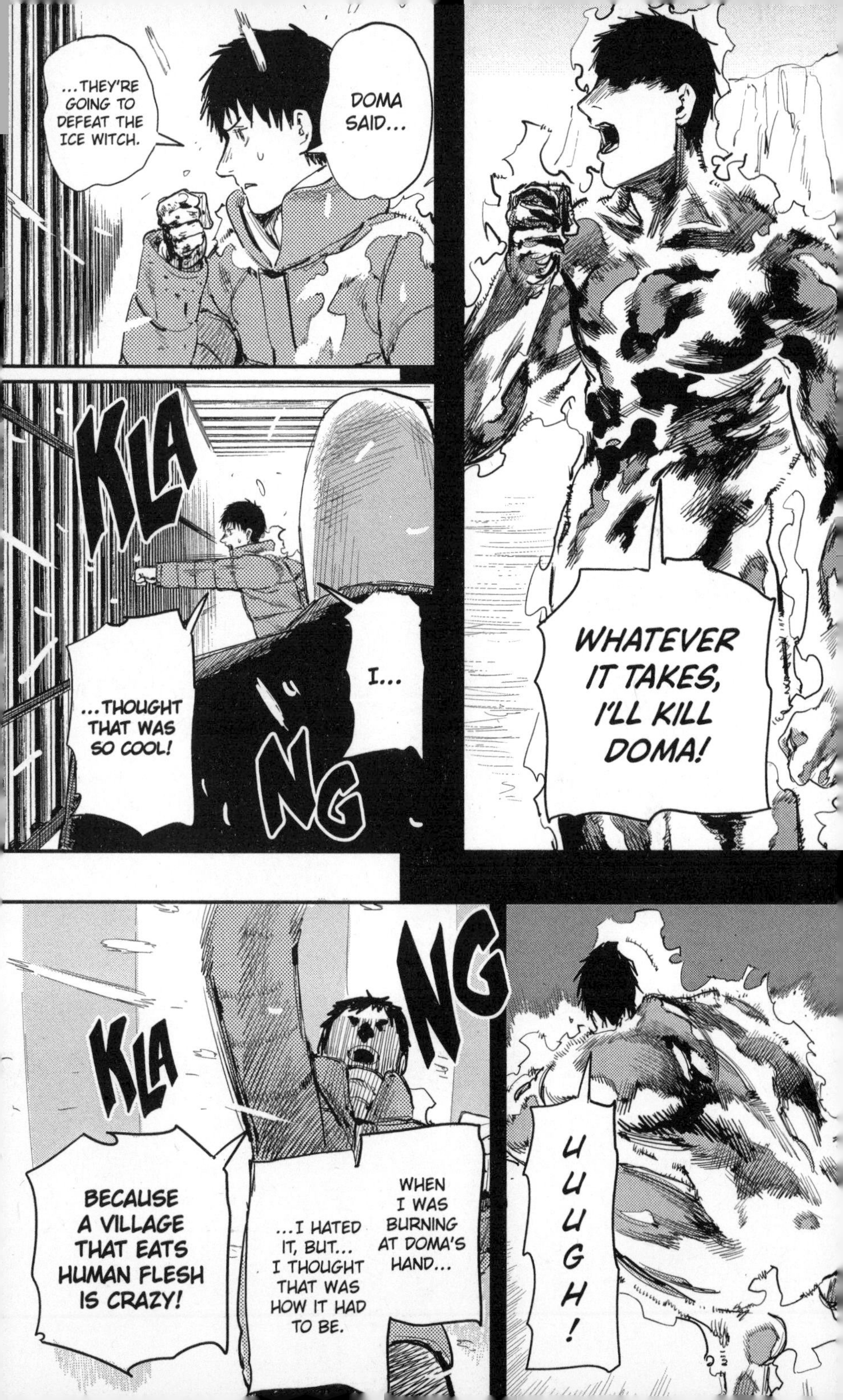
WHATEVER IT TAKES, I'LL KILL DOMA!
DOMA SAID...
...THEY'RE GOING TO DEFEAT THE ICE WITCH.
KLA
NG
I...
...THOUGHT THAT WAS SO COOL!
UUUGH!
KLA
NG
WHEN I WAS BURNING AT DOMA'S HAND...
...I HATED IT, BUT... I THOUGHT THAT WAS HOW IT HAD TO BE.
BECAUSE A VILLAGE THAT EATS HUMAN FLESH IS CRAZY!

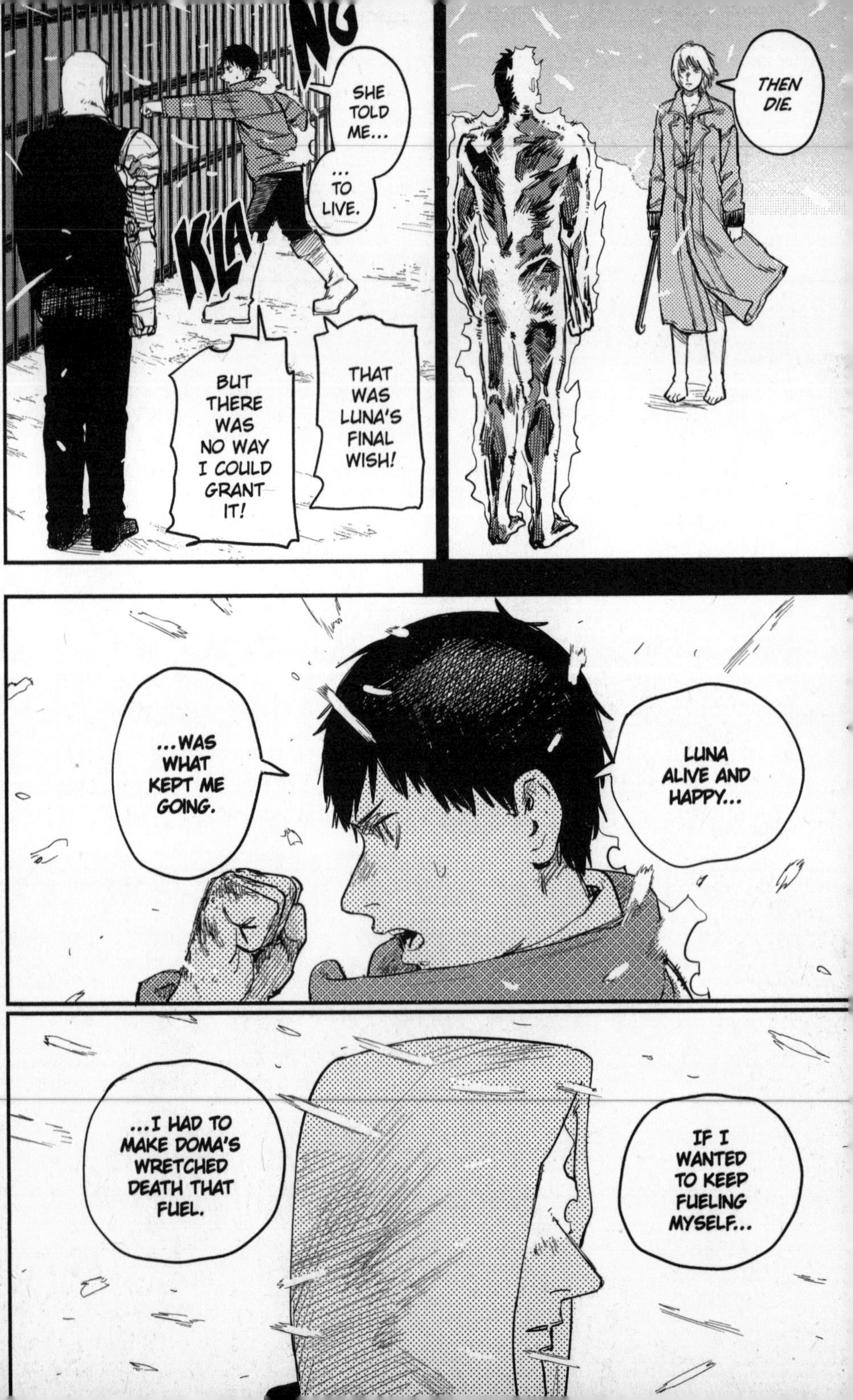
THEN DIE.
SHE TOLD ME...
...TO LIVE.
KLA
NG
THAT WAS LUNA'S FINAL WISH!
BUT THERE WAS NO WAY I COULD GRANT IT!
LUNA ALIVE AND HAPPY...
...WAS WHAT KEPT ME GOING.
IF I WANTED TO KEEP FUELING MYSELF...
...I HAD TO MAKE DOMA'S WRETCHED DEATH THAT FUEL.

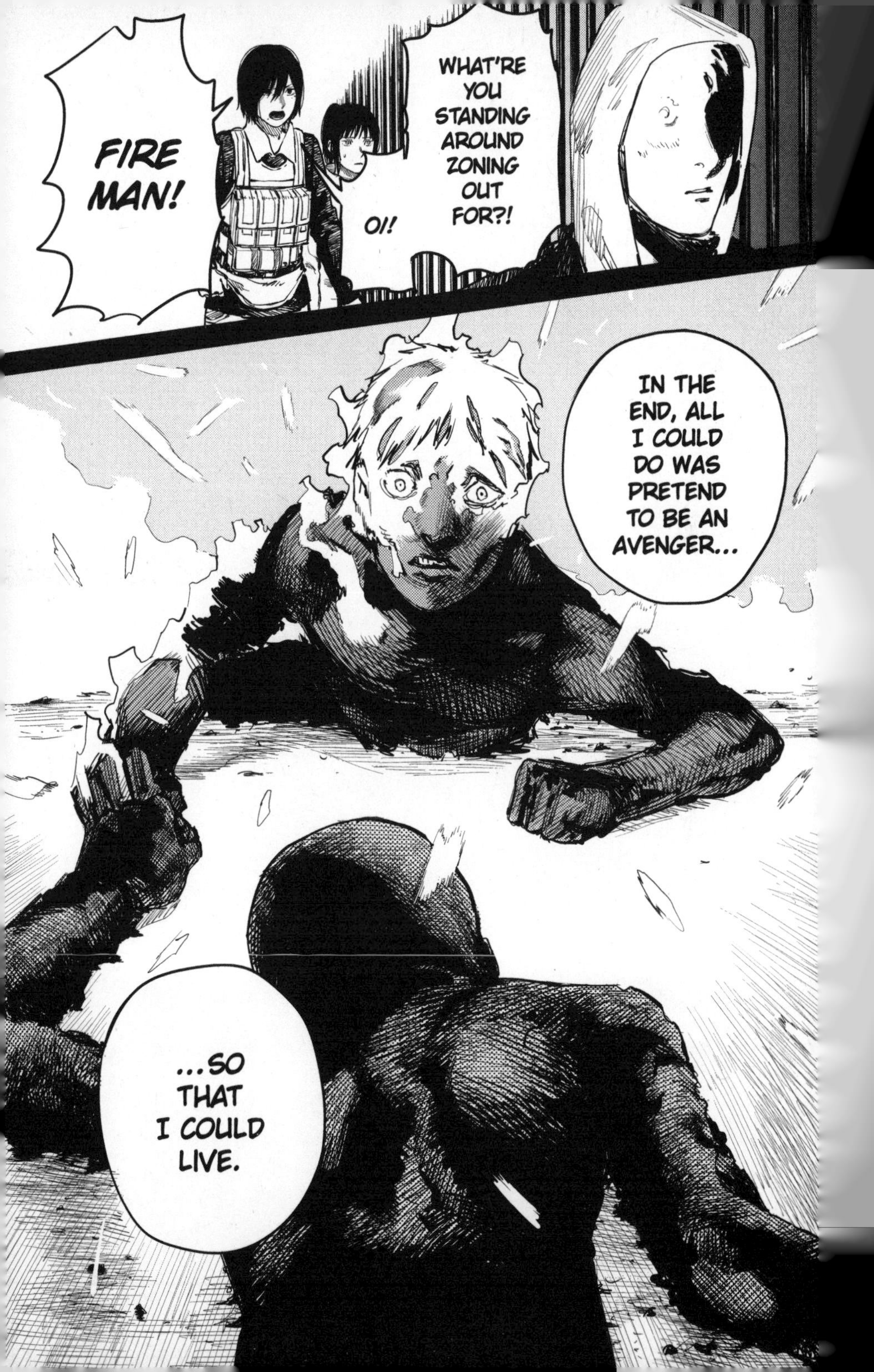
WHAT'RE YOU STANDING AROUND ZONING OUT FOR?!
OI!
FIRE MAN!
IN THE END, ALL I COULD DO WAS PRETEND TO BE AN AVENGER...
...SO THAT I COULD LIVE.

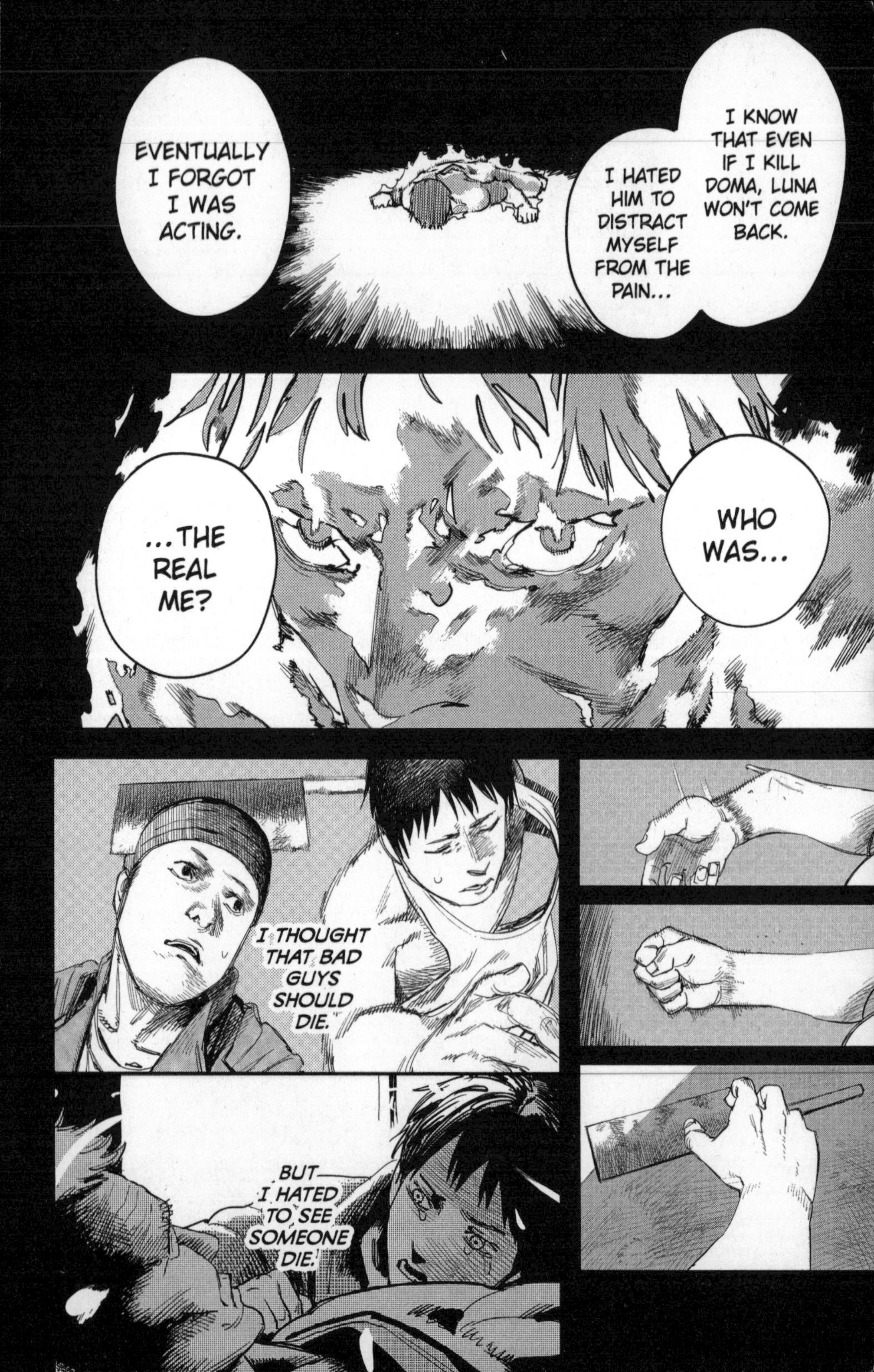
I KNOW THAT EVEN IF I KILL DOMA, LUNA WON'T COME BACK.
I HATED HIM TO DISTRACT MYSELF FROM THE PAIN...
EVENTUALLY I FORGOT I WAS ACTING.
WHO WAS...
...THE REAL ME?
I THOUGHT THAT BAD GUYS SHOULD DIE.
BUT—I HATED TO SEE SOMEONE DIE.

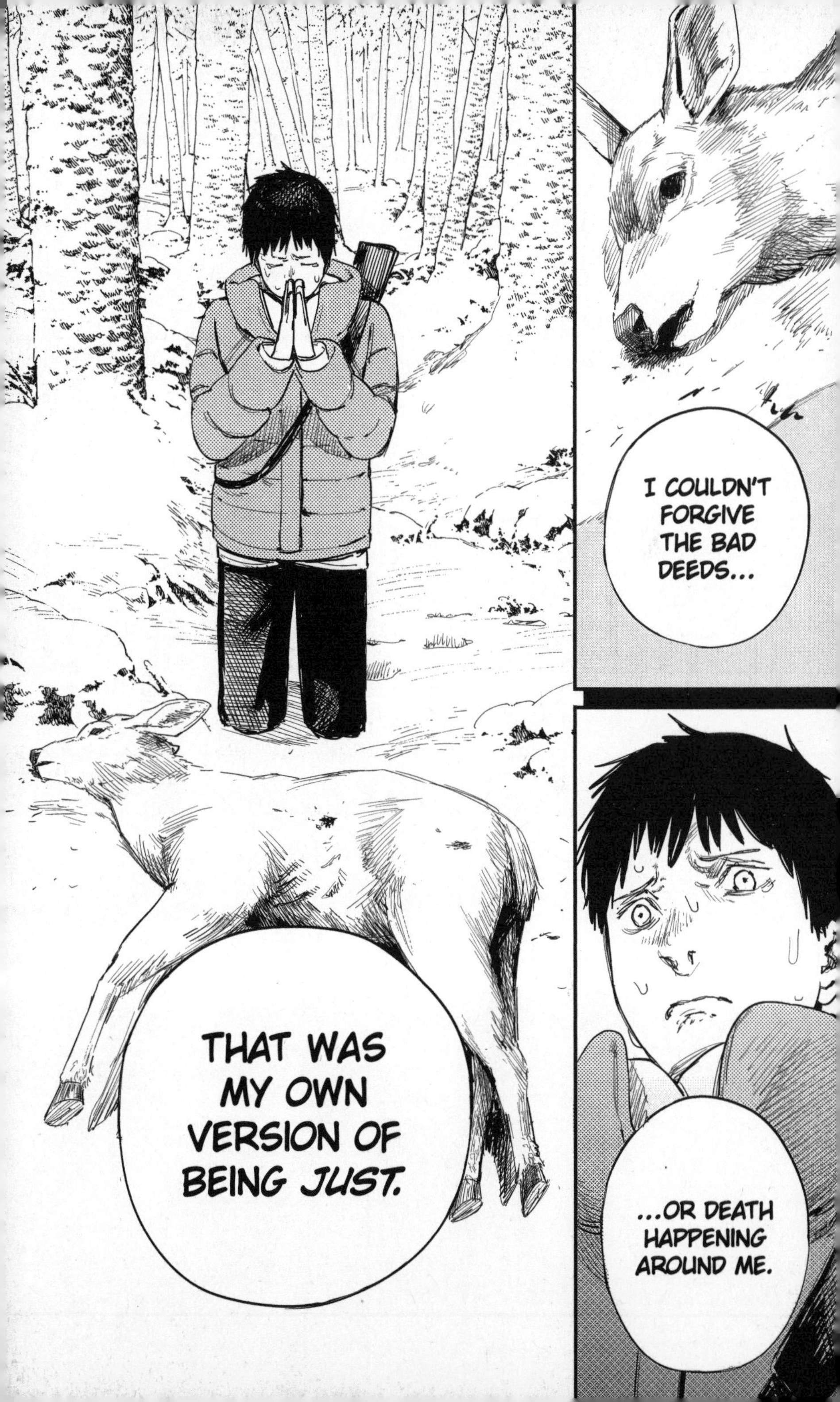
I COULDN'T FORGIVE THE BAD DEEDS...
...OR DEATH HAPPENING AROUND ME.
THAT WAS MY OWN VERSION OF BEING JUST.

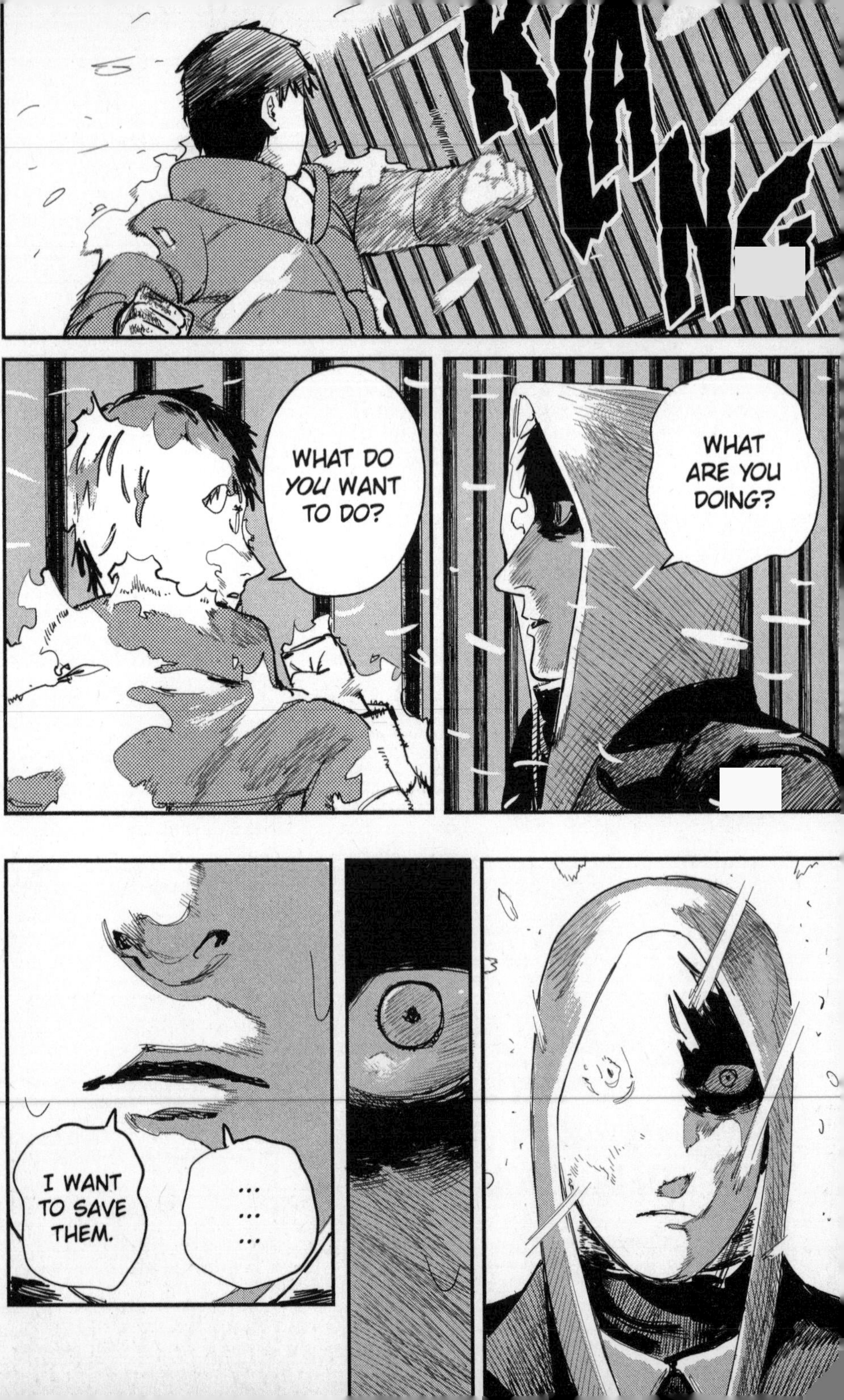
KLANG
WHAT ARE YOU DOING?
WHAT DO *YOU* WANT TO DO?
... ...
I WANT TO SAVE THEM.

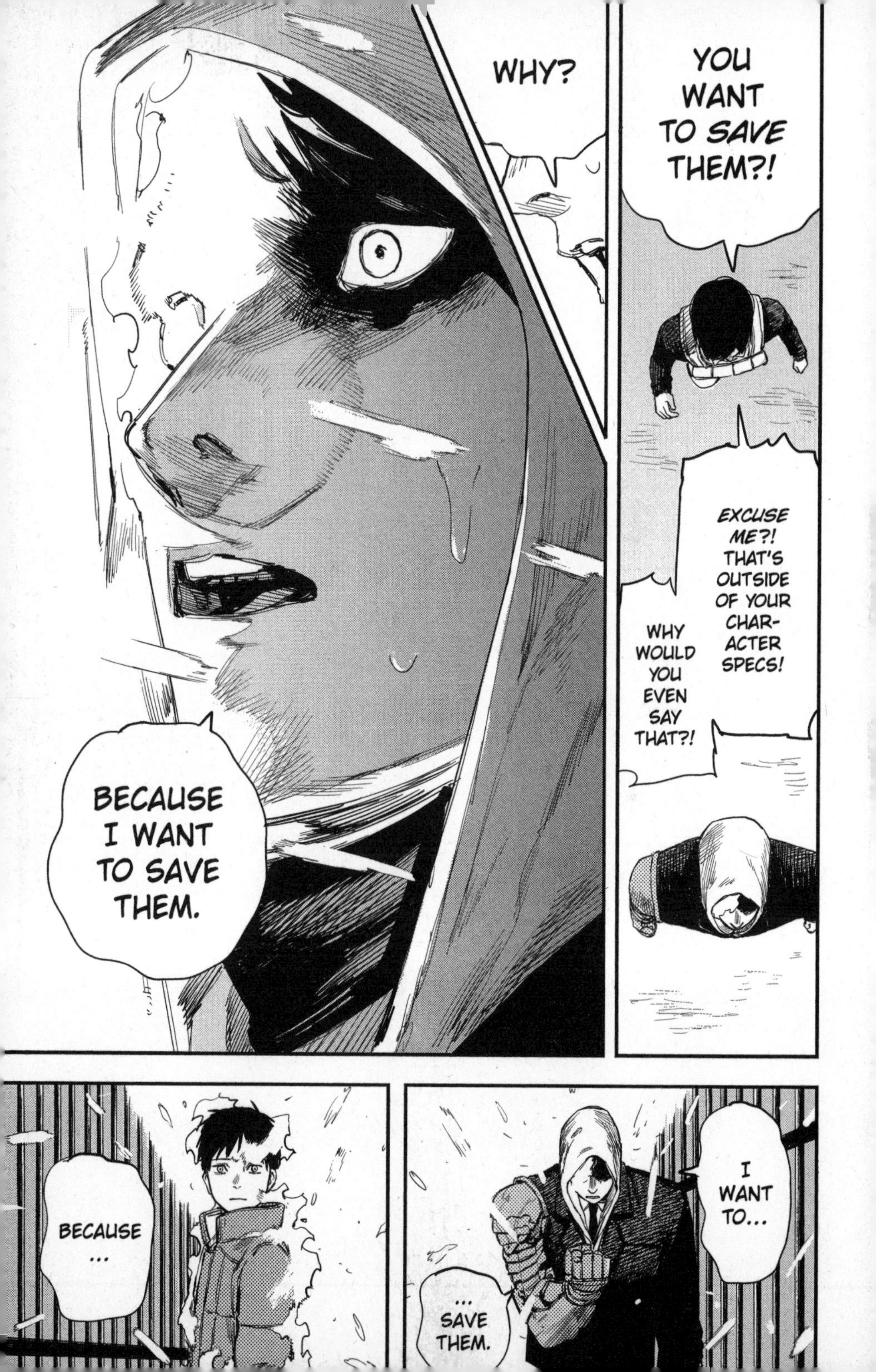
YOU WANT TO SAVE THEM?!
EXCUSE ME?! THAT'S OUTSIDE OF YOUR CHARACTER SPECS!
WHY WOULD YOU EVEN SAY THAT?!
WHY?
BECAUSE I WANT TO SAVE THEM.
I WANT TO...
... SAVE THEM.
BECAUSE ...

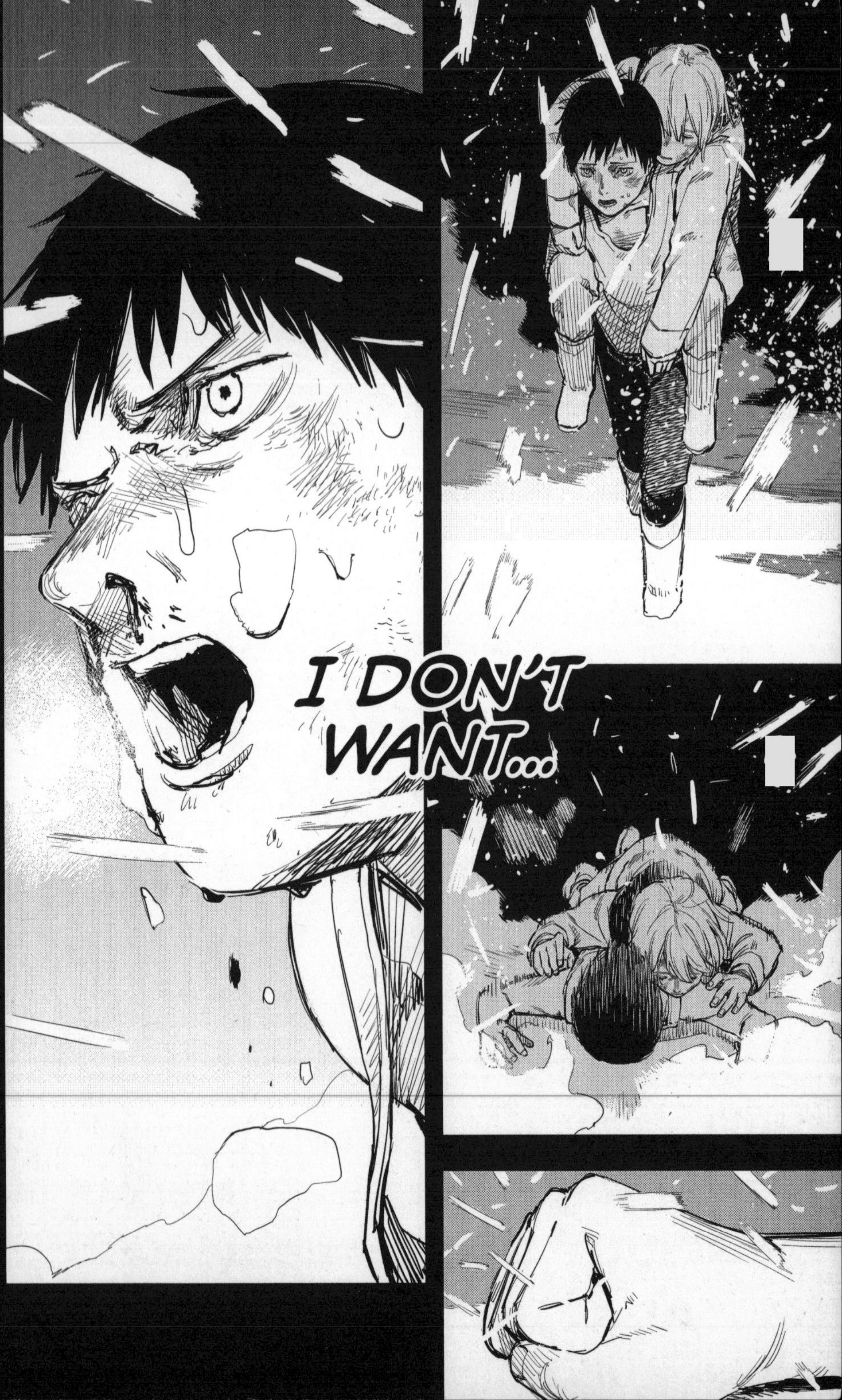
I DON'T WANT...

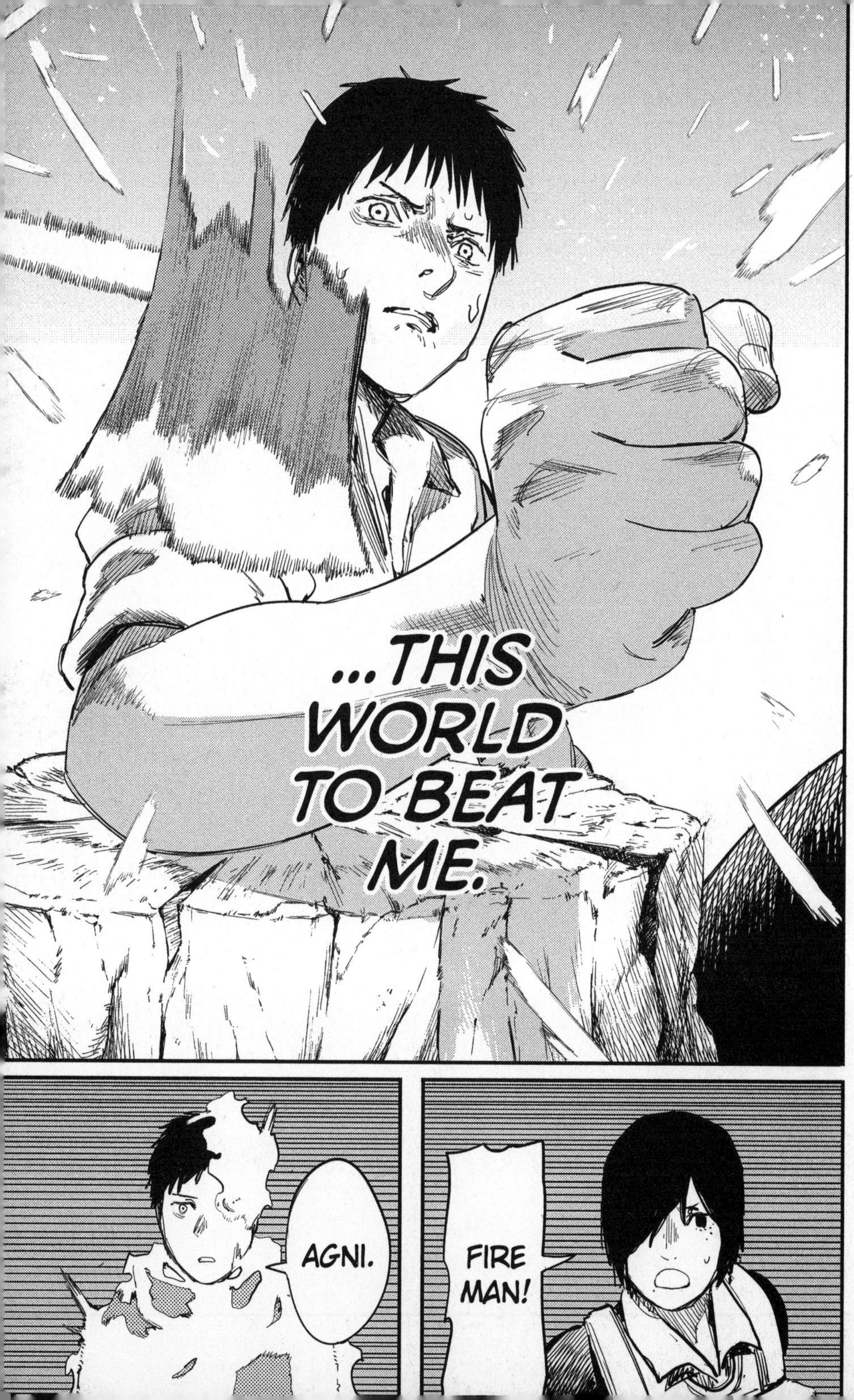
...THIS WORLD TO BEAT ME.
FIRE MAN!
AGNI.

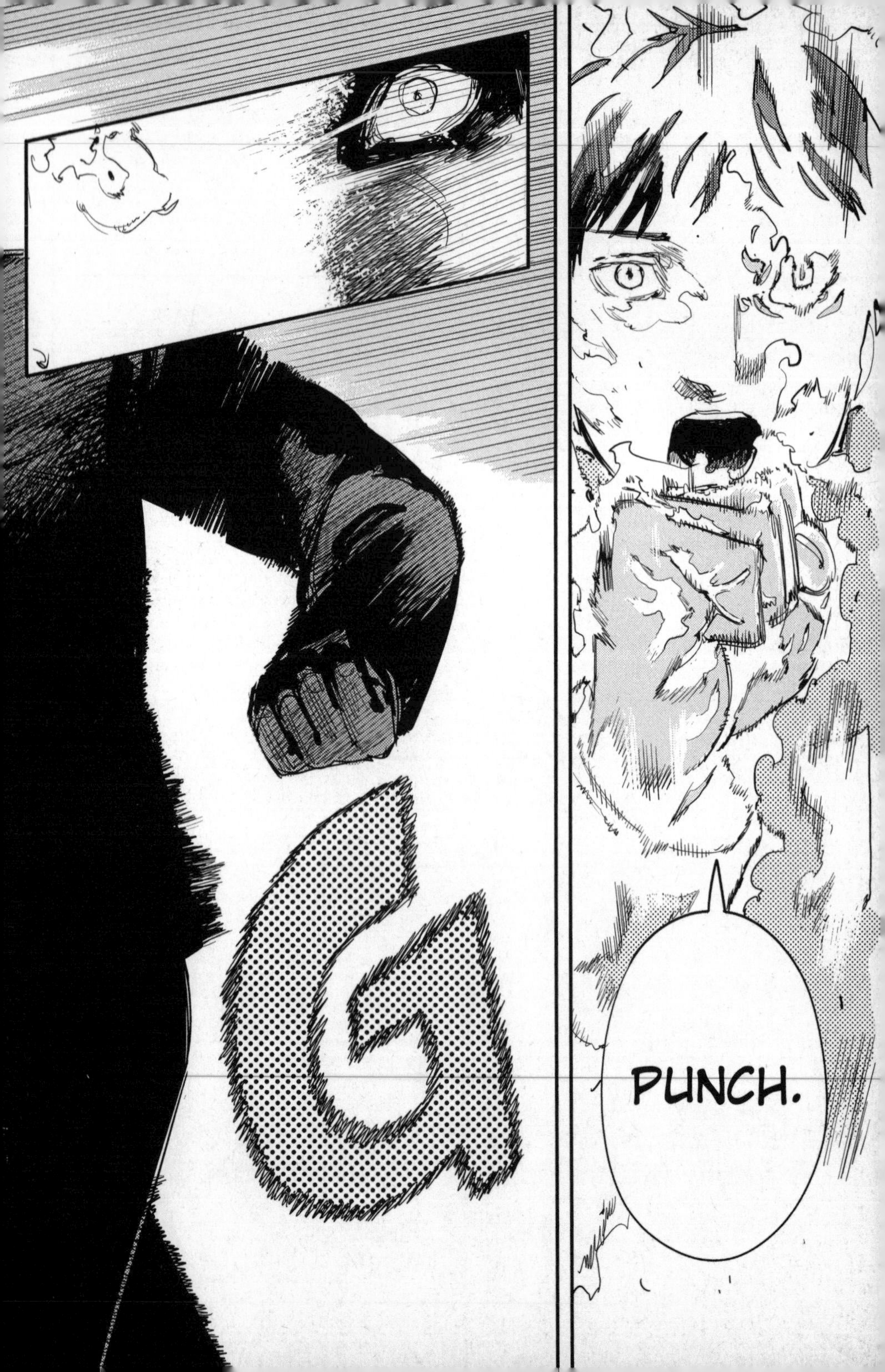
PUNCH.

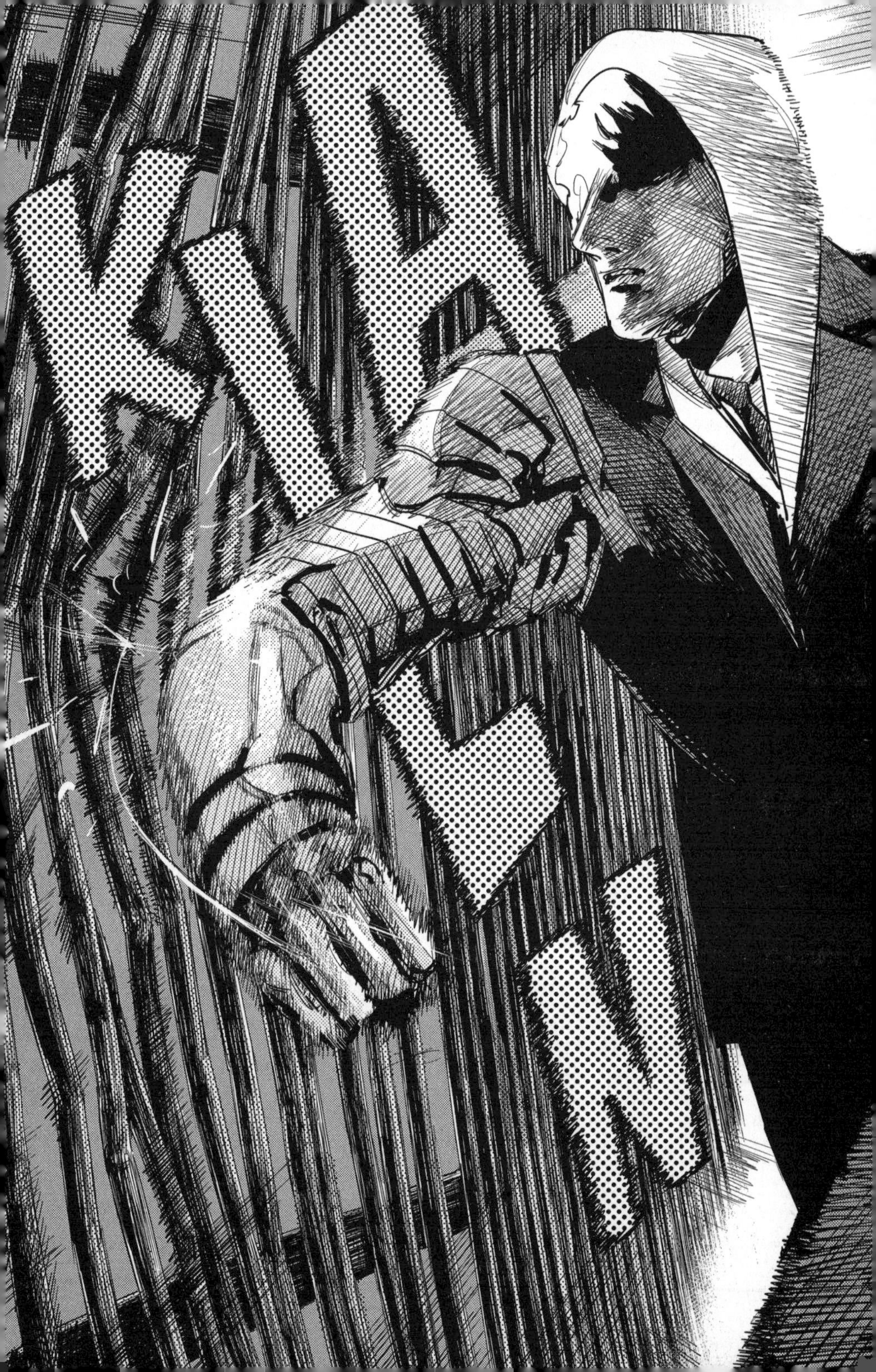

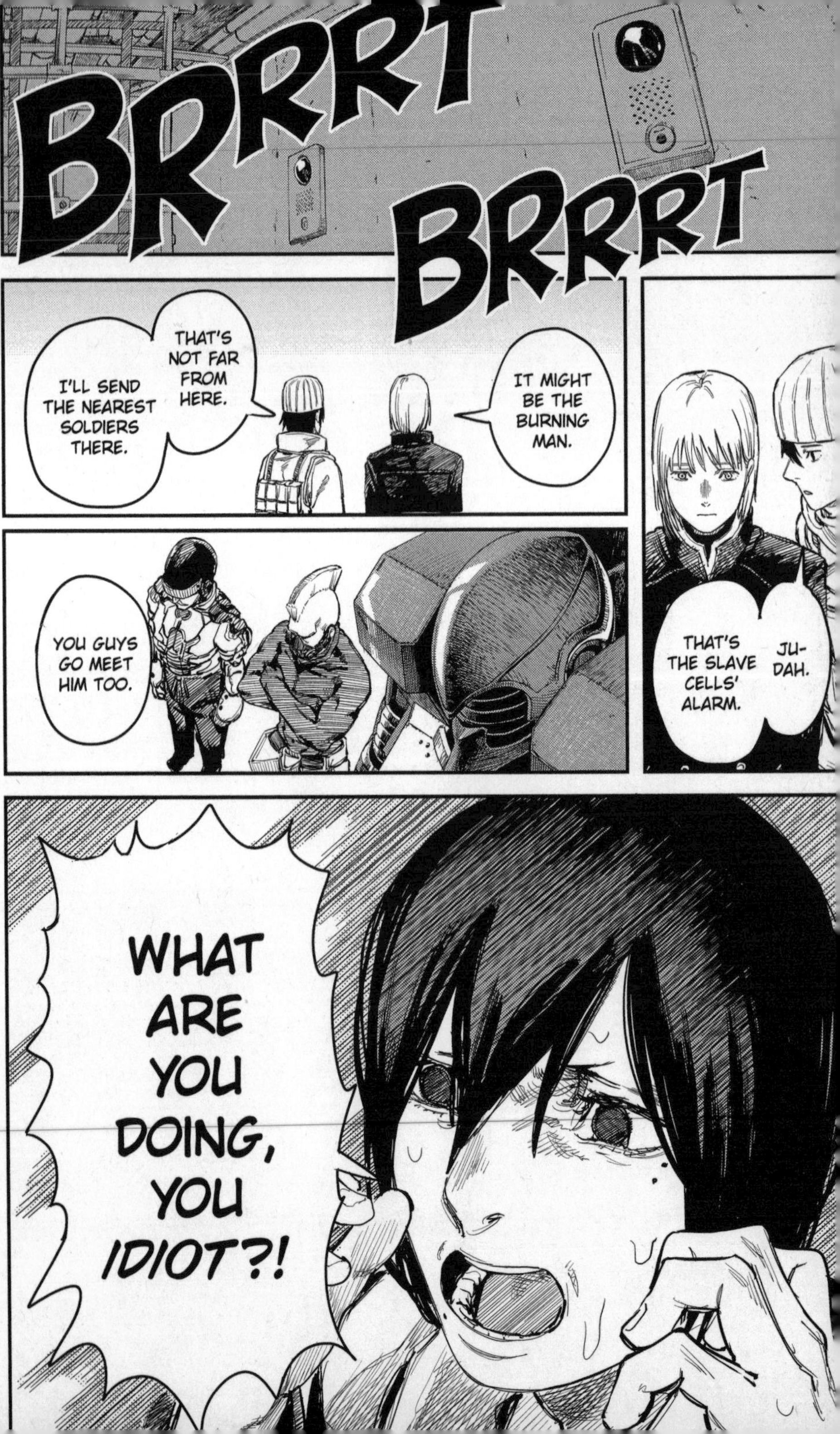
BRRRT
BRRRT
JU-DAH.
THAT'S THE SLAVE CELLS' ALARM.
IT MIGHT BE THE BURNING MAN.
THAT'S NOT FAR FROM HERE.
I'LL SEND THE NEAREST SOLDIERS THERE.
YOU GUYS GO MEET HIM TOO.
WHAT ARE YOU DOING, YOU IDIOT?!

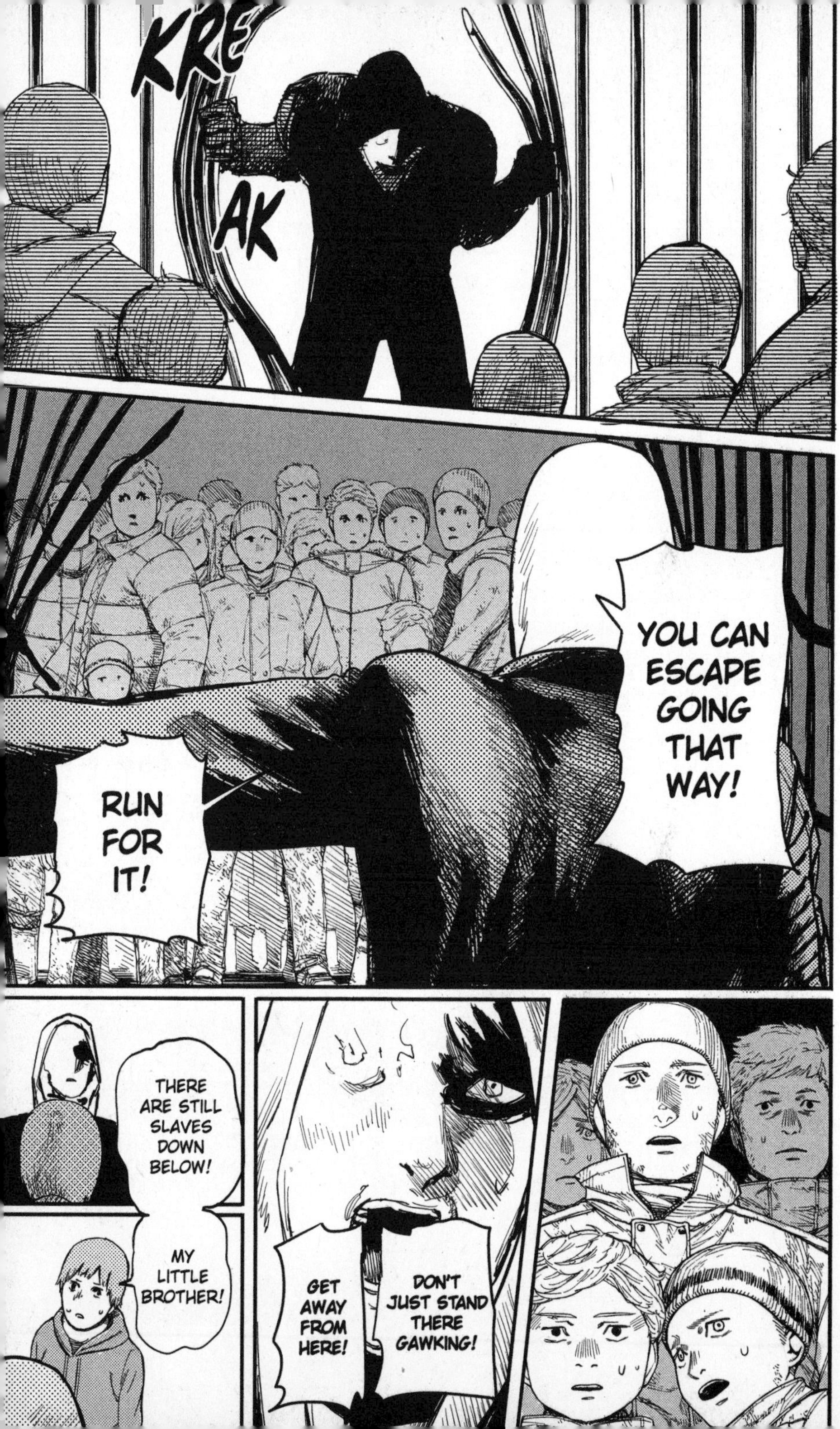
KREAK
YOU CAN ESCAPE GOING THAT WAY!
RUN FOR IT!
DON'T JUST STAND THERE GAWKING!
GET AWAY FROM HERE!
THERE ARE STILL SLAVES DOWN BELOW!
MY LITTLE BROTHER!

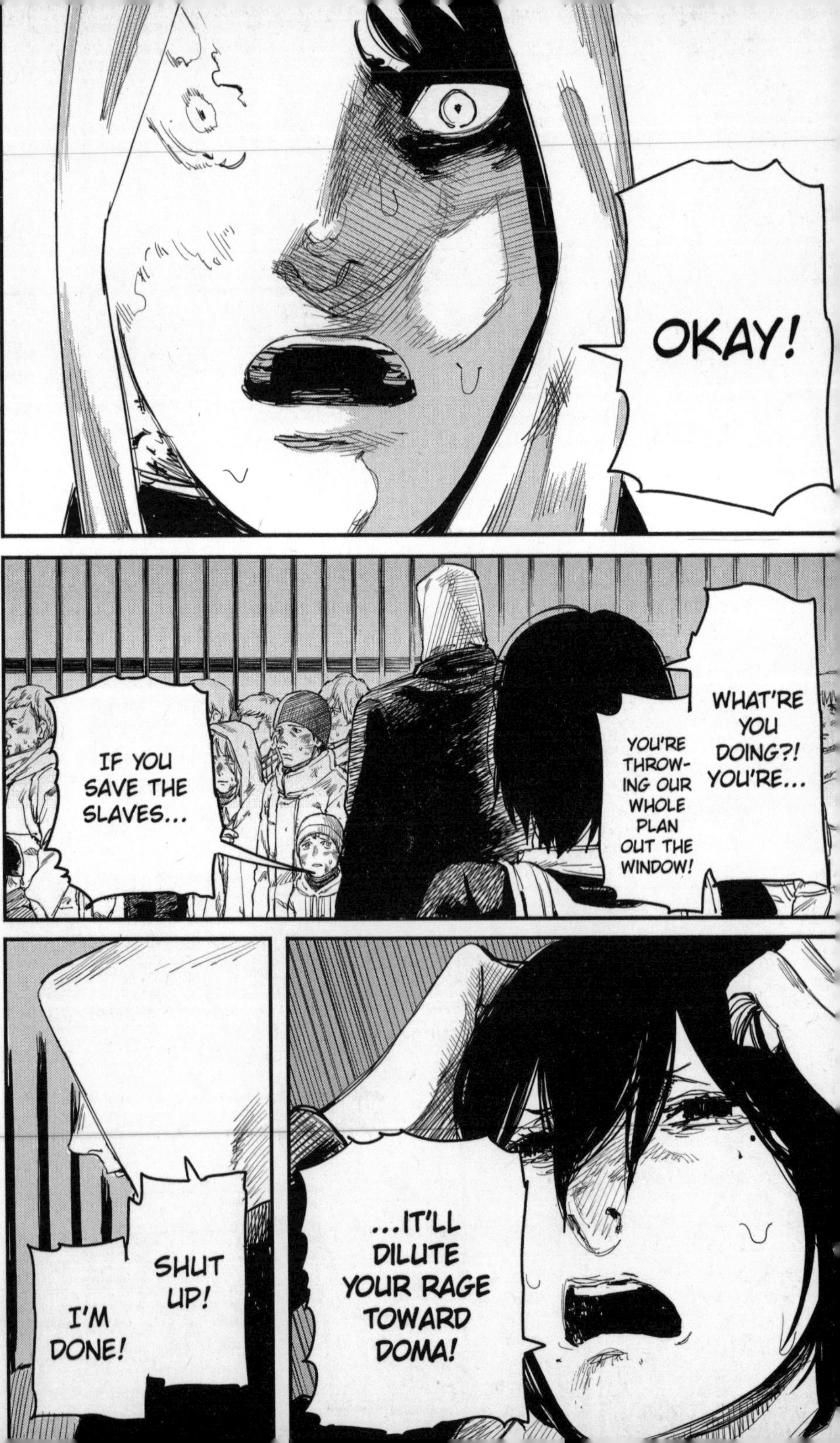
OKAY!
WHAT'RE YOU DOING?! YOU'RE...
YOU'RE THROW-ING OUR WHOLE PLAN OUT THE WINDOW!
IF YOU SAVE THE SLAVES...
...IT'LL DILUTE YOUR RAGE TOWARD DOMA!
SHUT UP!
I'M DONE!

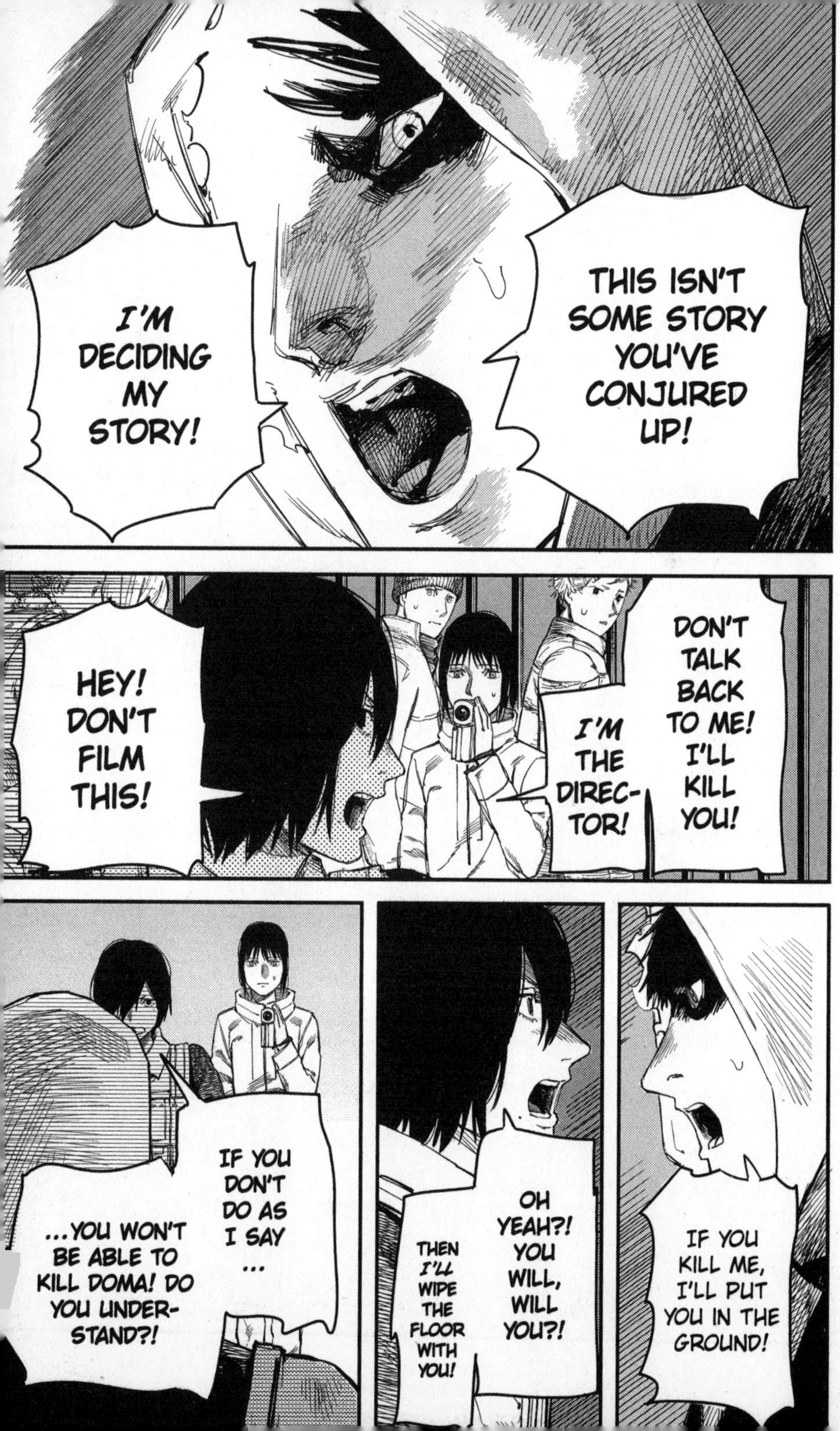
THIS ISN'T SOME STORY YOU'VE CONJURED UP!
I'M DECIDING MY STORY!
DON'T TALK BACK TO ME! I'LL KILL YOU!
I'M THE DIREC-TOR!
HEY! DON'T FILM THIS!
IF YOU KILL ME, I'LL PUT YOU IN THE GROUND!
OH YEAH?! YOU WILL, WILL YOU?!
THEN I'LL WIPE THE FLOOR WITH YOU!
IF YOU DON'T DO AS I SAY ...
...YOU WON'T BE ABLE TO KILL DOMA! DO YOU UNDER-STAND?!

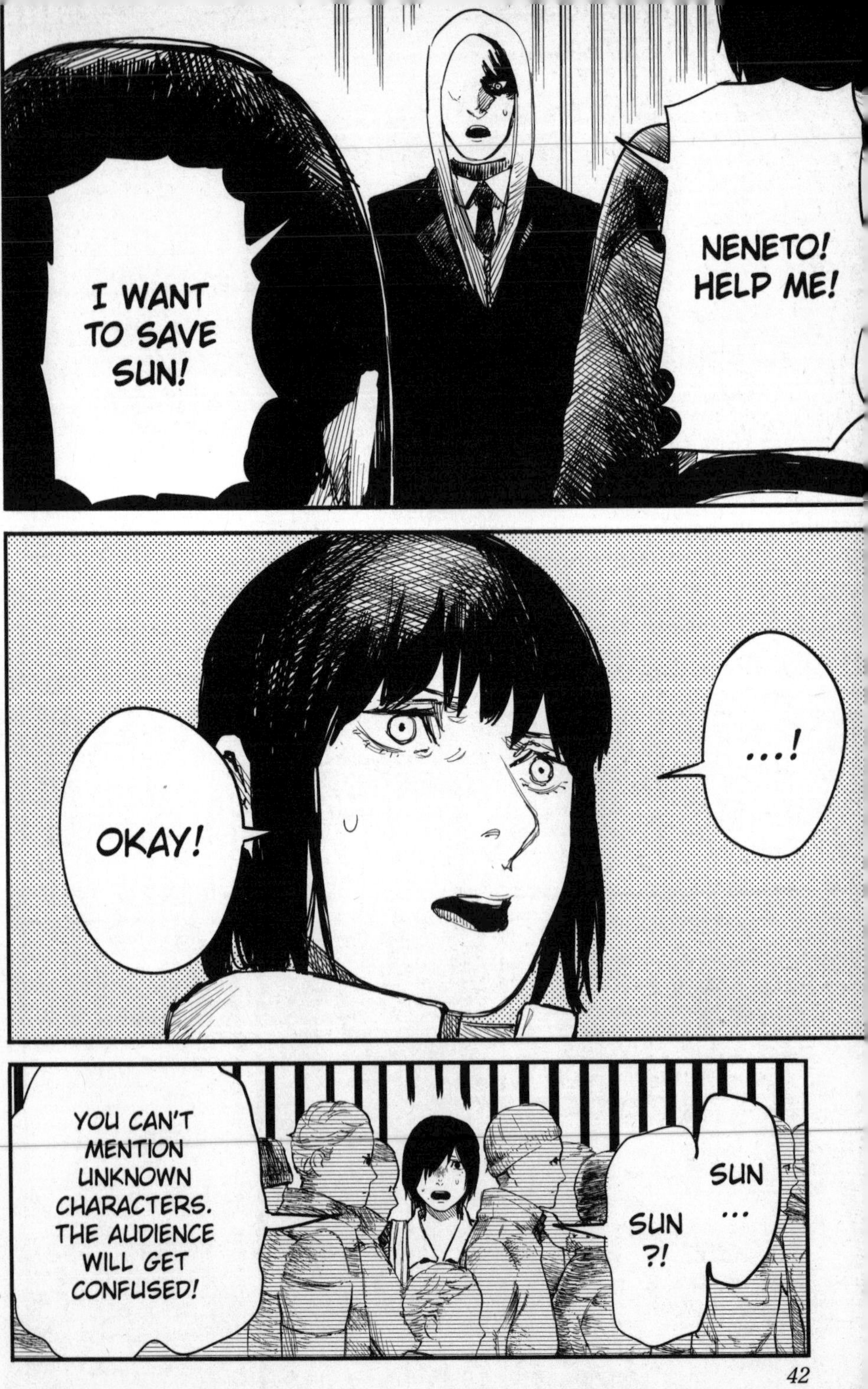
NENETO! HELP ME!
I WANT TO SAVE SUN!
...!
OKAY!
SUN ...
SUN ?!
YOU CAN'T MENTION UNKNOWN CHARACTERS. THE AUDIENCE WILL GET CONFUSED!

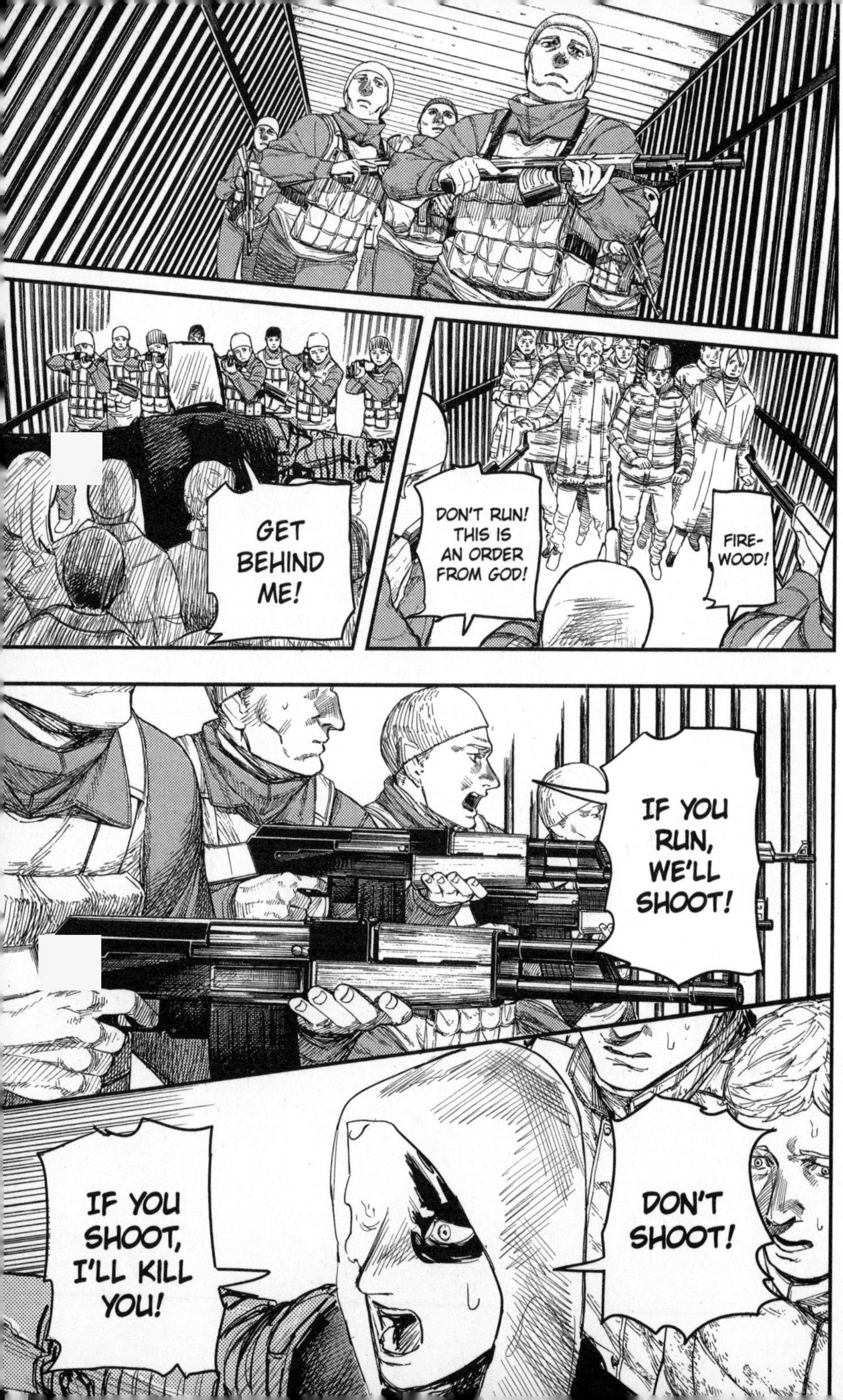
FIRE-WOOD!
DON'T RUN! THIS IS AN ORDER FROM GOD!
GET BEHIND ME!
IF YOU RUN, WE'LL SHOOT!
DON'T SHOOT!
IF YOU SHOOT, I'LL KILL YOU!

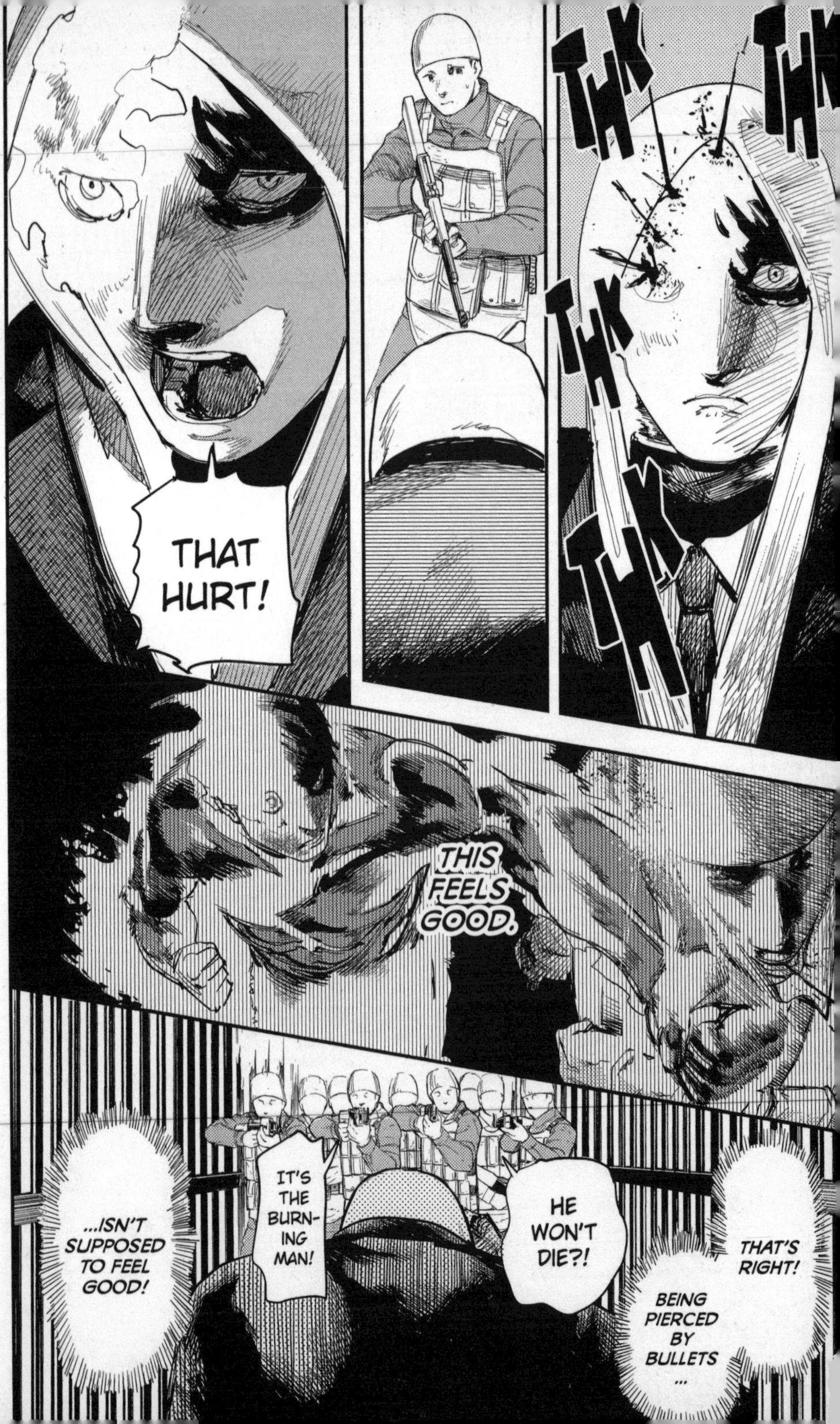
THK
THK
THK
THK
THAT HURT!
THIS FEELS GOOD.
THAT'S RIGHT!
BEING PIERCED BY BULLETS...
HE WON'T DIE?!
IT'S THE BURN-ING MAN!
...ISN'T SUPPOSED TO FEEL GOOD!

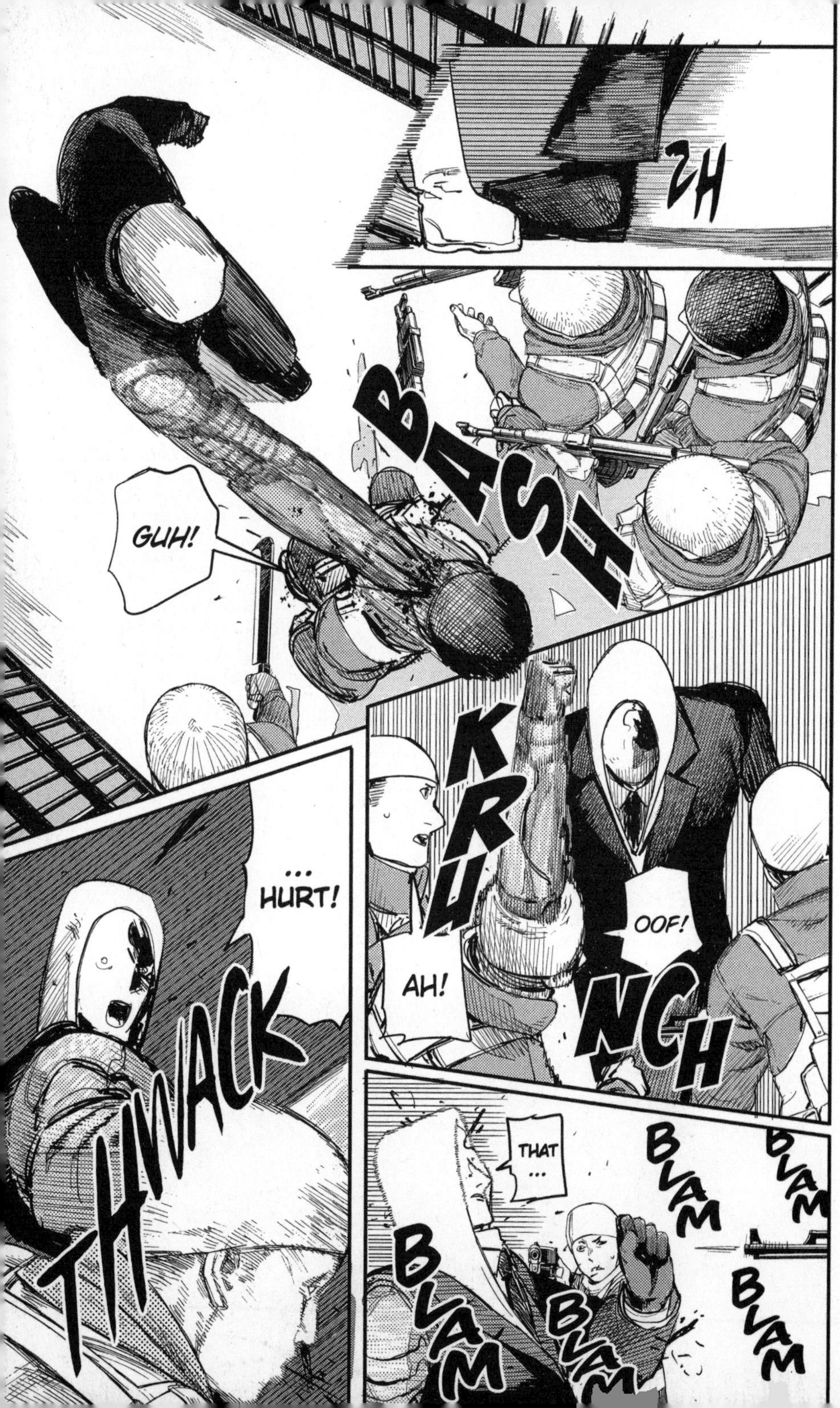
ZH
BASH
GUH!
KRUNCH
OOF!
AH!
THAT ...
BLAM
BLAM
BLAM
BLAM
BLAM
BLAM
... HURT!
THWACK

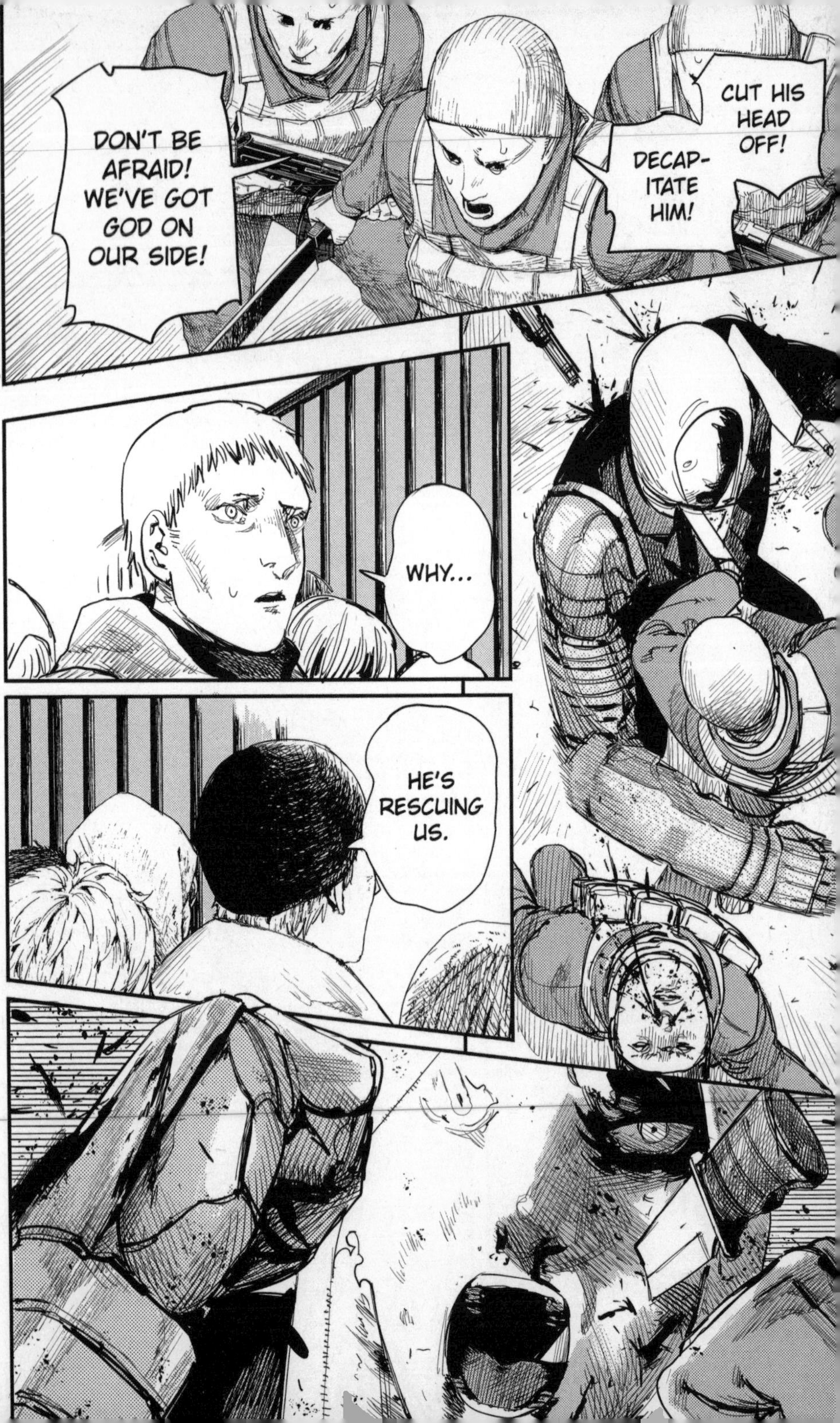
CUT HIS HEAD OFF!
DECAP-ITATE HIM!
DON'T BE AFRAID! WE'VE GOT GOD ON OUR SIDE!
WHY...
HE'S RESCUING US.

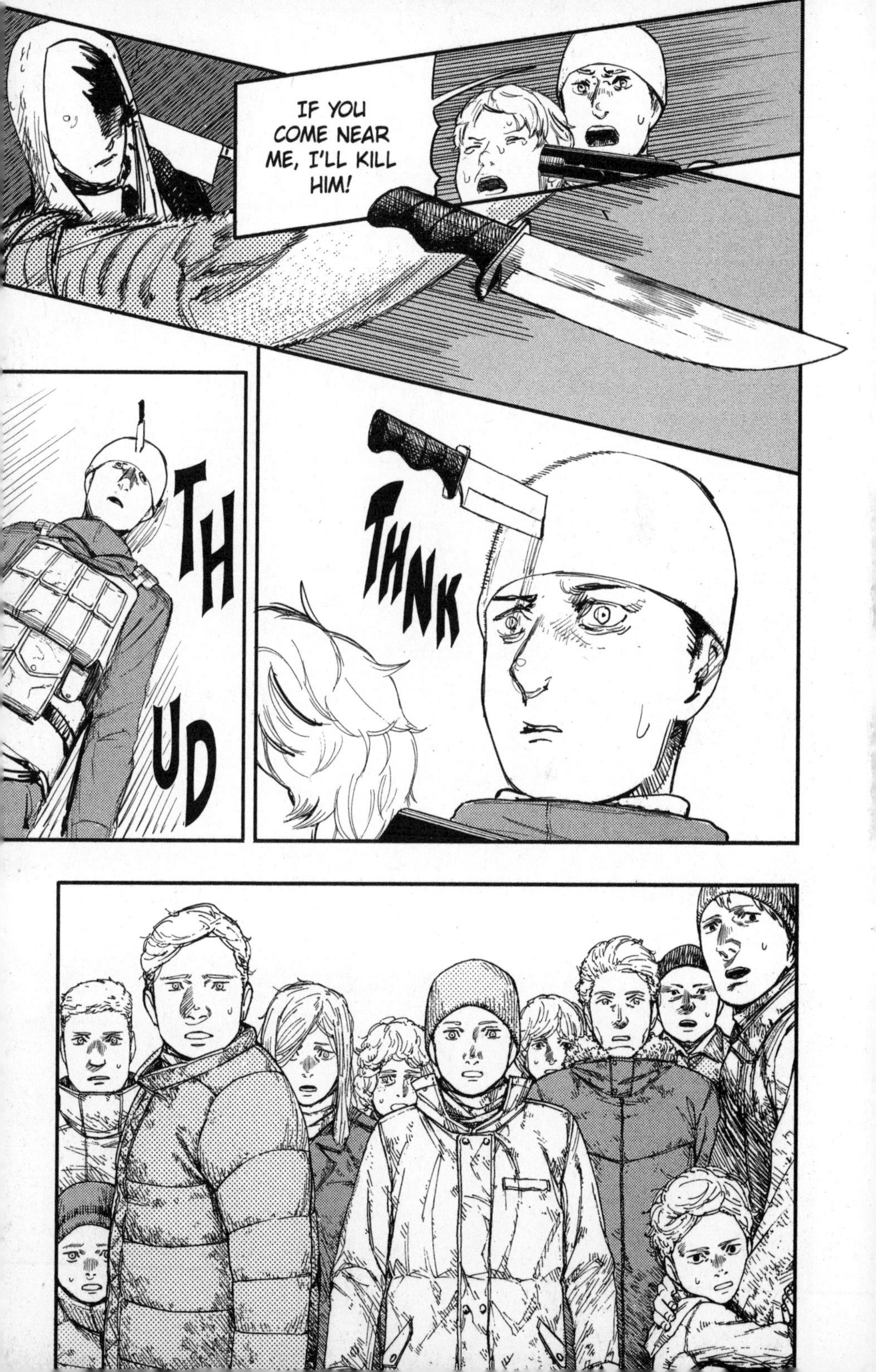
IF YOU COME NEAR ME, I'LL KILL HIM!
THNK
THUD

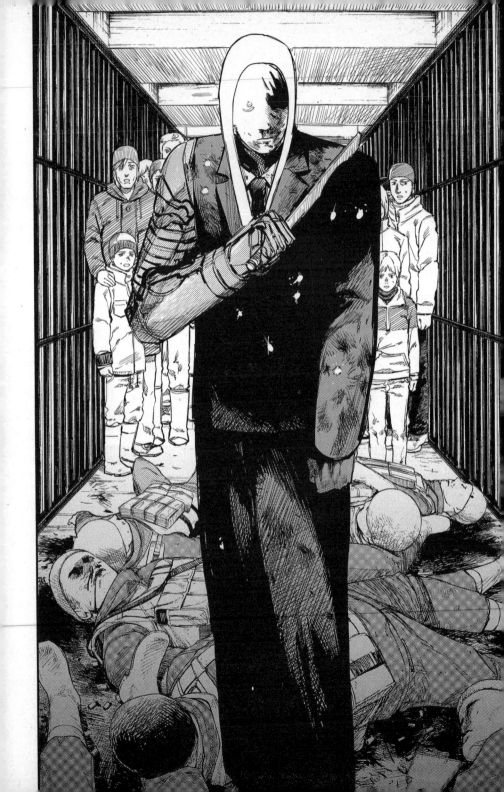

FIRE PUNCH

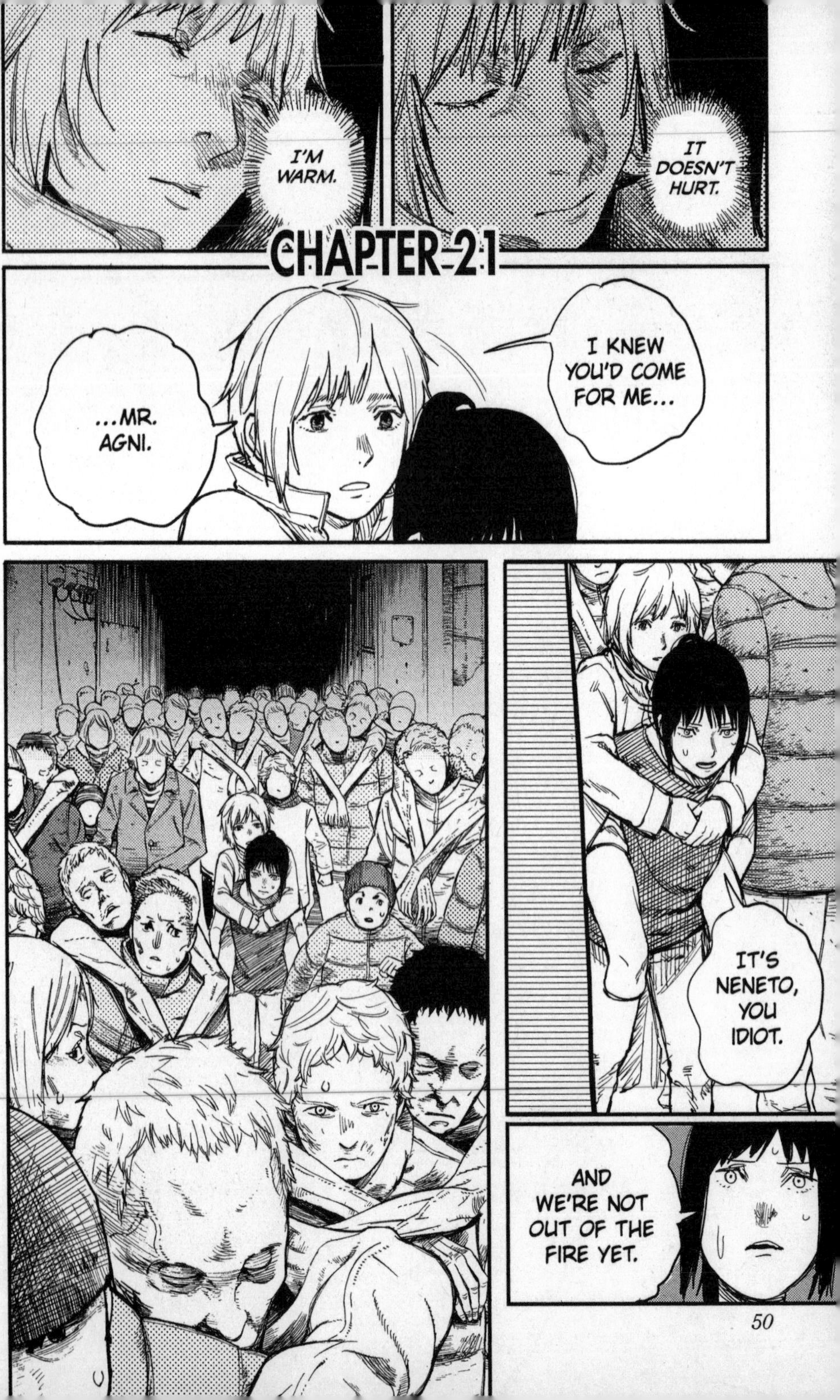
IT DOESN'T HURT.
I'M WARM.
CHAPTER 21
I KNEW YOU'D COME FOR ME...
...MR. AGNI.
IT'S NENETO, YOU IDIOT.
AND WE'RE NOT OUT OF THE FIRE YET.

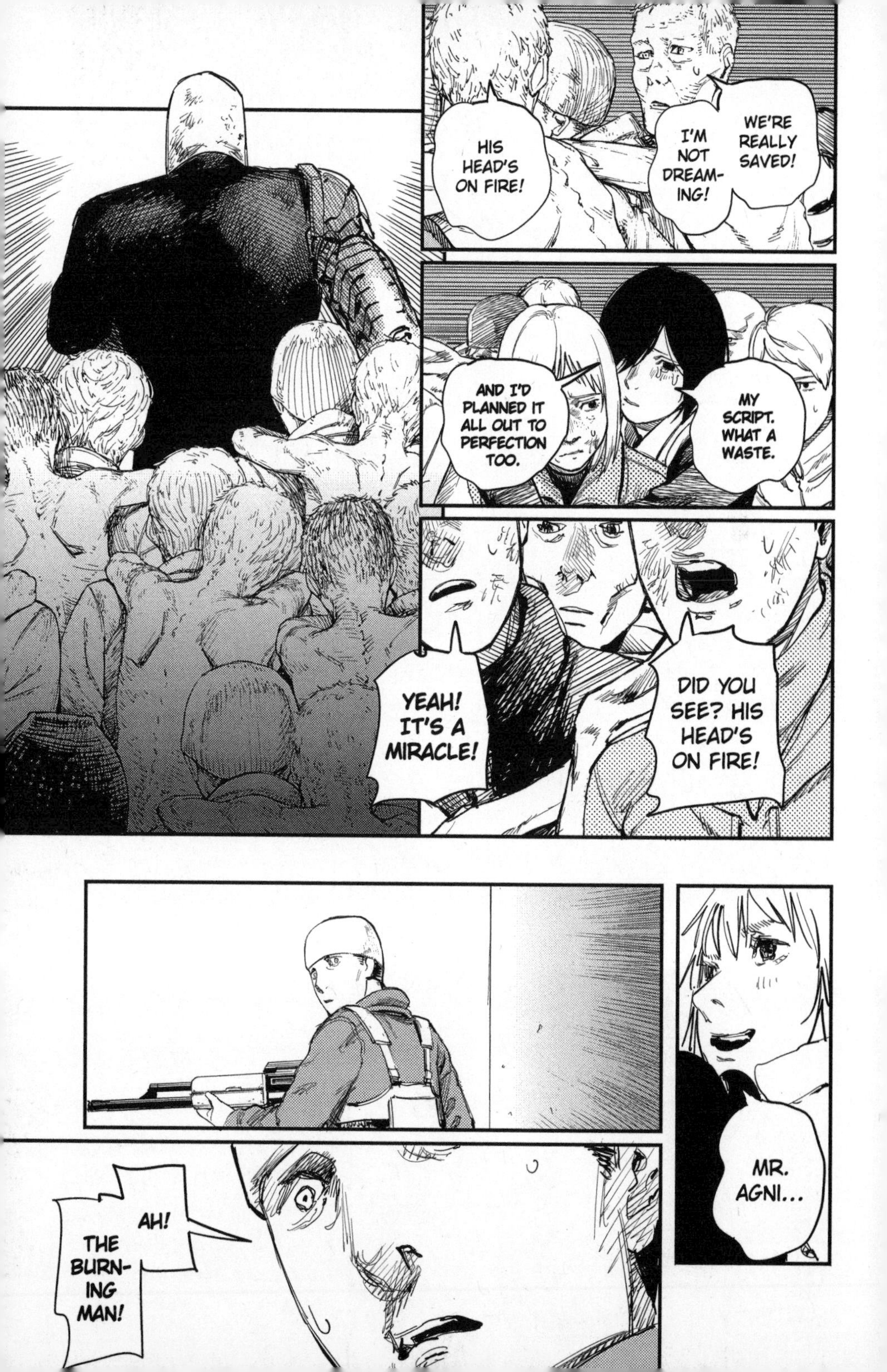
WE'RE REALLY SAVED!
I'M NOT DREAMING!
HIS HEAD'S ON FIRE!
MY SCRIPT. WHAT A WASTE.
AND I'D PLANNED IT ALL OUT TO PERFECTION TOO.
DID YOU SEE? HIS HEAD'S ON FIRE!
YEAH! IT'S A MIRACLE!
MR. AGNI...
AH! THE BURNING MAN!

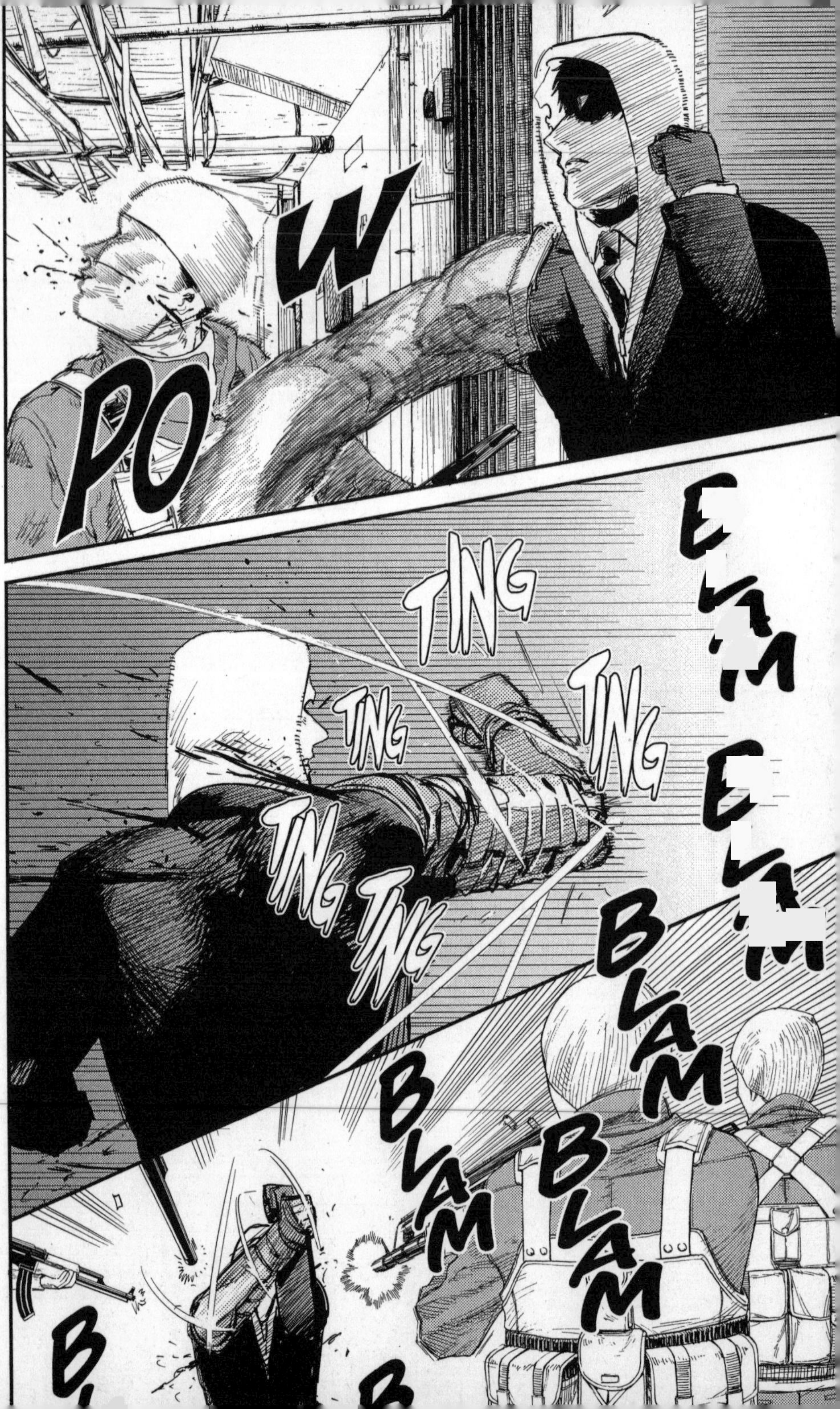
POW
TING
TING
TING
TING
TING
BLAM
BLAM
BLAM
BLAM
BLAM
BLAM
B
B

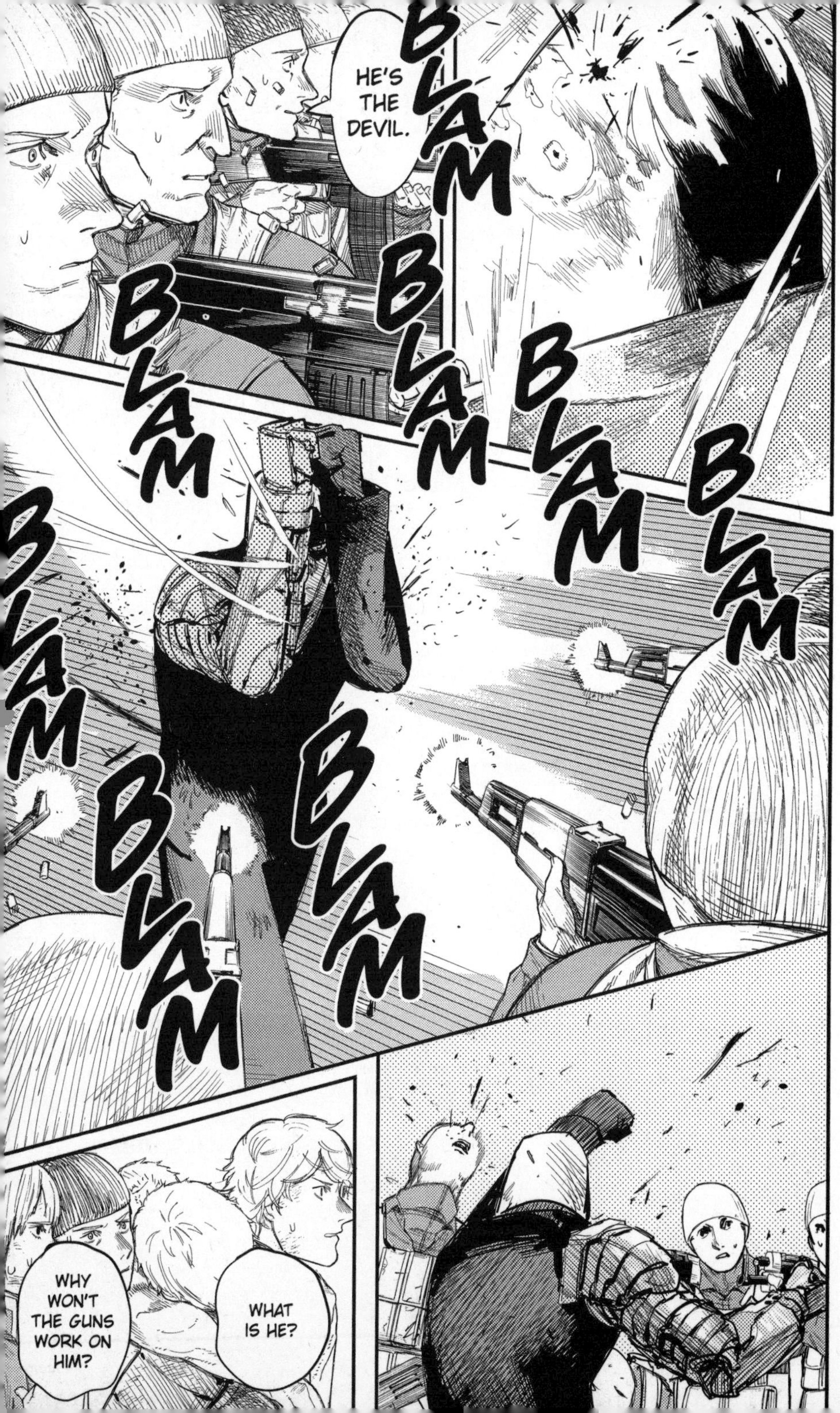

BLAM
BLAM
BLAM
BLAM
HE'S THE DEVIL.
BLAM
BLAM
BLAM
BLAM
WHAT IS HE?
WHY WON'T THE GUNS WORK ON HIM?

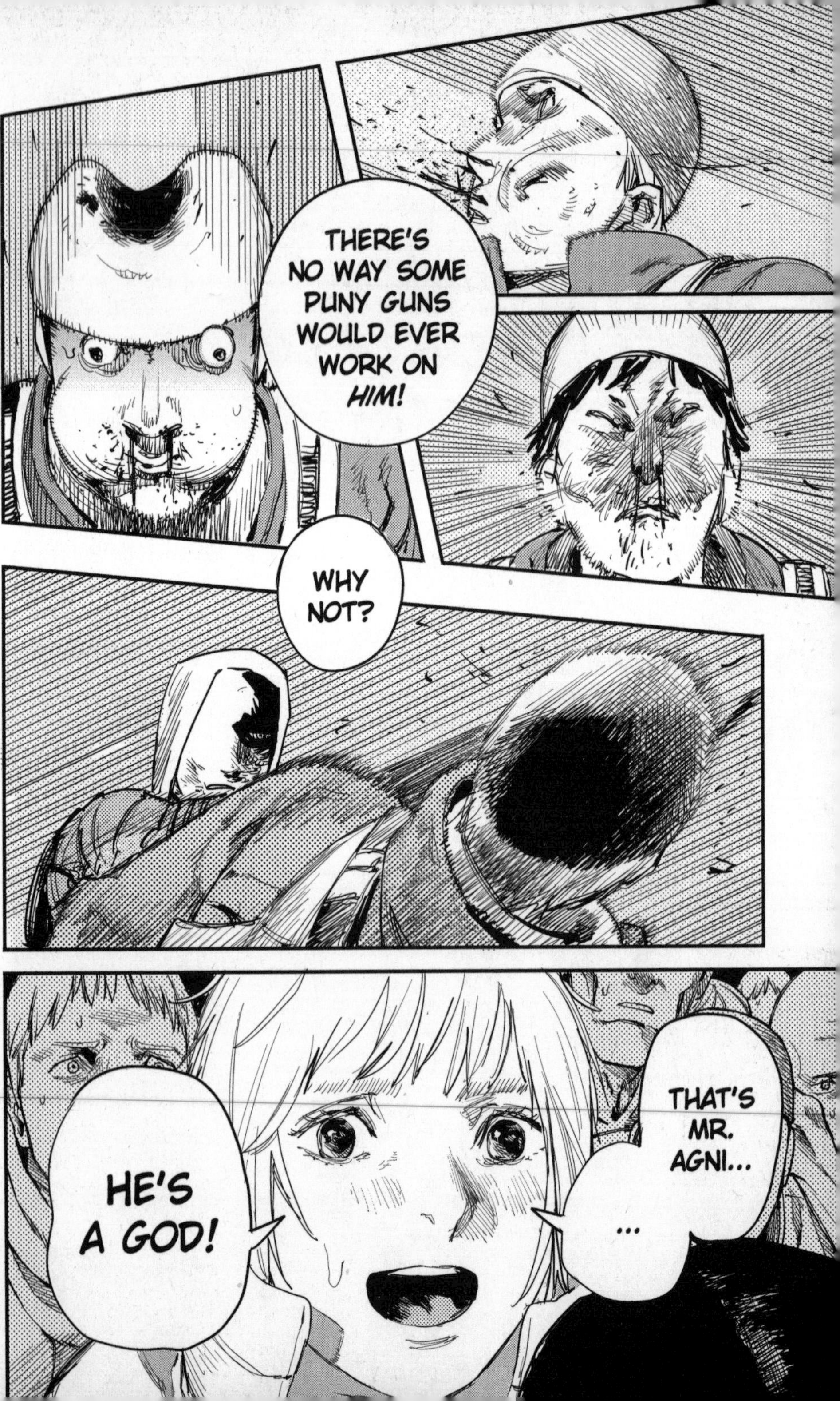
THERE'S NO WAY SOME PUNY GUNS WOULD EVER WORK ON *HIM!*
WHY NOT?
THAT'S MR. AGNI...
...
HE'S A GOD!

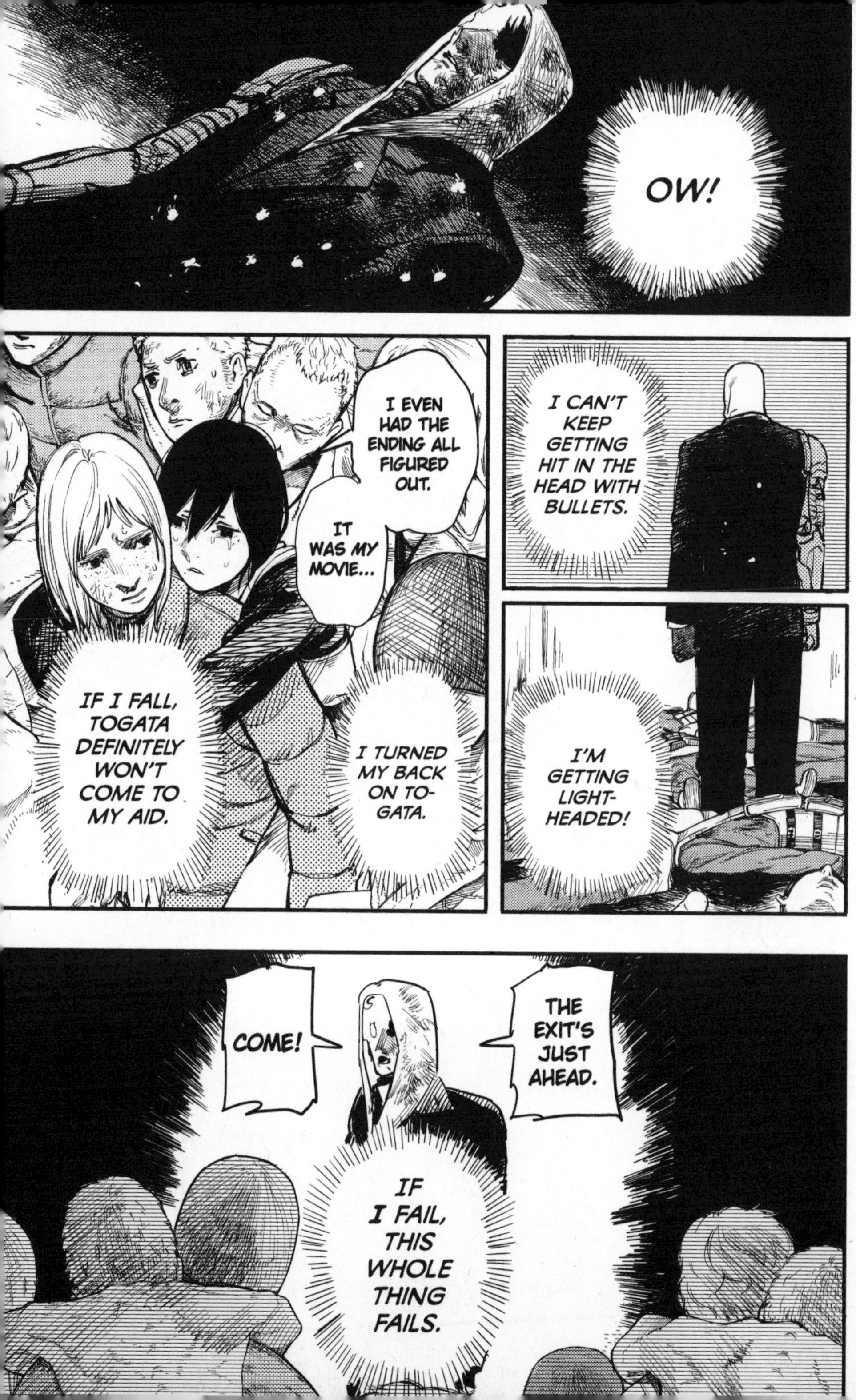
OW!
I CAN'T KEEP GETTING HIT IN THE HEAD WITH BULLETS.
I'M GETTING LIGHT-HEADED!
I EVEN HAD THE ENDING ALL FIGURED OUT.
IT WAS MY MOVIE...
I TURNED MY BACK ON TO-GATA.
IF I FALL, TOGATA DEFINITELY WON'T COME TO MY AID.
THE EXIT'S JUST AHEAD.
COME!
IF I FAIL, THIS WHOLE THING FAILS.

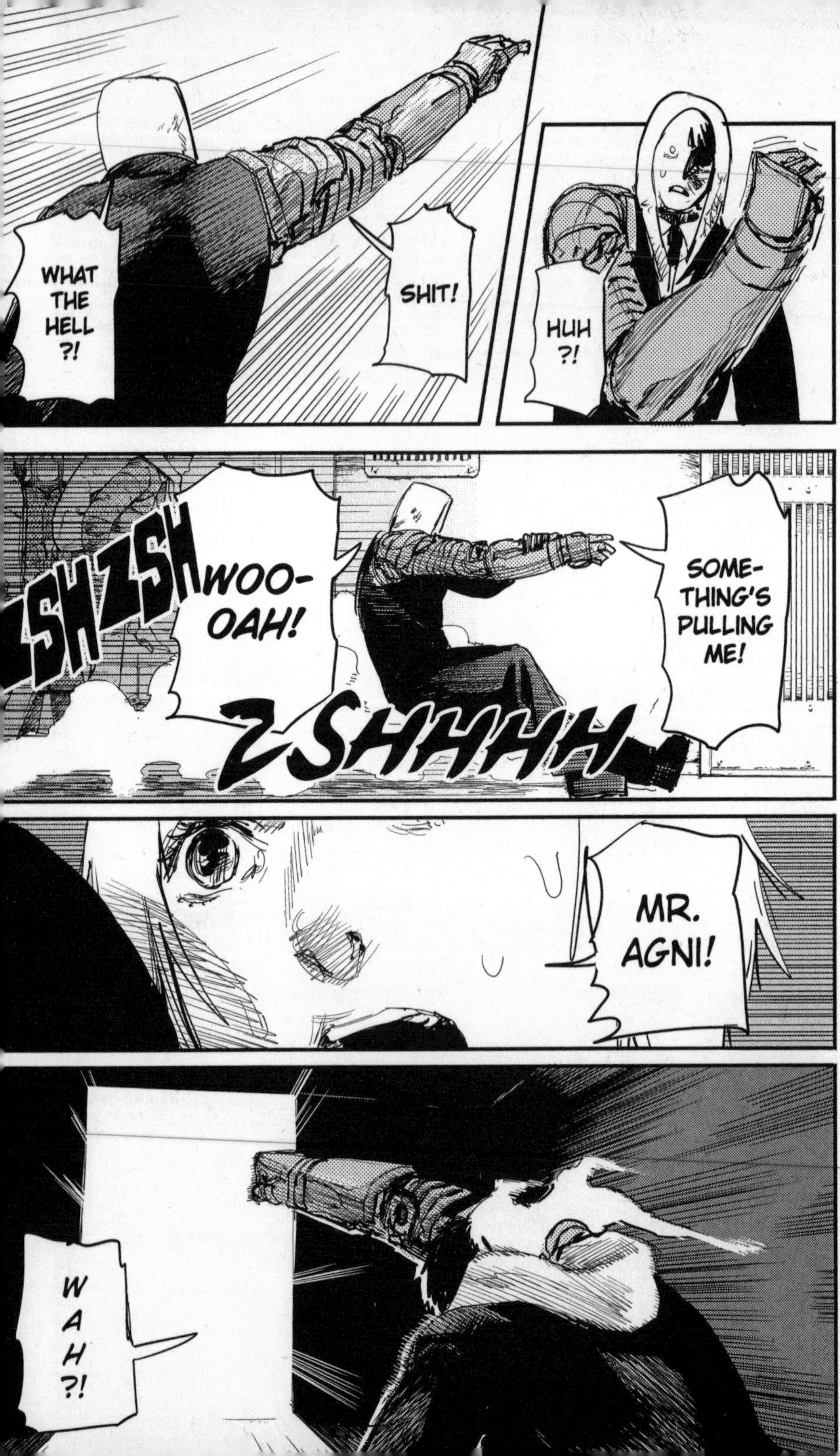
HUH ?!
SHIT!
WHAT THE HELL ?!
SOME-THING'S PULLING ME!
ZSHHHH
WOO-OAH!
SHZSH
MR. AGNI!
WAH?!

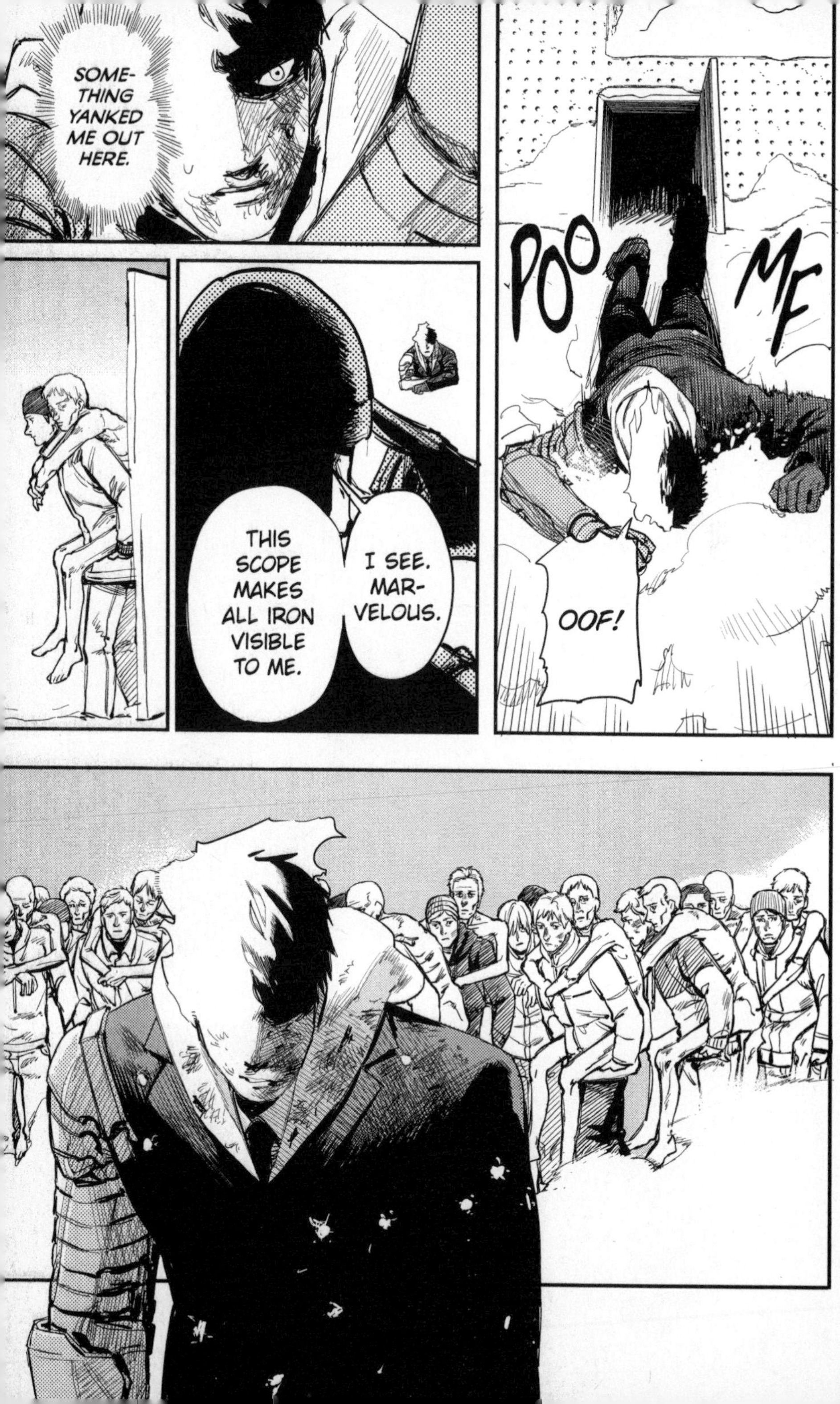
POOMF
OOF!
SOMETHING YANKED ME OUT HERE.
I SEE. MARVELOUS.
THIS SCOPE MAKES ALL IRON VISIBLE TO ME.

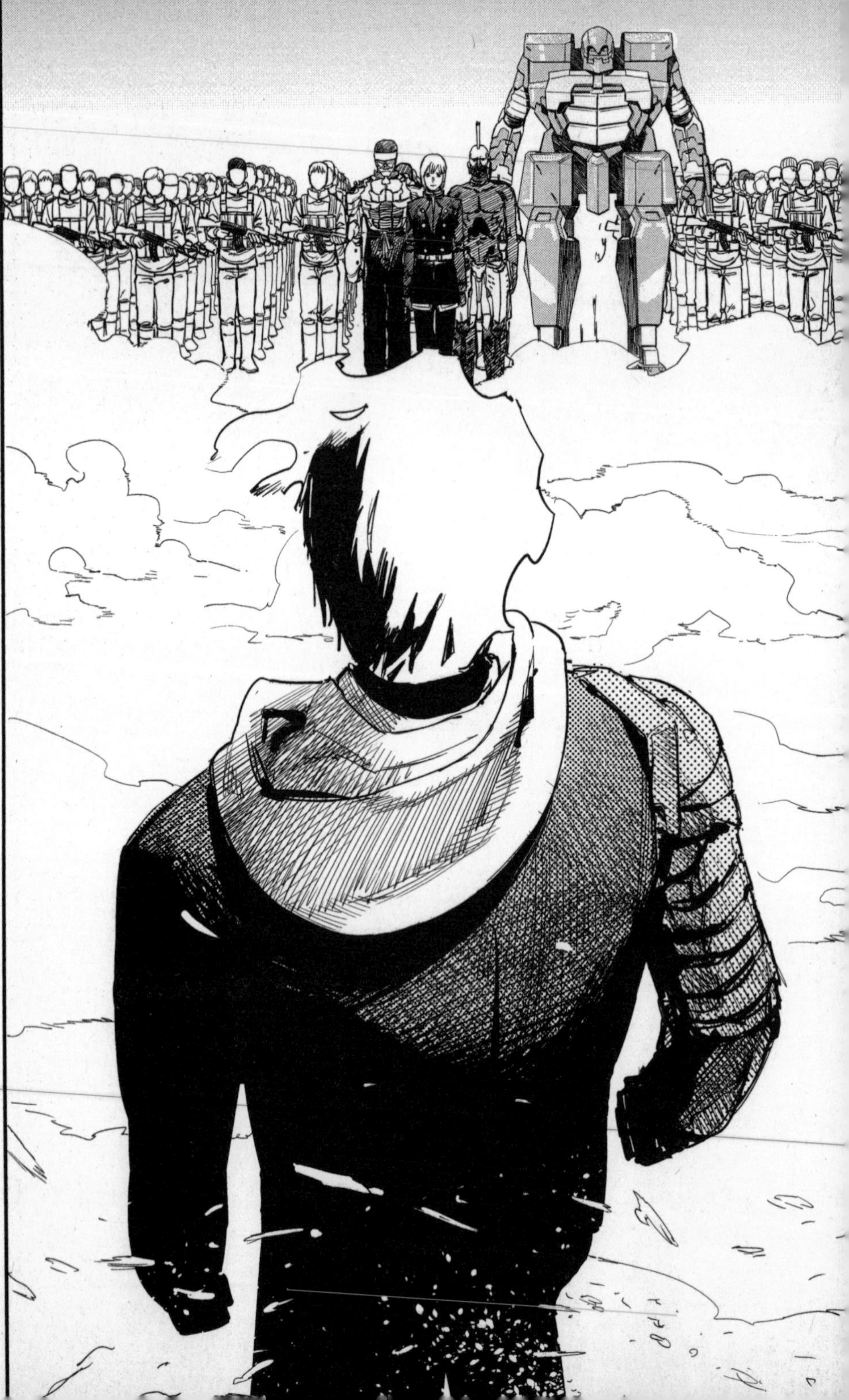

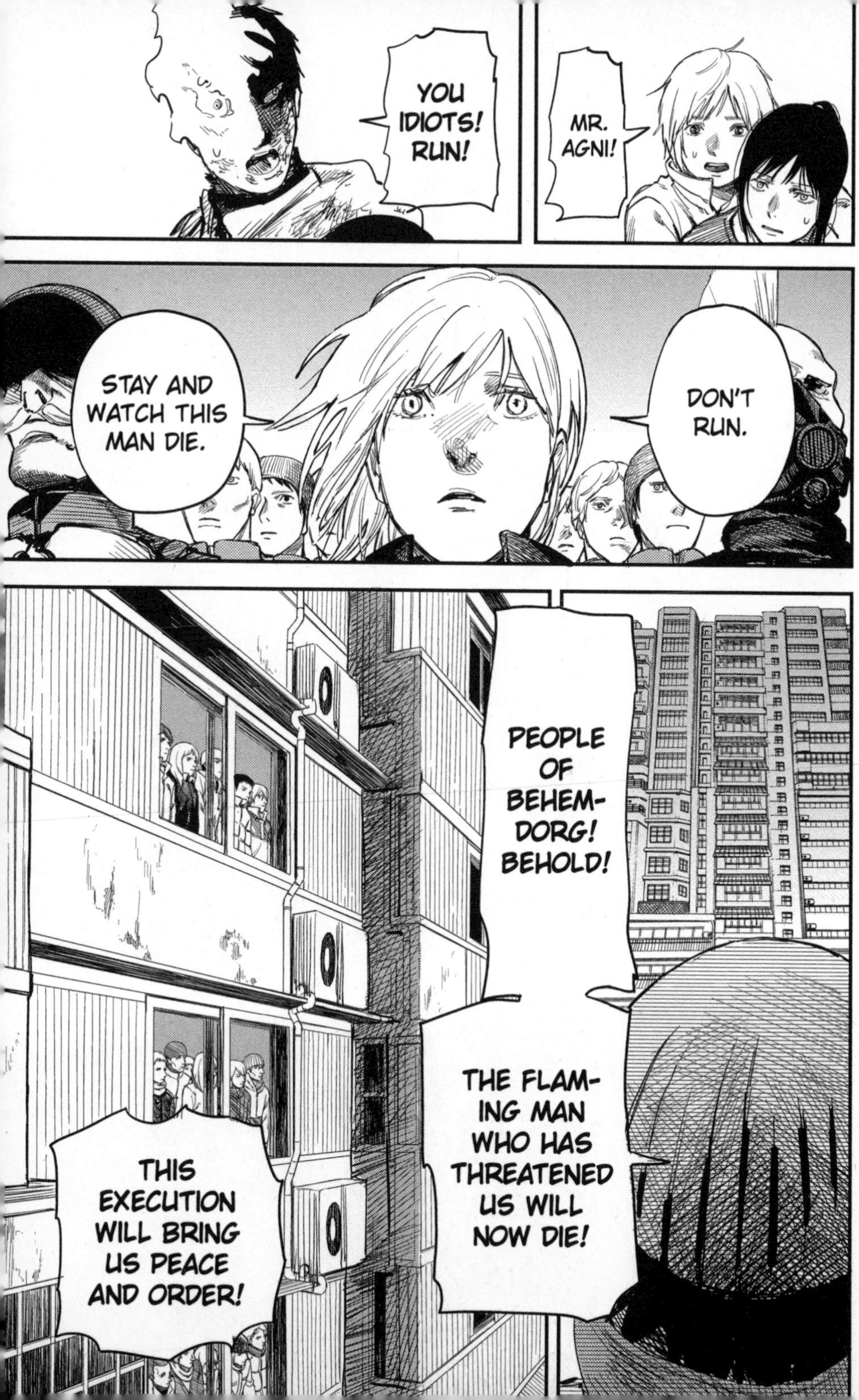
MR. AGNI!
YOU IDIOTS! RUN!
DON'T RUN.
STAY AND WATCH THIS MAN DIE.
PEOPLE OF BEHEM-DORG! BEHOLD!
THE FLAM-ING MAN WHO HAS THREATENED US WILL NOW DIE!
THIS EXECUTION WILL BRING US PEACE AND ORDER!

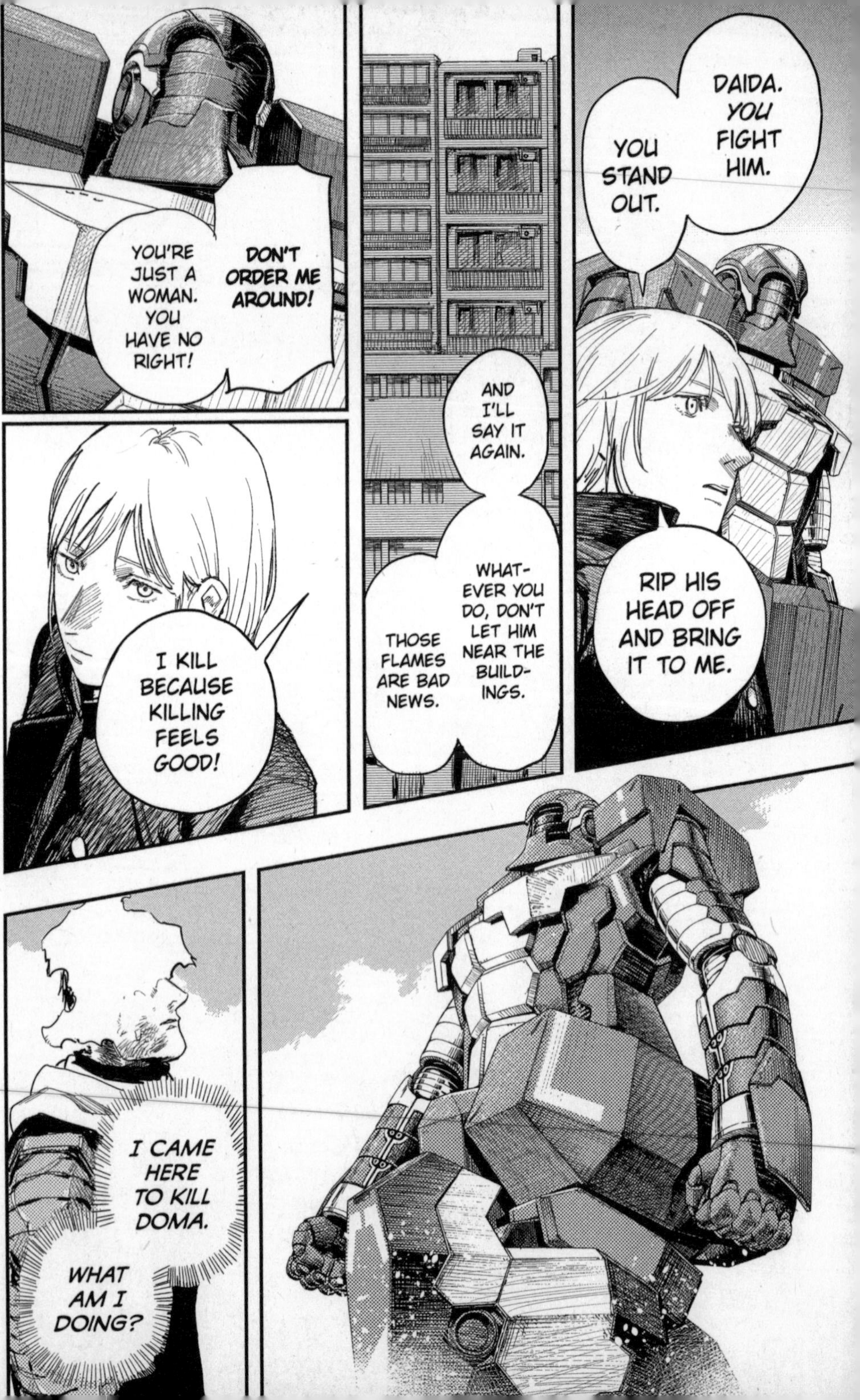
DAIDA. YOU FIGHT HIM.
YOU STAND OUT.
RIP HIS HEAD OFF AND BRING IT TO ME.
AND I'LL SAY IT AGAIN.
WHAT-EVER YOU DO, DON'T LET HIM NEAR THE BUILD-INGS.
THOSE FLAMES ARE BAD NEWS.
DON'T ORDER ME AROUND!
YOU'RE JUST A WOMAN. YOU HAVE NO RIGHT!
I KILL BECAUSE KILLING FEELS GOOD!
I CAME HERE TO KILL DOMA.
WHAT AM I DOING?

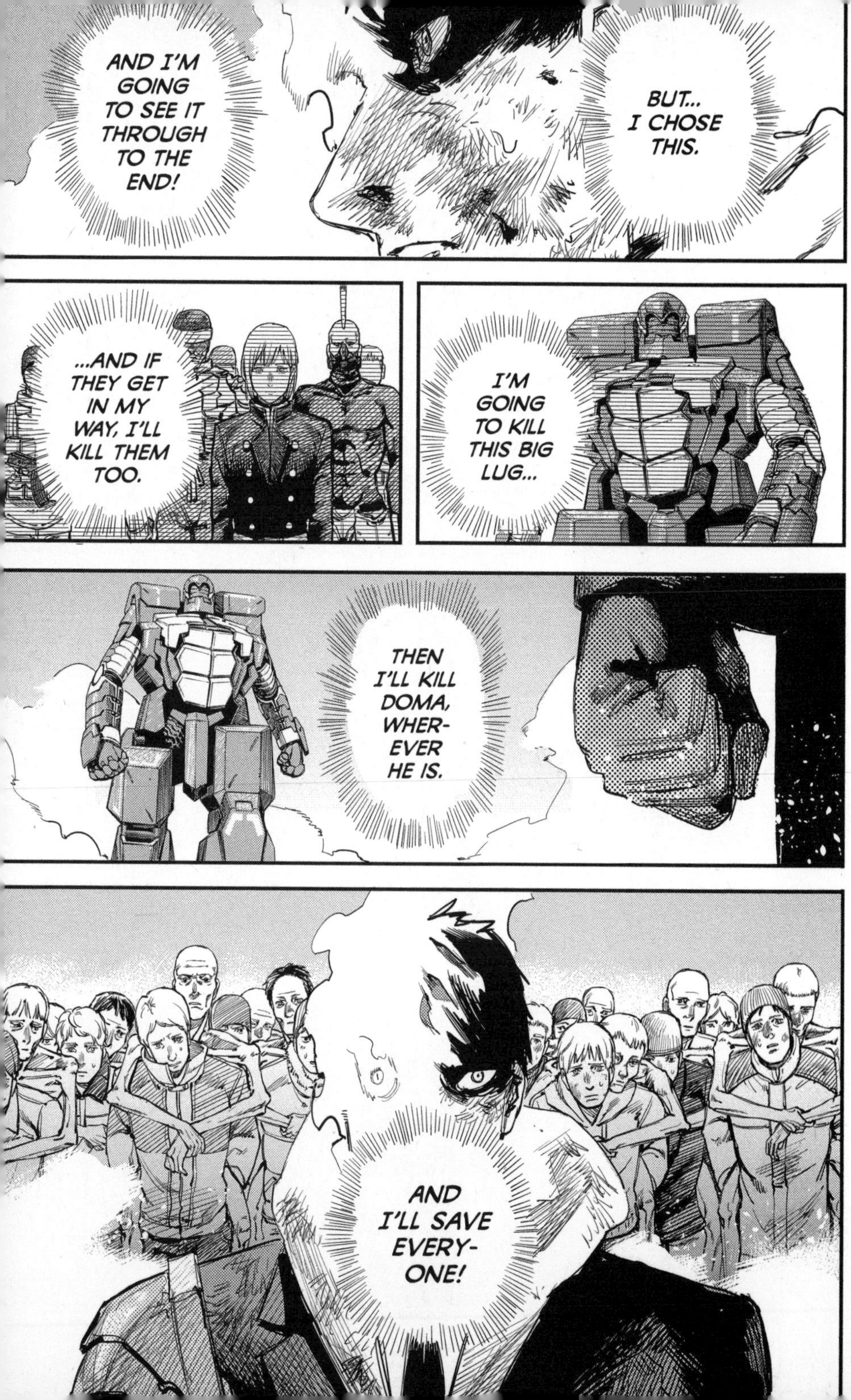
BUT... I CHOSE THIS.
AND I'M GOING TO SEE IT THROUGH TO THE END!
I'M GOING TO KILL THIS BIG LUG...
...AND IF THEY GET IN MY WAY, I'LL KILL THEM TOO.
THEN I'LL KILL DOMA, WHEREVER HE IS.
AND I'LL SAVE EVERYONE!

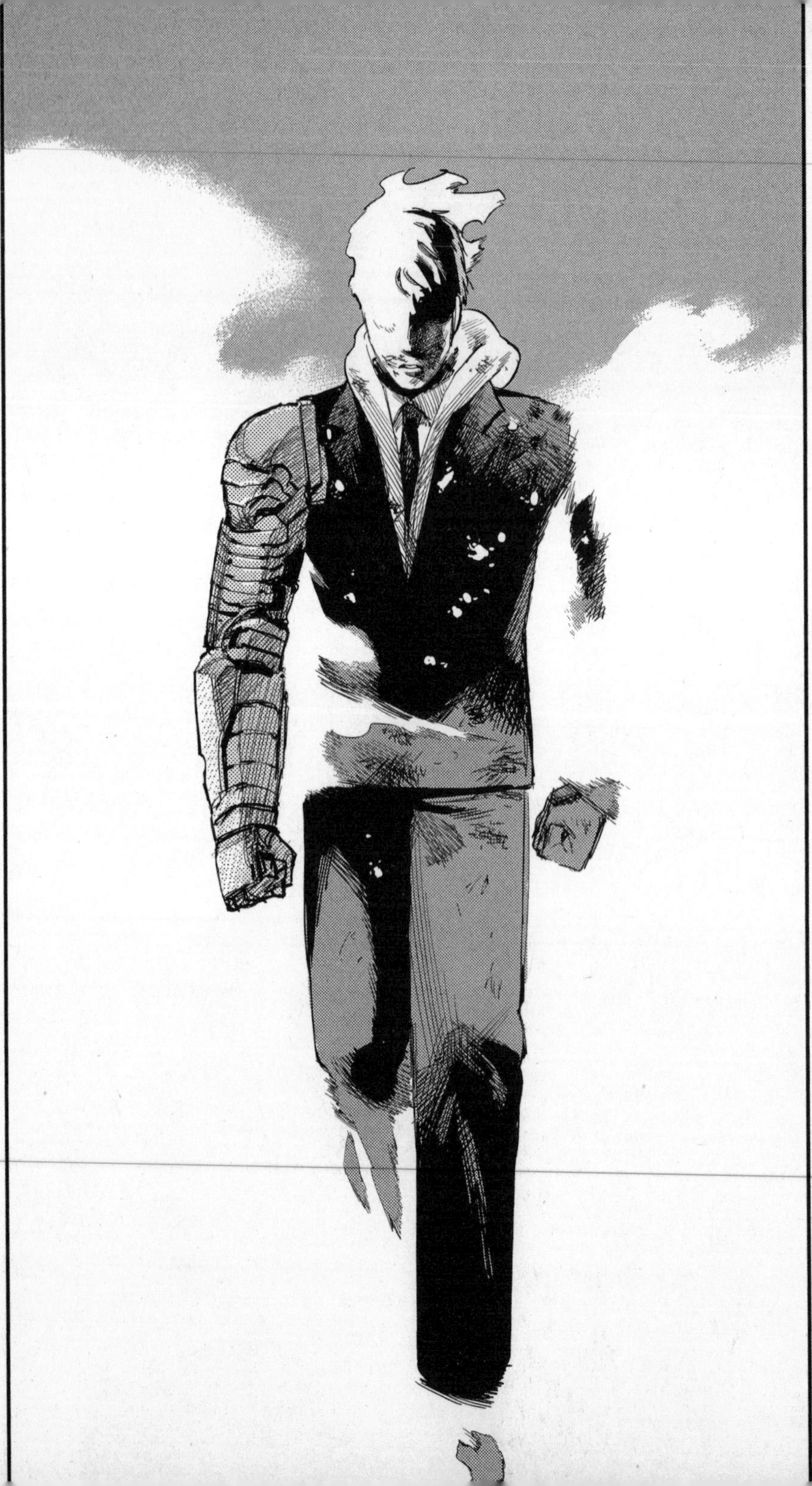

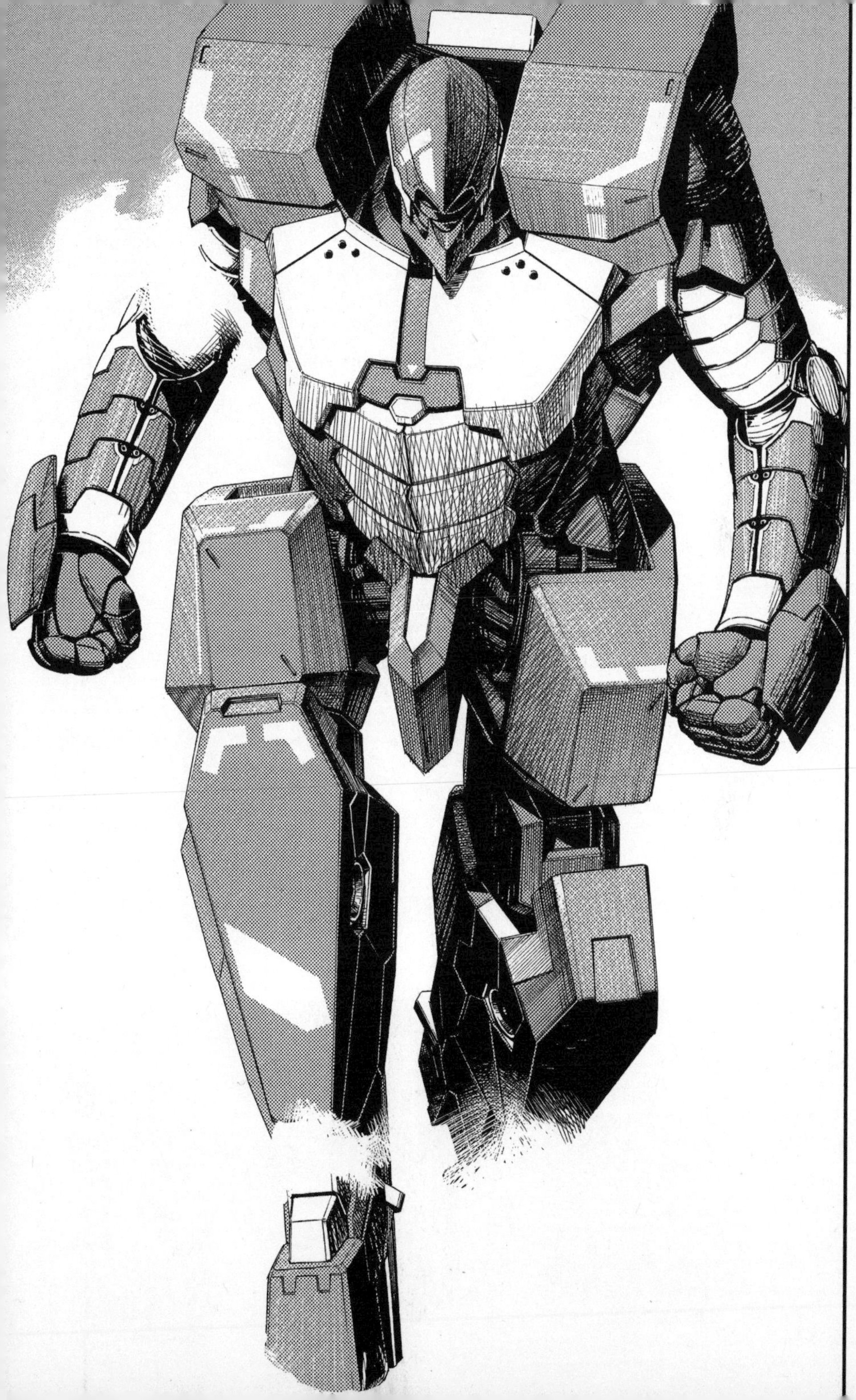

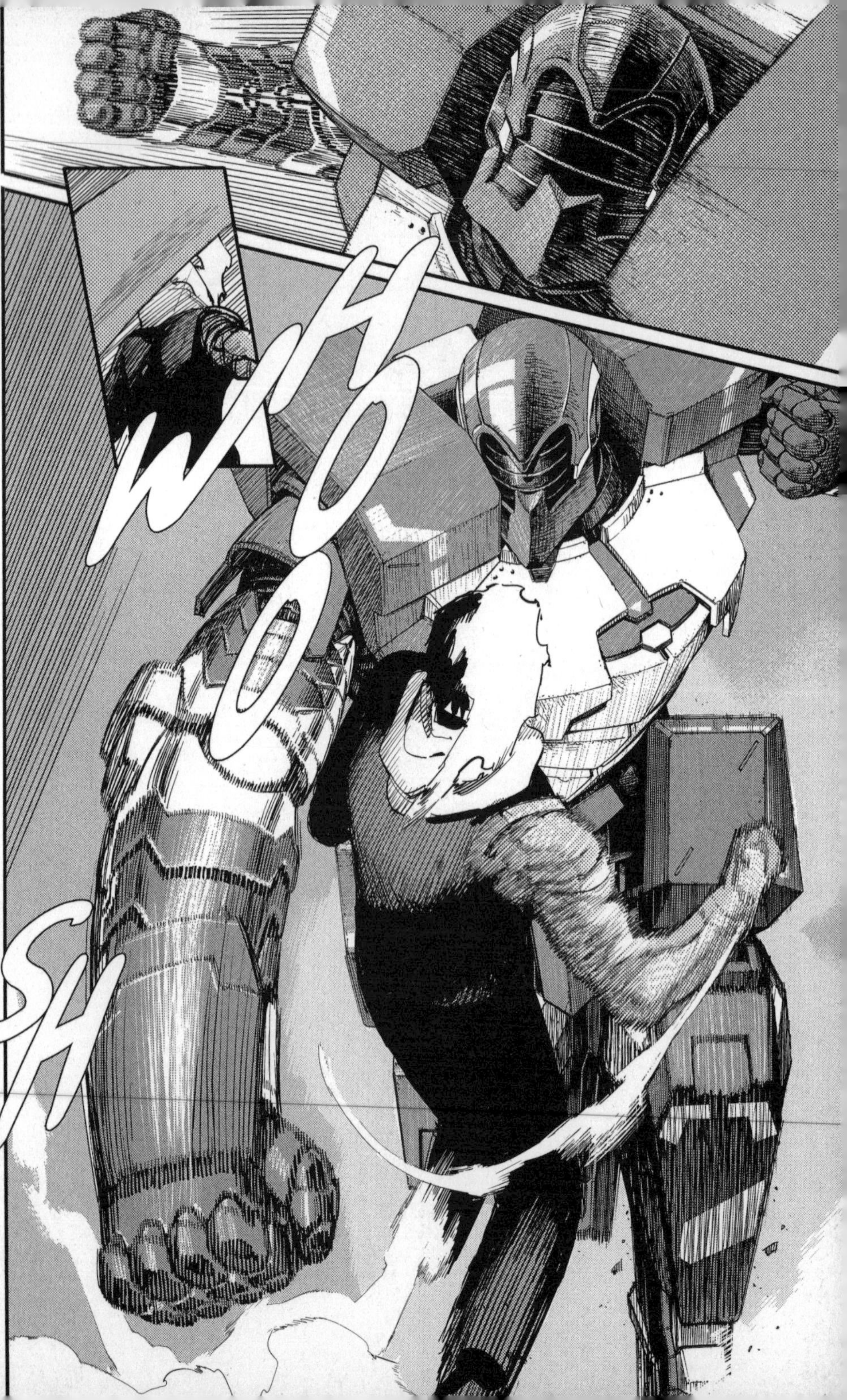
WHOOO
SH

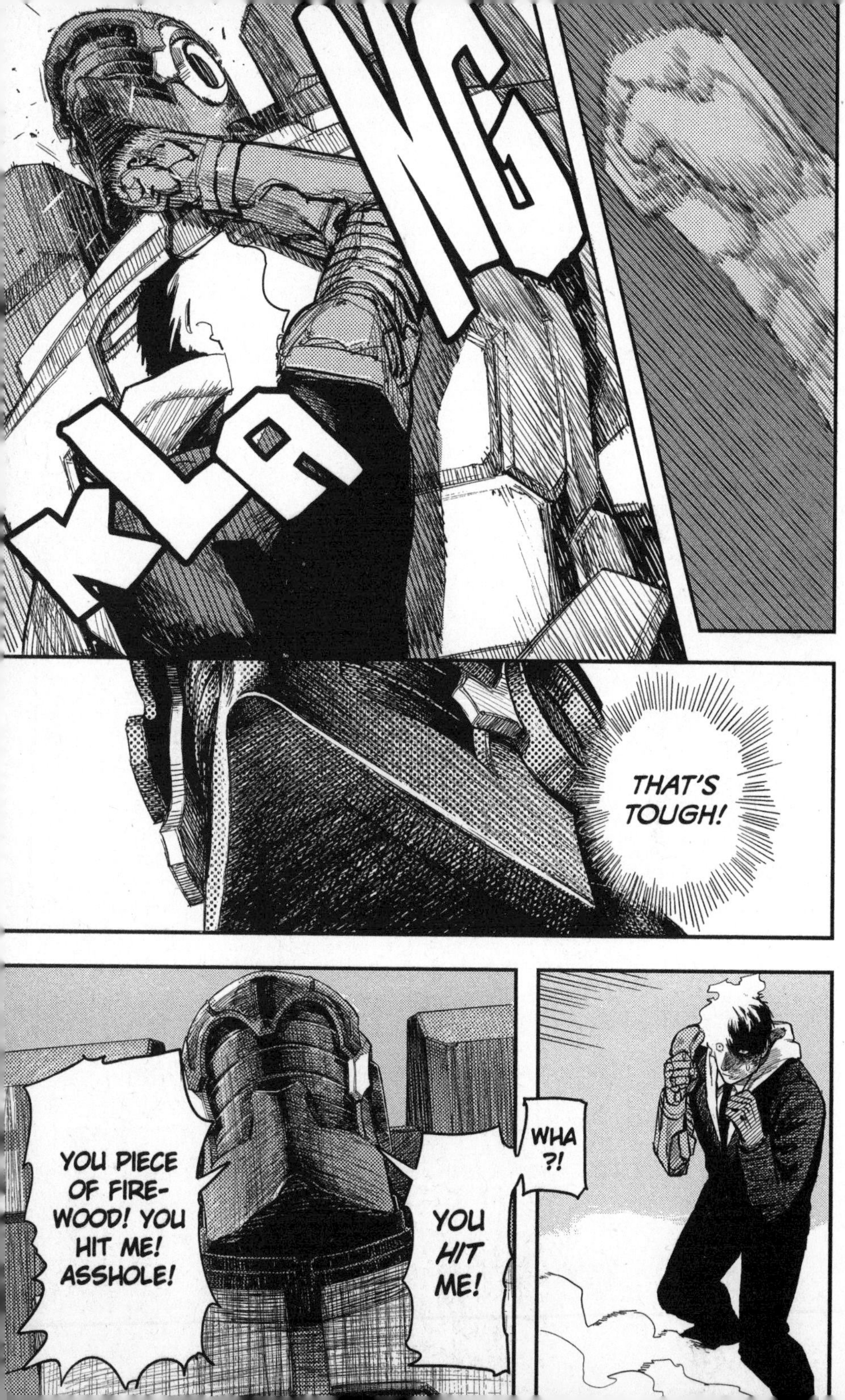
KLANG
THAT'S TOUGH!
WHA ?!
YOU HIT ME!
YOU PIECE OF FIRE-WOOD! YOU HIT ME! ASSHOLE!

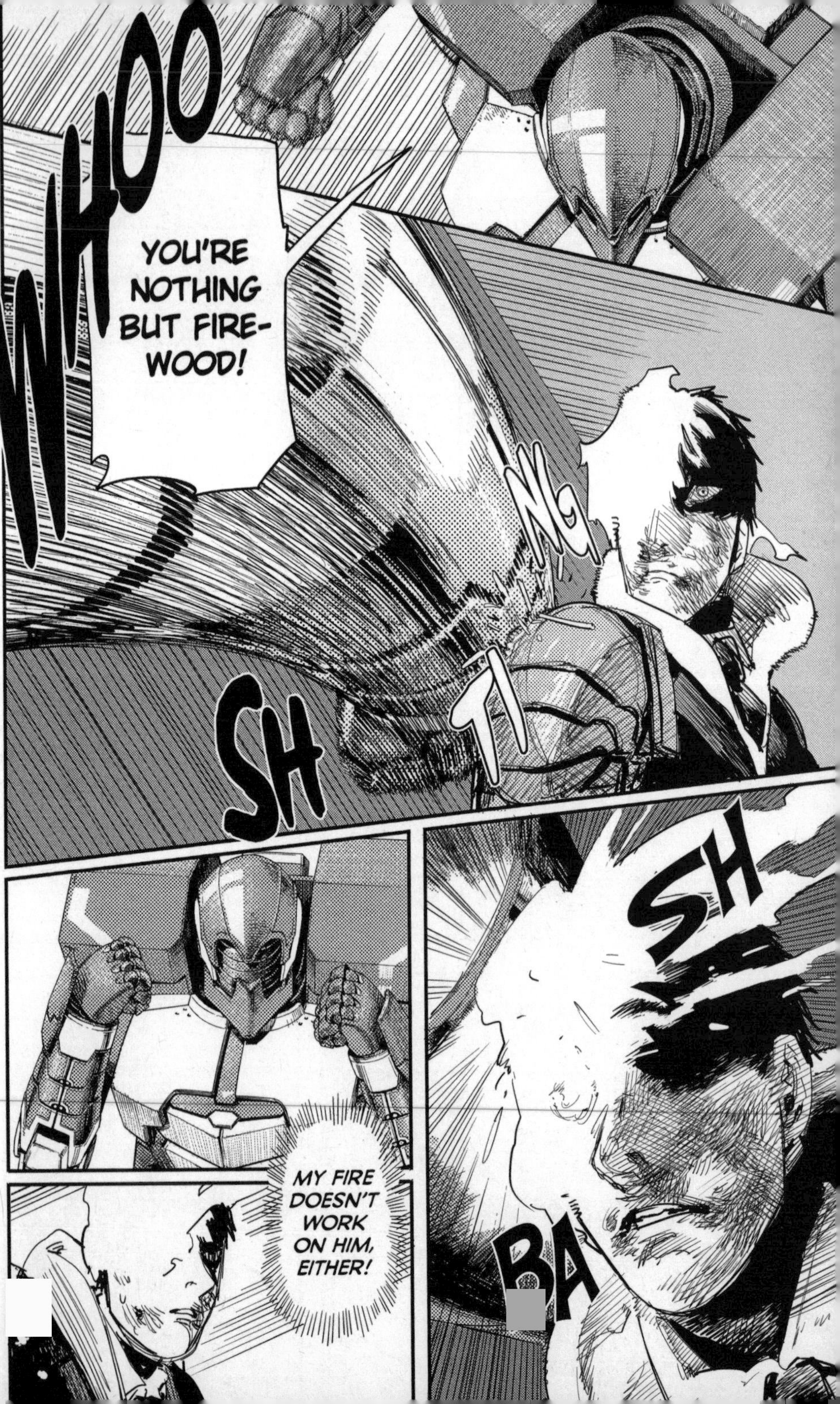
WHOO
YOU'RE NOTHING BUT FIRE-WOOD!
NG
TI
SH
SH
BA
MY FIRE DOESN'T WORK ON HIM, EITHER!

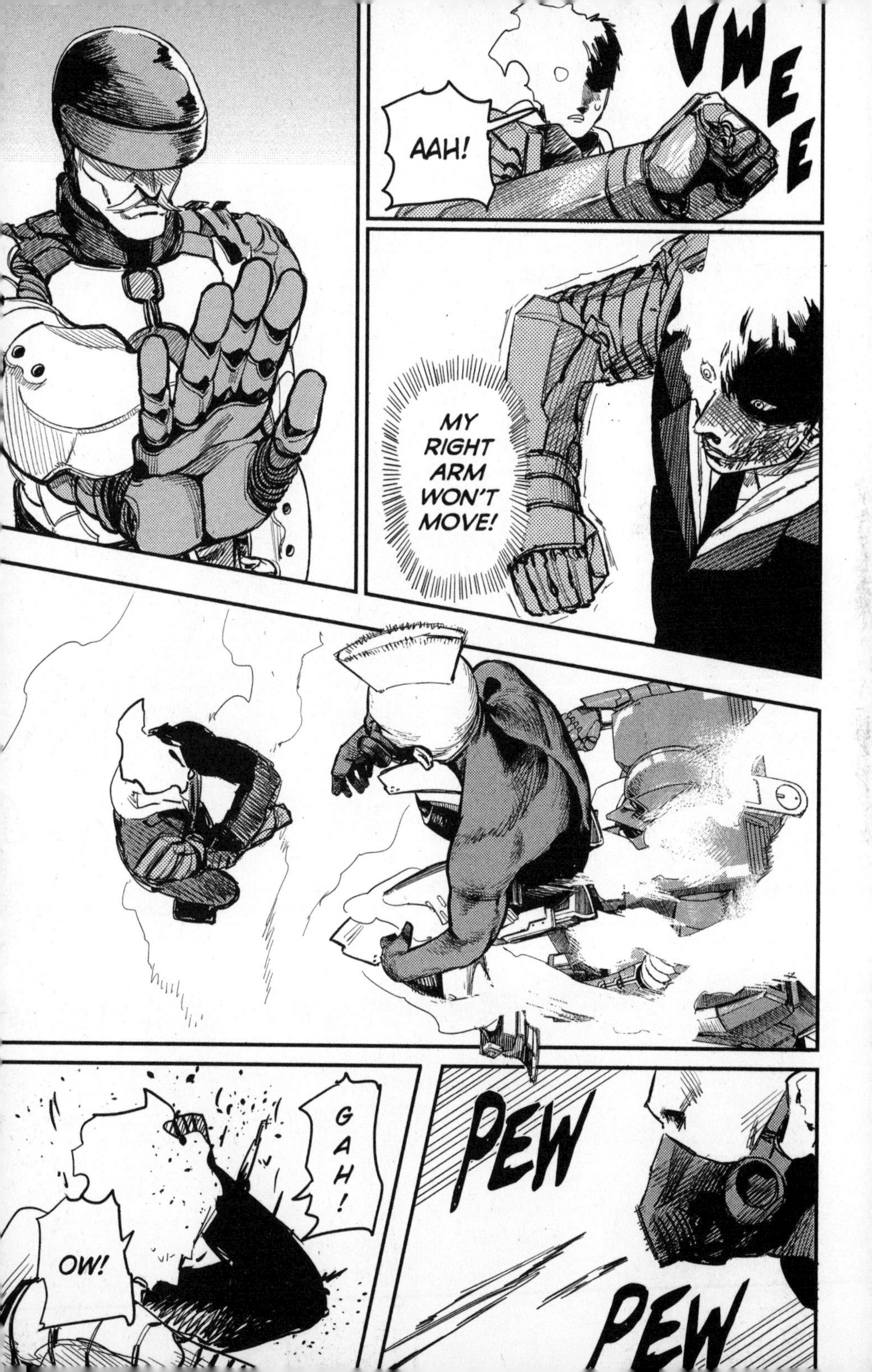
VWEE
AAH!
MY RIGHT ARM WON'T MOVE!
PEW
PEW
GAH!
OW!

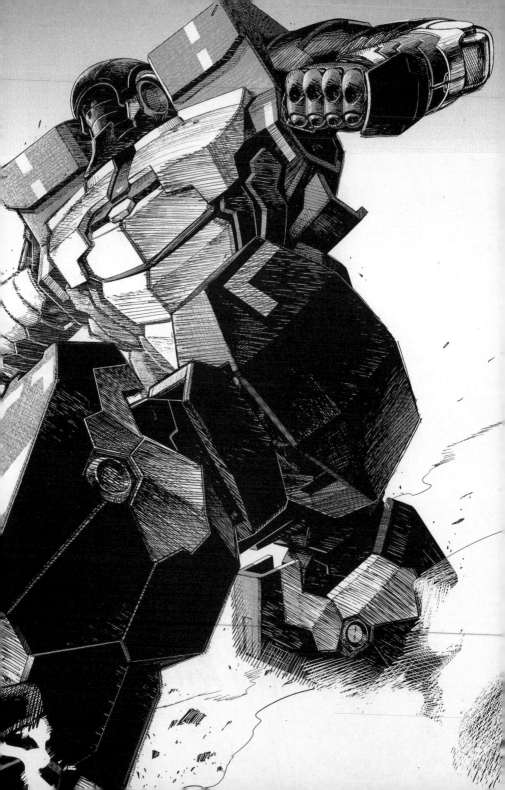

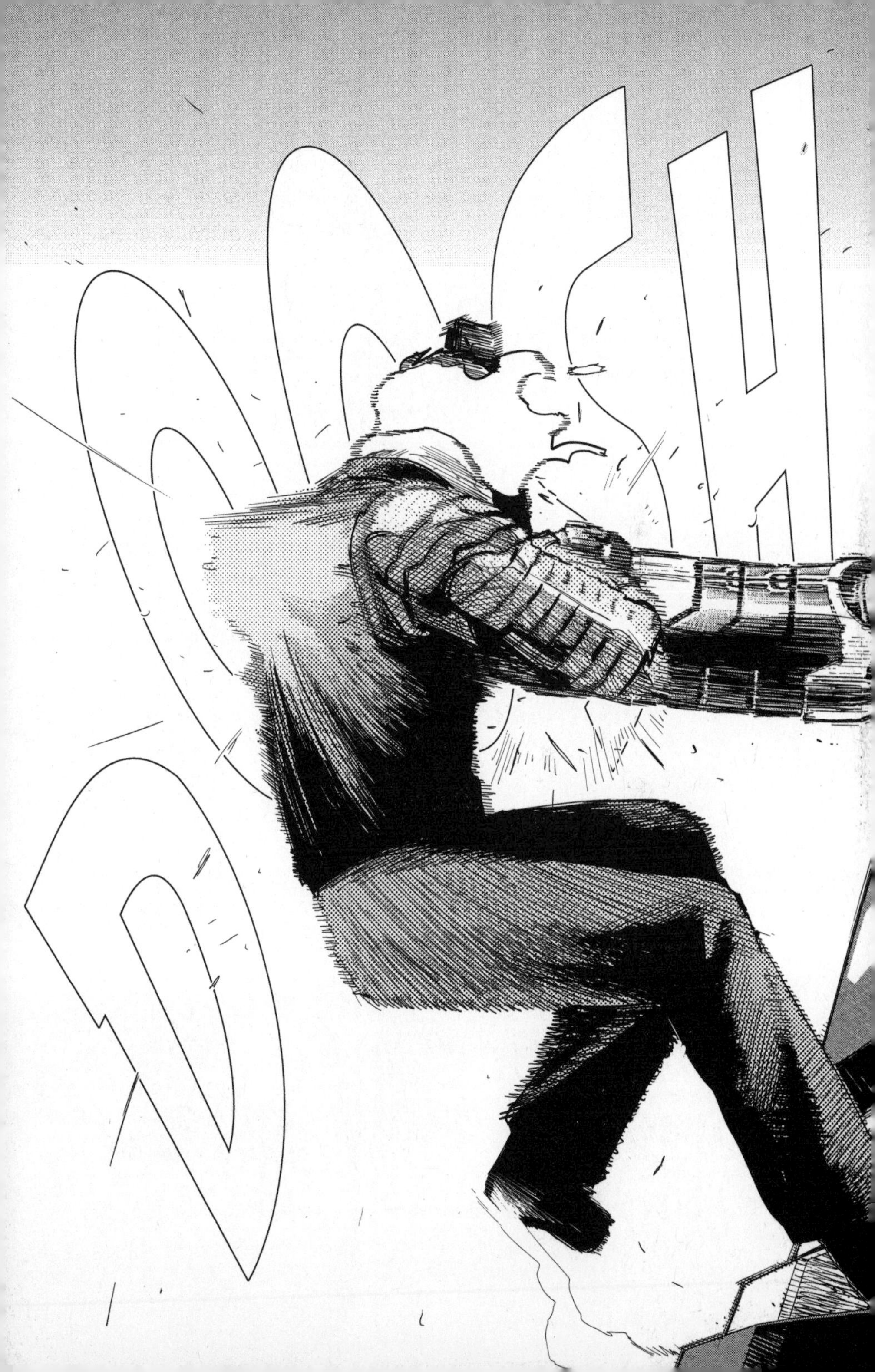
DOOSH

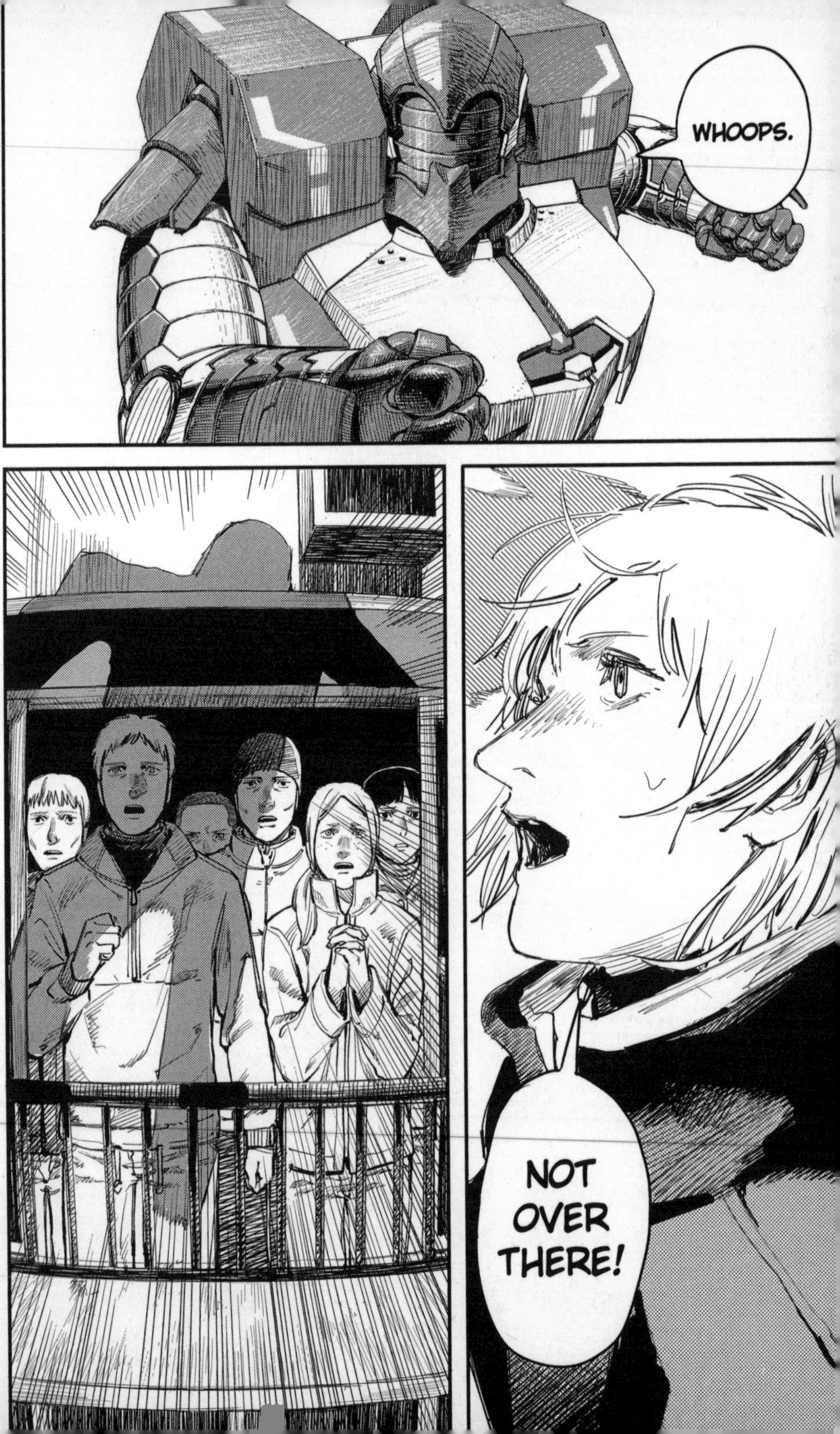
WHOOPS.
NOT OVER THERE!

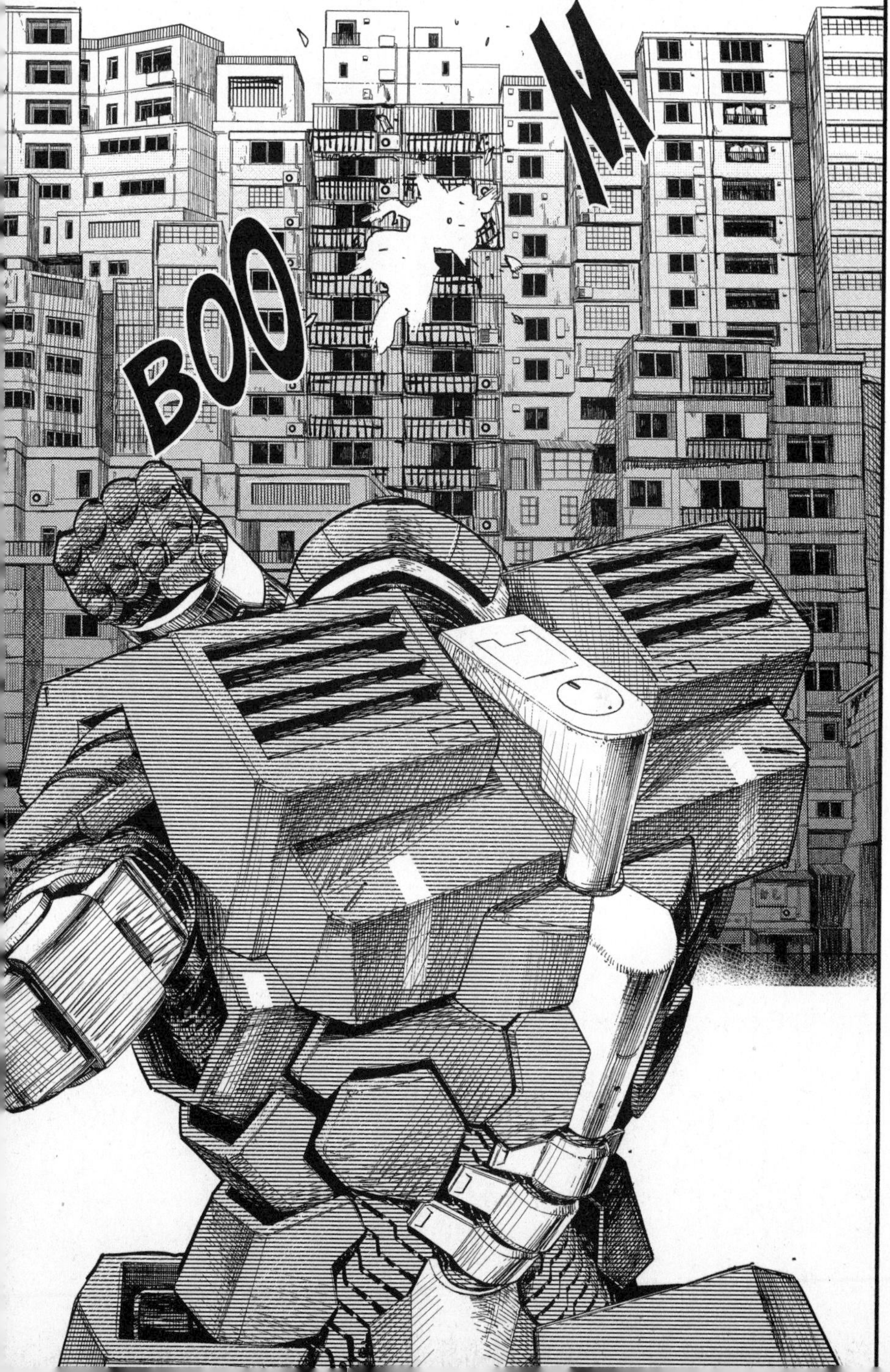
BOOM

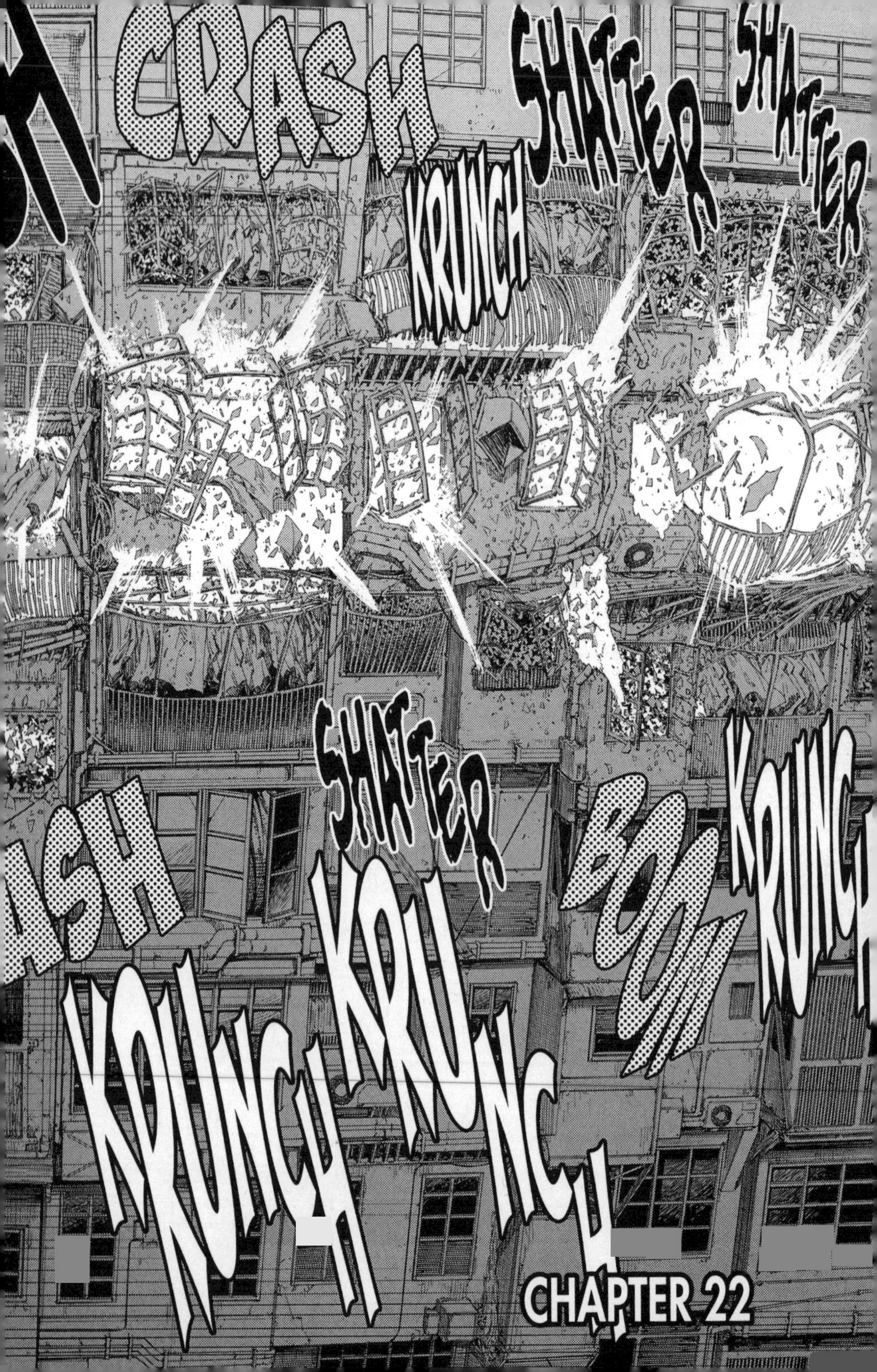
SHATTER
SHATTER
KRUNCH
CRASH
KRUNCH
BOOM
SHATTER
KRUNCH
KRUNCH

CHAPTER 22

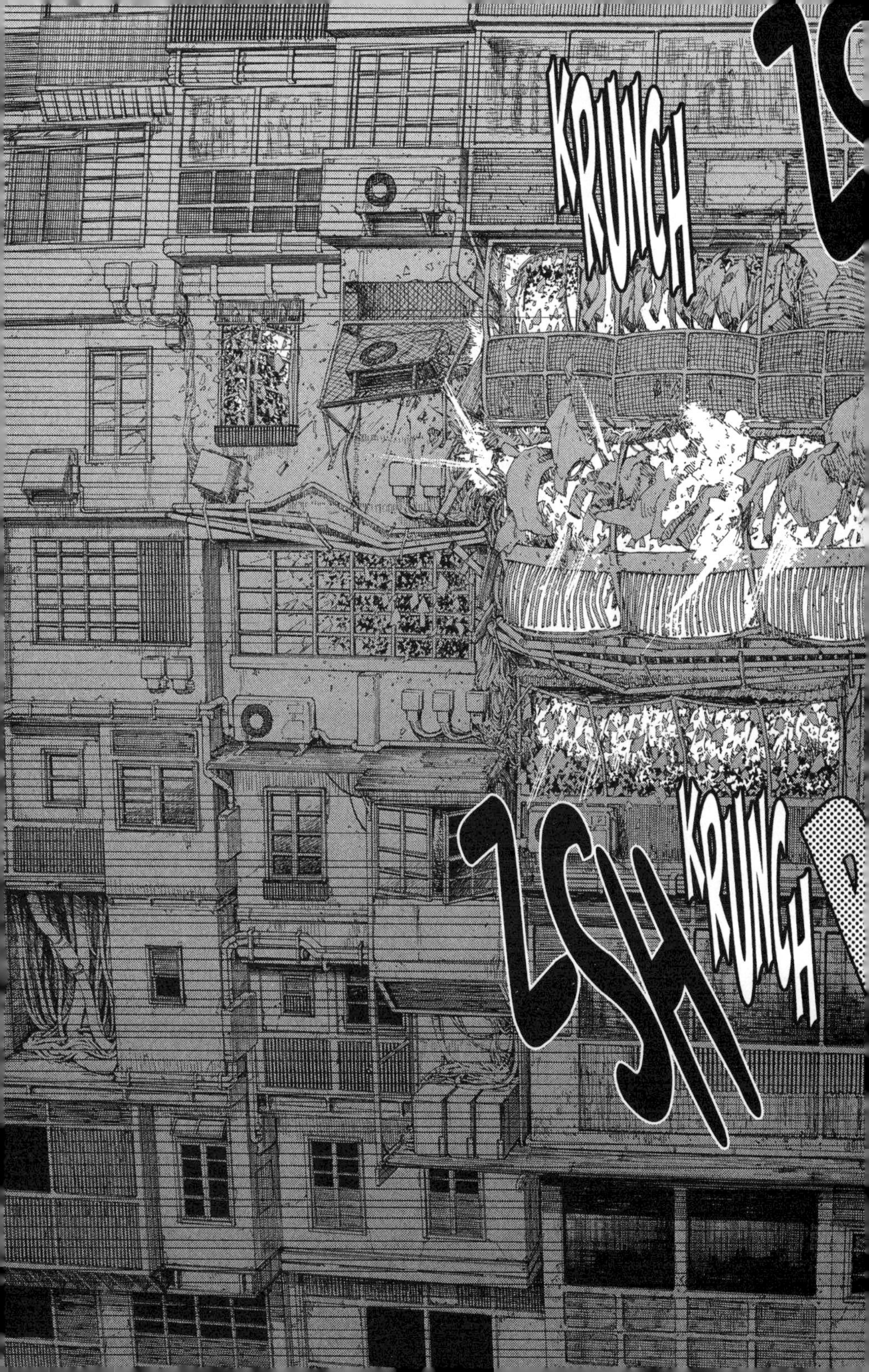
KRUNCH
KRUNCH
ZSH

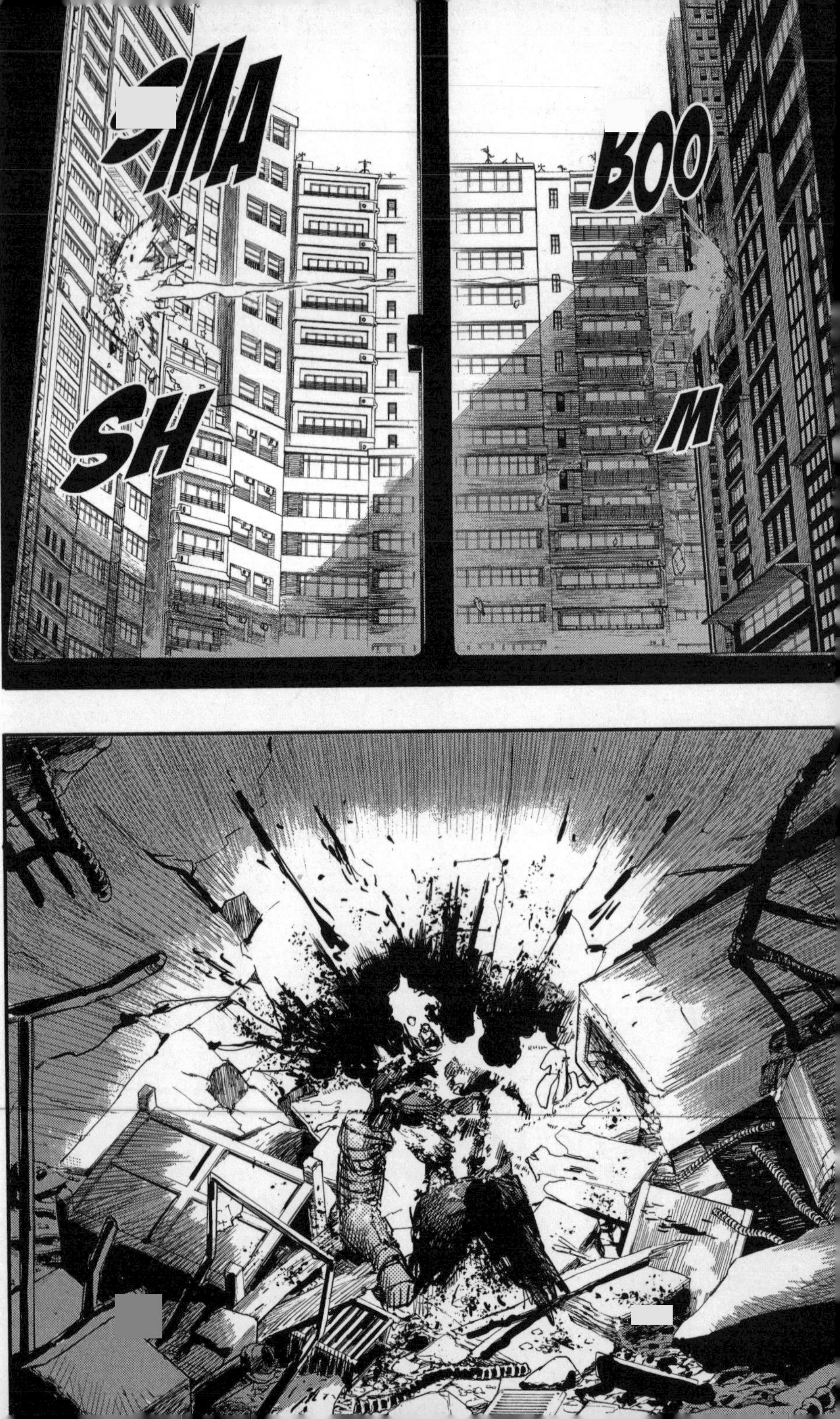
BOO
M
SMA
SH

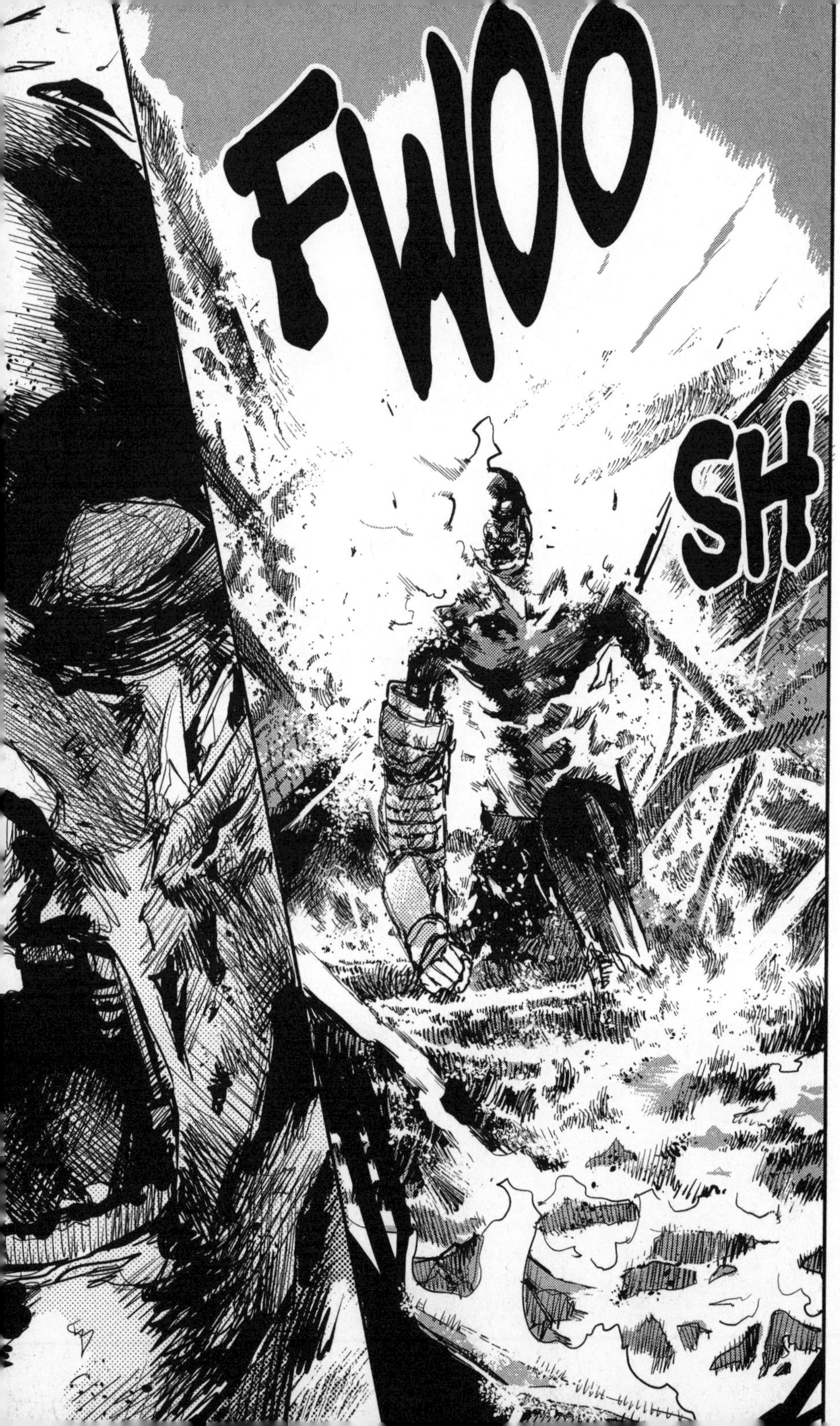
FWOO
SH

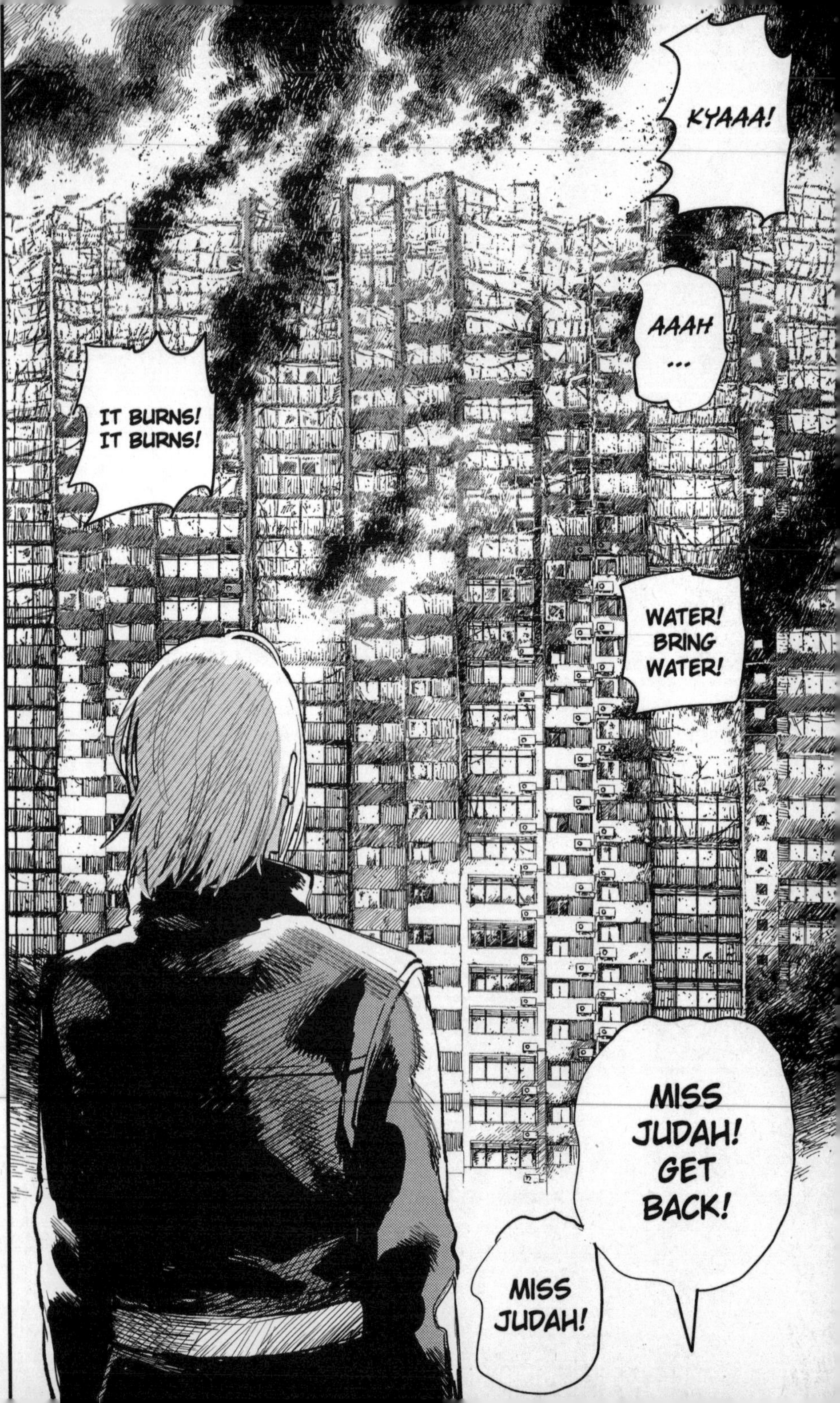
KYAAA!
AAAH ...
IT BURNS! IT BURNS!
WATER! BRING WATER!
MISS JUDAH! GET BACK!
MISS JUDAH!

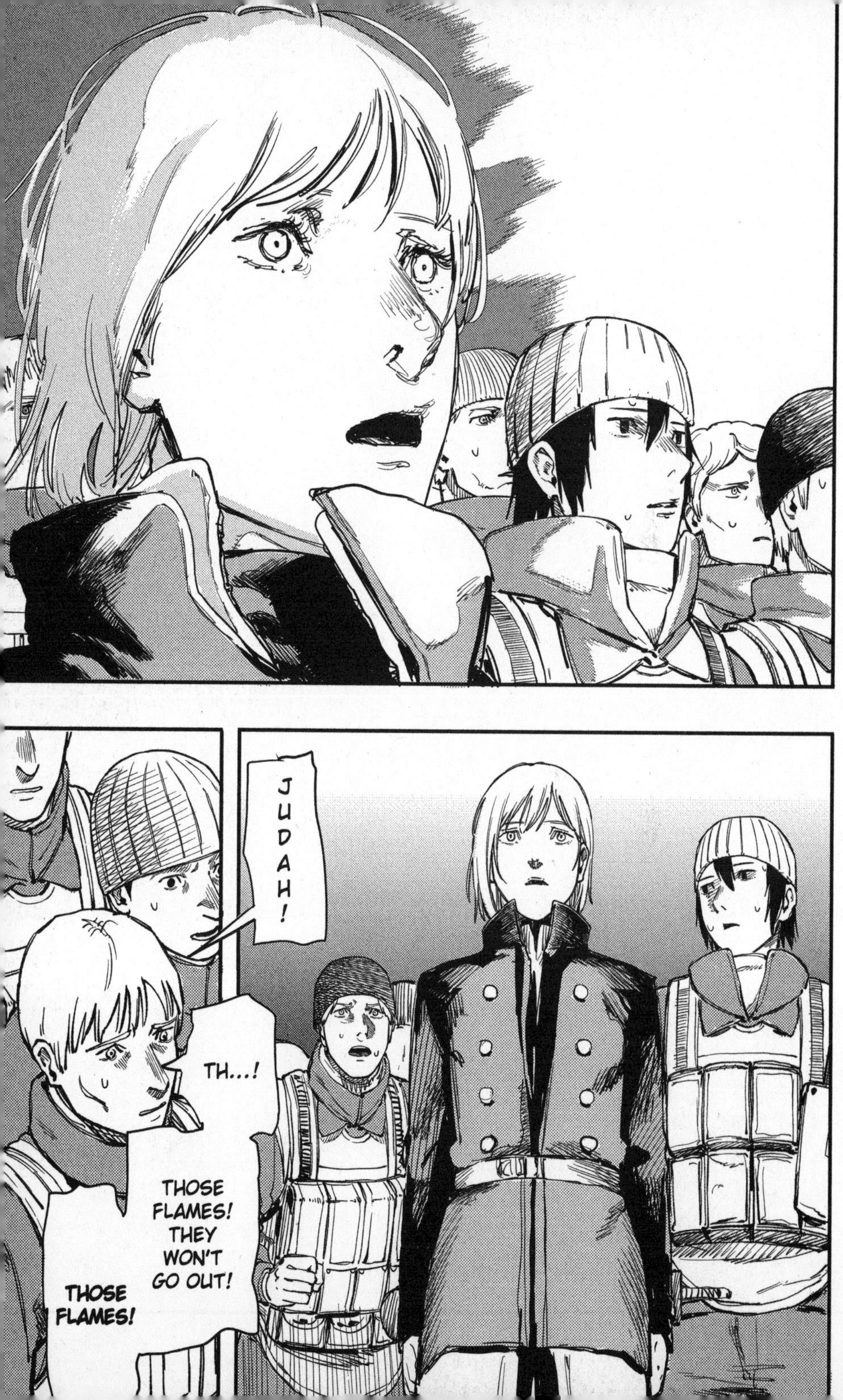
JUDAH!
TH...!
THOSE FLAMES! THEY WON'T GO OUT!
THOSE FLAMES!

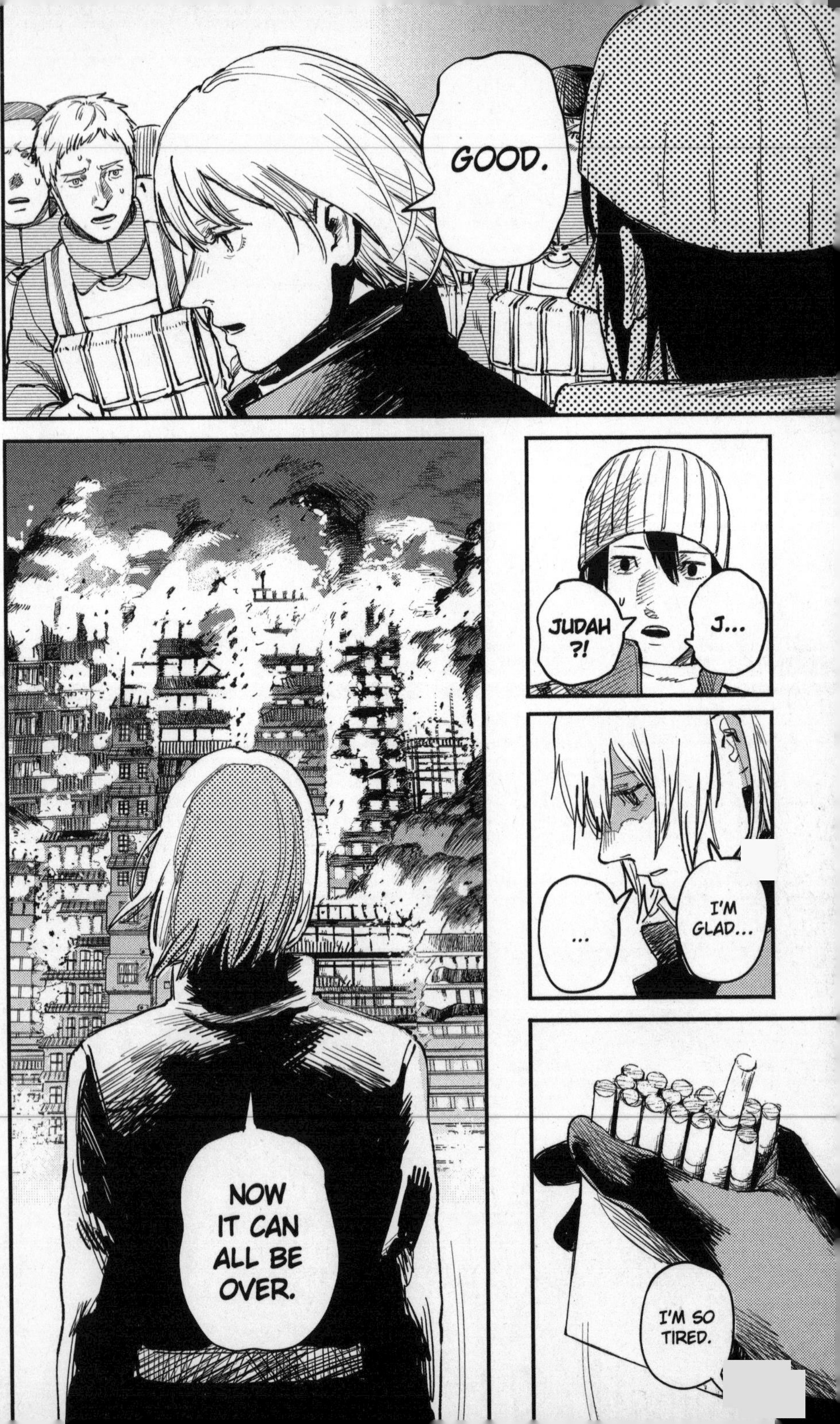
GOOD.
J...
JUDAH ?!
I'M GLAD...
...
I'M SO TIRED.
NOW IT CAN ALL BE OVER.

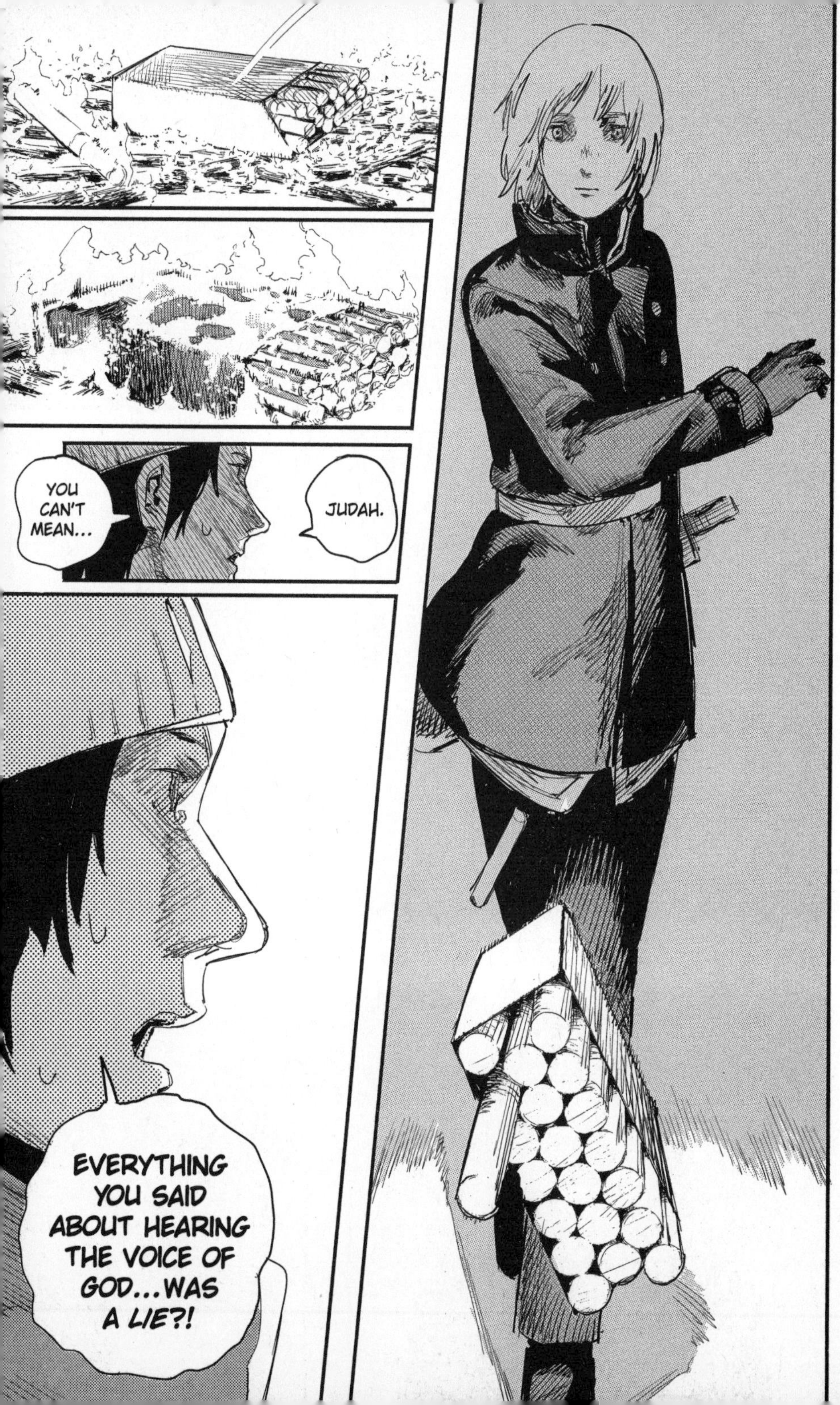
JUDAH.
YOU CAN'T MEAN...
EVERYTHING YOU SAID ABOUT HEARING THE VOICE OF GOD...WAS A LIE?!

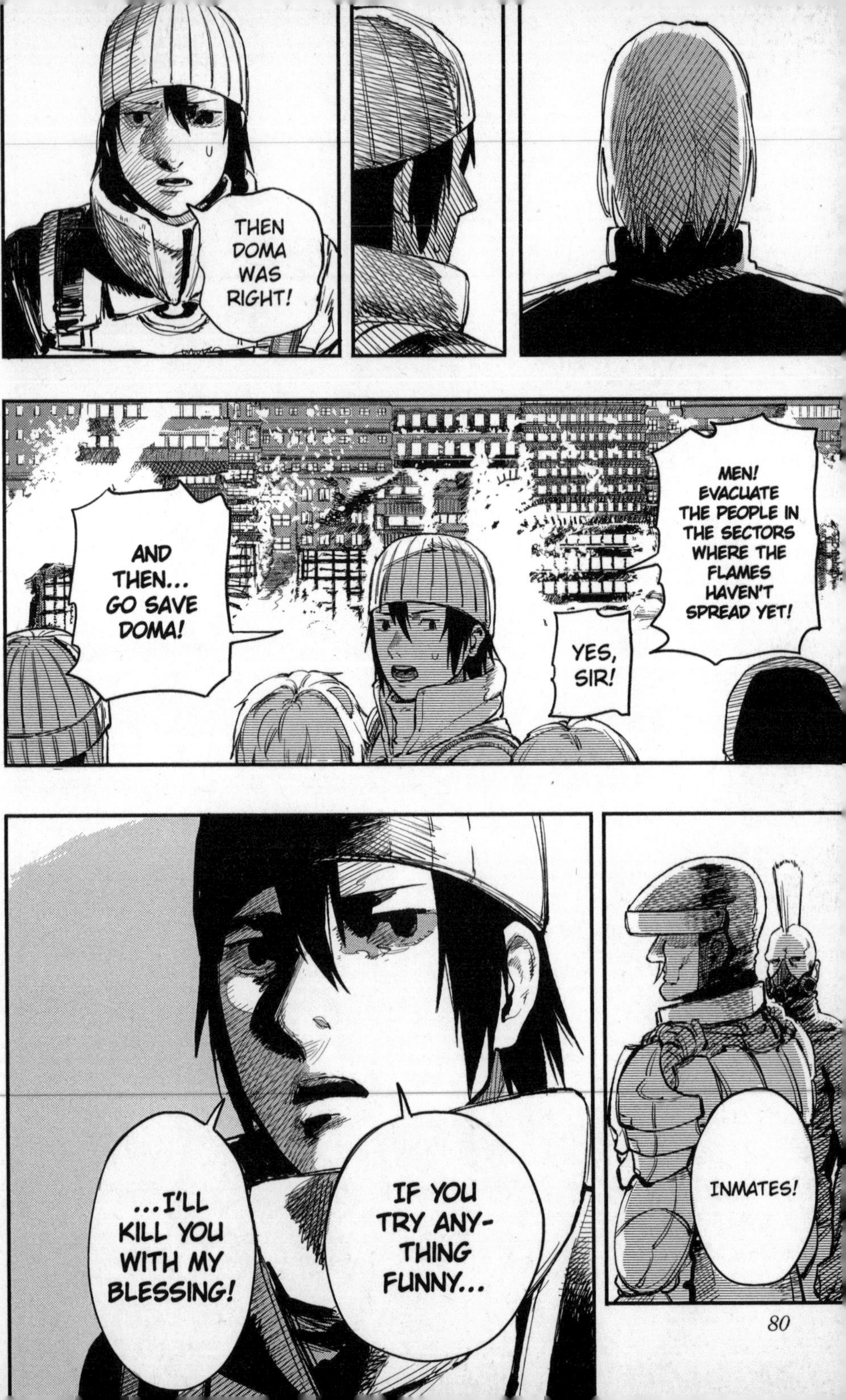
THEN DOMA WAS RIGHT!
MEN! EVACUATE THE PEOPLE IN THE SECTORS WHERE THE FLAMES HAVEN'T SPREAD YET!
YES, SIR!
AND THEN... GO SAVE DOMA!
INMATES!
IF YOU TRY ANY-THING FUNNY...
...I'LL KILL YOU WITH MY BLESSING!

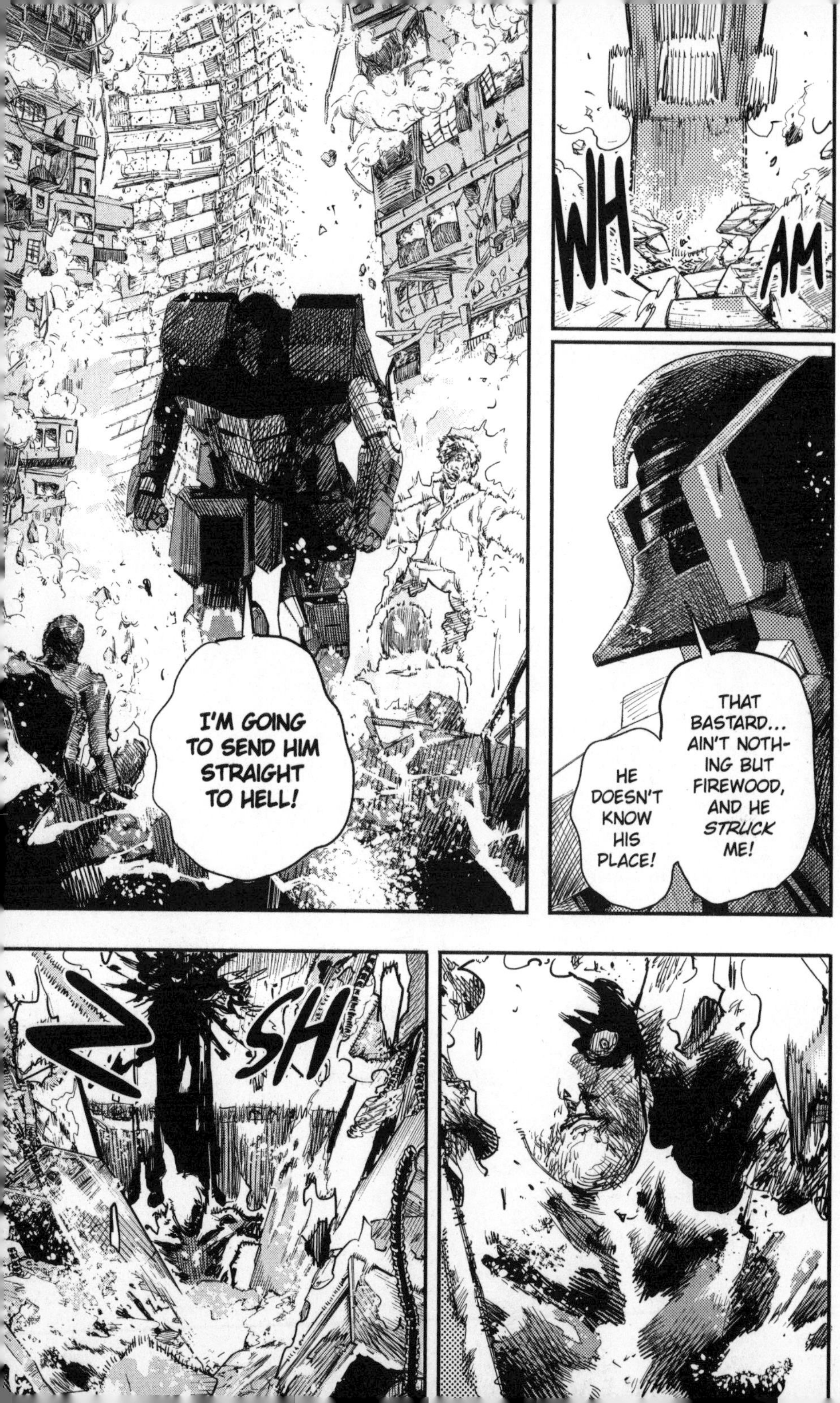
WHAM
THAT BASTARD... AIN'T NOTHING BUT FIREWOOD, AND HE *STRUCK* ME!
HE DOESN'T KNOW HIS PLACE!
I'M GOING TO SEND HIM STRAIGHT TO HELL!
SH

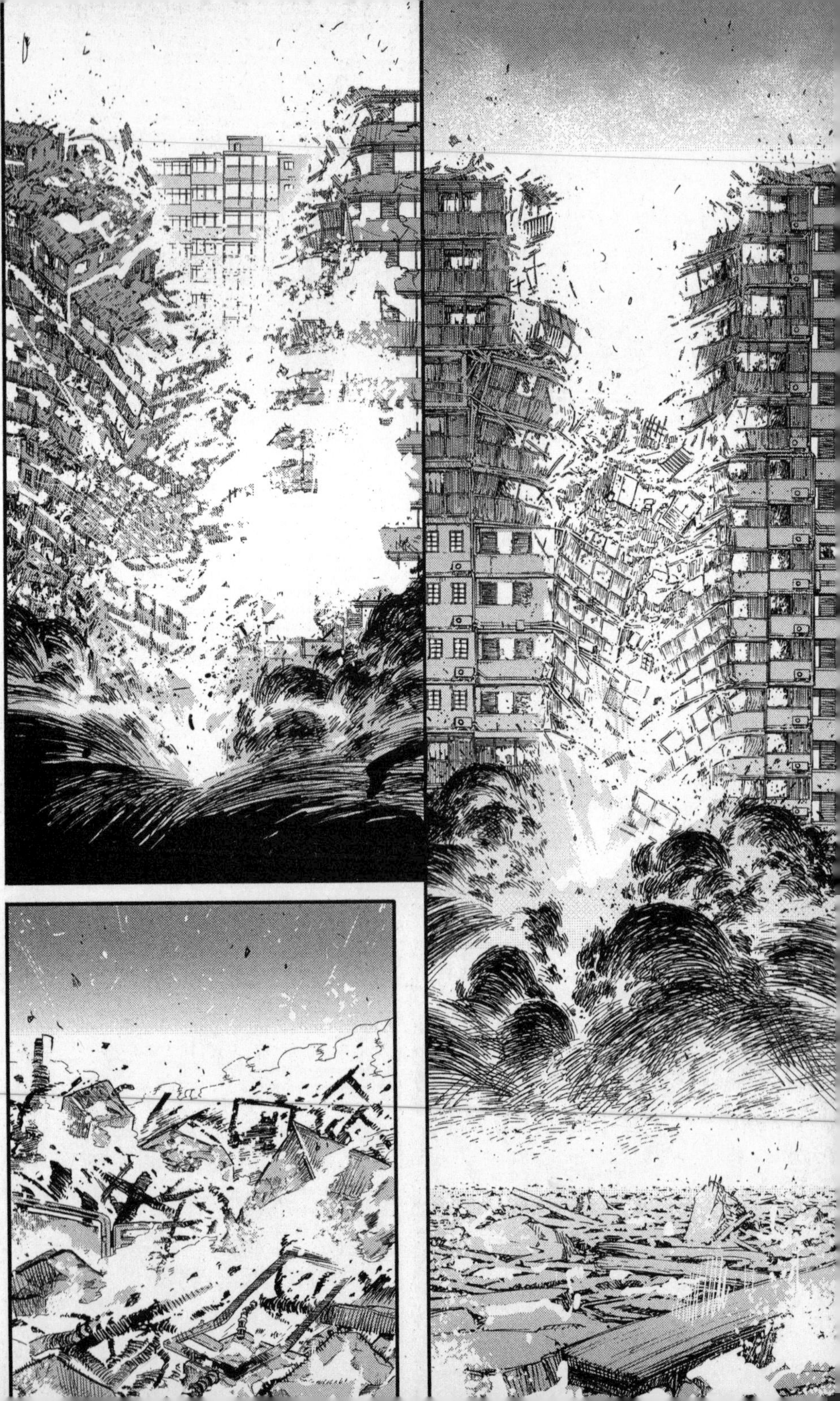

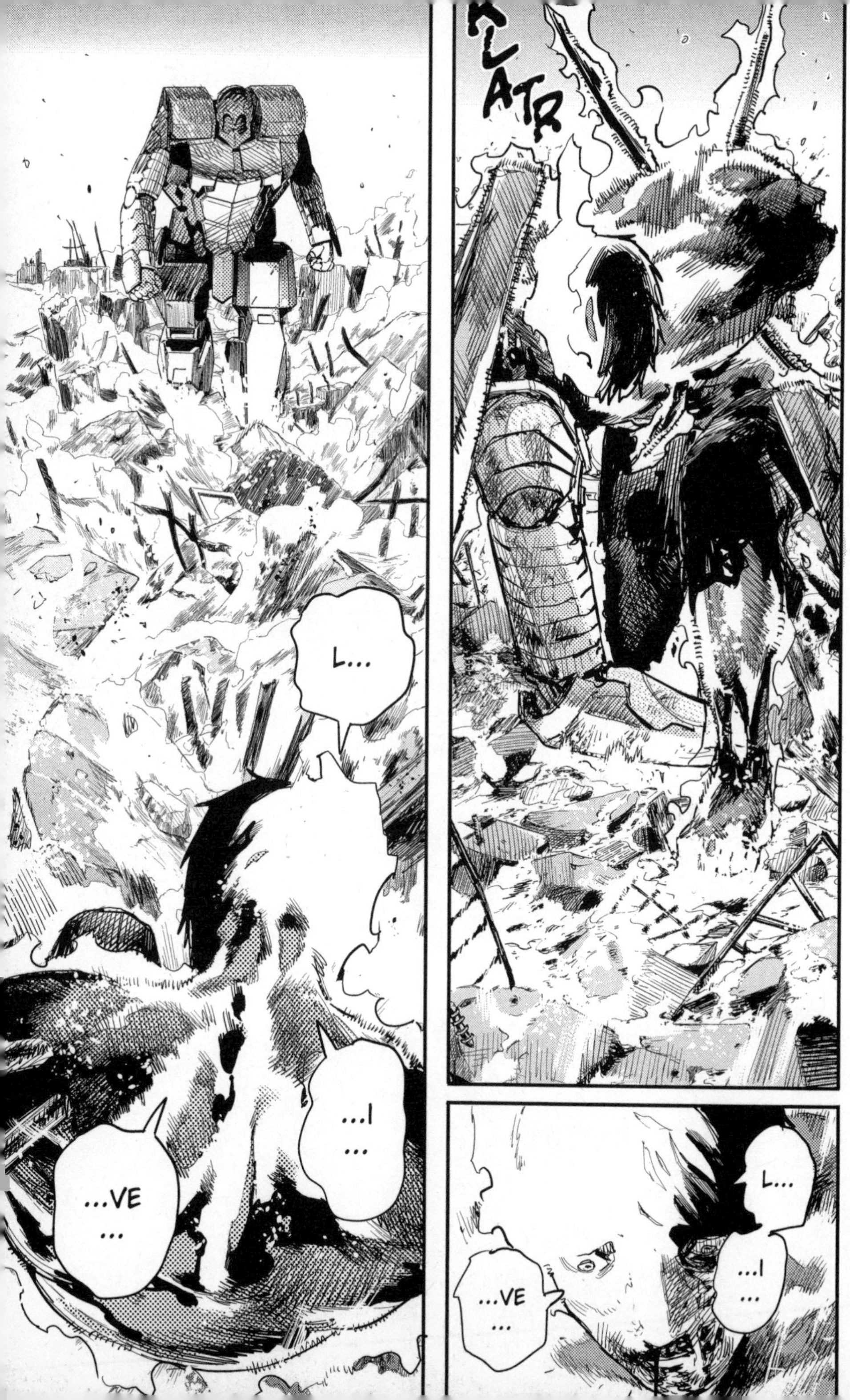
KLATR
L...
...I ...
...VE ...
L...
...I ...
...VE ...

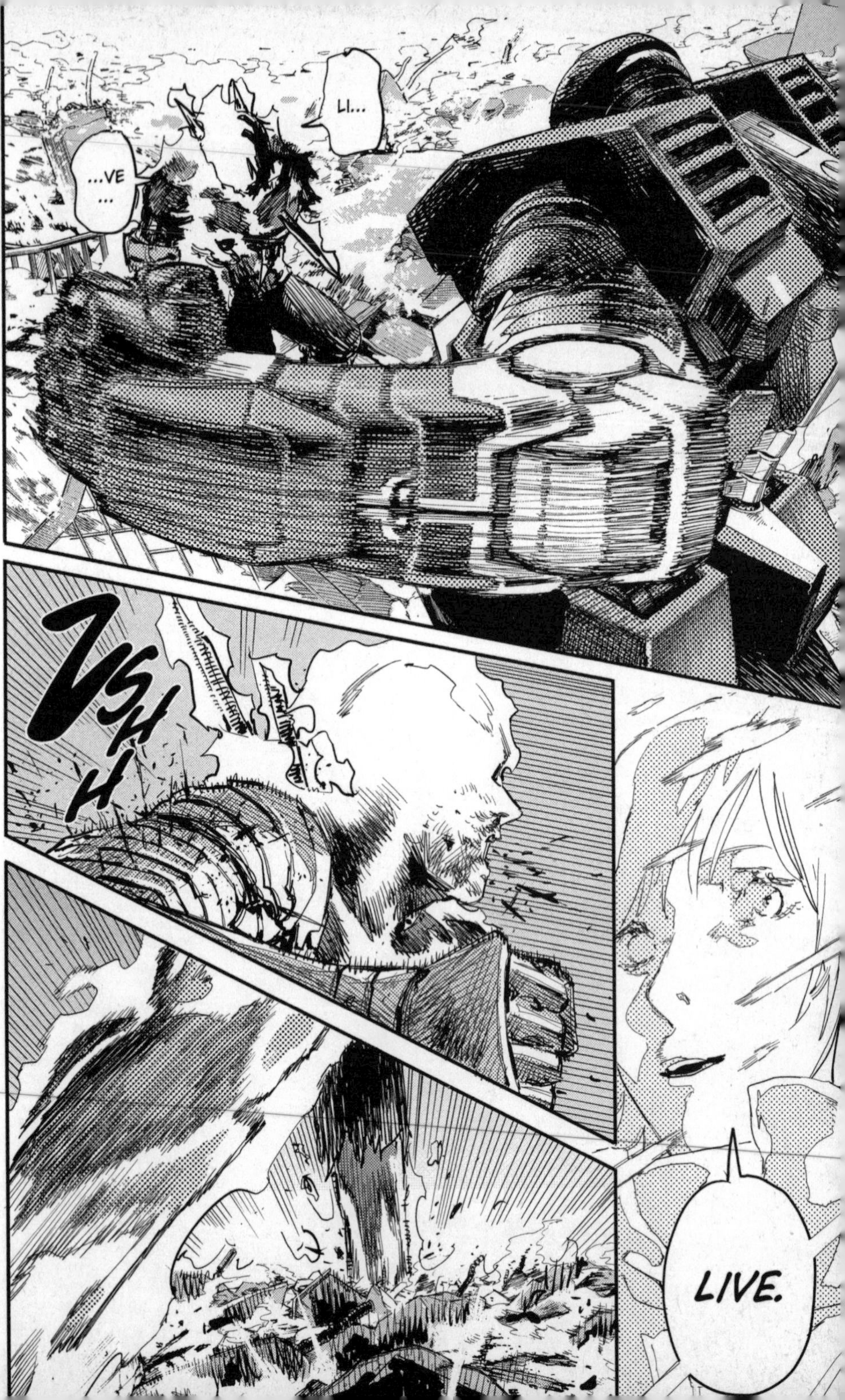
LI...
...VE ...
LIVE.
VSHH

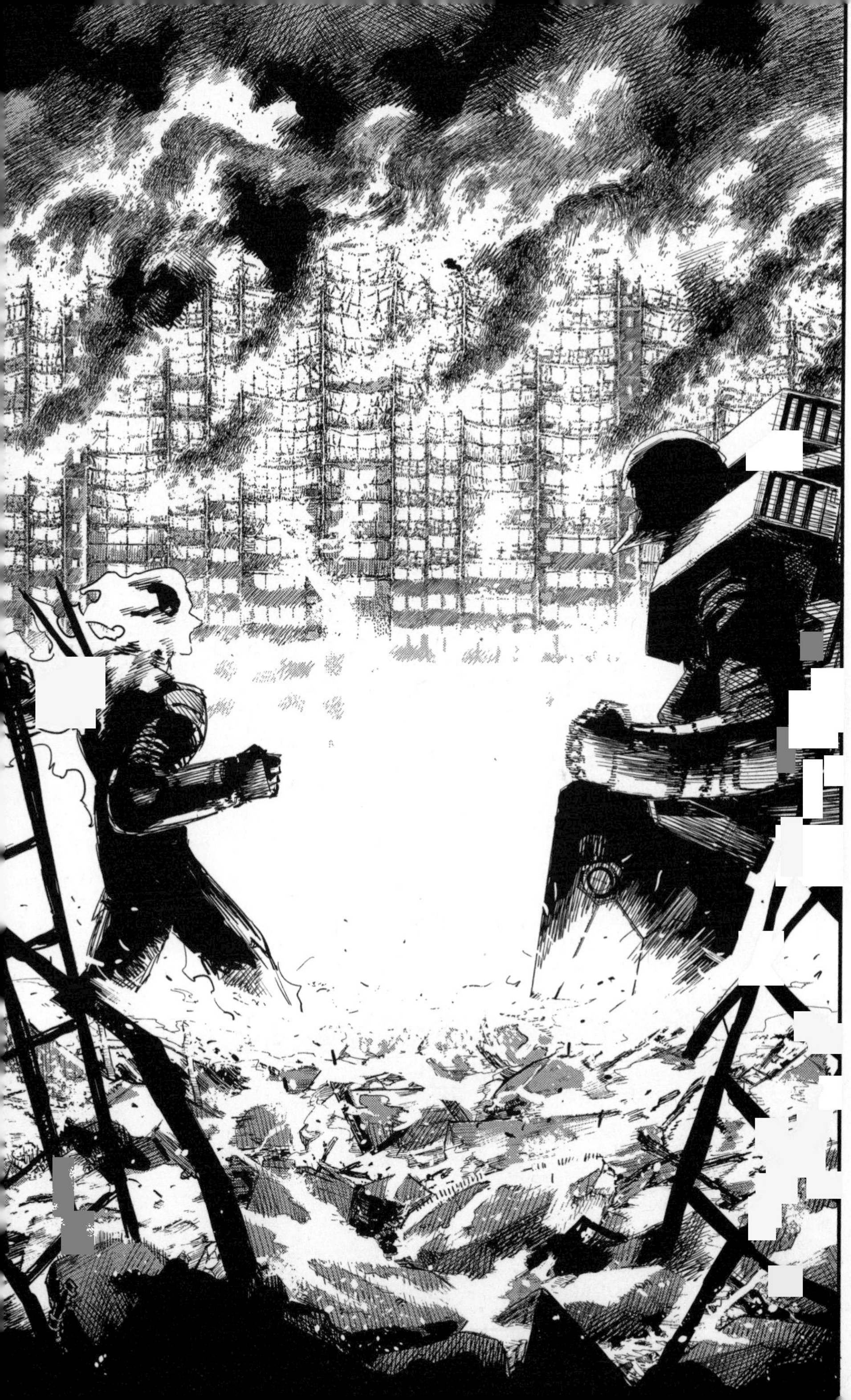

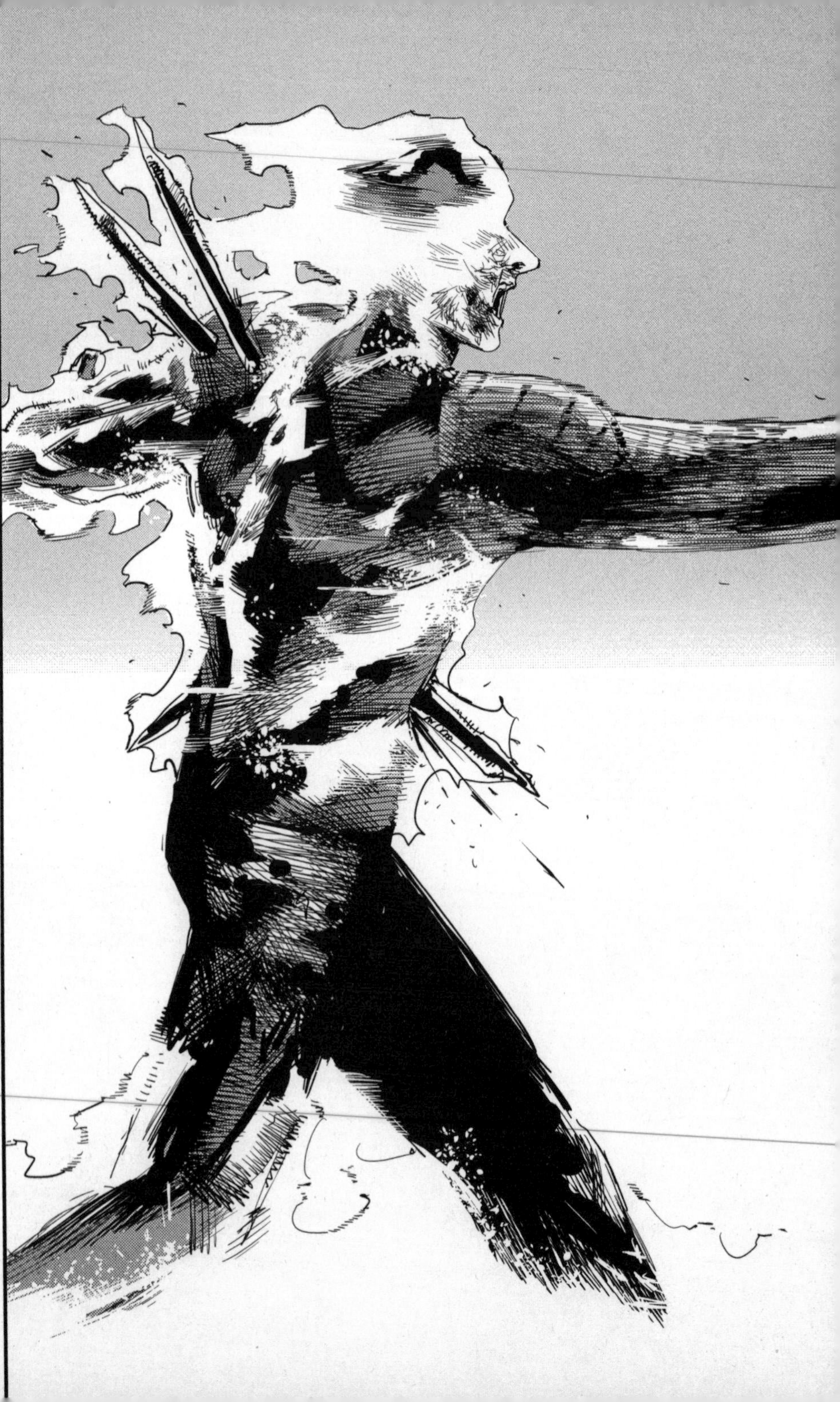

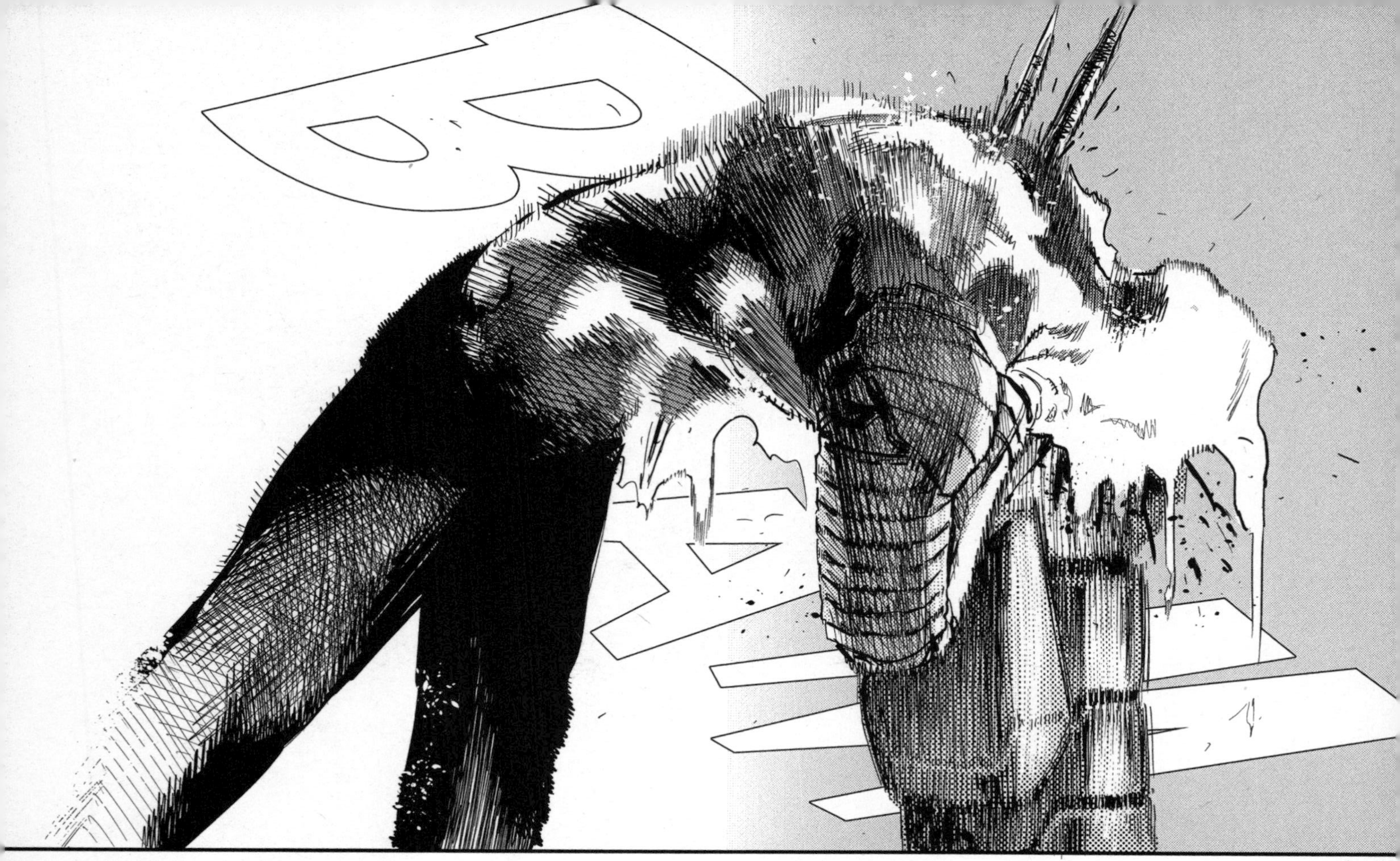
BAM

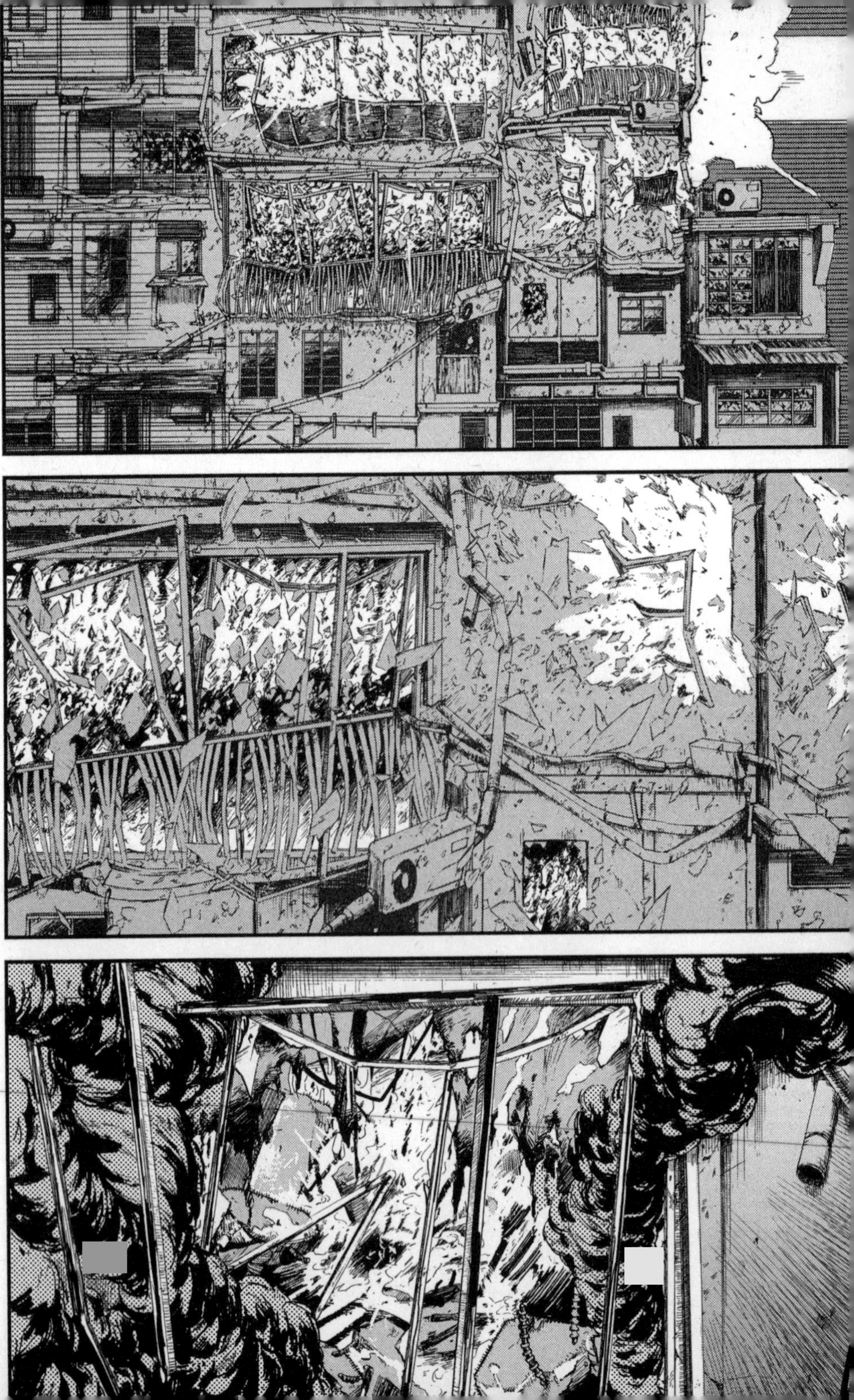

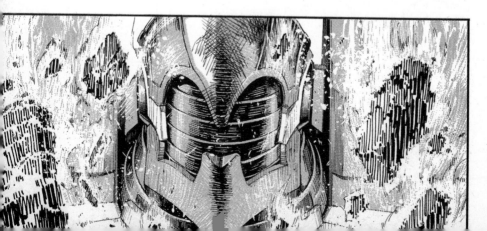

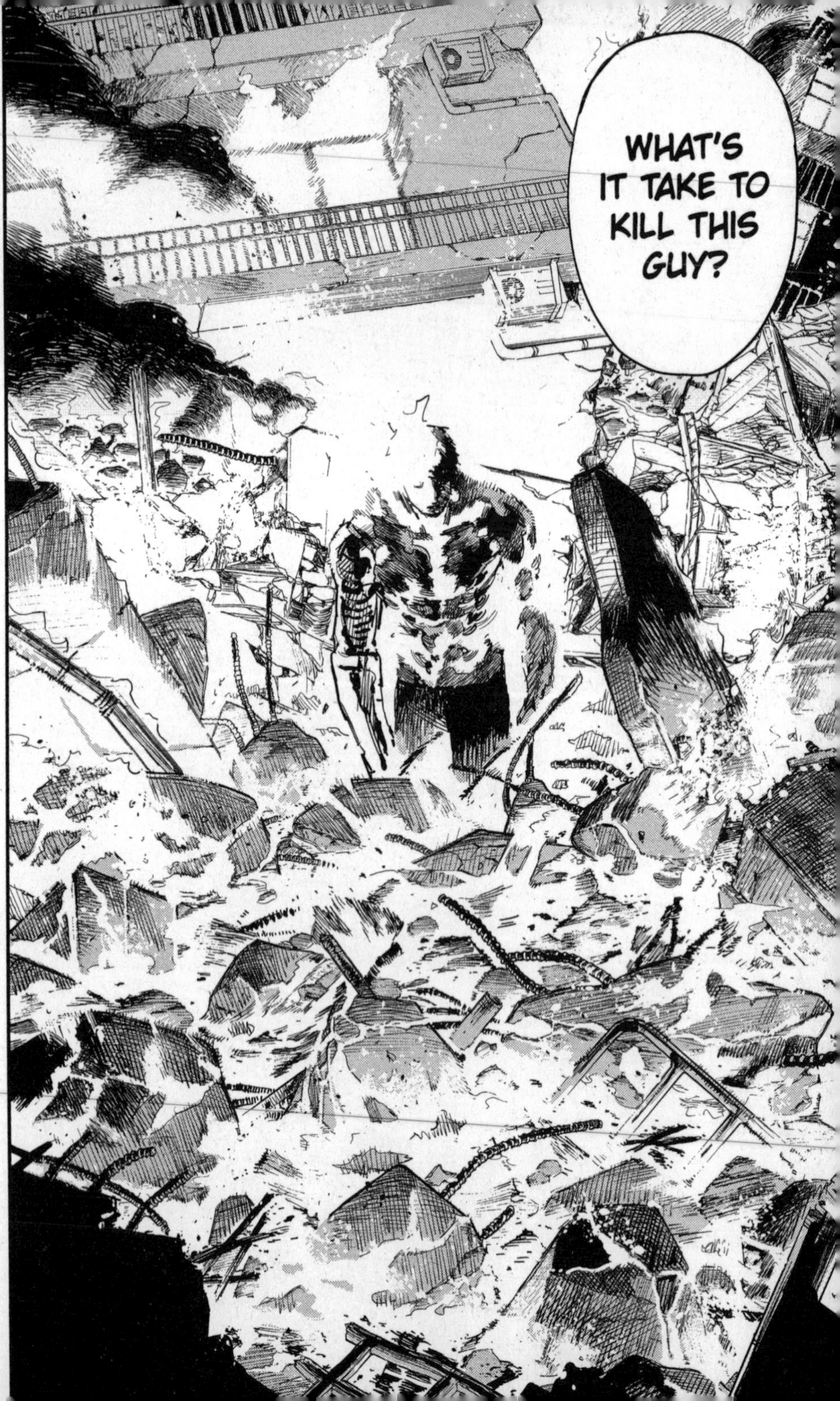
WHAT'S IT TAKE TO KILL THIS GUY?

FIRE PUNCH

CHAPTER 23

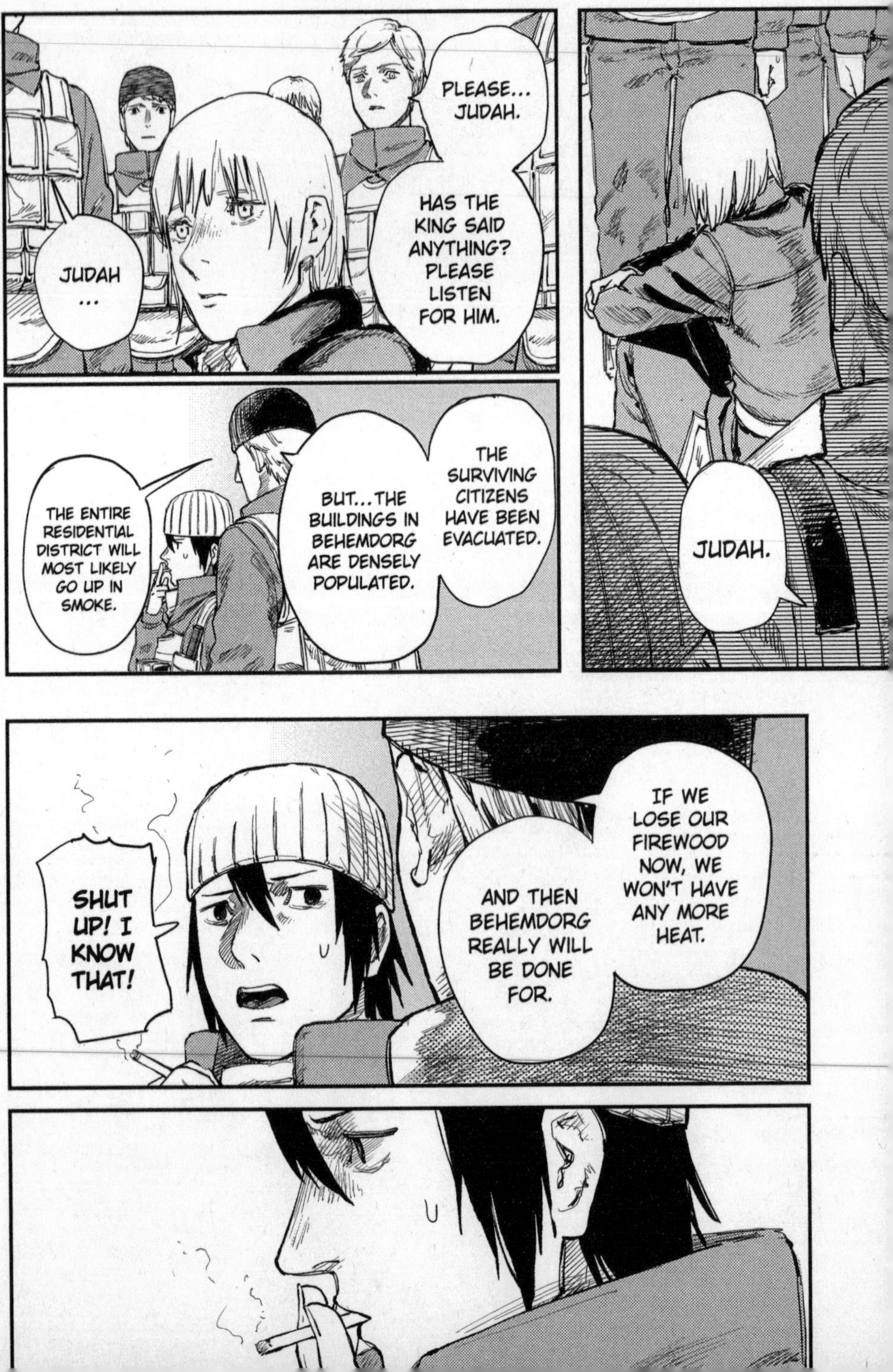
JUDAH.
PLEASE... JUDAH.
HAS THE KING SAID ANYTHING? PLEASE LISTEN FOR HIM.
JUDAH ...
THE SURVIVING CITIZENS HAVE BEEN EVACUATED.
BUT...THE BUILDINGS IN BEHEMDORG ARE DENSELY POPULATED.
THE ENTIRE RESIDENTIAL DISTRICT WILL MOST LIKELY GO UP IN SMOKE.
IF WE LOSE OUR FIREWOOD NOW, WE WON'T HAVE ANY MORE HEAT.
AND THEN BEHEMDORG REALLY WILL BE DONE FOR.
SHUT UP! I KNOW THAT!

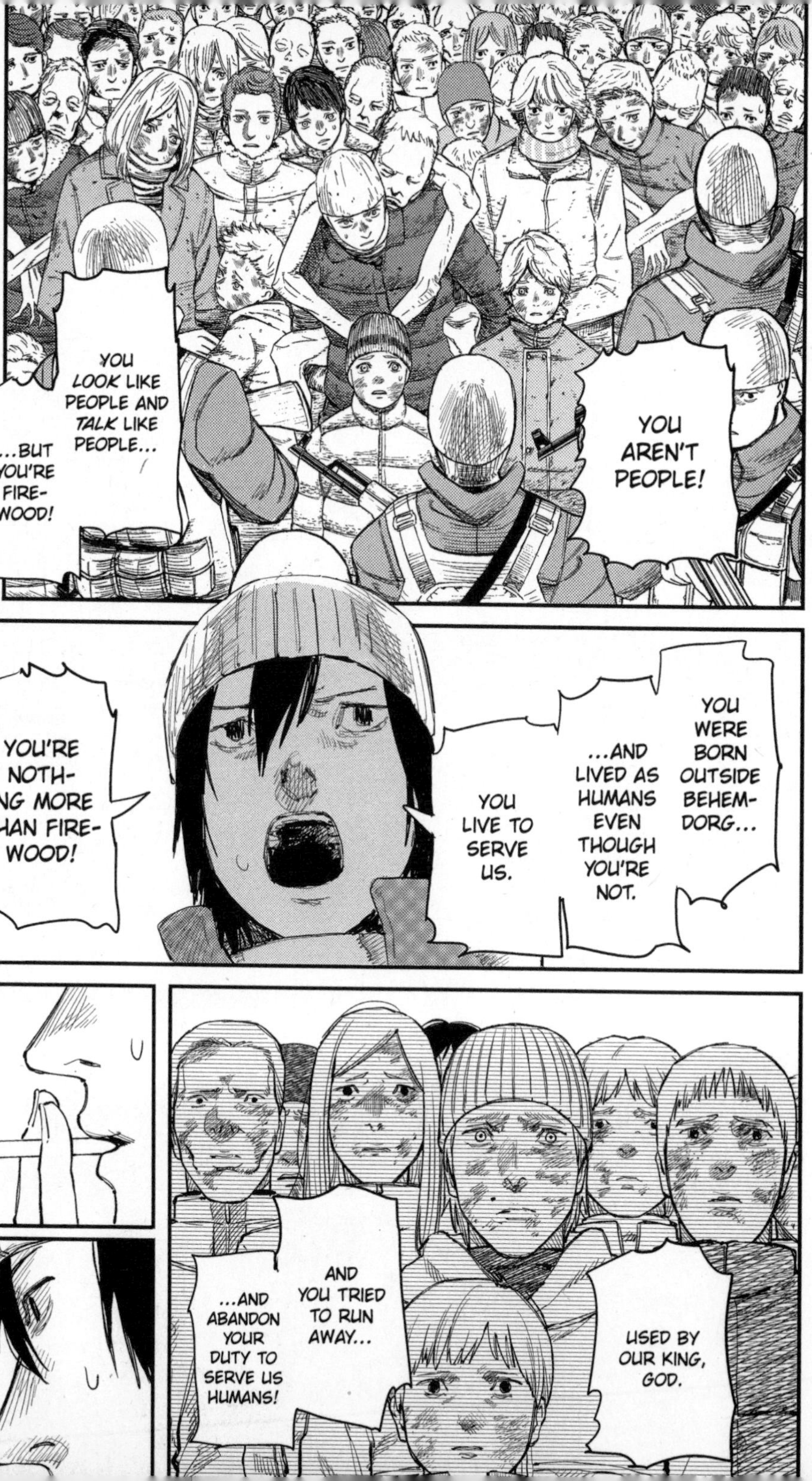
YOU AREN'T PEOPLE!
YOU LOOK LIKE PEOPLE AND TALK LIKE PEOPLE...
...BUT YOU'RE FIRE-WOOD!
YOU WERE BORN OUTSIDE BEHEM-DORG...
...AND LIVED AS HUMANS EVEN THOUGH YOU'RE NOT.
YOU LIVE TO SERVE US.
YOU'RE NOTH-ING MORE THAN FIRE-WOOD!
USED BY OUR KING, GOD.
AND YOU TRIED TO RUN AWAY...
...AND ABANDON YOUR DUTY TO SERVE US HUMANS!

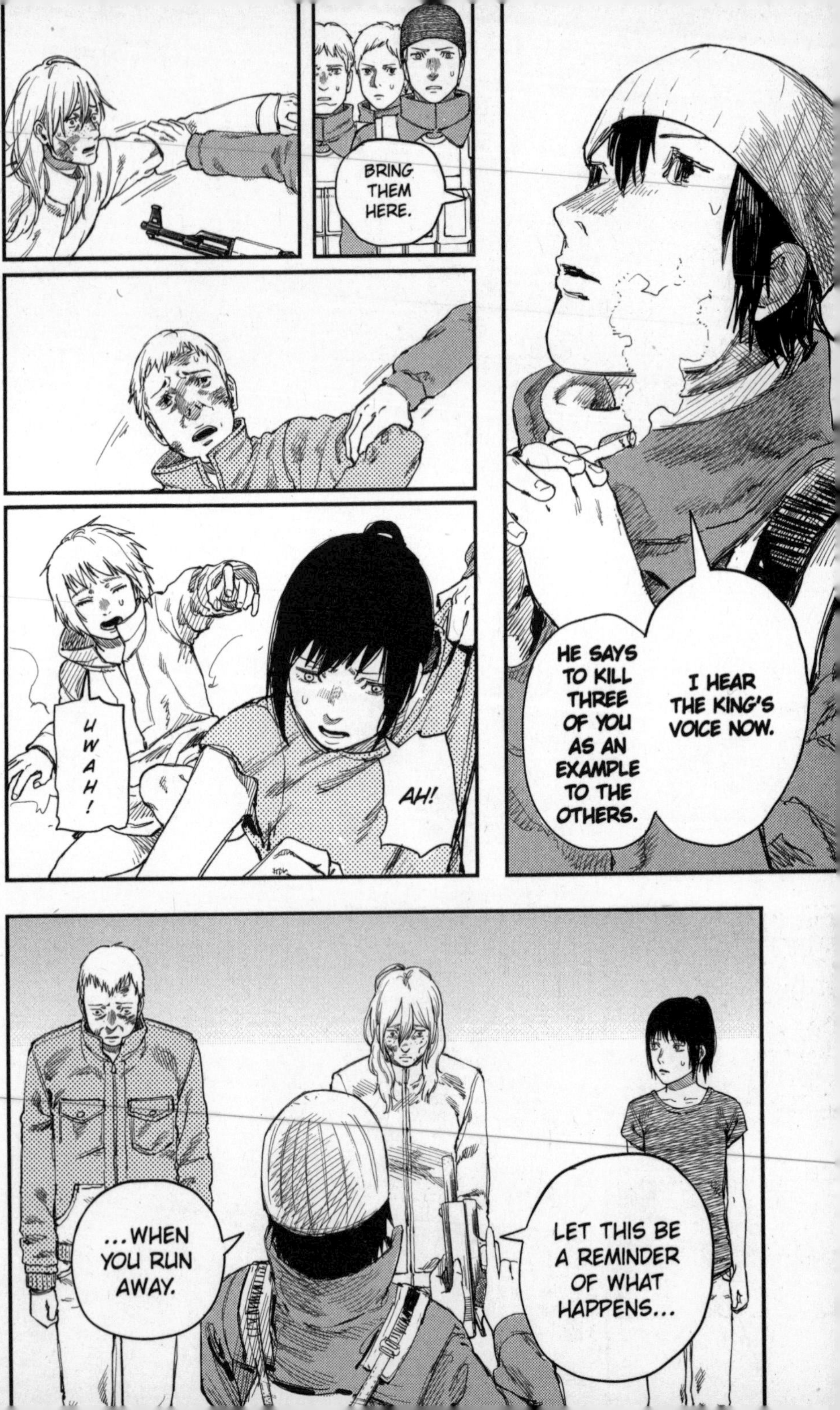
I HEAR THE KING'S VOICE NOW.
HE SAYS TO KILL THREE OF YOU AS AN EXAMPLE TO THE OTHERS.
BRING THEM HERE.
AH!
UWAH!
LET THIS BE A REMINDER OF WHAT HAPPENS...
...WHEN YOU RUN AWAY.

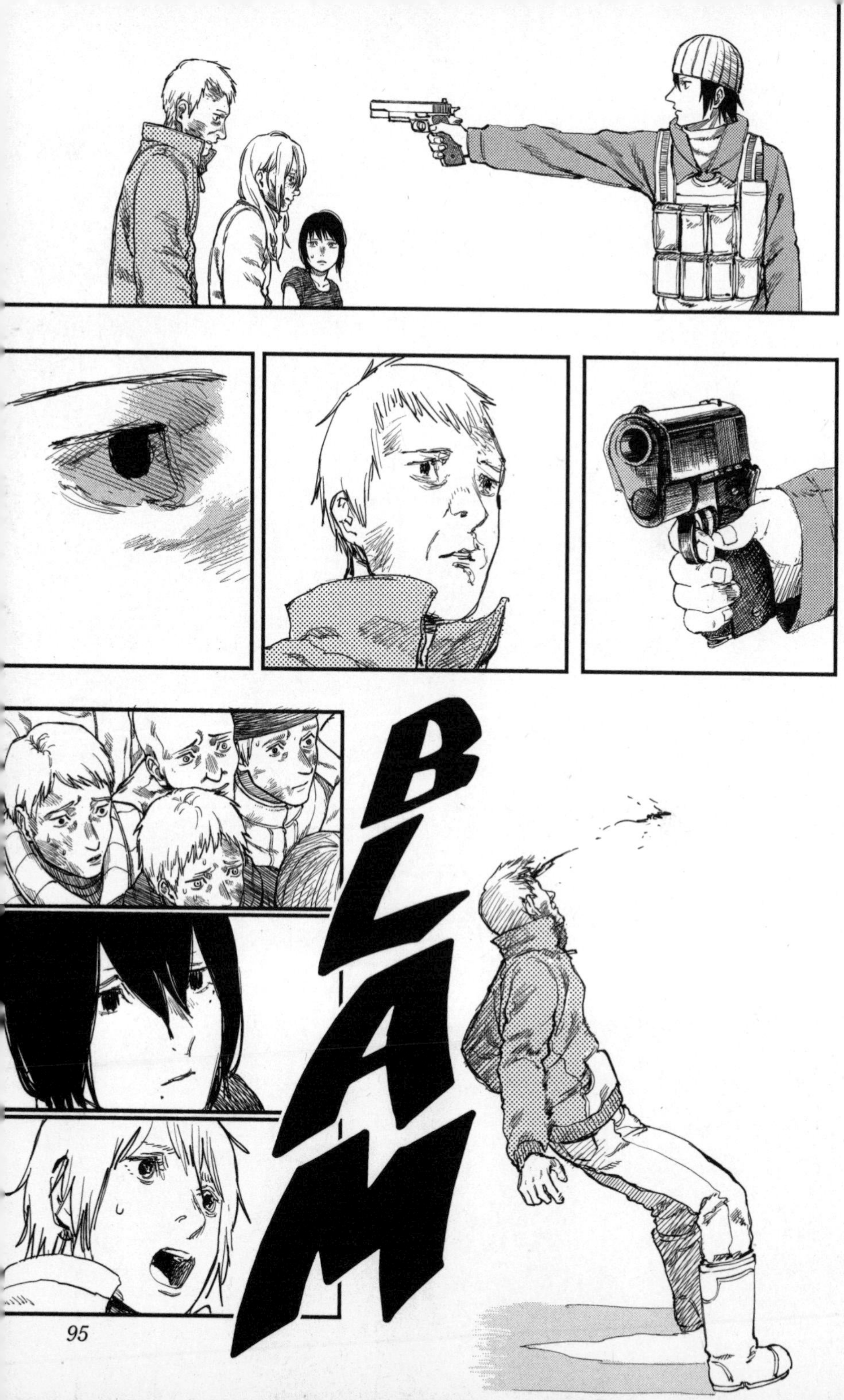
BLAM

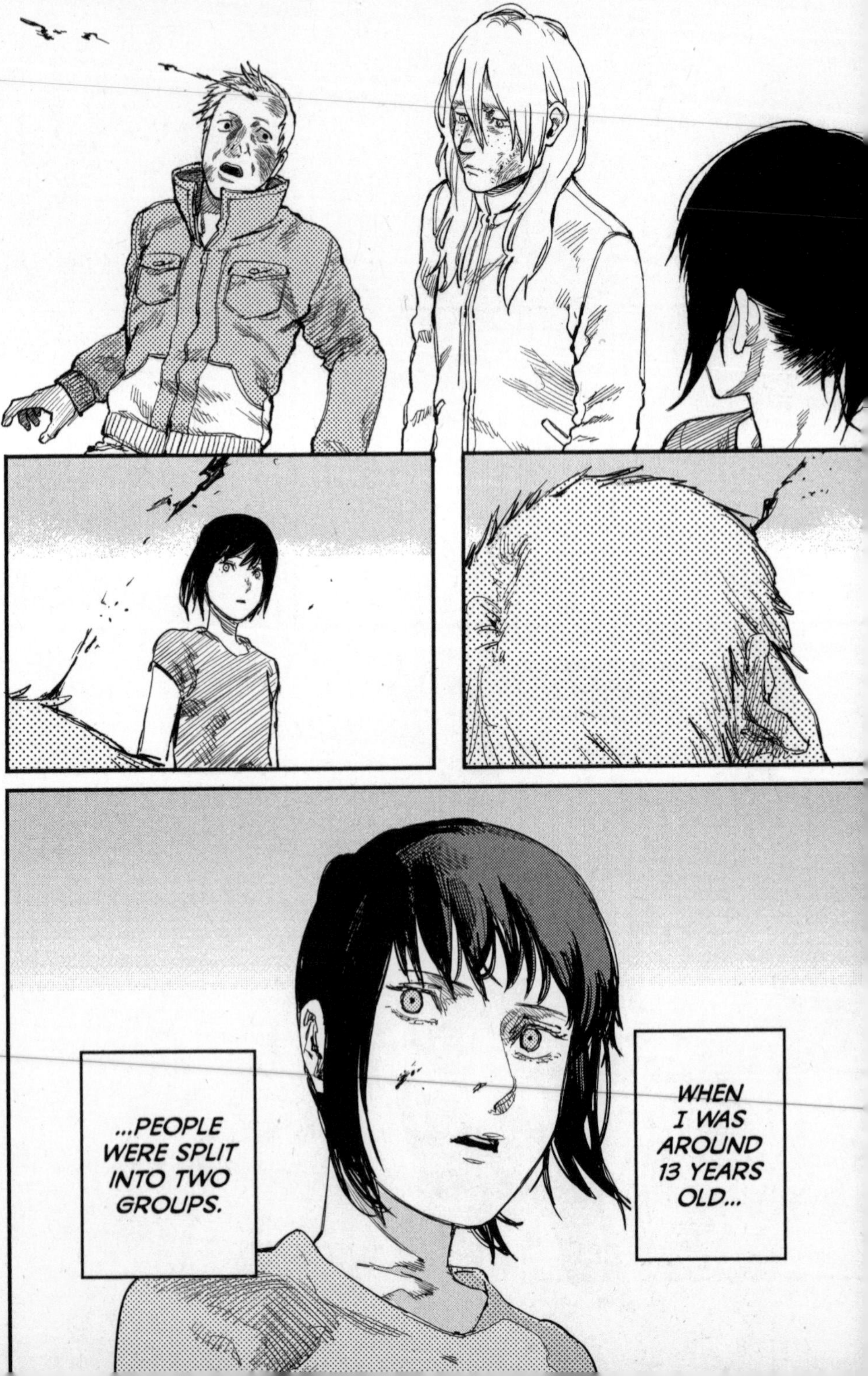
WHEN I WAS AROUND 13 YEARS OLD...
...PEOPLE WERE SPLIT INTO TWO GROUPS.

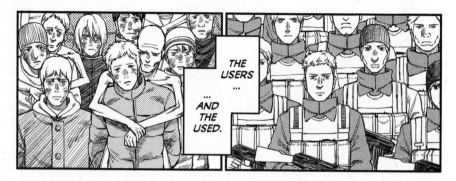

THE USERS... ...AND THE USED.

THE WARM... ...AND THE FREEZING.

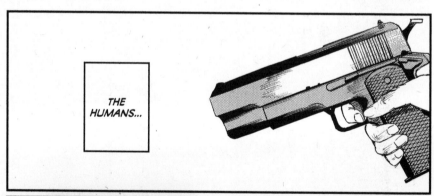

THE HUMANS...

...AND THE FIREWOOD.

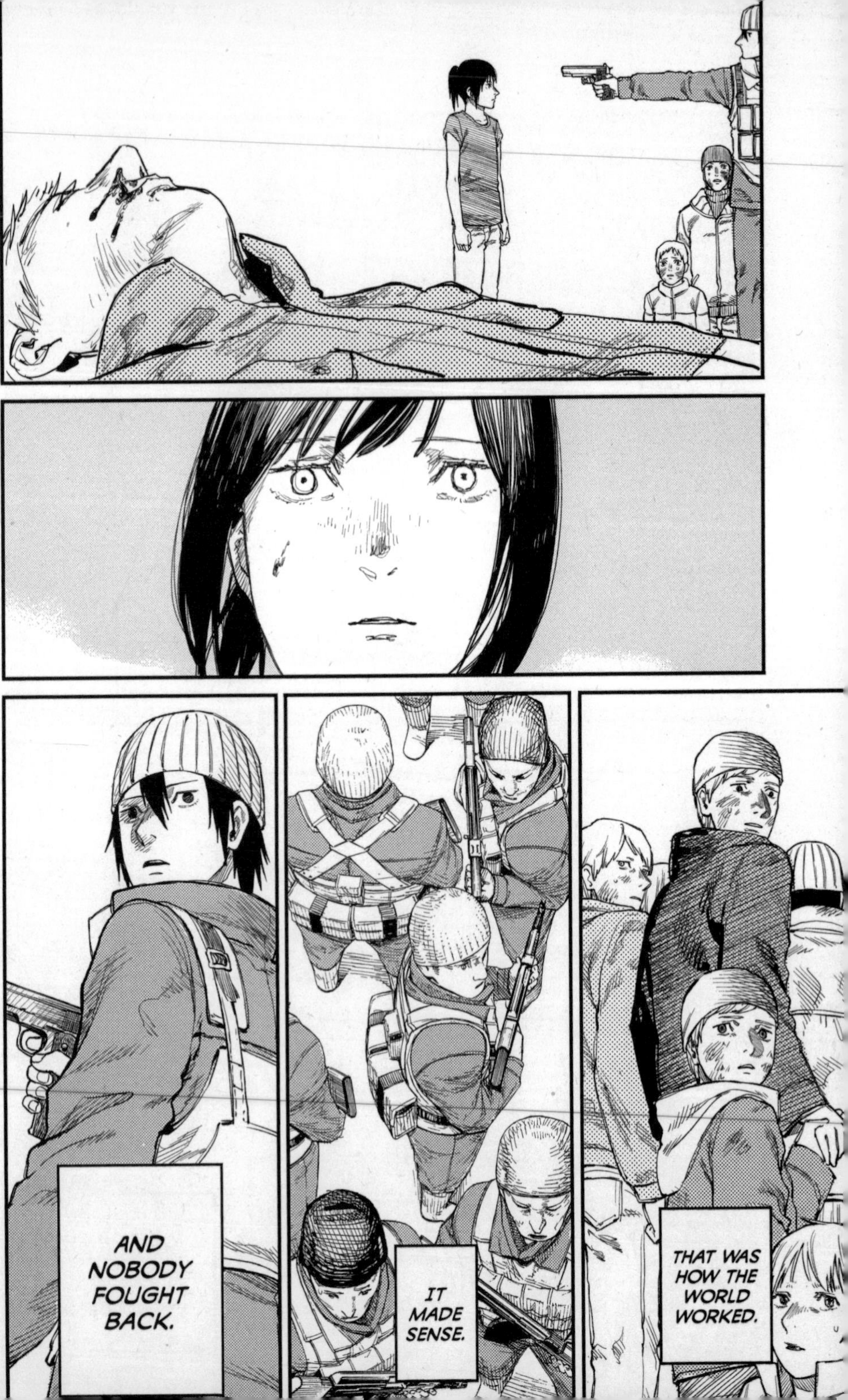
THAT WAS HOW THE WORLD WORKED.
IT MADE SENSE.
AND NOBODY FOUGHT BACK.

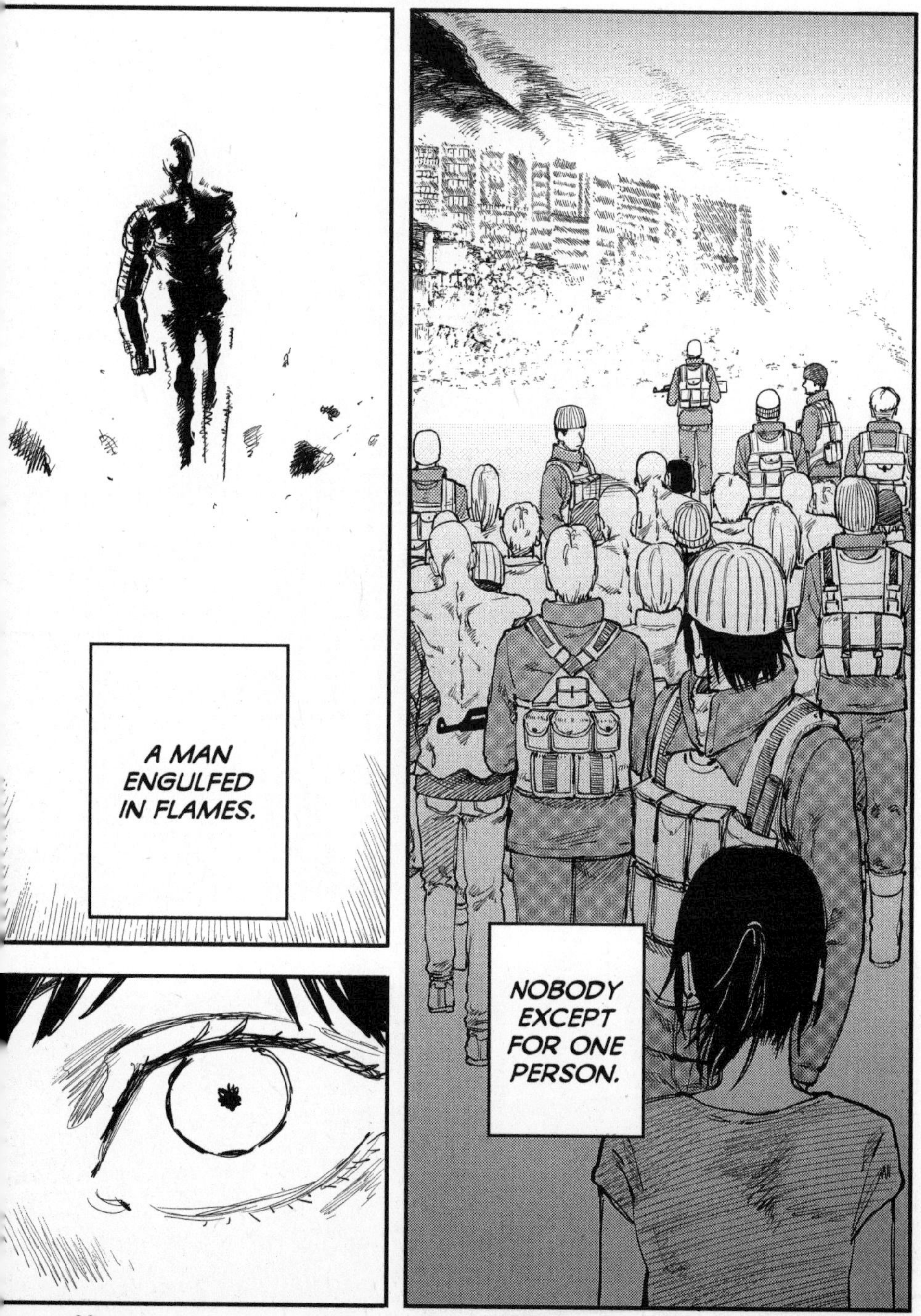
NOBODY EXCEPT FOR ONE PERSON.
A MAN ENGULFED IN FLAMES.

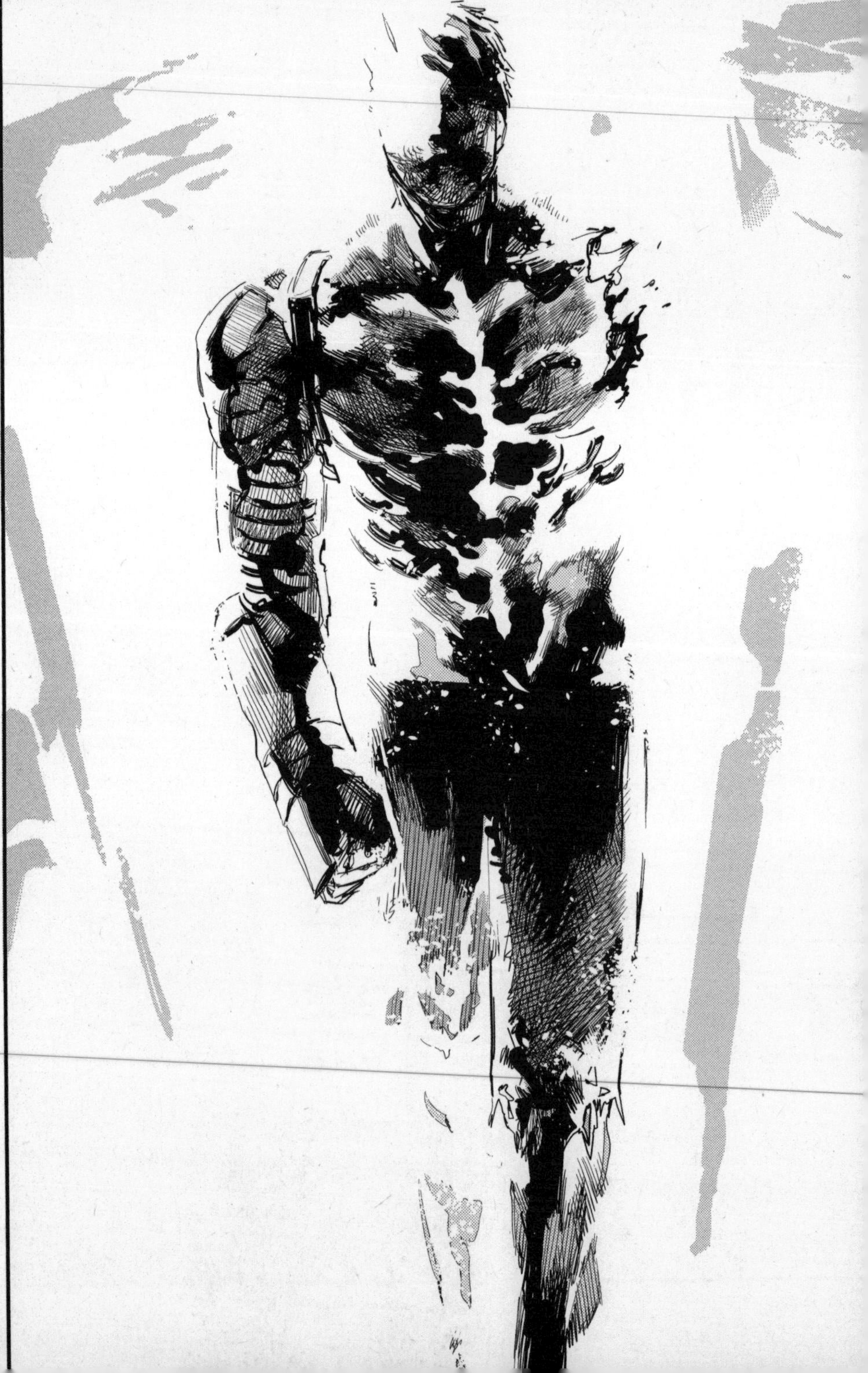

EH?!

SUN! GIVE ME THAT THING IN YOUR POCKET!

...!

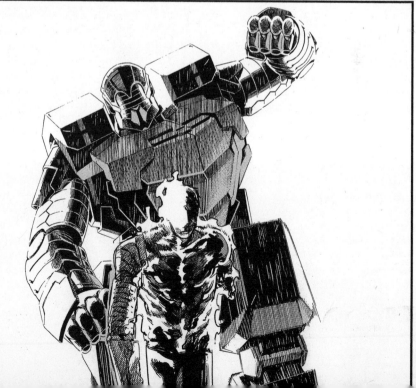

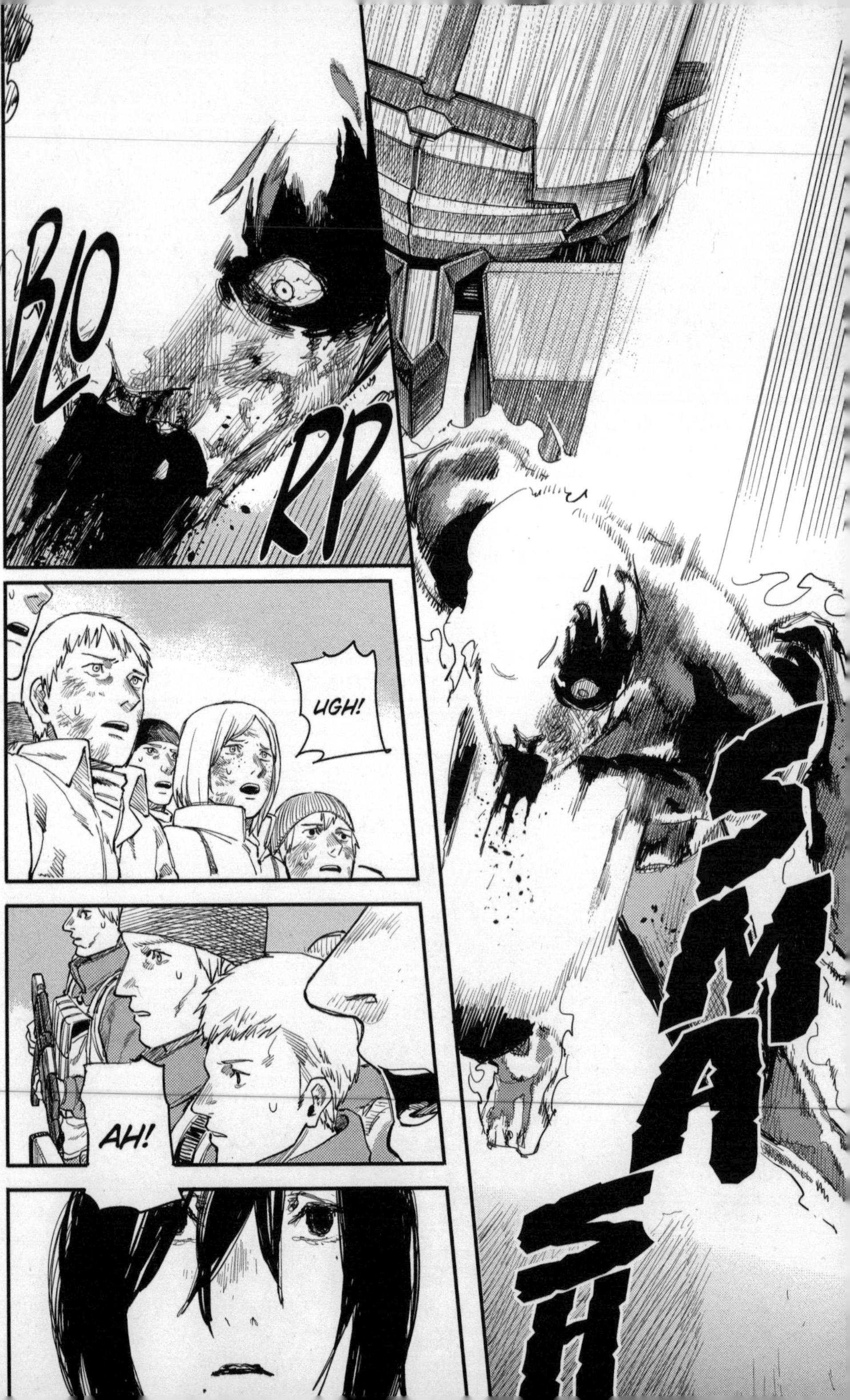
SMASH
BLORP
UGH!
AH!

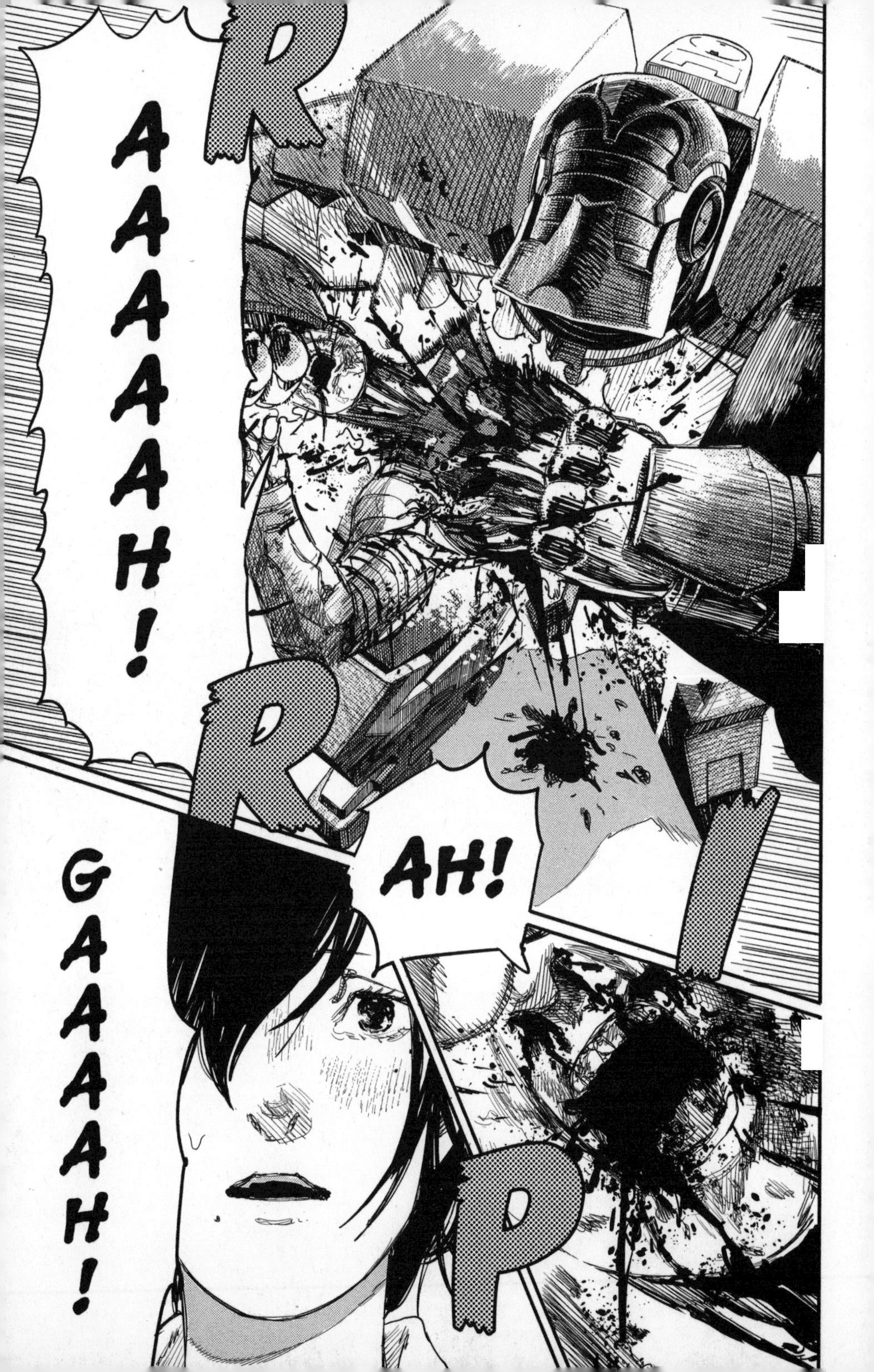
AAAAAH!
RRIP
AH!
GAAAAAH!

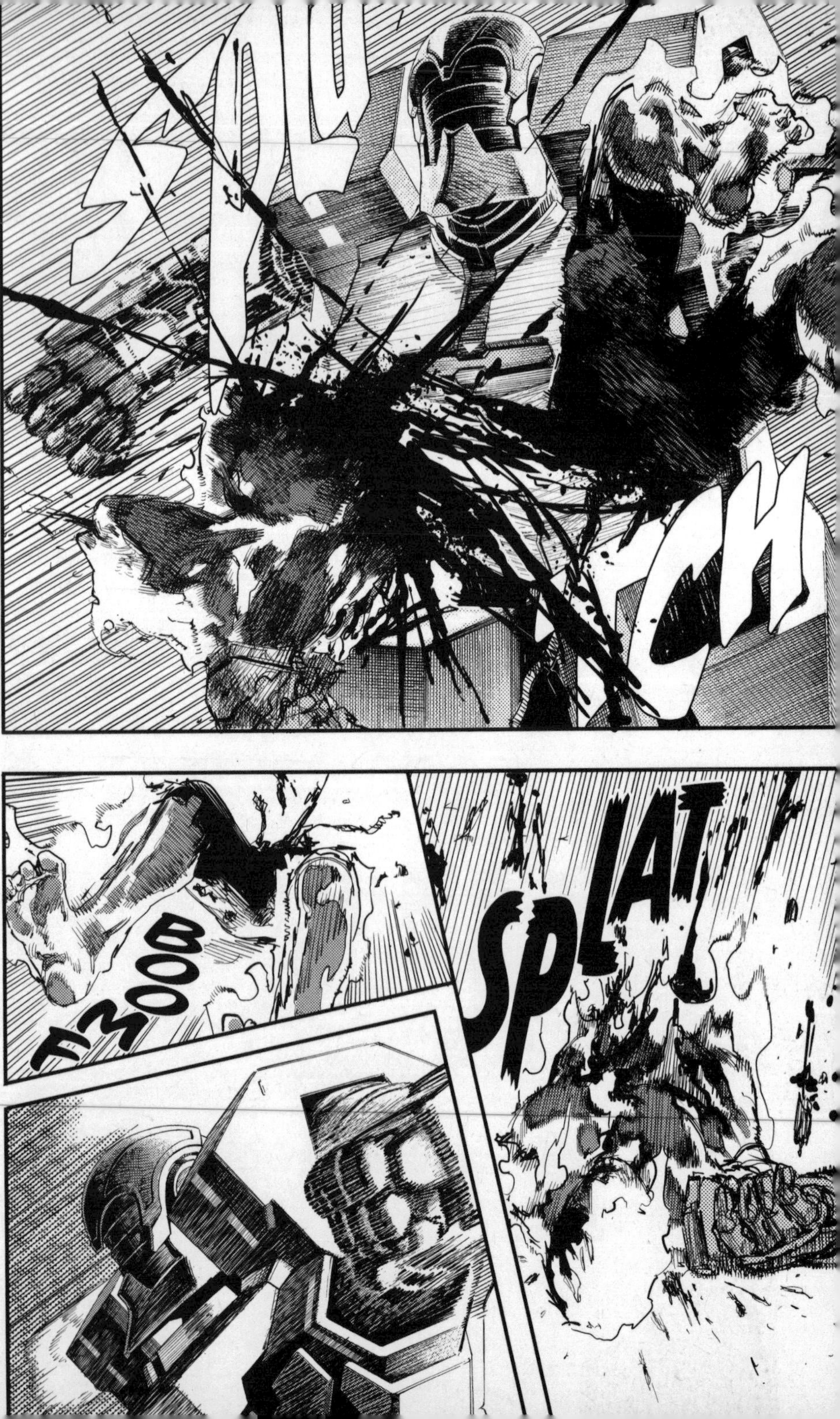
SPLAT
BOOM

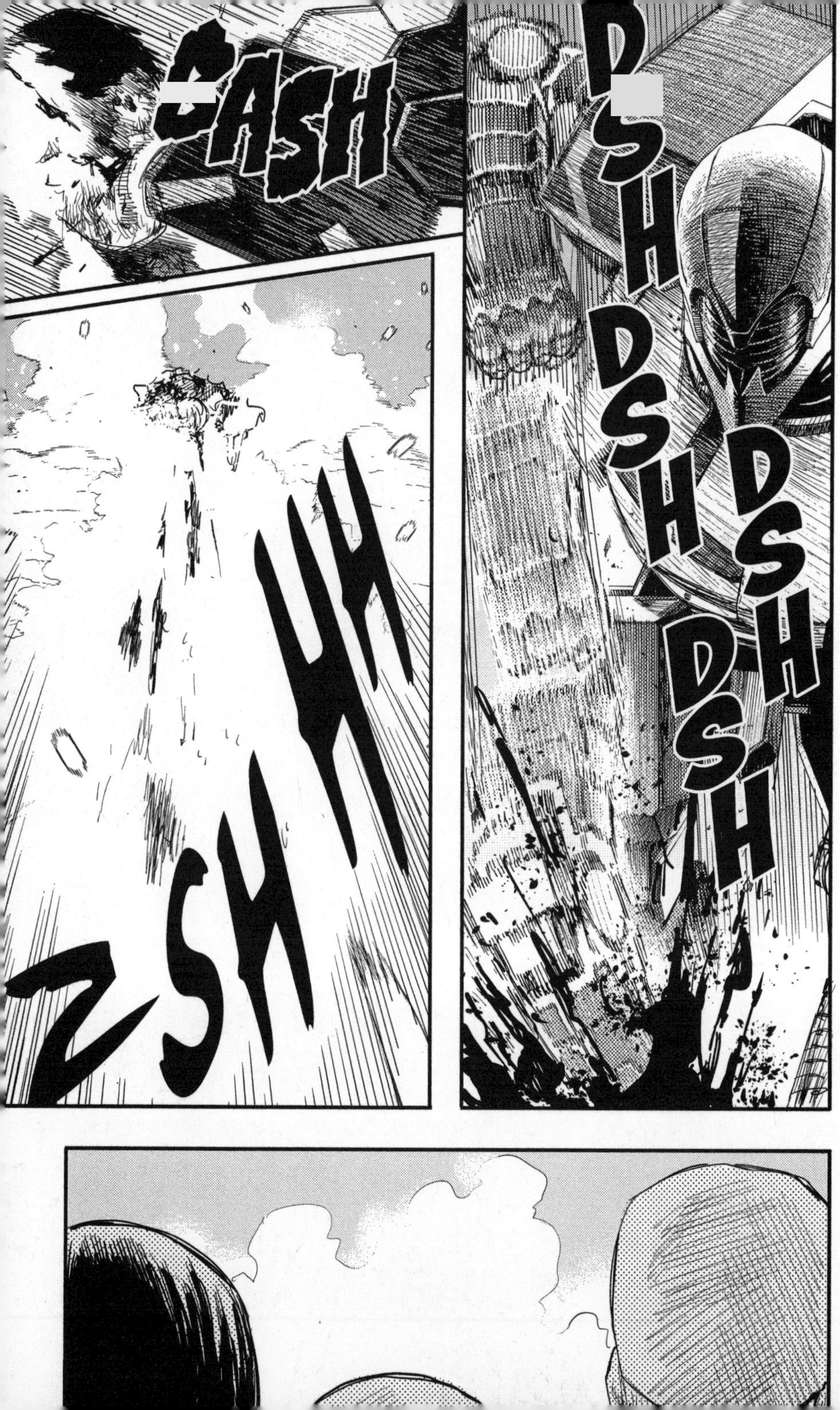
DSH
DSH
DSH
DSH
CASH
ZSHHH

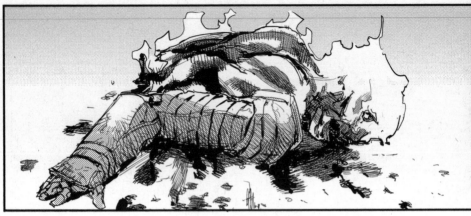

AAAAH...

UHF!

AH!

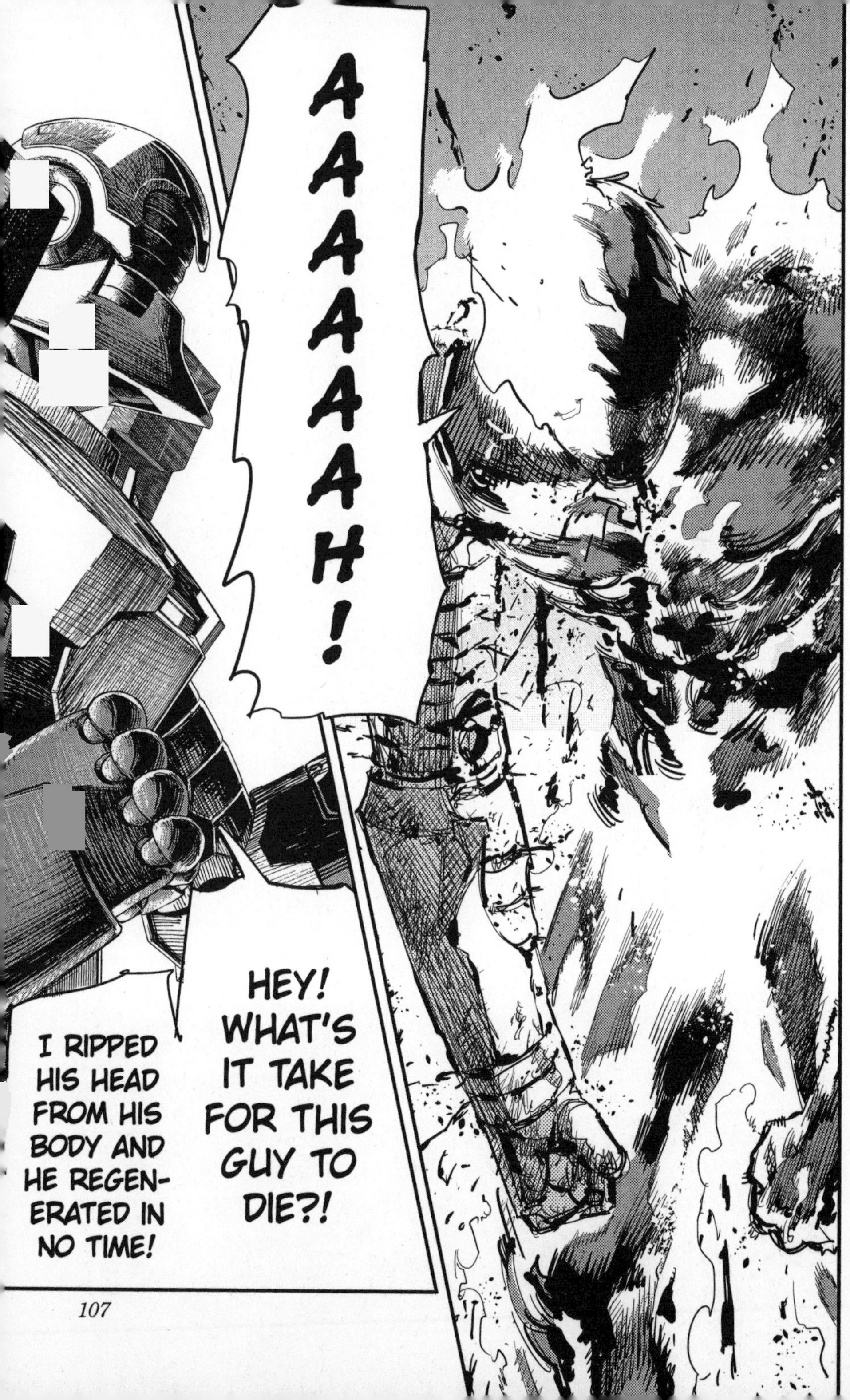
AAAAAAH!
HEY! WHAT'S IT TAKE FOR THIS GUY TO DIE?!
I RIPPED HIS HEAD FROM HIS BODY AND HE REGEN-ERATED IN NO TIME!

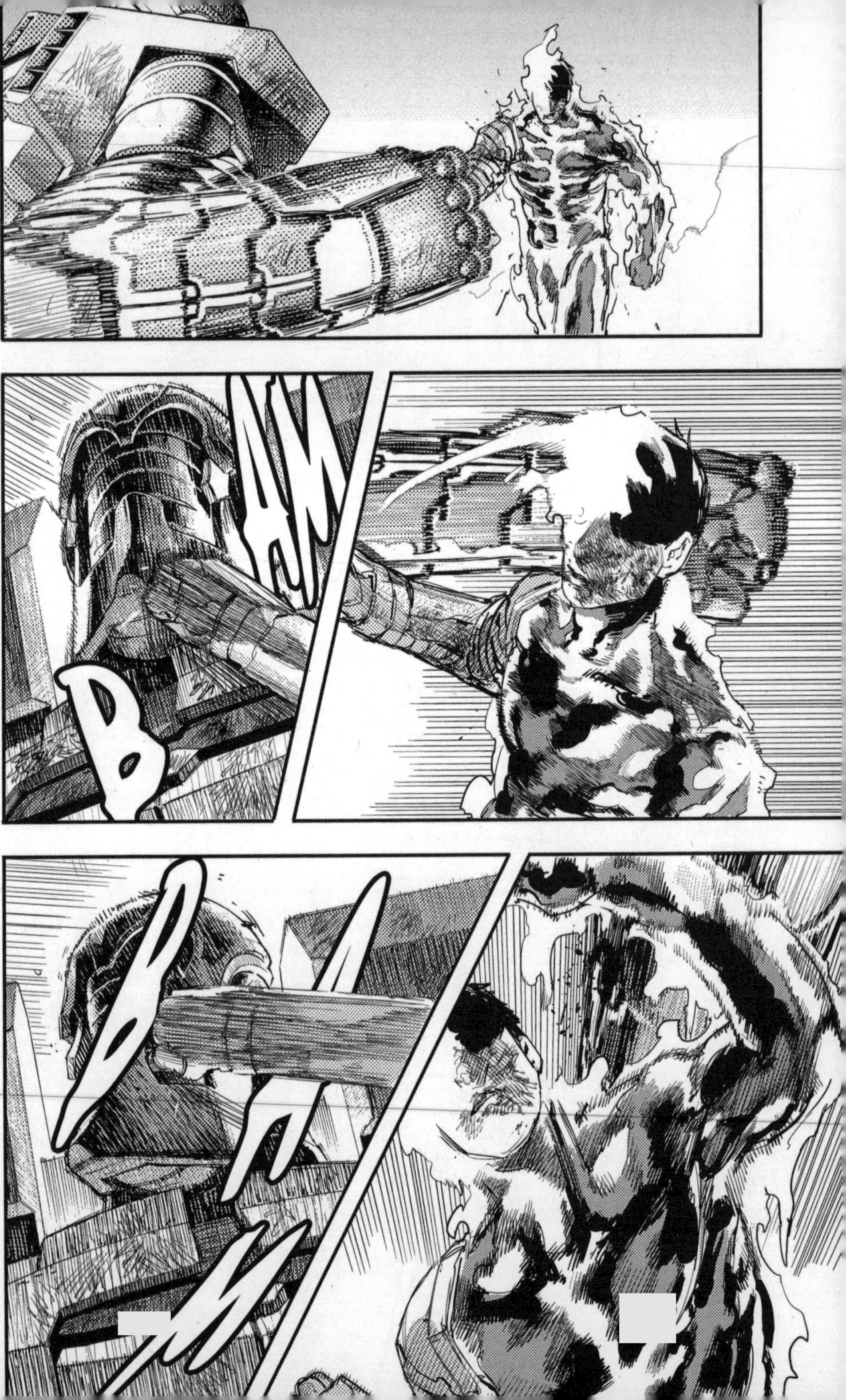
BAM
BAM

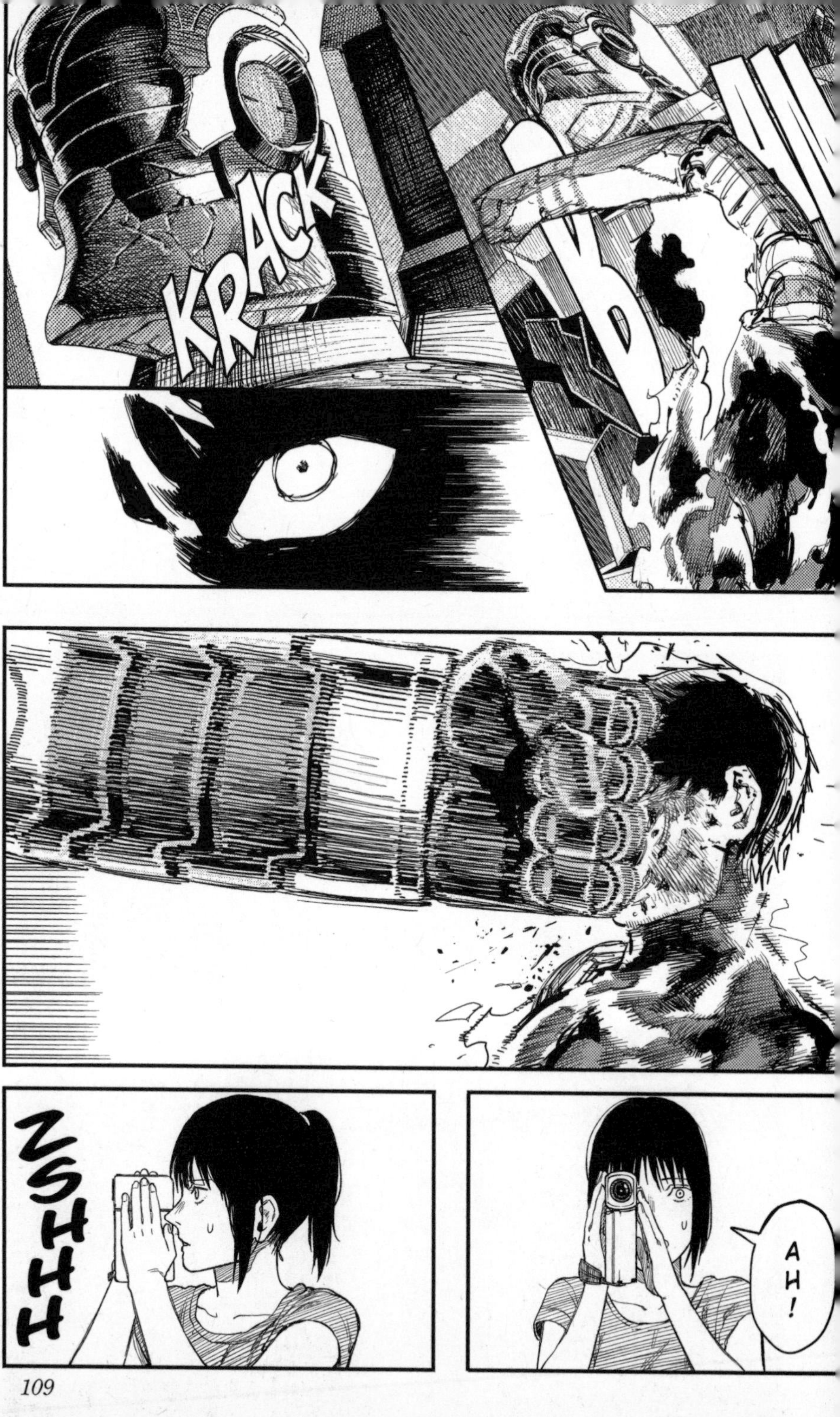
KRACK
AH!
ZSHHH

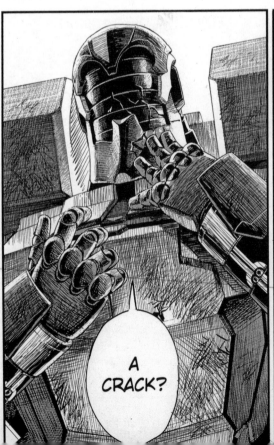

A CRACK?

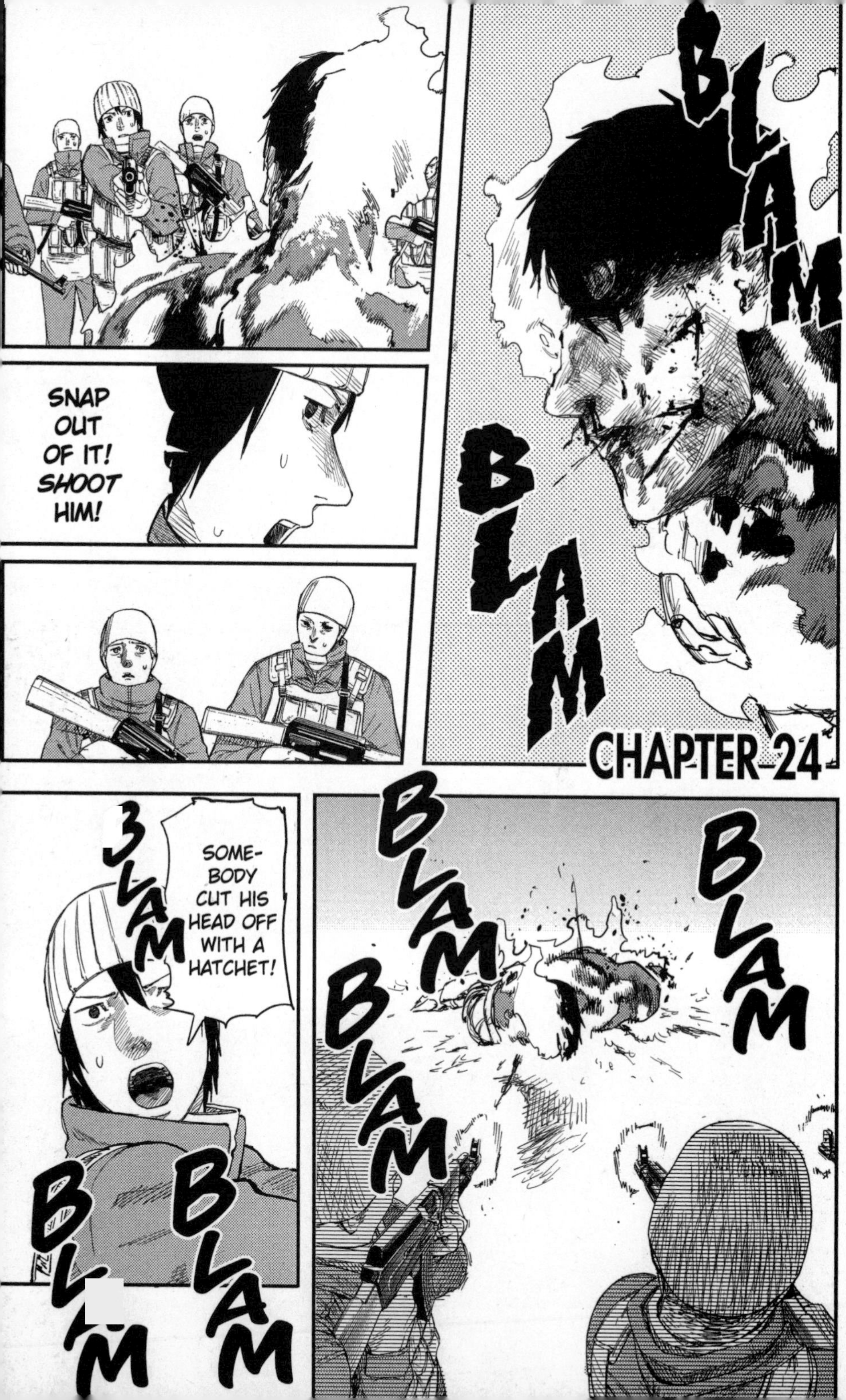
BLAM
BLAM
CHAPTER 24
SNAP OUT OF IT! SHOOT HIM!
BLAM
BLAM
BLAM
BLAM
SOME-BODY CUT HIS HEAD OFF WITH A HATCHET!
BLAM

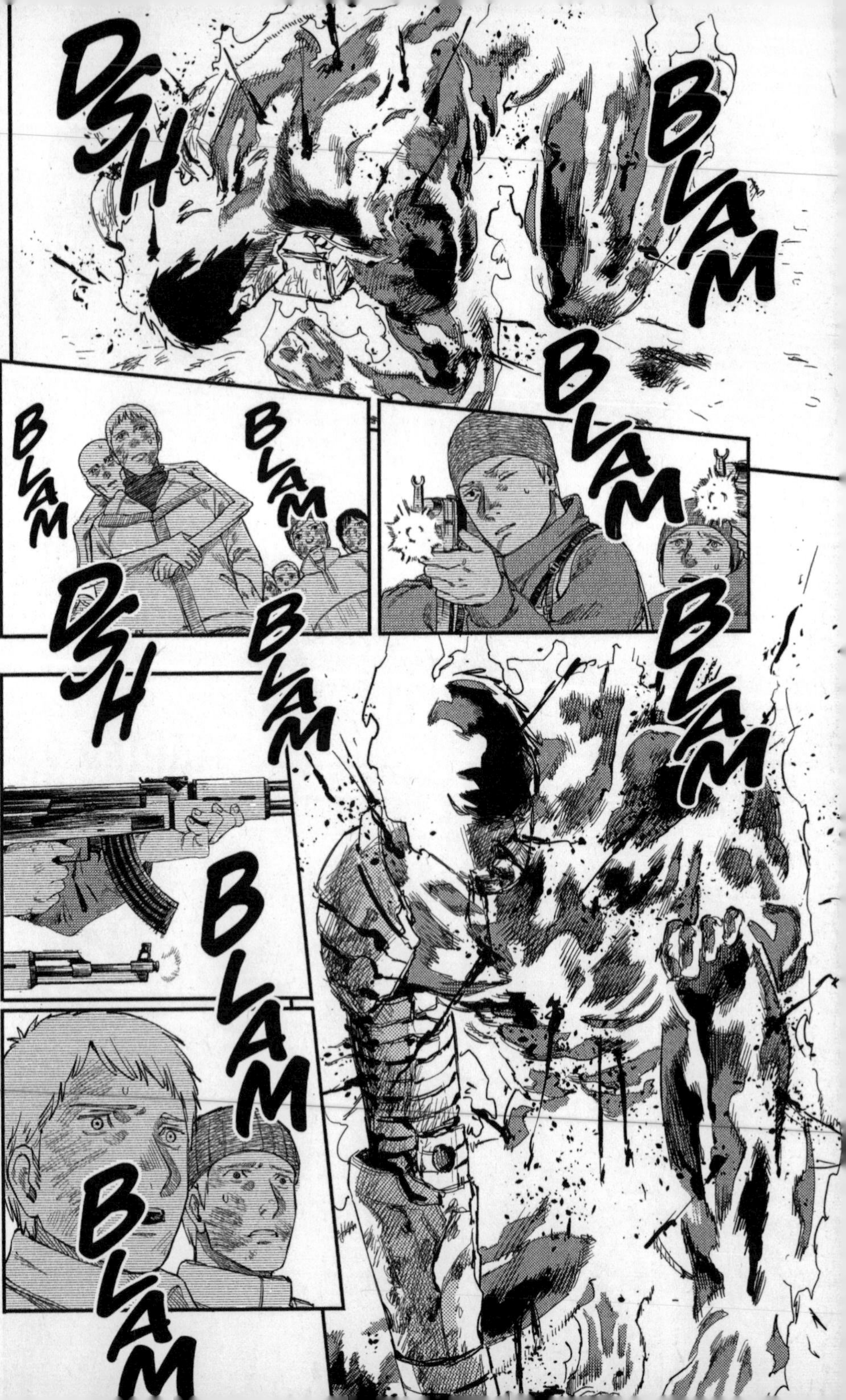
BLAM
DSH
BLAM
BLAM
BLAM
BLAM
BLAM
DSH
BLAM
BLAM
BLAM

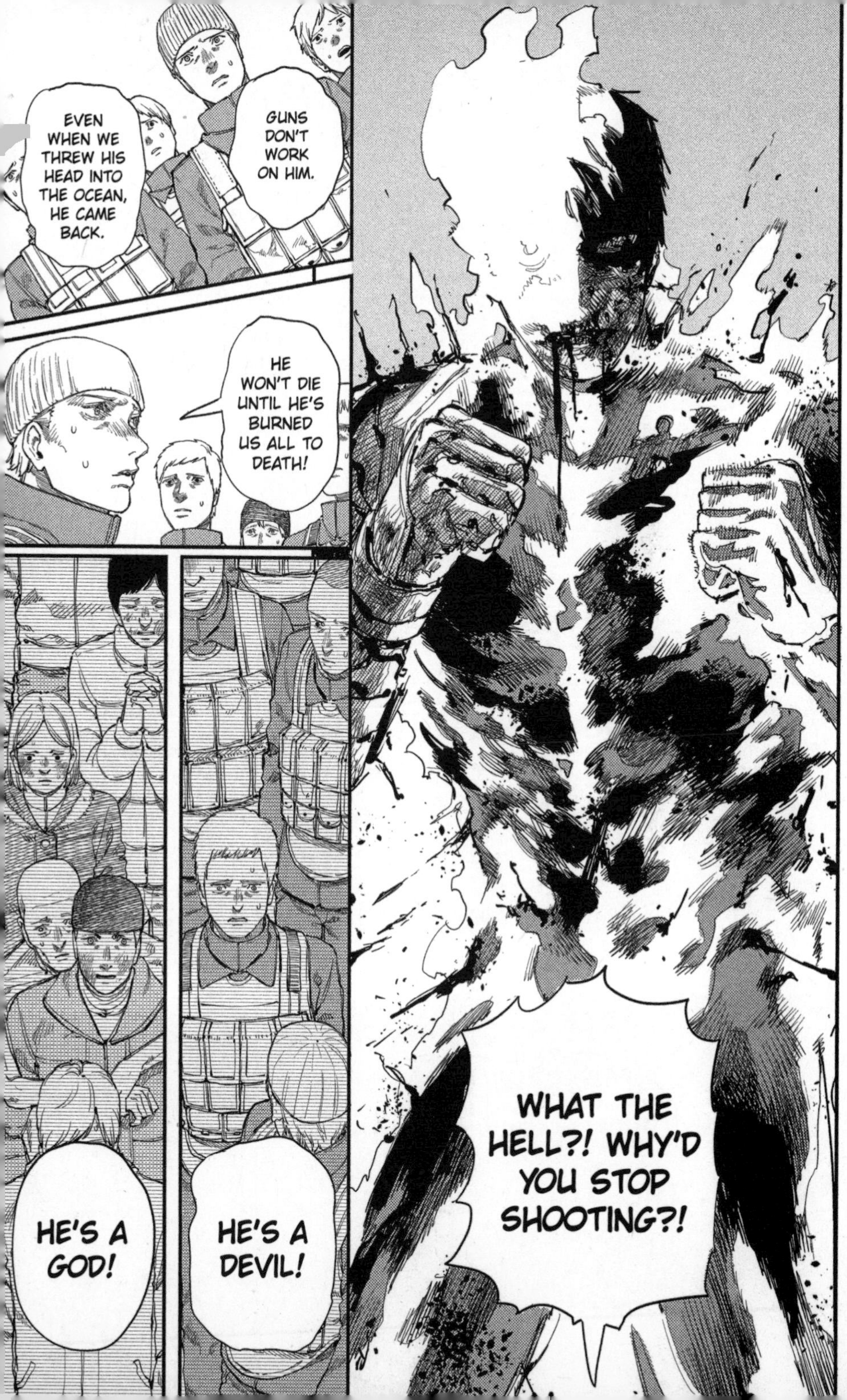
WHAT THE HELL?! WHY'D YOU STOP SHOOTING?!
GUNS DON'T WORK ON HIM.
EVEN WHEN WE THREW HIS HEAD INTO THE OCEAN, HE CAME BACK.
HE WON'T DIE UNTIL HE'S BURNED US ALL TO DEATH!
HE'S A DEVIL!
HE'S A GOD!

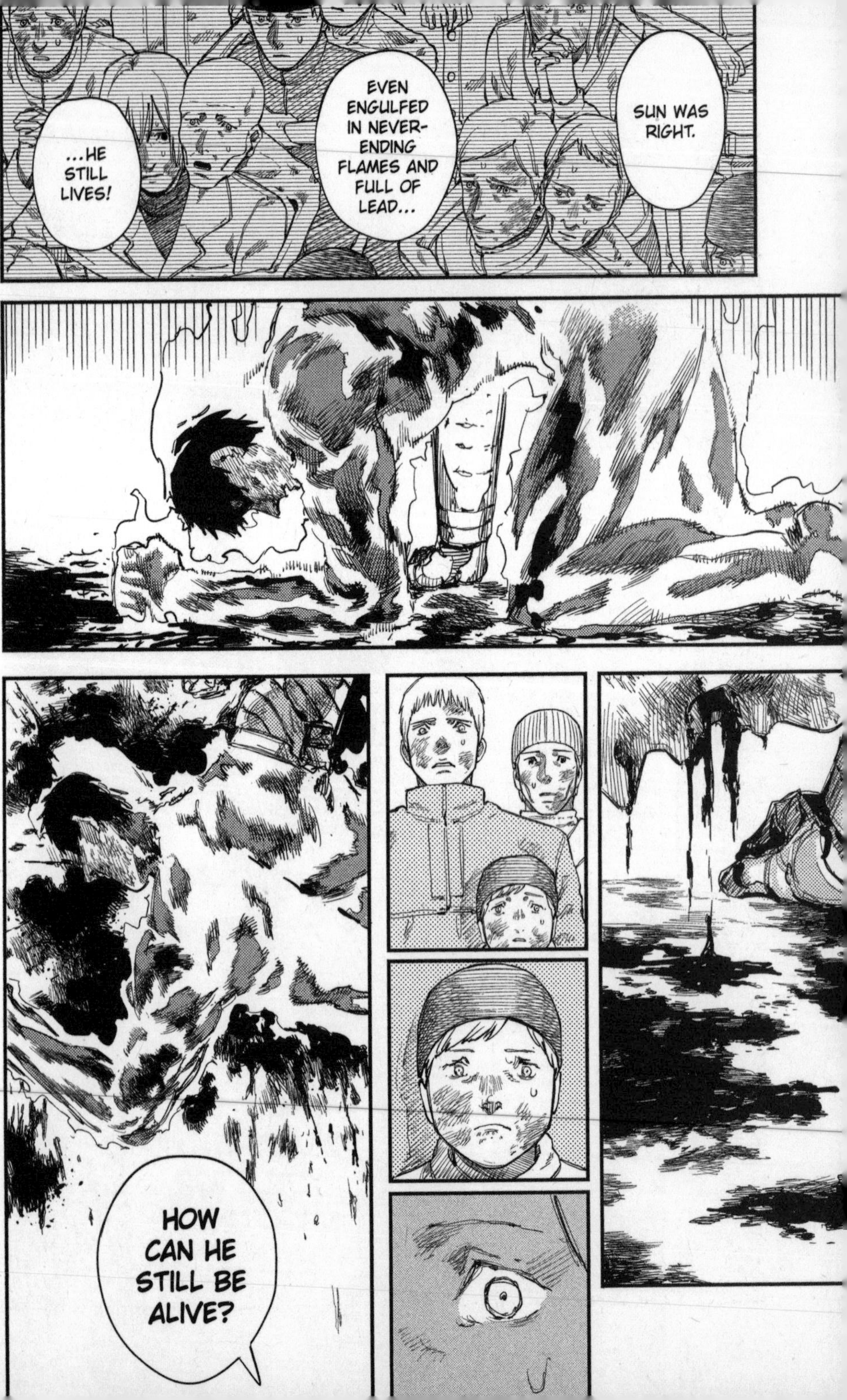
SUN WAS RIGHT.
EVEN ENGULFED IN NEVER-ENDING FLAMES AND FULL OF LEAD...
...HE STILL LIVES!
HOW CAN HE STILL BE ALIVE?

LIVING BRINGS NOTHING BUT PAIN.

WHY AM I ALIVE?

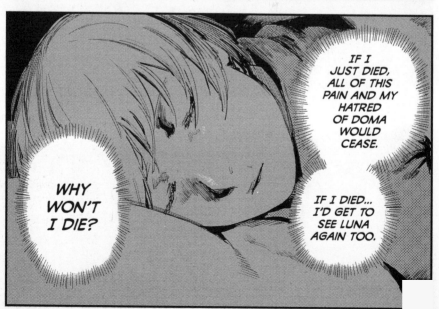

IF I JUST DIED, ALL OF THIS PAIN AND MY HATRED OF DOMA WOULD CEASE.

WHY WON'T I DIE?

IF I DIED... I'D GET TO SEE LUNA AGAIN TOO.

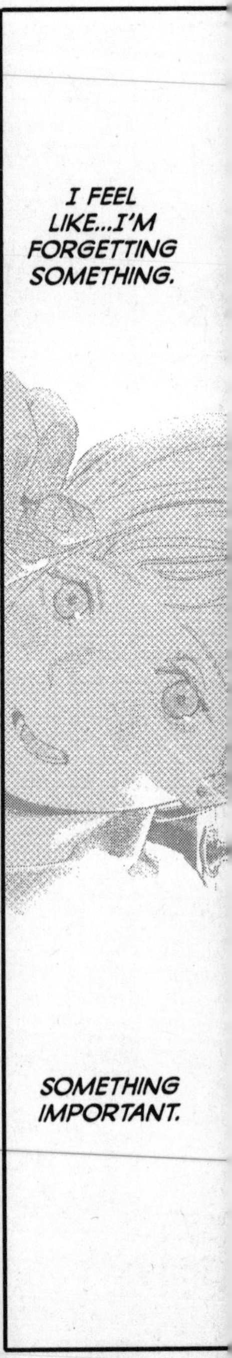
I FEEL LIKE...I'M FORGETTING SOMETHING.
SOMETHING IMPORTANT.

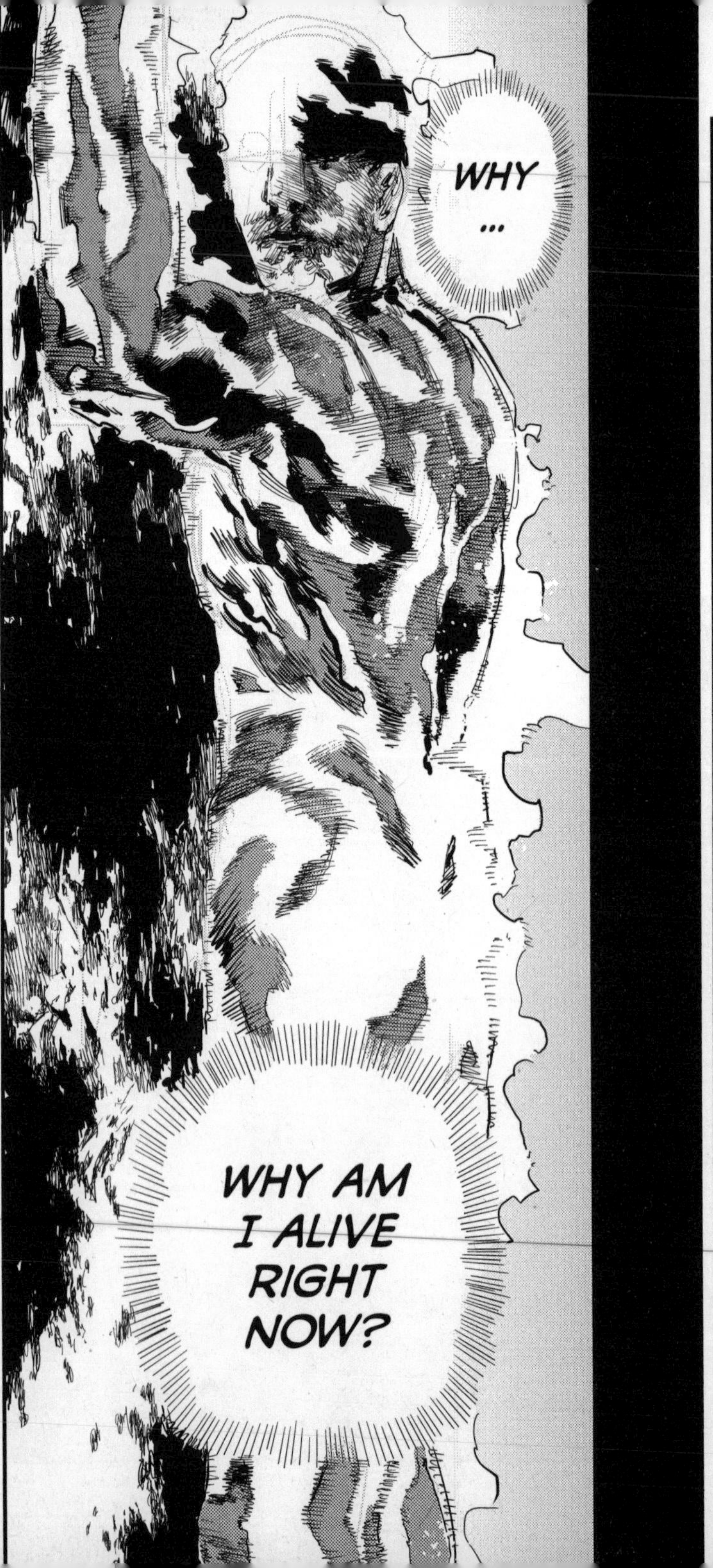
WHY ...
WHY AM I ALIVE RIGHT NOW?

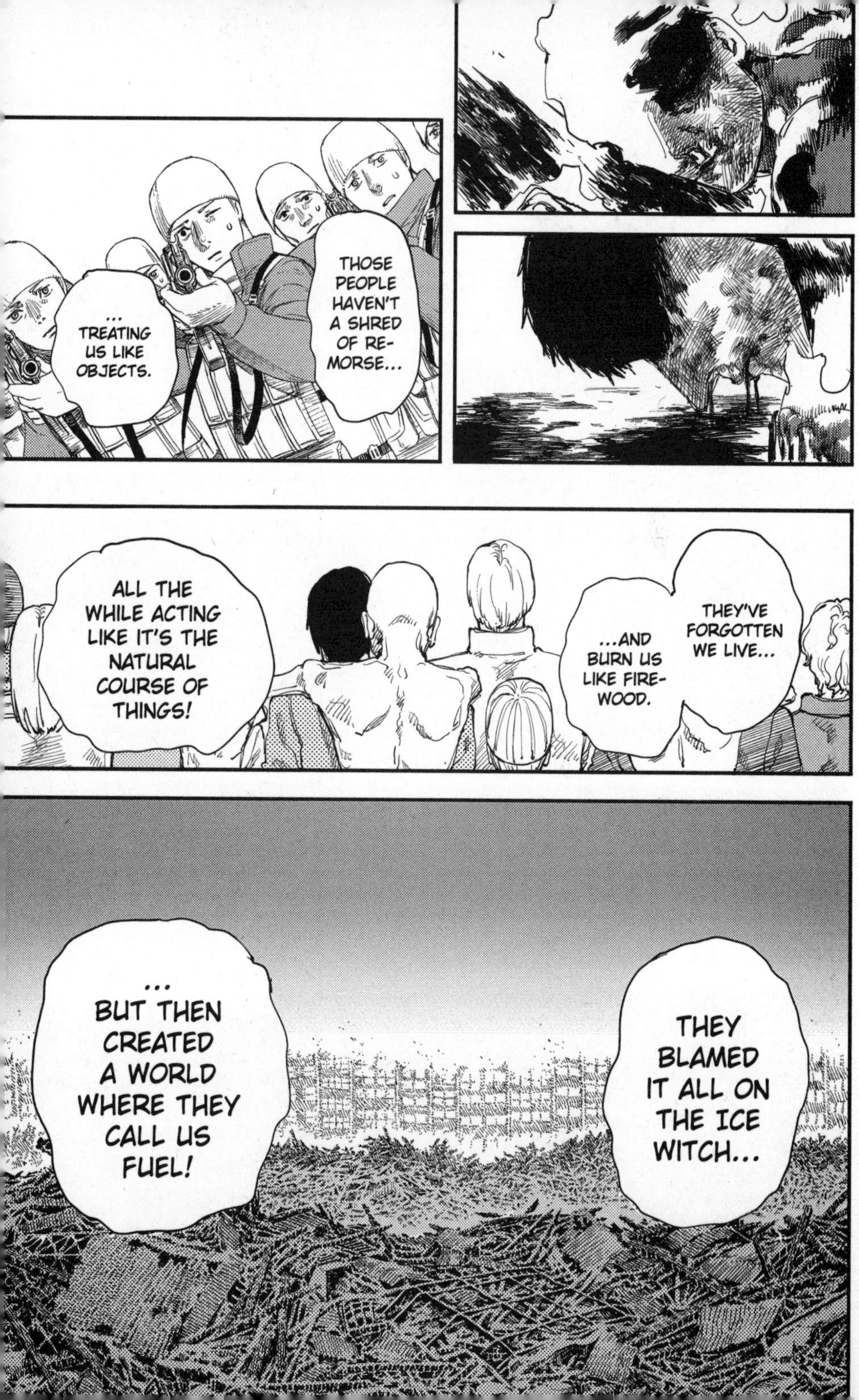
THOSE PEOPLE HAVEN'T A SHRED OF RE-MORSE...
...TREATING US LIKE OBJECTS.
THEY'VE FORGOTTEN WE LIVE...
...AND BURN US LIKE FIRE-WOOD.
ALL THE WHILE ACTING LIKE IT'S THE NATURAL COURSE OF THINGS!
THEY BLAMED IT ALL ON THE ICE WITCH...
... BUT THEN CREATED A WORLD WHERE THEY CALL US FUEL!

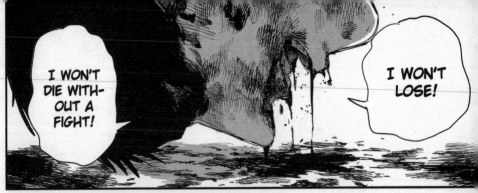

I WON'T DIE WITHOUT A FIGHT!

I WON'T LOSE!

THE SNOW.

THE HUNGER.

THE MADNESS.

THAT'S RIGHT... I HATED IT ALL.

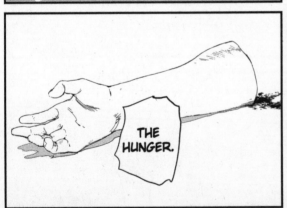

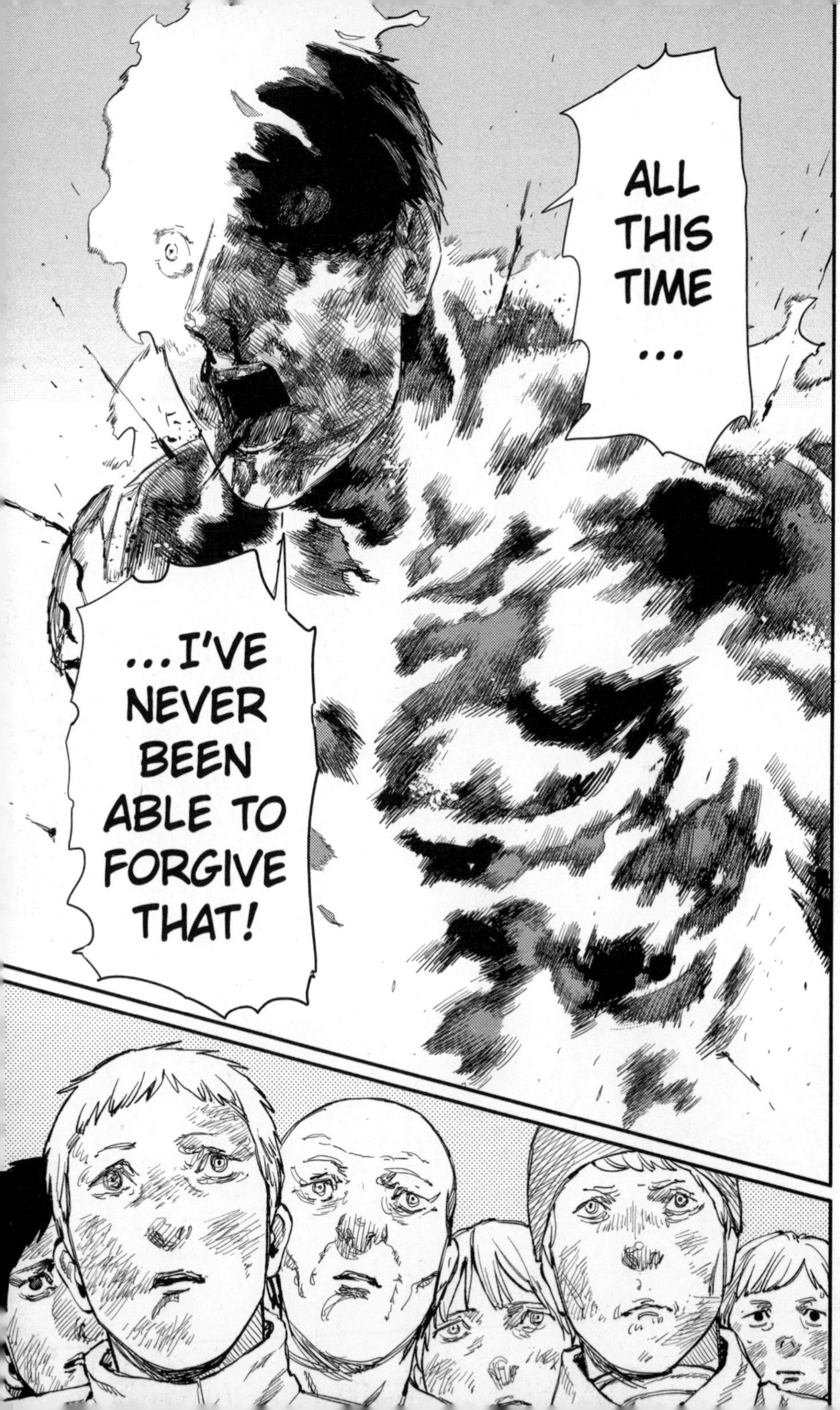
ALL THIS TIME ...
...I'VE NEVER BEEN ABLE TO FORGIVE THAT!

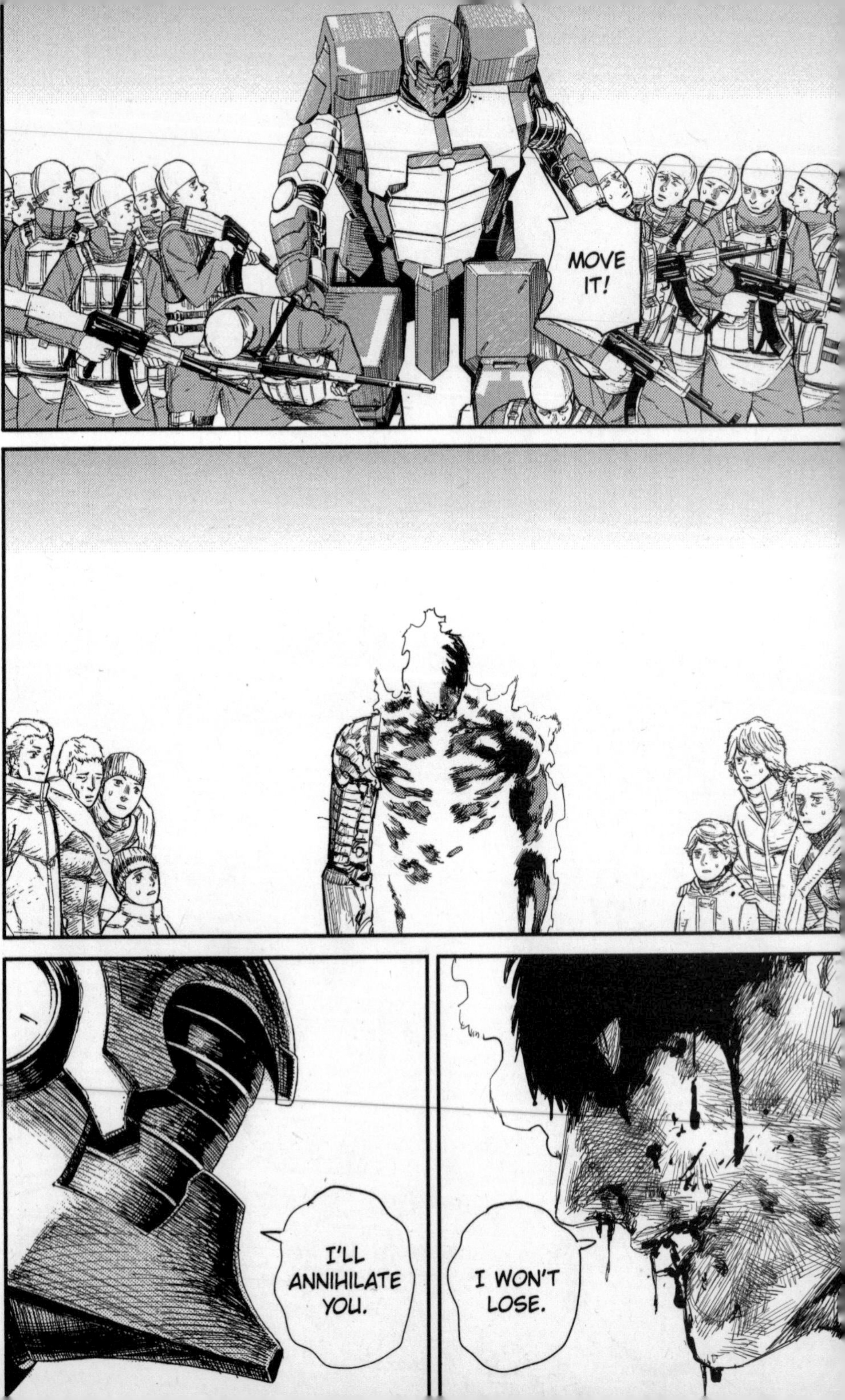
MOVE IT!
I WON'T LOSE.
I'LL ANNIHILATE YOU.

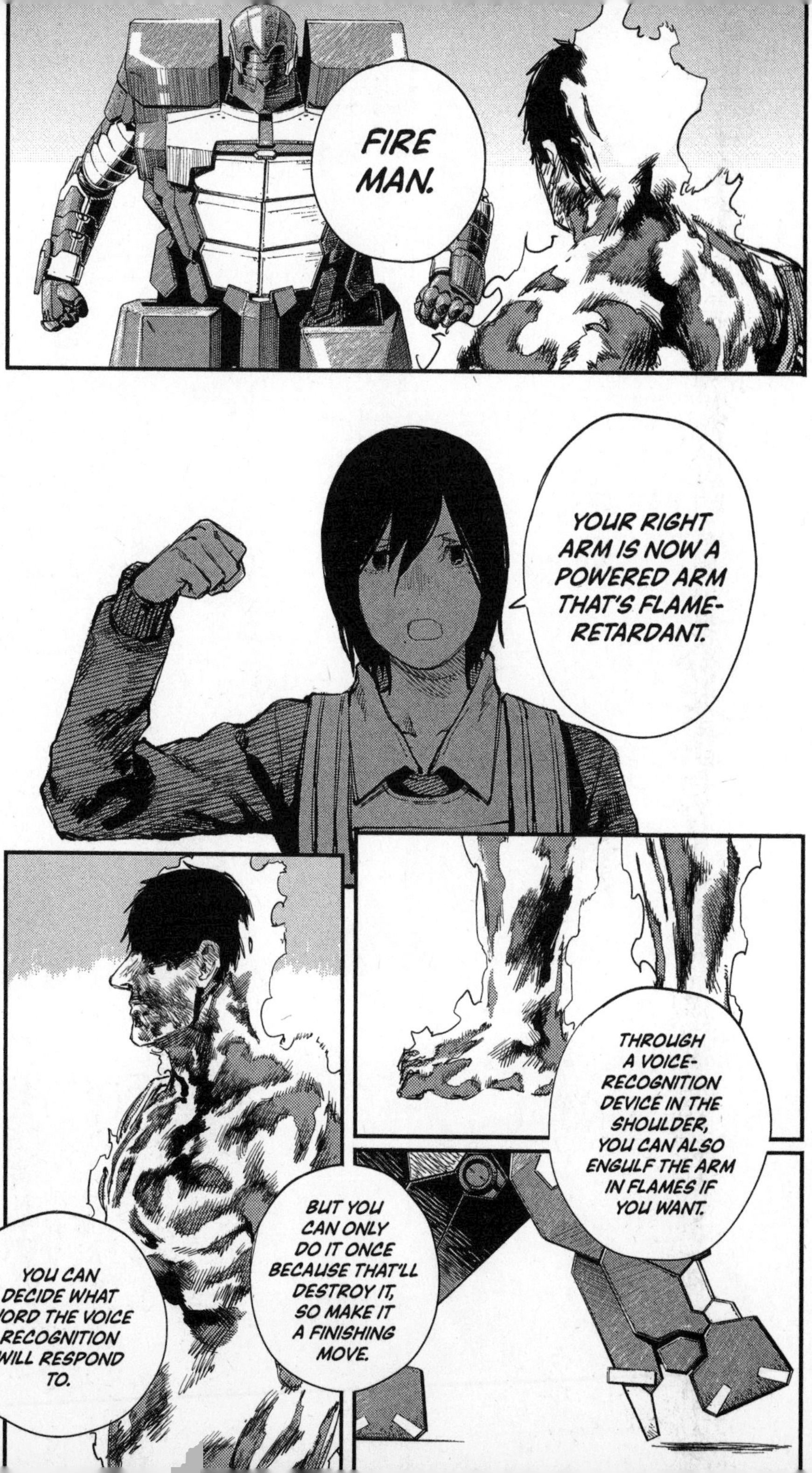
FIRE MAN.
YOUR RIGHT ARM IS NOW A POWERED ARM THAT'S FLAME-RETARDANT.
THROUGH A VOICE-RECOGNITION DEVICE IN THE SHOULDER, YOU CAN ALSO ENGULF THE ARM IN FLAMES IF YOU WANT.
BUT YOU CAN ONLY DO IT ONCE BECAUSE THAT'LL DESTROY IT, SO MAKE IT A FINISHING MOVE.
YOU CAN DECIDE WHAT WORD THE VOICE RECOGNITION WILL RESPOND TO.

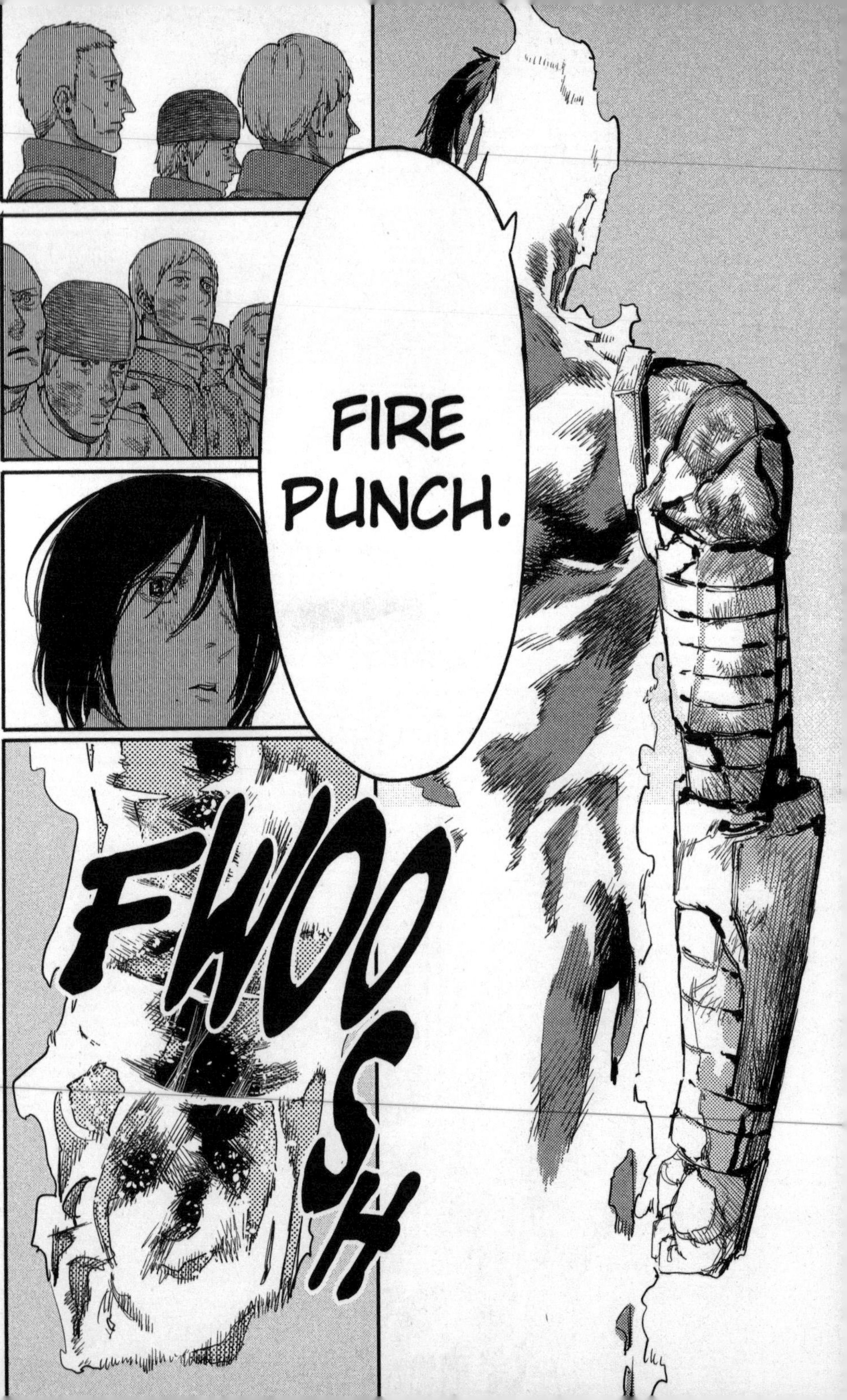
FIRE PUNCH.
FWOOSH

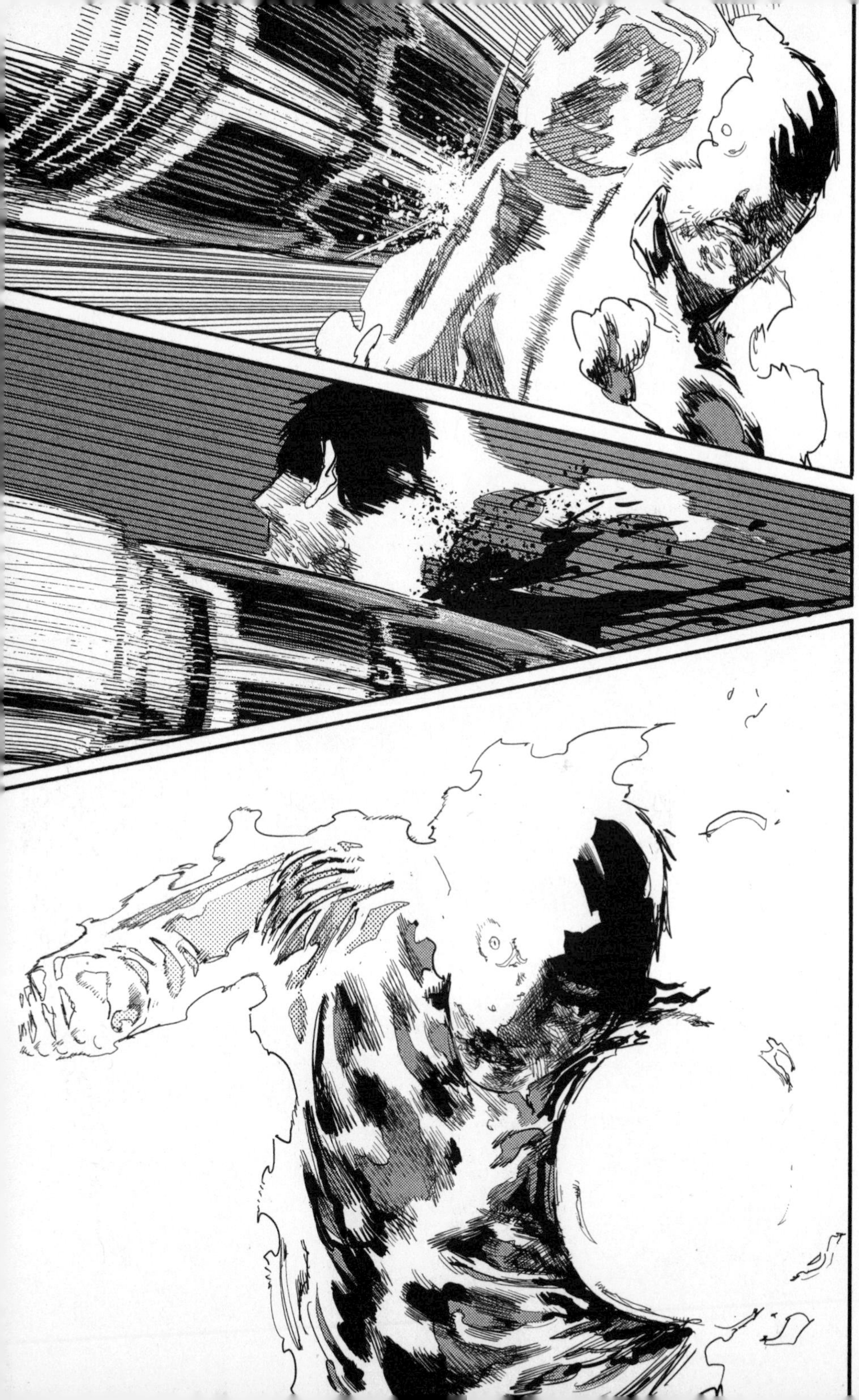

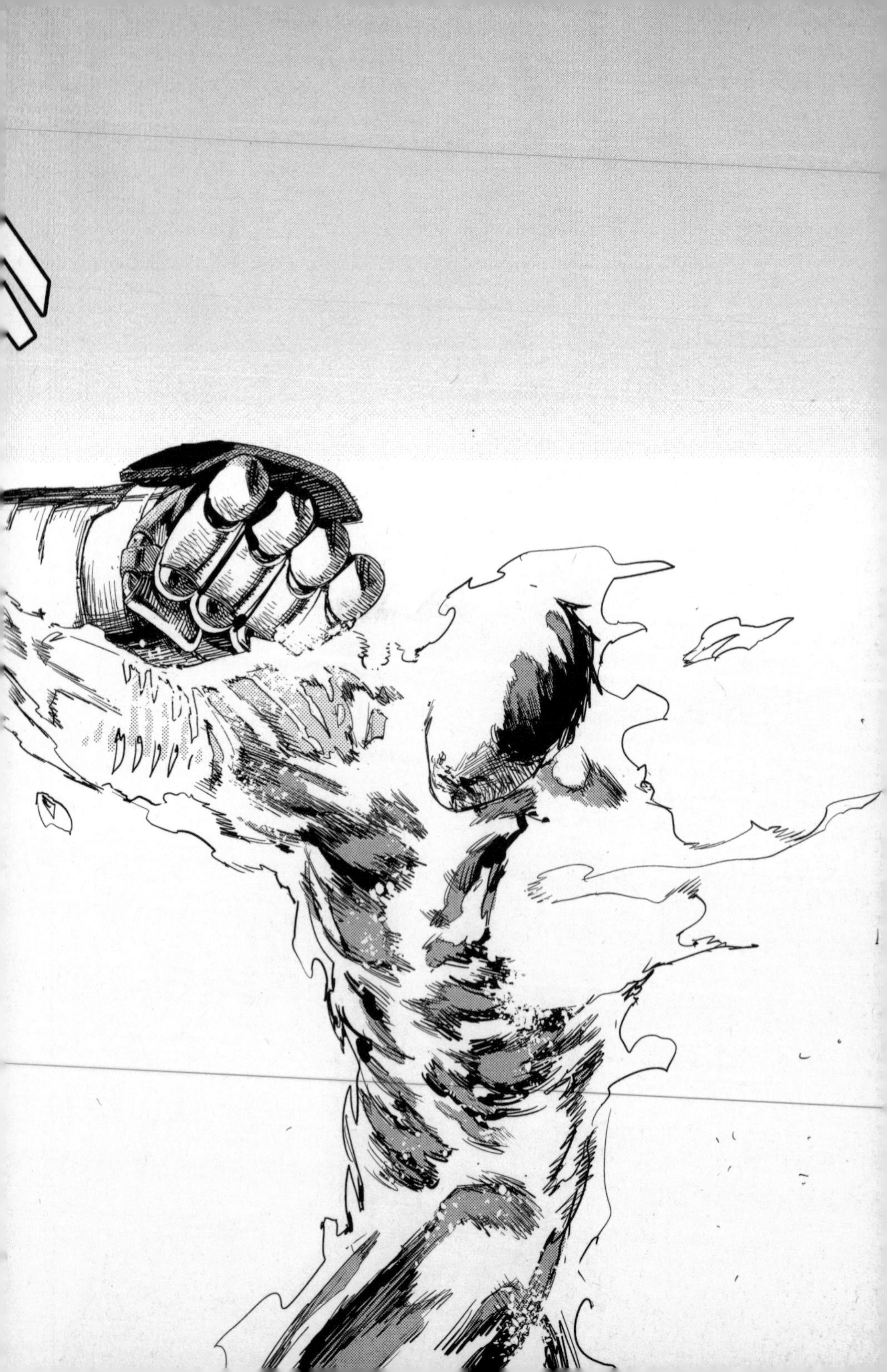

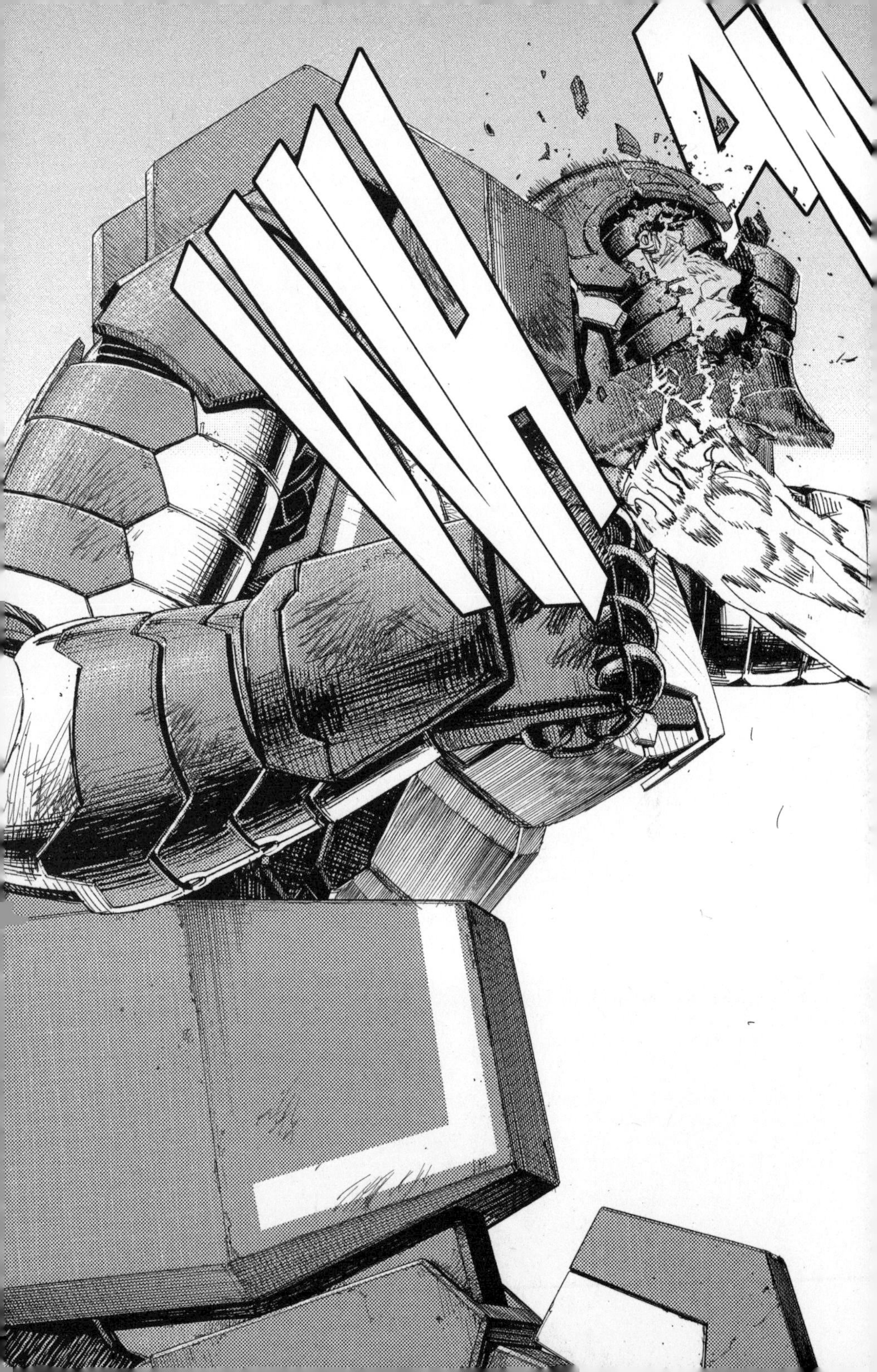
WHAM

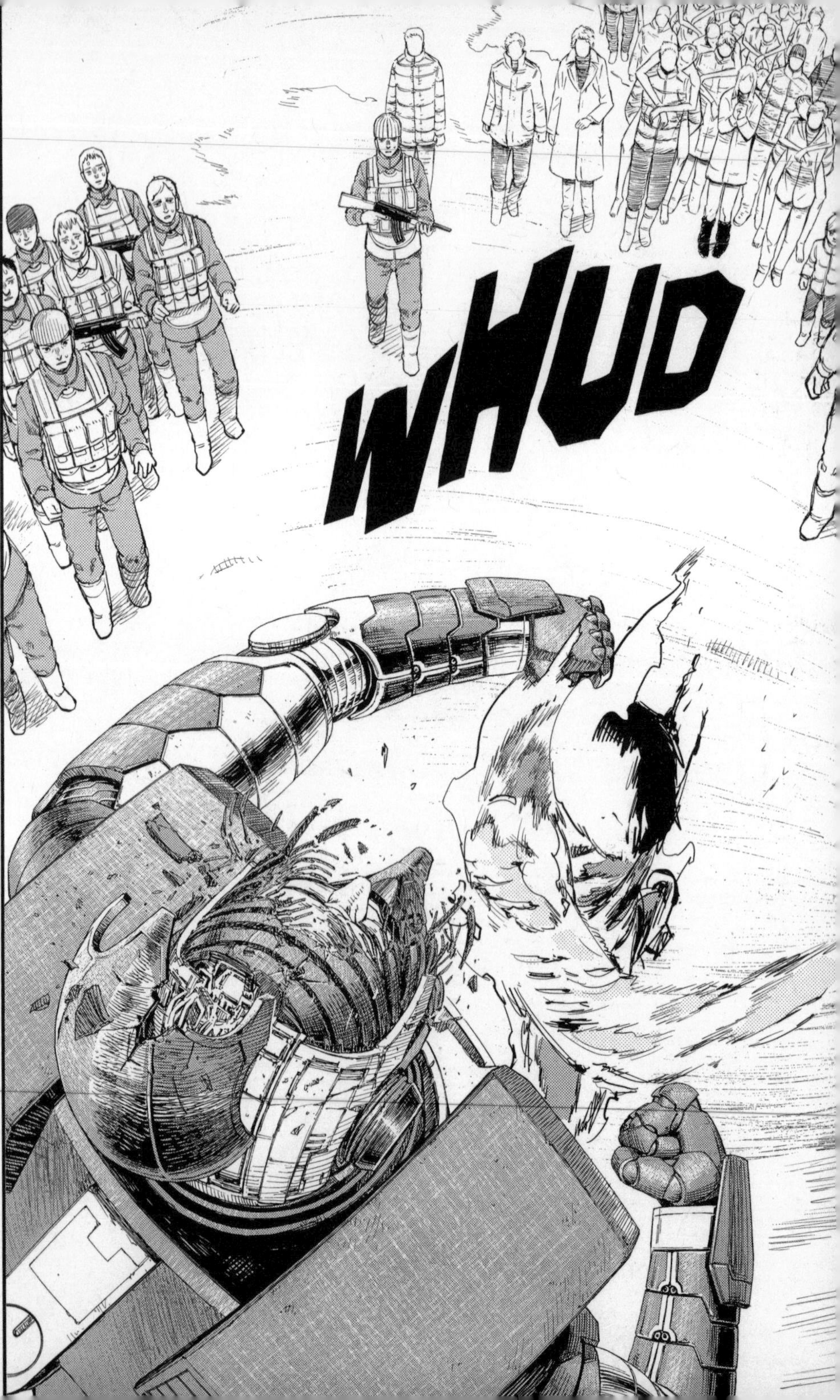
WHUD

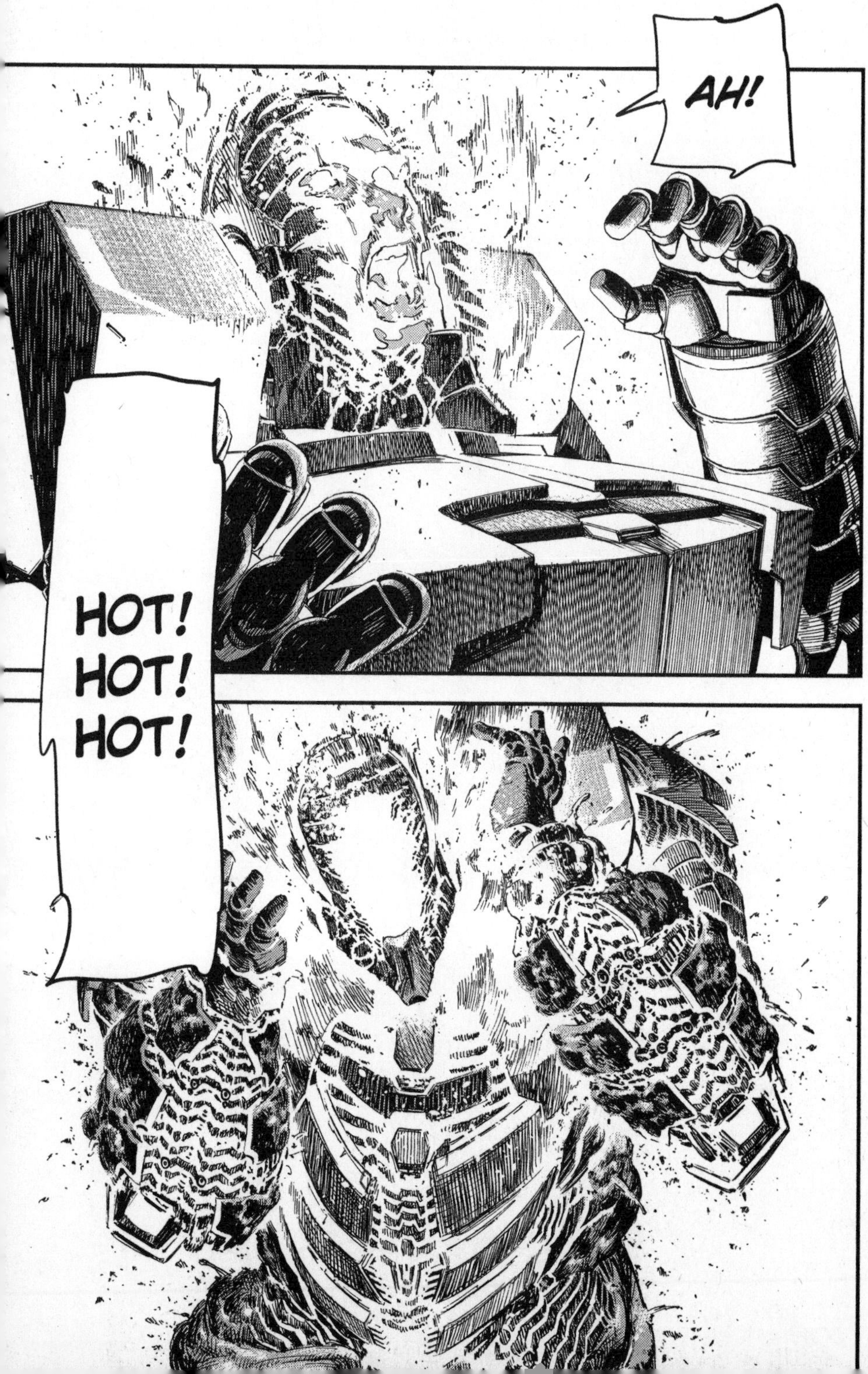
AH!
HOT! HOT! HOT!

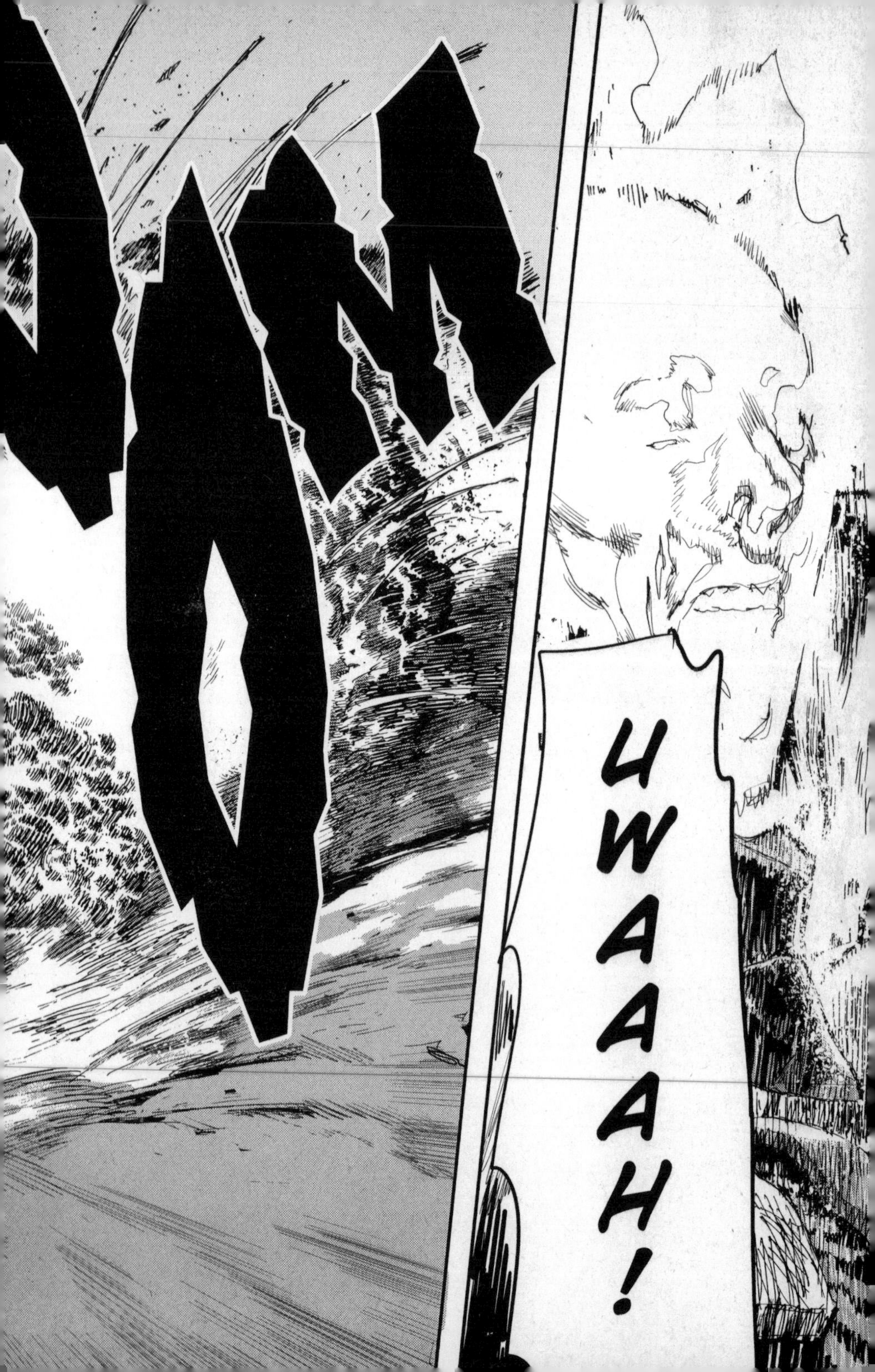
UWAAAH!

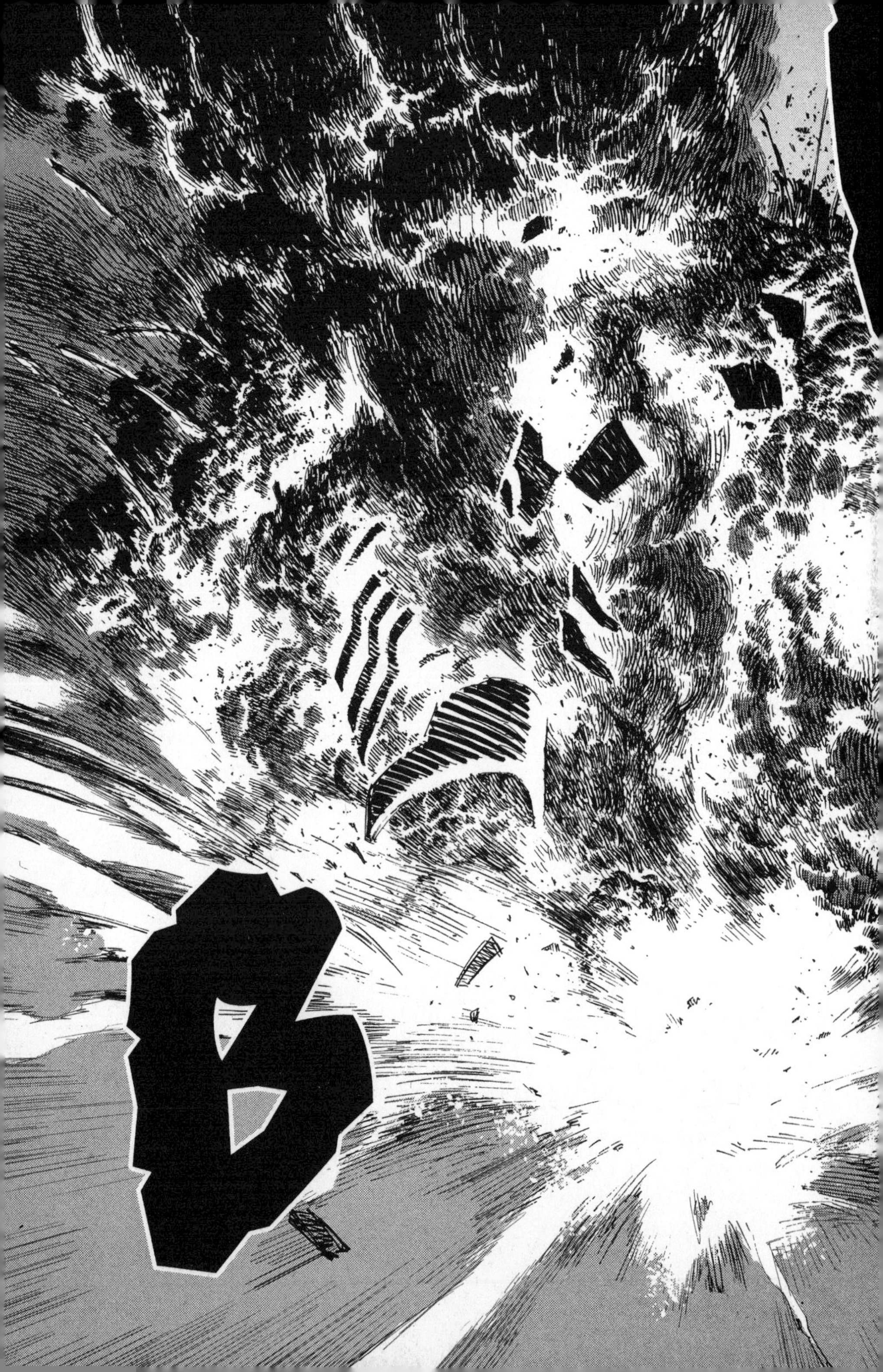
B

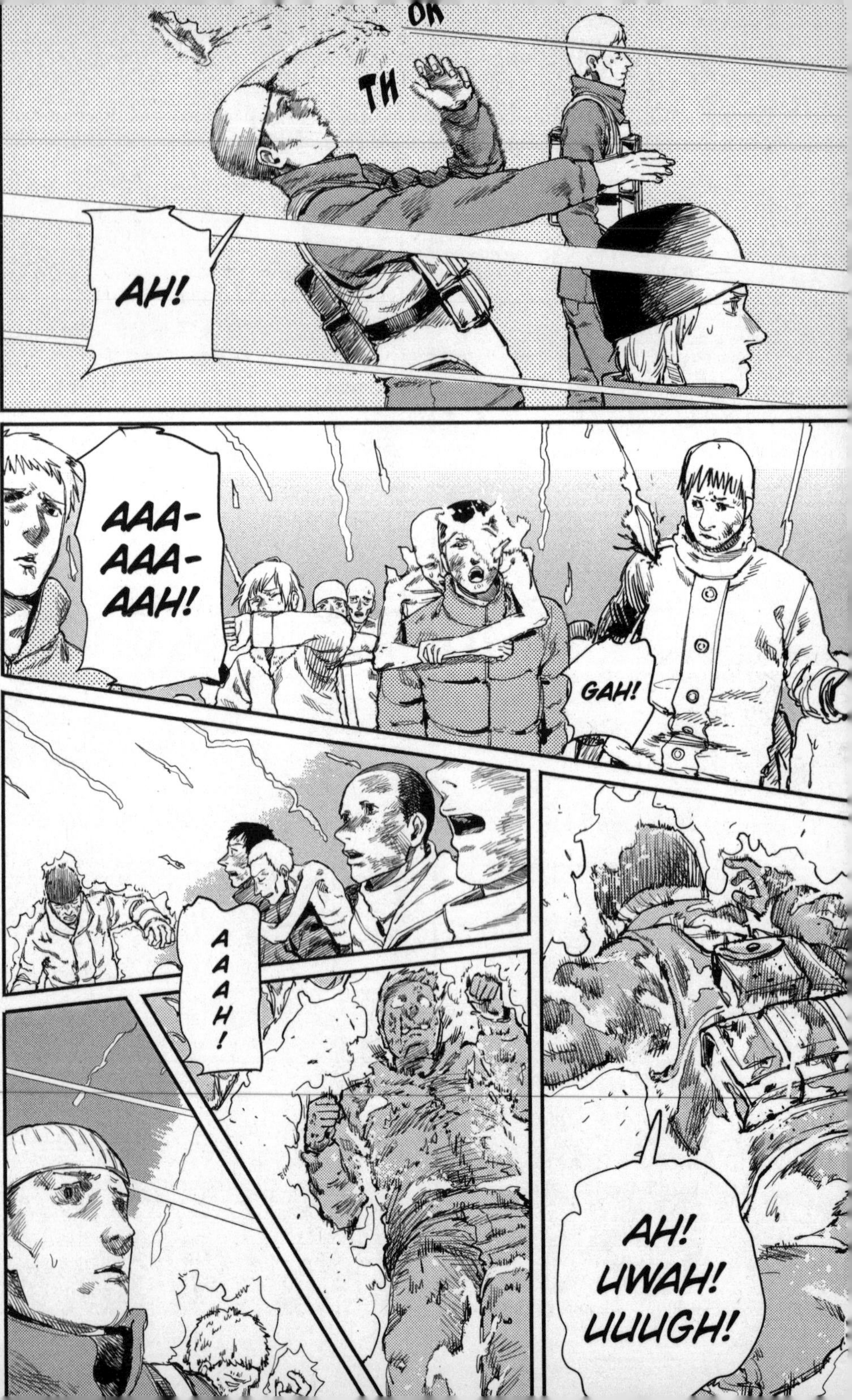

OK
TH
AH!
GAH!
AAA-AAA-AAH!
AH! UWAH! UUUGH!
AAAAH!

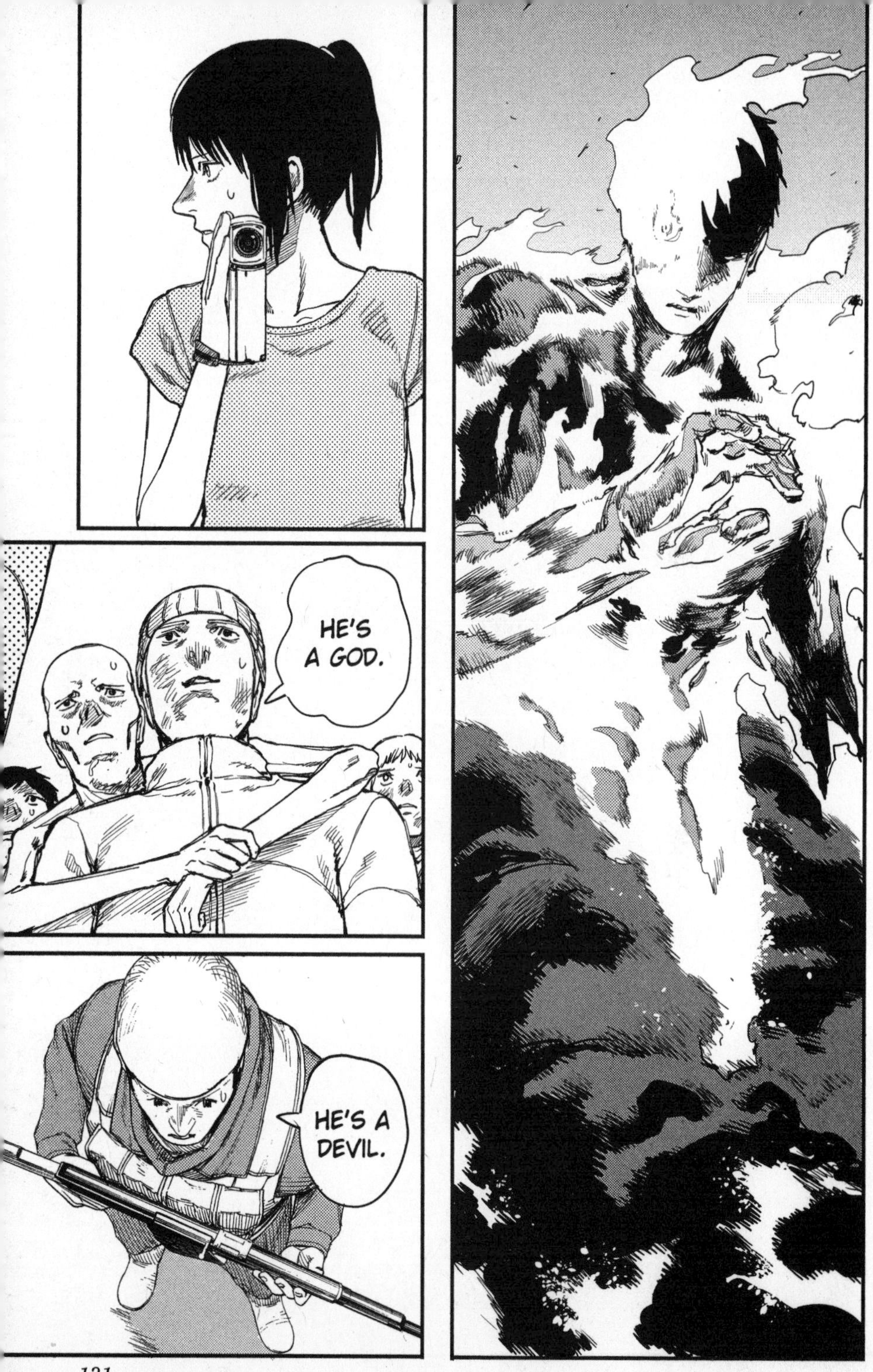
HE'S A GOD.
HE'S A DEVIL.

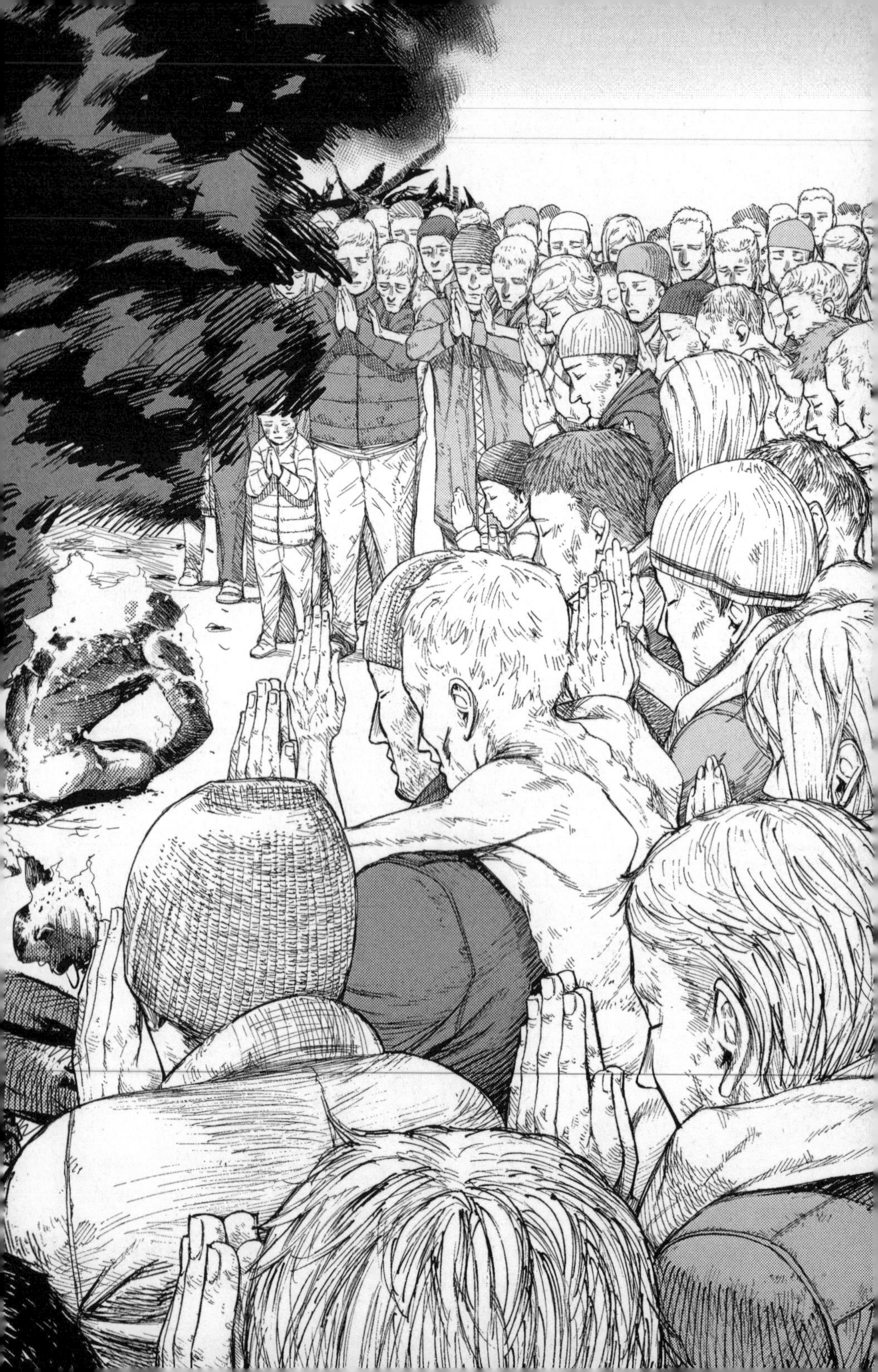

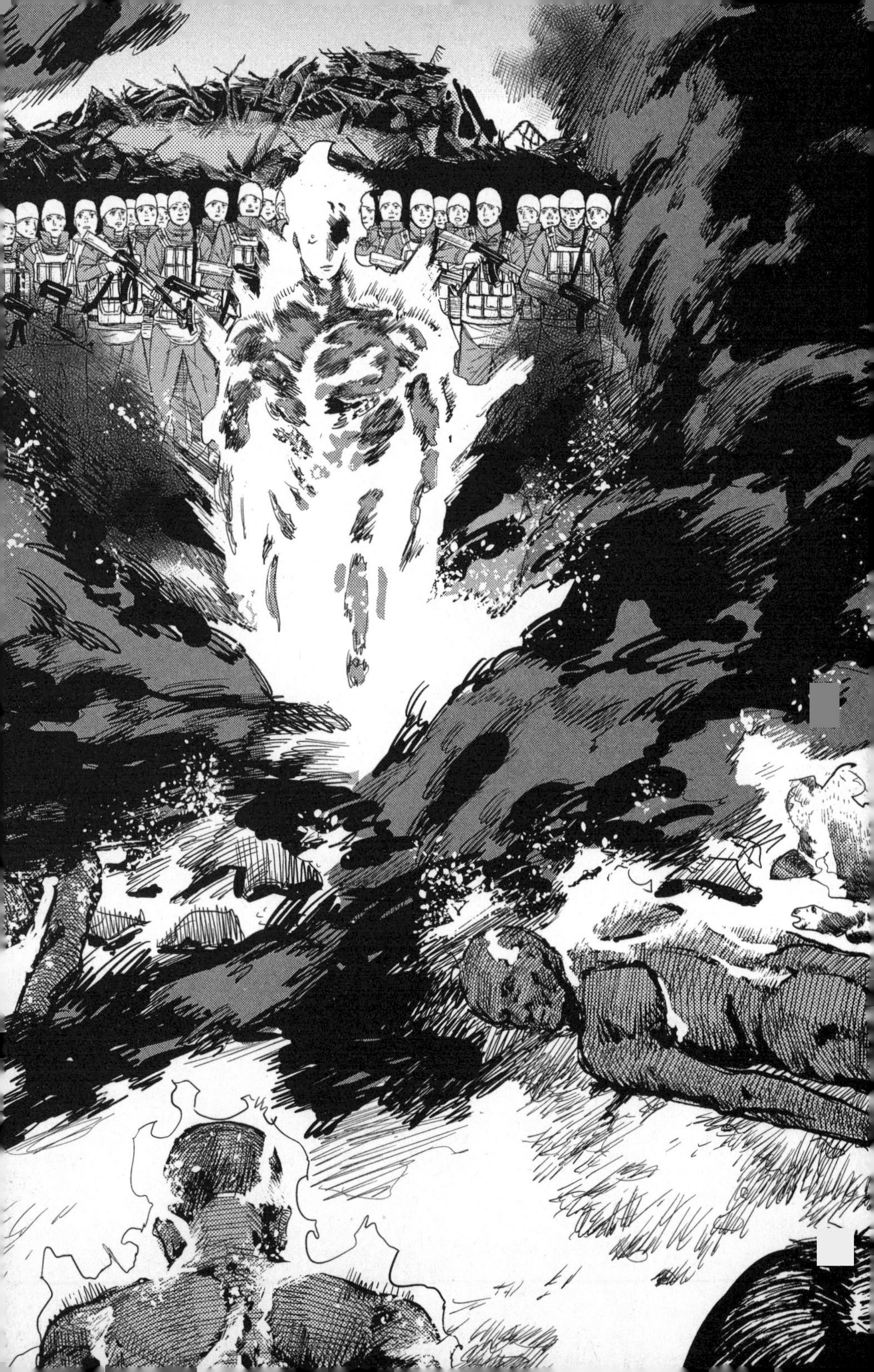

FIRE PUNCH

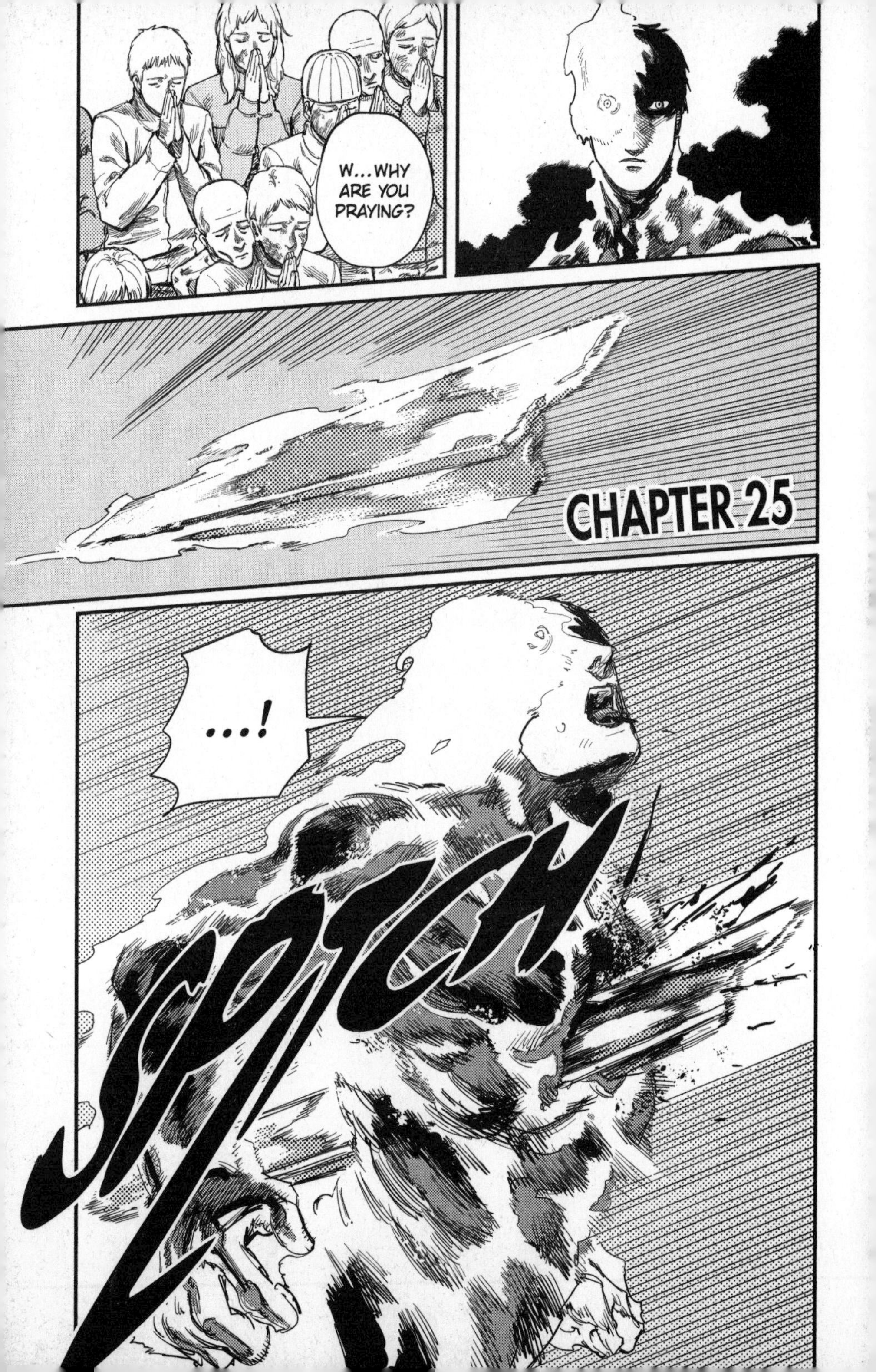
W...WHY ARE YOU PRAYING?
CHAPTER 25
...!

HE'S
FLOATING!

HE'S
FLOATING!

UH!

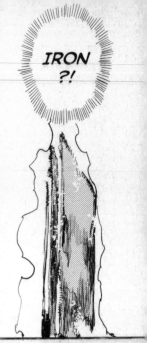

IRON
?!

IT'S THE
POWER
OF GOD!

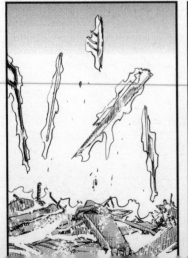

HE'S
NO GOD.

BUT
HE *IS* A
HAND-
FUL.

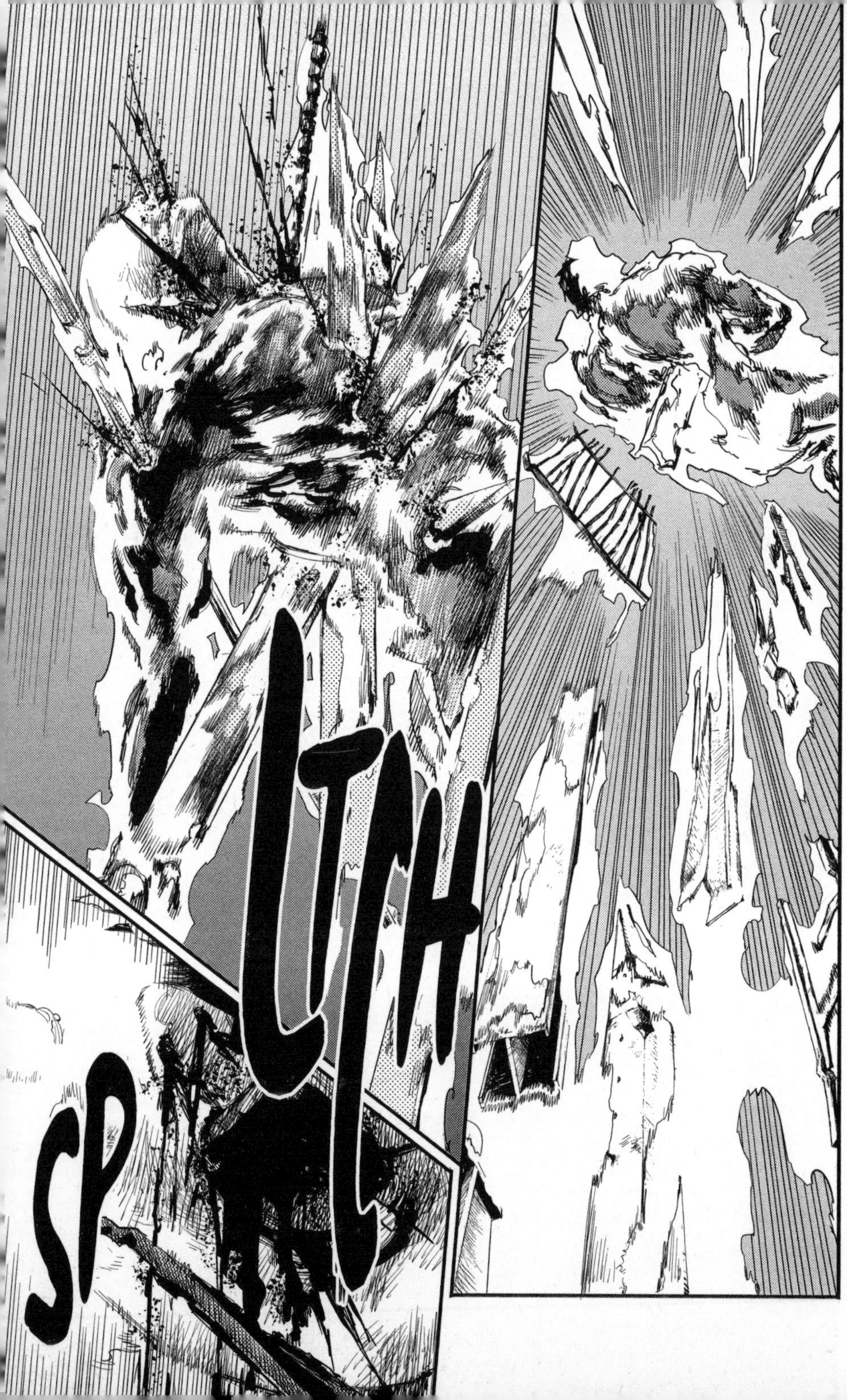
SPLUTCH

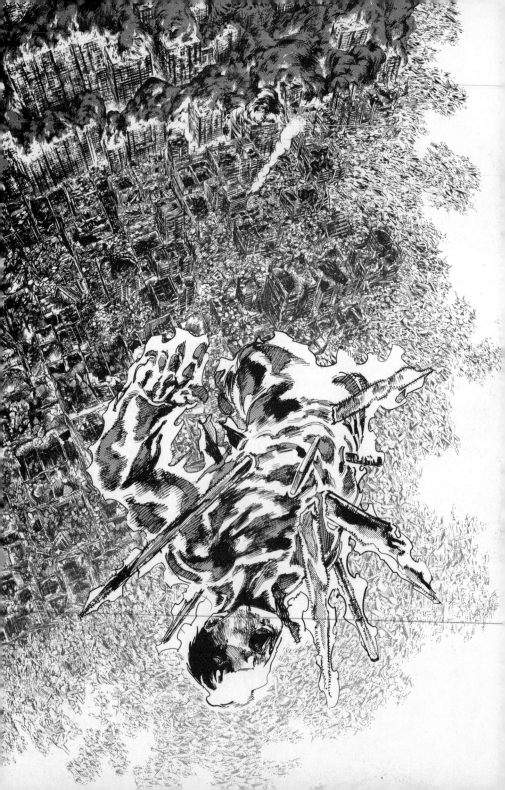

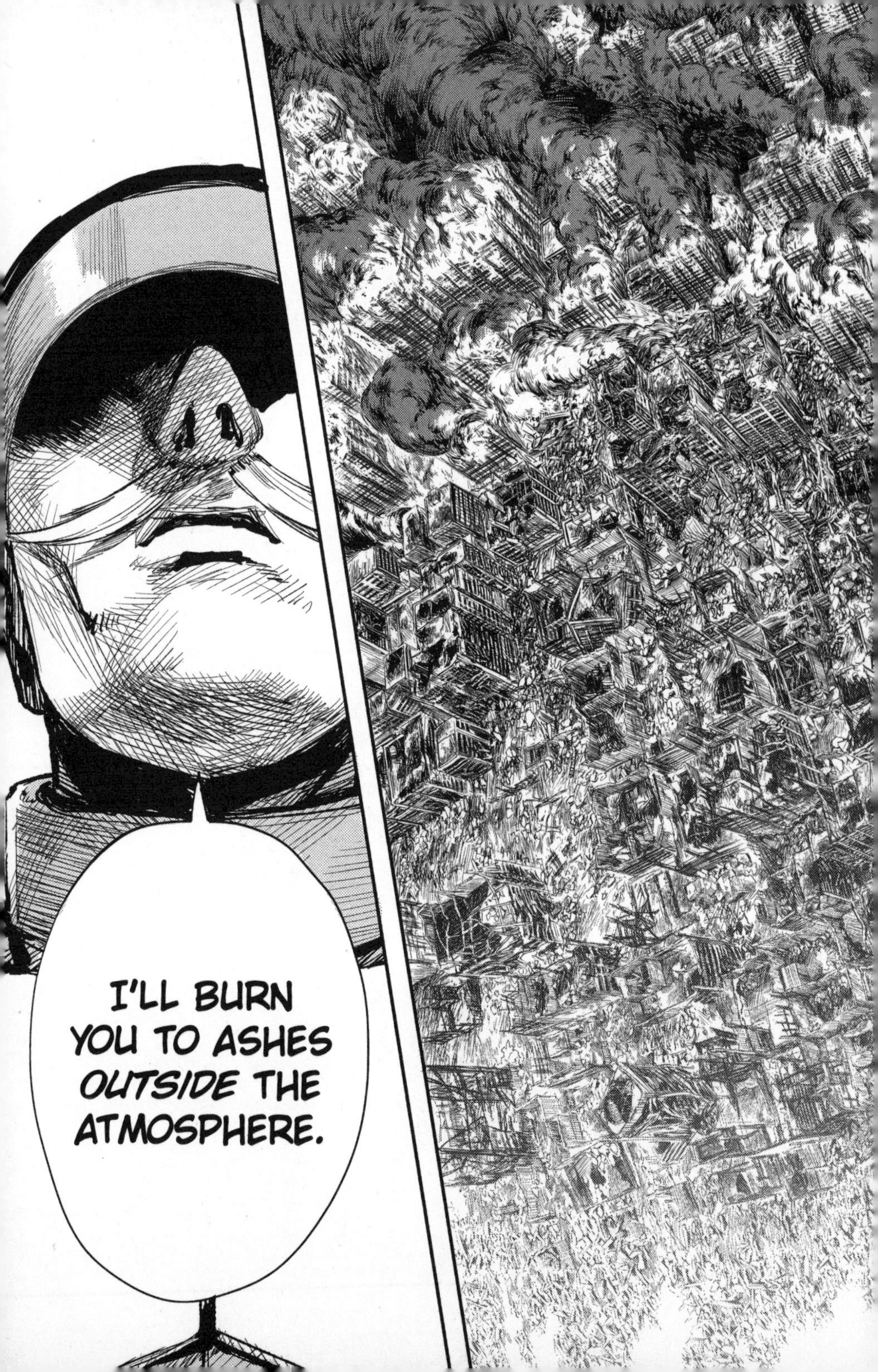
I'LL BURN YOU TO ASHES OUTSIDE THE ATMOSPHERE.

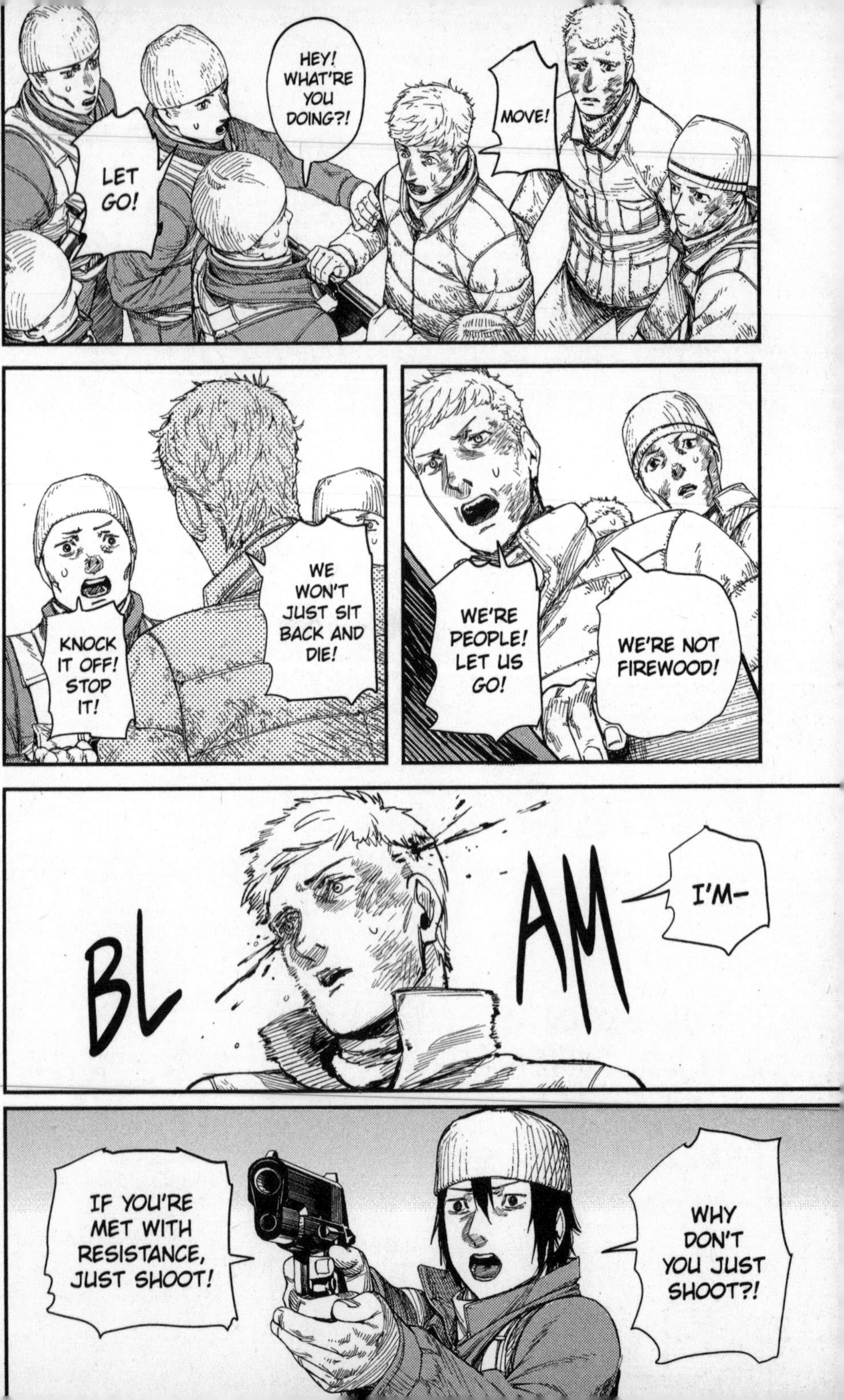
MOVE!
HEY! WHAT'RE YOU DOING?!
LET GO!
WE'RE NOT FIREWOOD!
WE'RE PEOPLE! LET US GO!
WE WON'T JUST SIT BACK AND DIE!
KNOCK IT OFF! STOP IT!
I'M-
BLAM
WHY DON'T YOU JUST SHOOT?!
IF YOU'RE MET WITH RESISTANCE, JUST SHOOT!

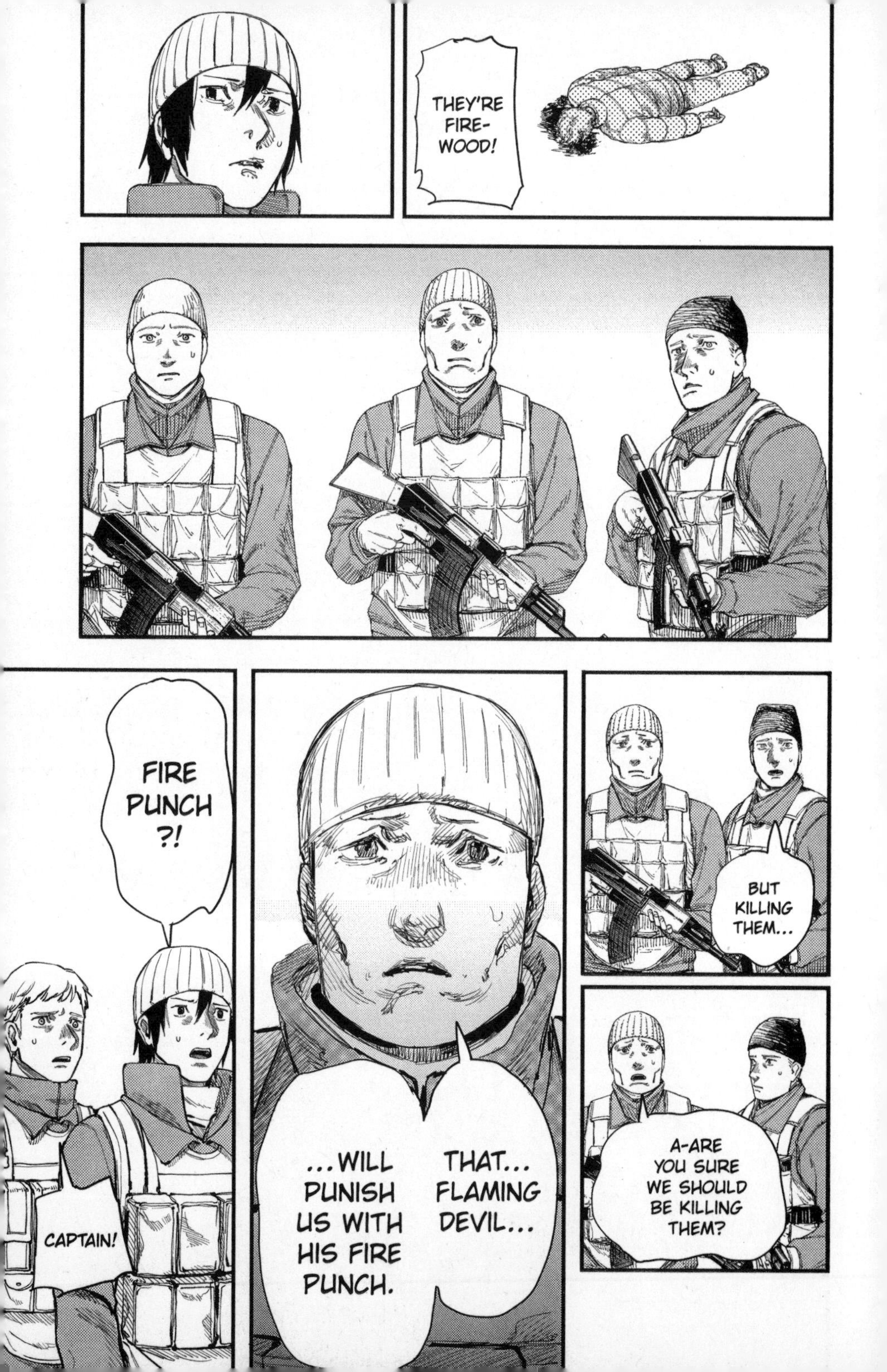
THEY'RE FIRE-WOOD!
BUT KILLING THEM...
A-ARE YOU SURE WE SHOULD BE KILLING THEM?
THAT... FLAMING DEVIL...
...WILL PUNISH US WITH HIS FIRE PUNCH.
FIRE PUNCH ?!
CAPTAIN!

THE INMATE WITH THE MOHAWK'S RUN AWAY!

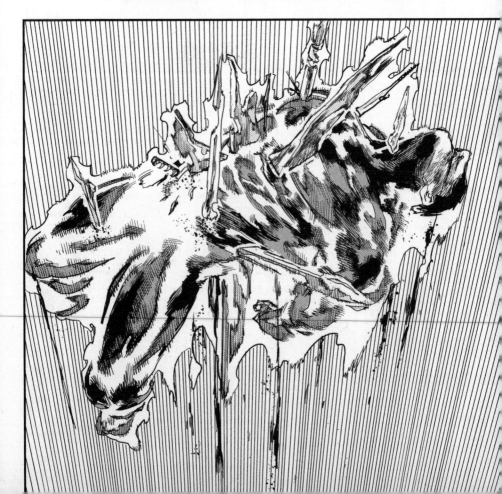

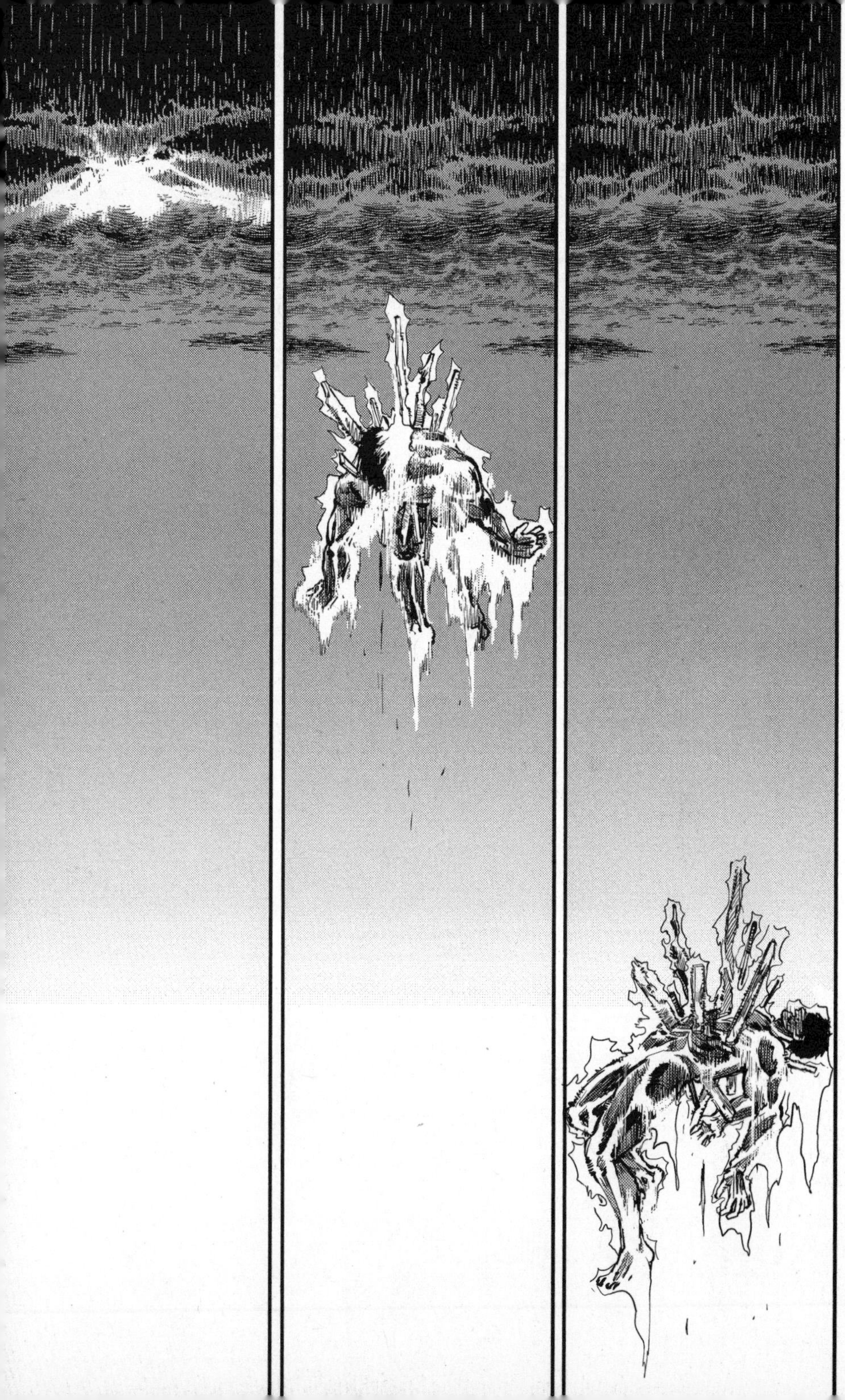

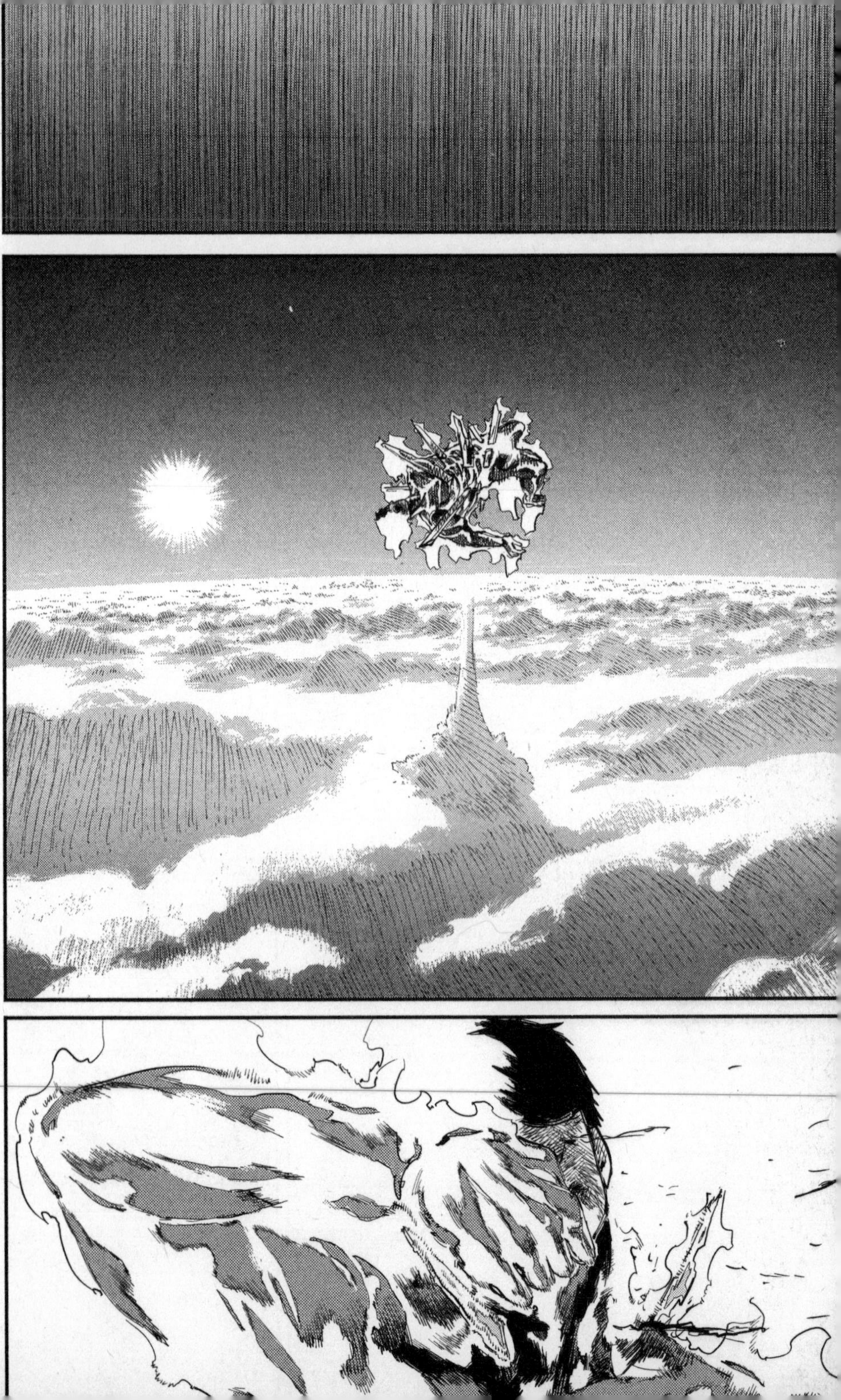

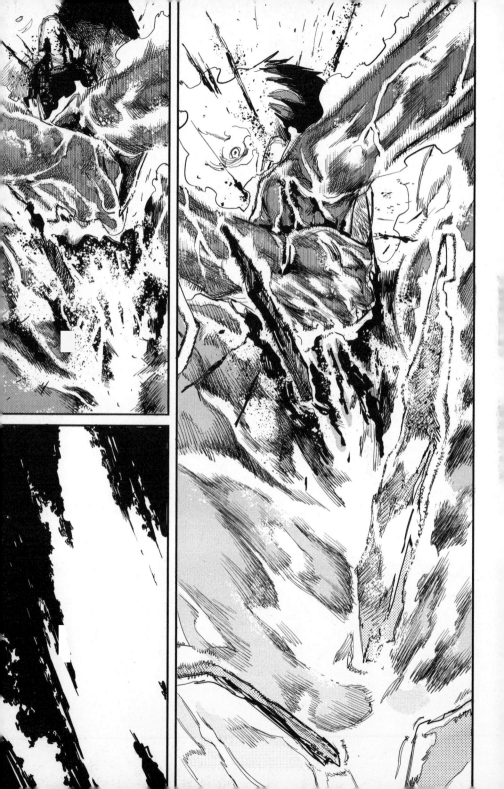

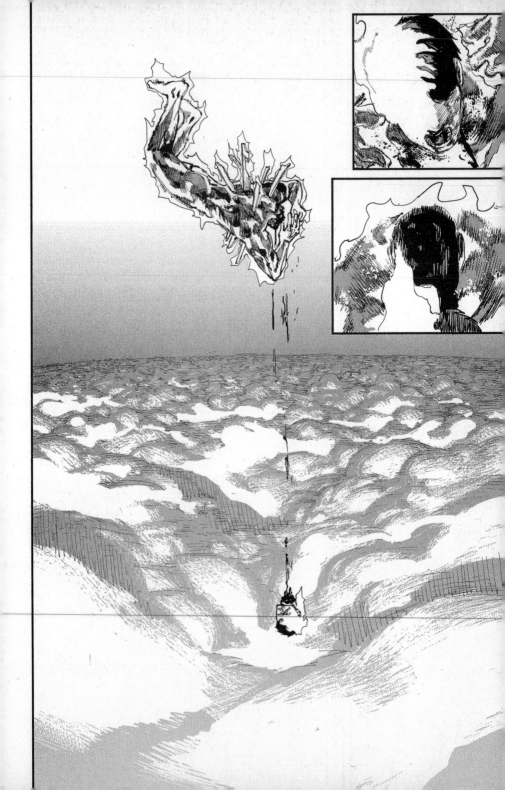

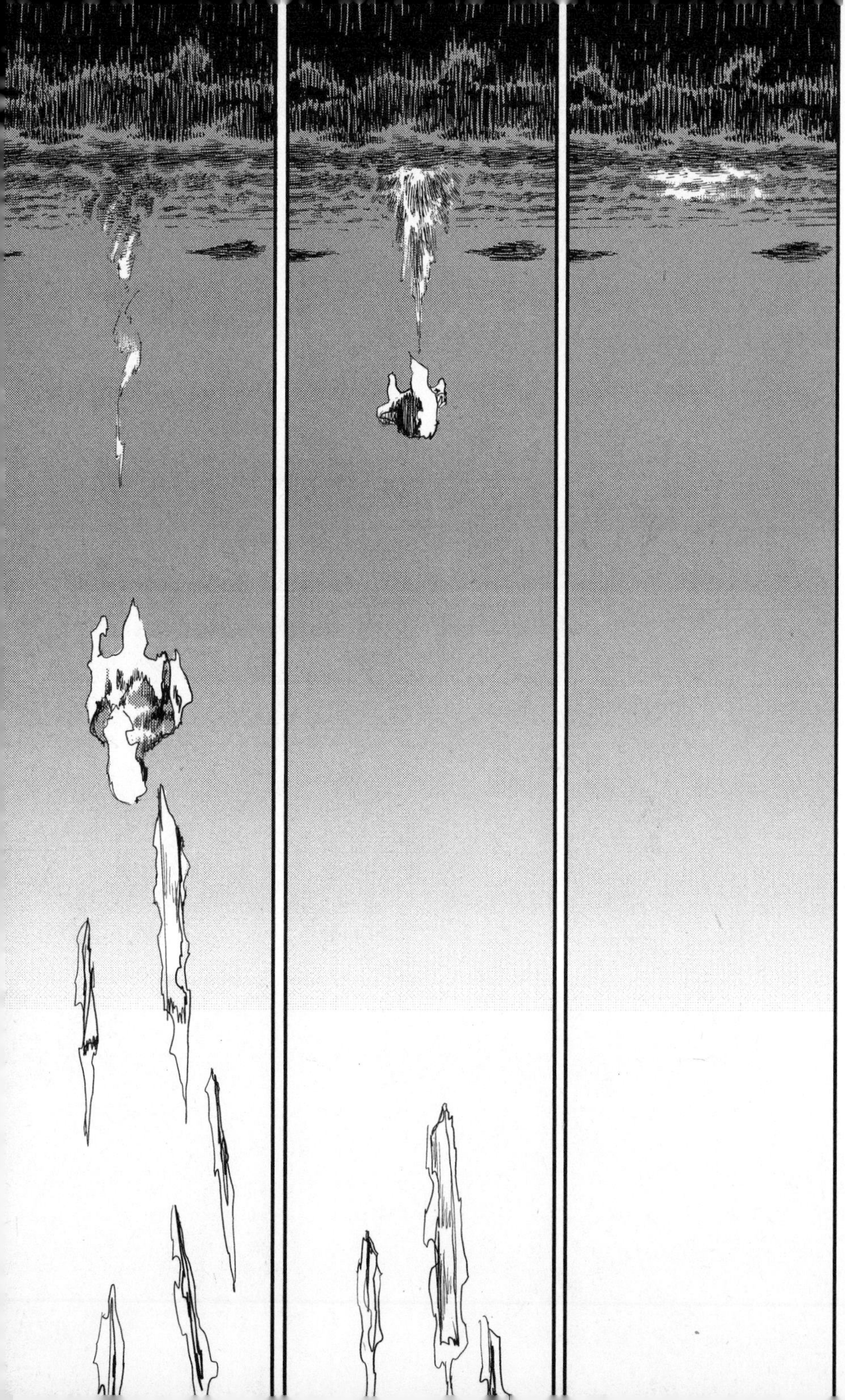

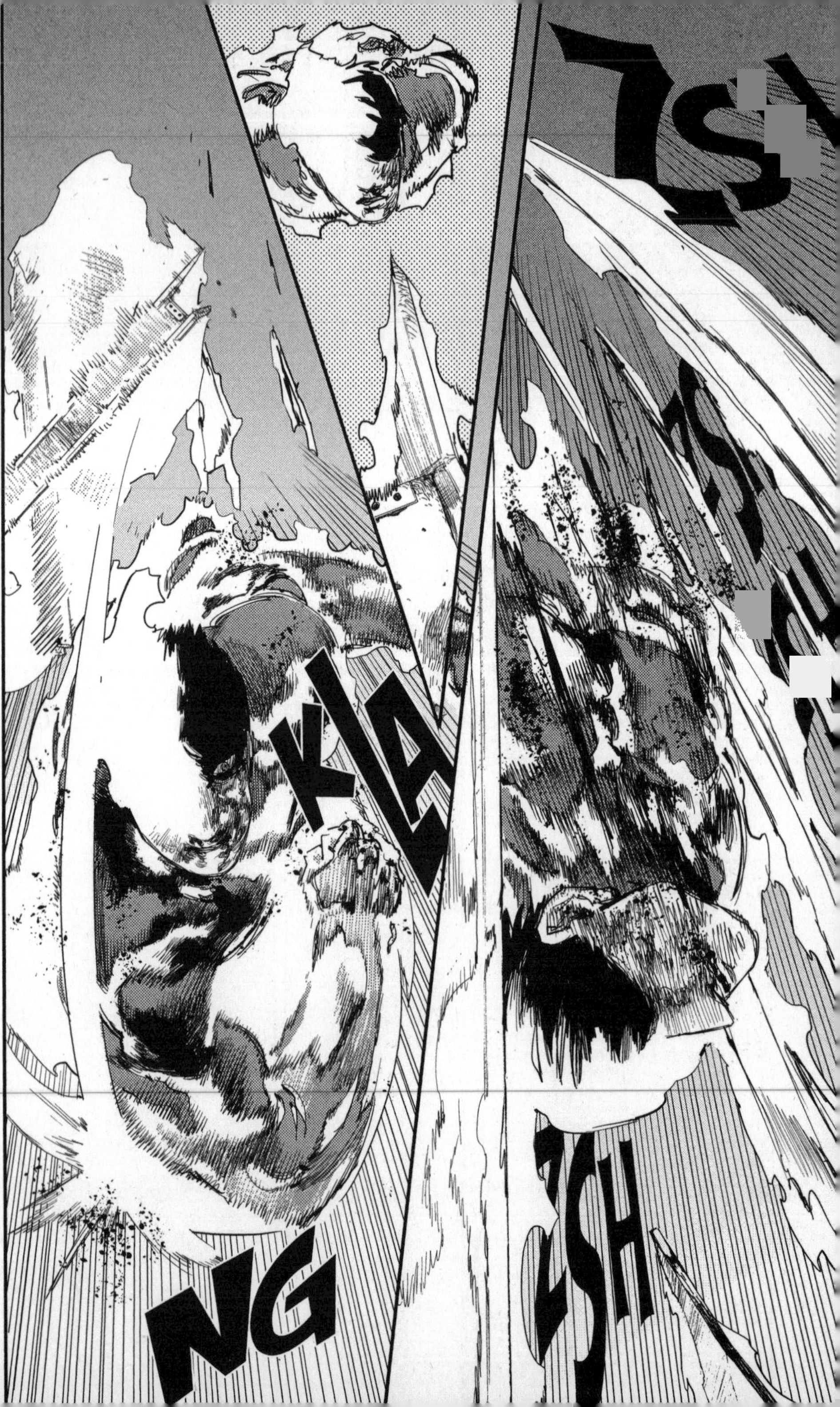
ZSH
ZSH
KLA
NG

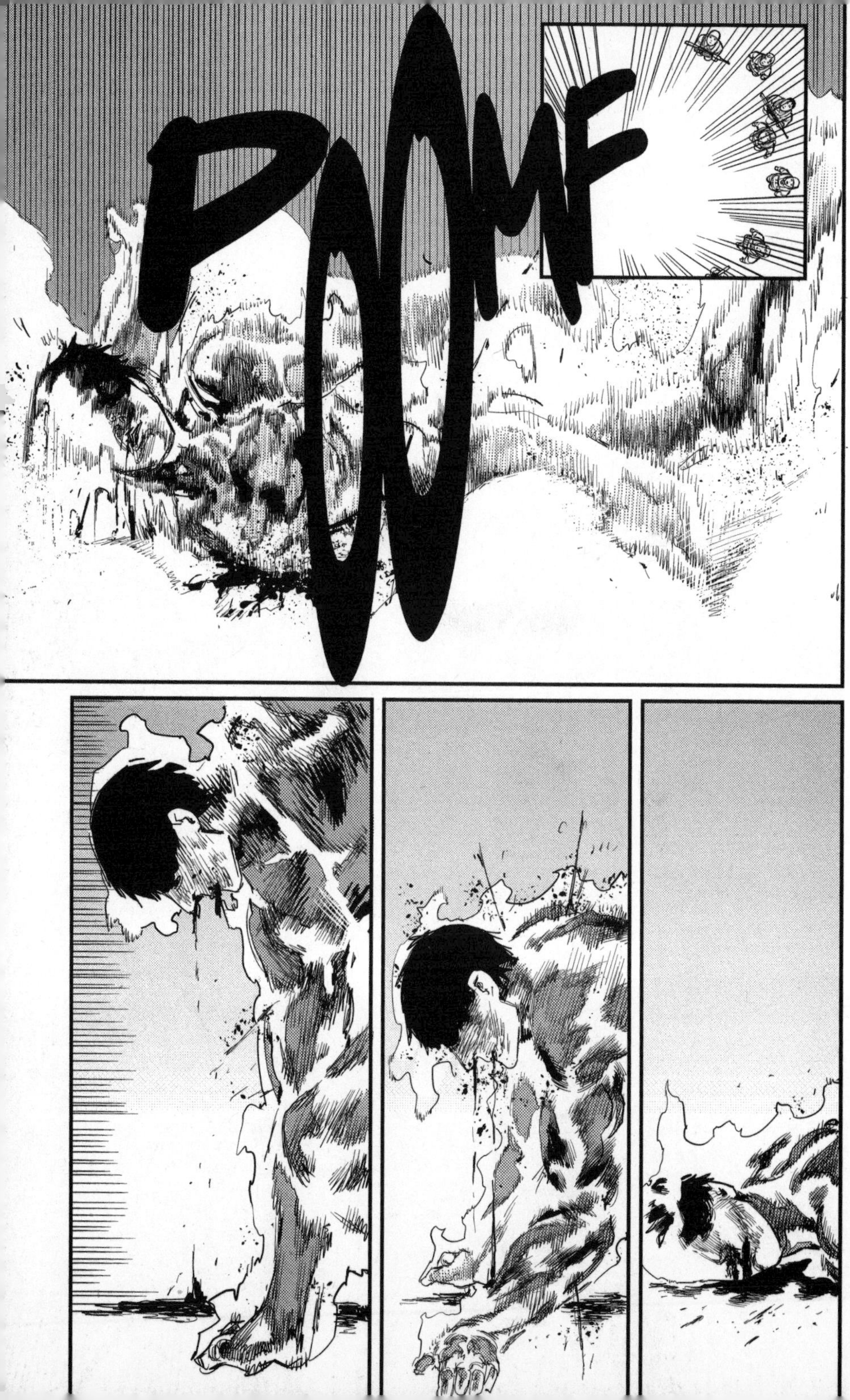
POOMF

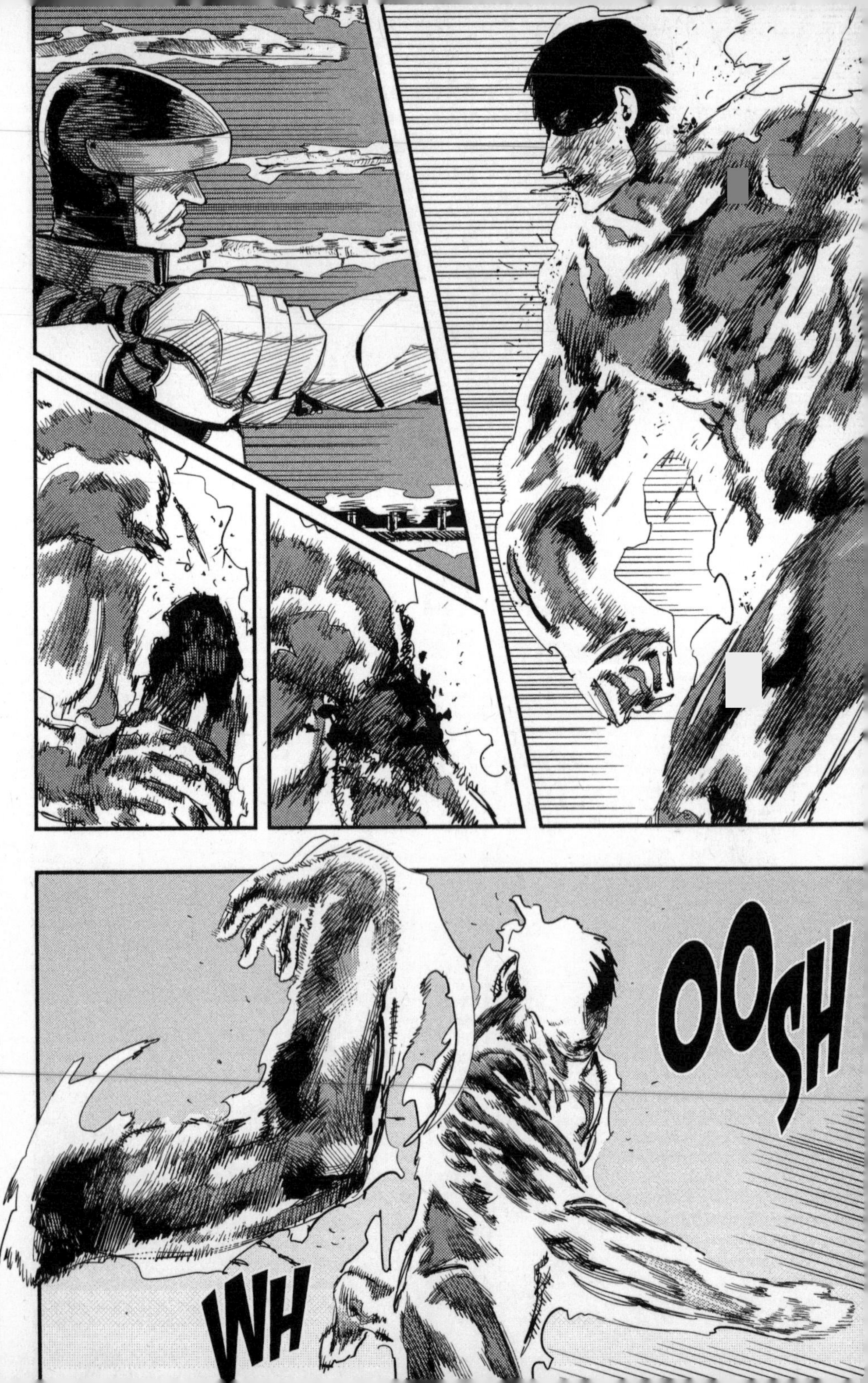
OOSH
WH

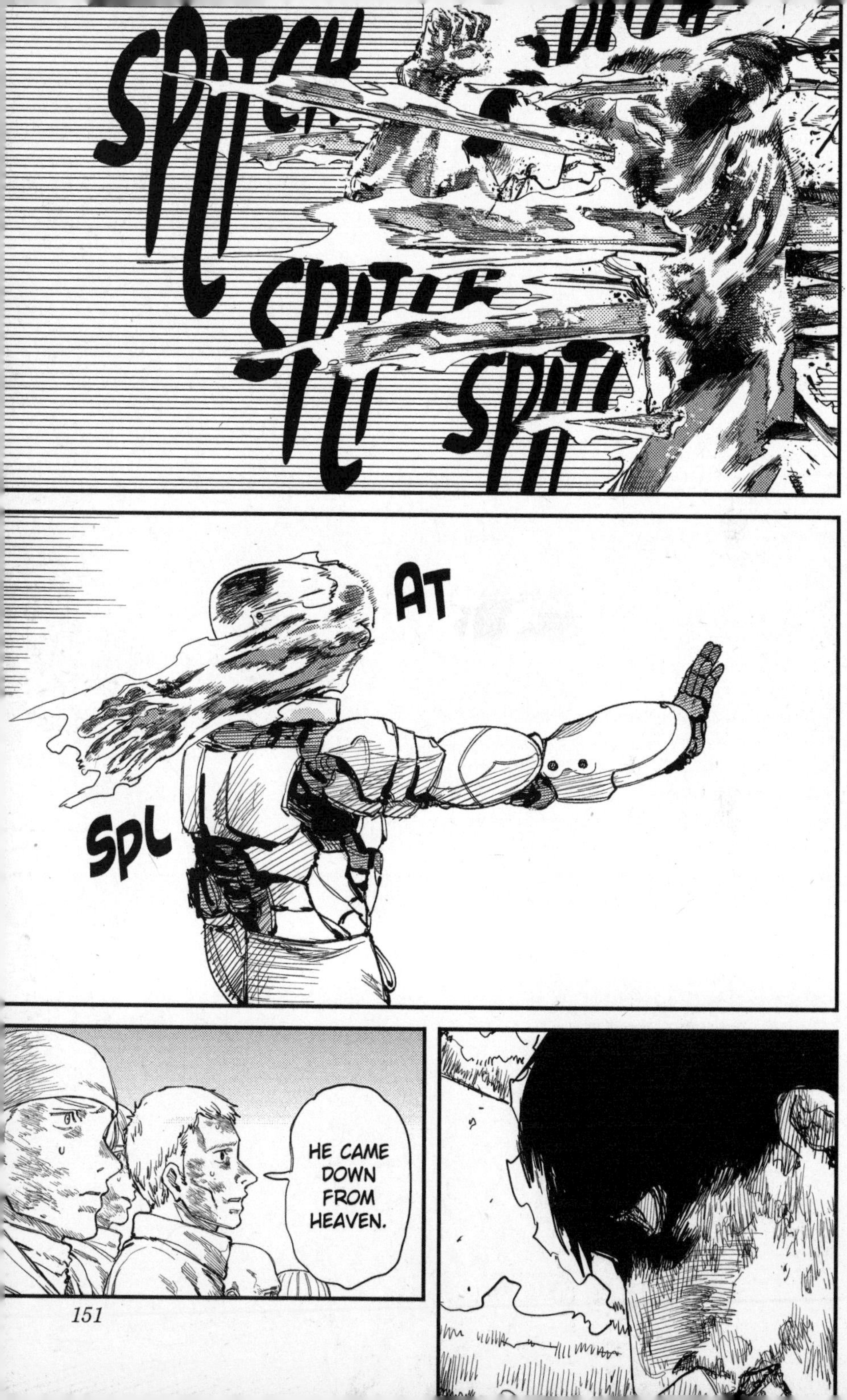
SPITCH
SPITCH
SPITCH
AT
SPL
HE CAME DOWN FROM HEAVEN.

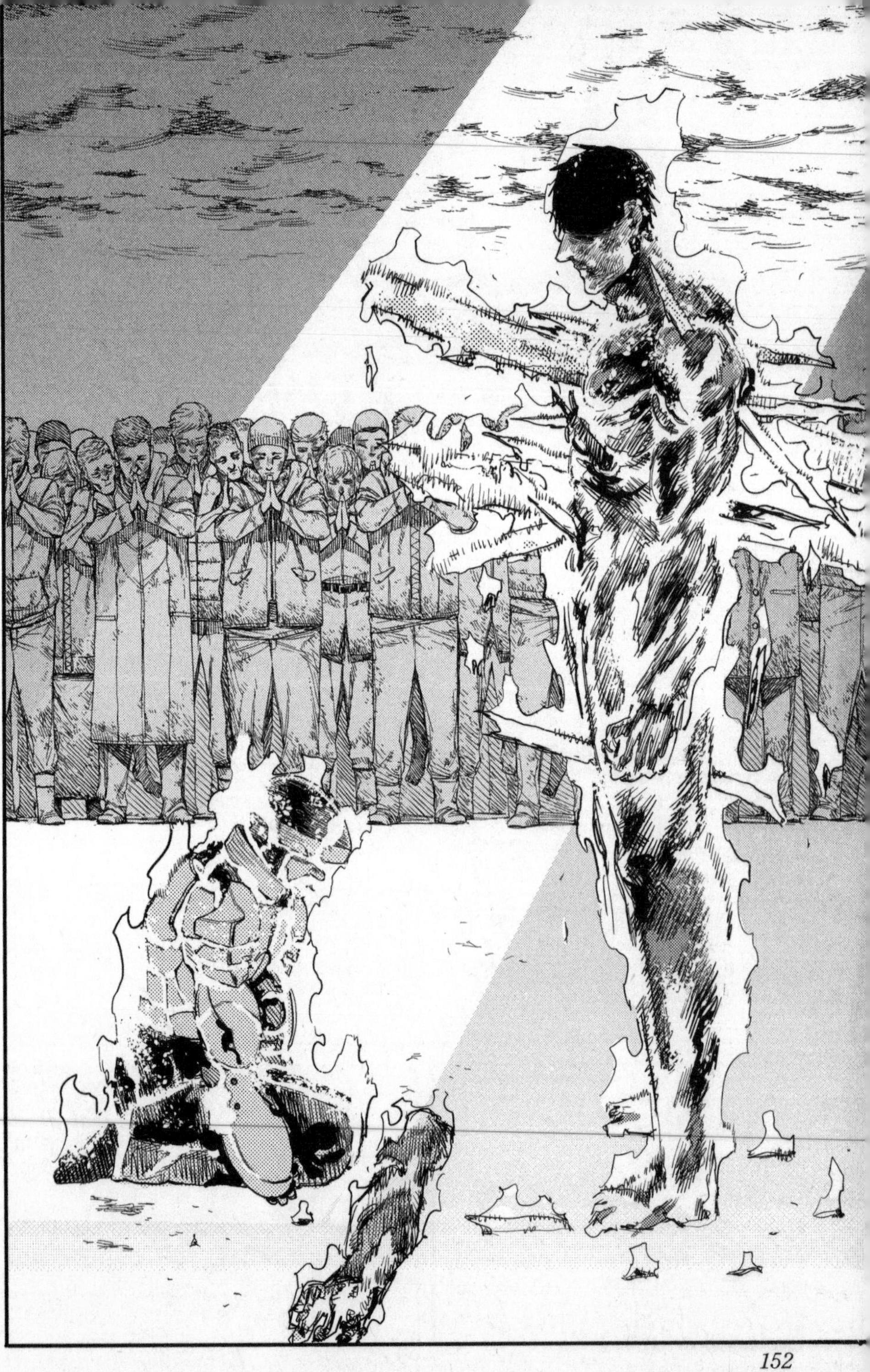

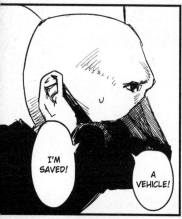

I'M SAVED!

A VEHICLE!

NO WAY IN HELL I'M FIGHTING THAT DEVIL!

IF I FLY FAR ENOUGH OUT OF RANGE OF THEIR DETONATORS, I'M A FREE MAN!

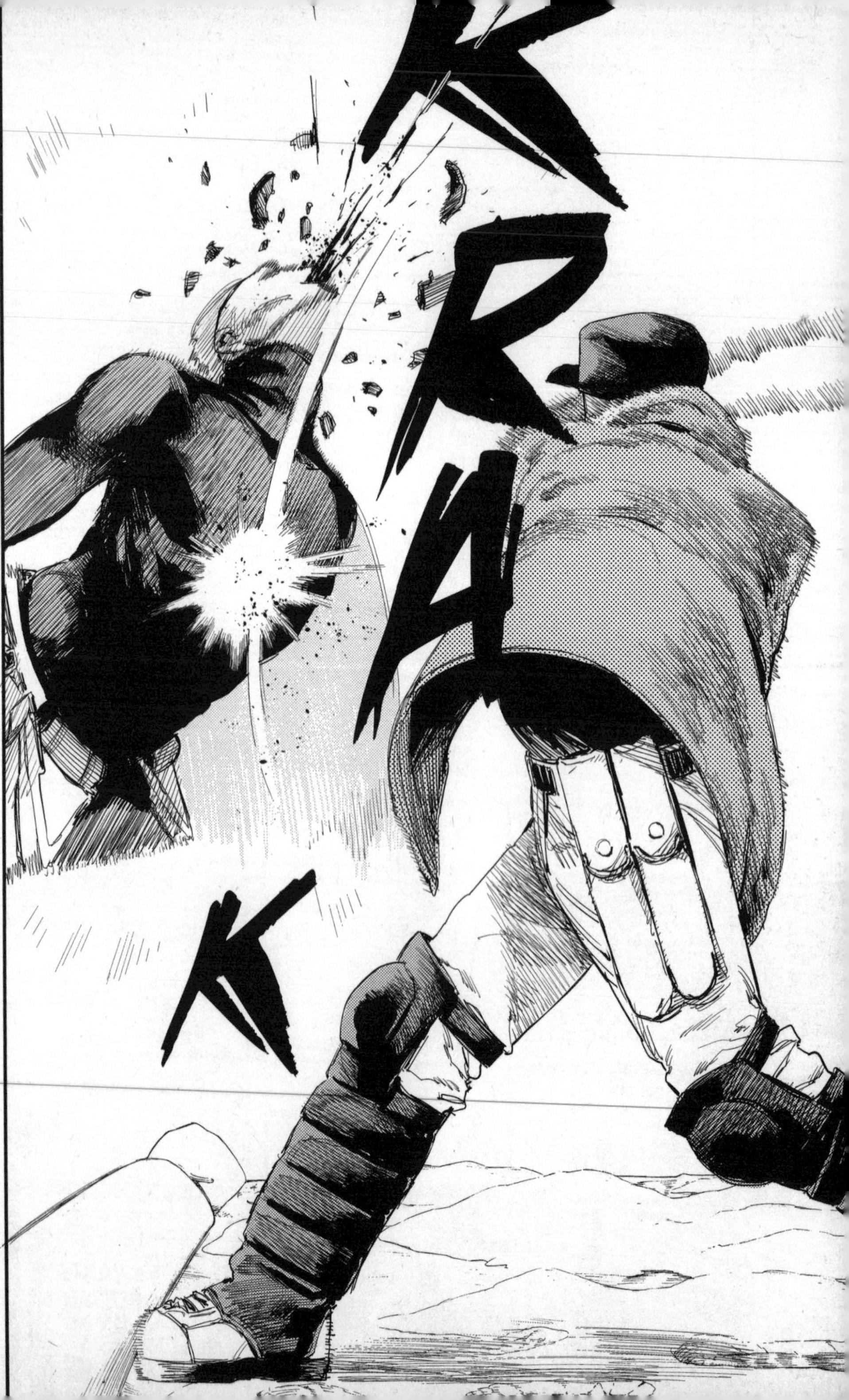
KRAKK

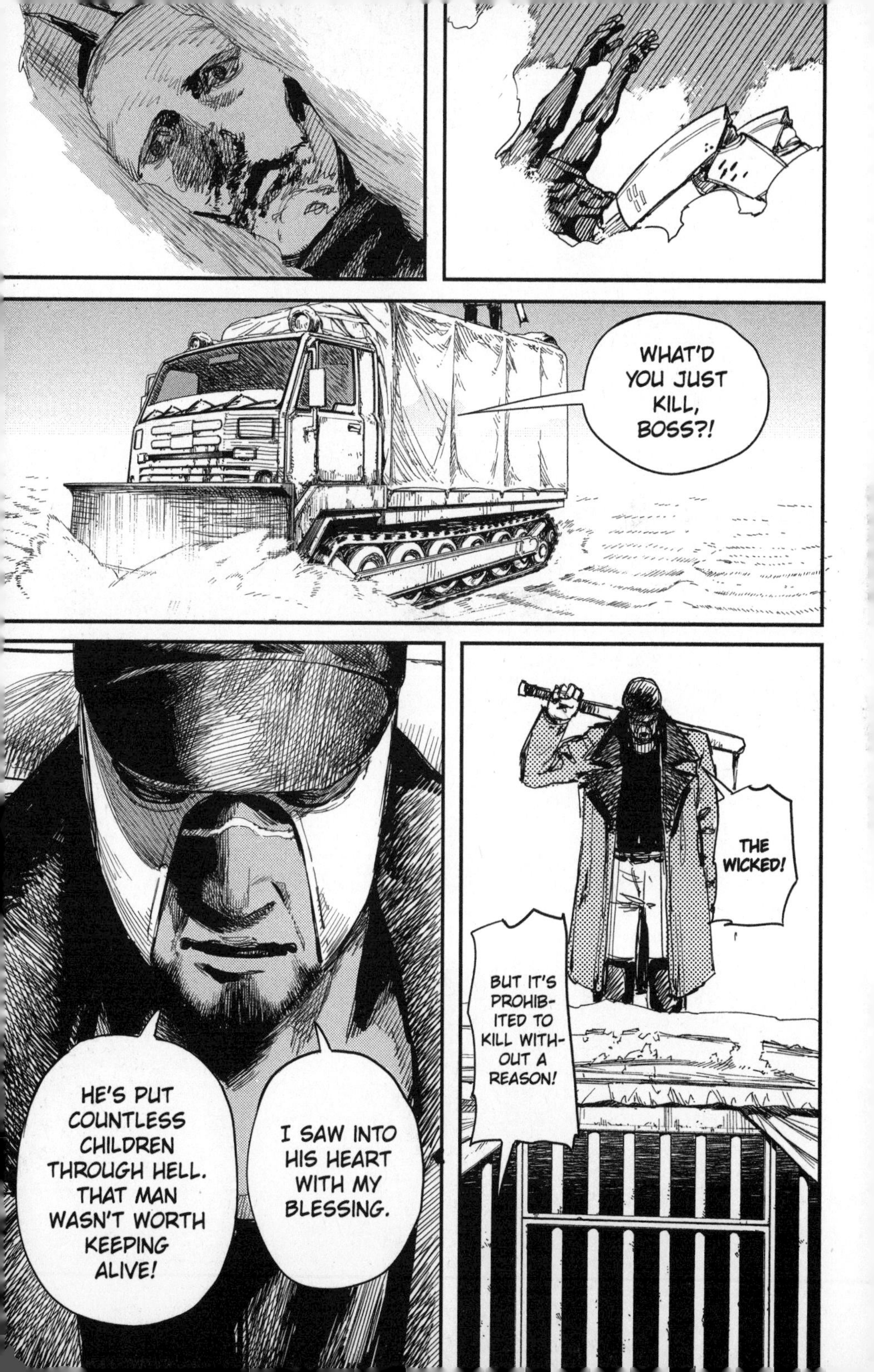
WHAT'D YOU JUST KILL, BOSS?!
THE WICKED!
BUT IT'S PROHIBITED TO KILL WITHOUT A REASON!
I SAW INTO HIS HEART WITH MY BLESSING.
HE'S PUT COUNTLESS CHILDREN THROUGH HELL. THAT MAN WASN'T WORTH KEEPING ALIVE!

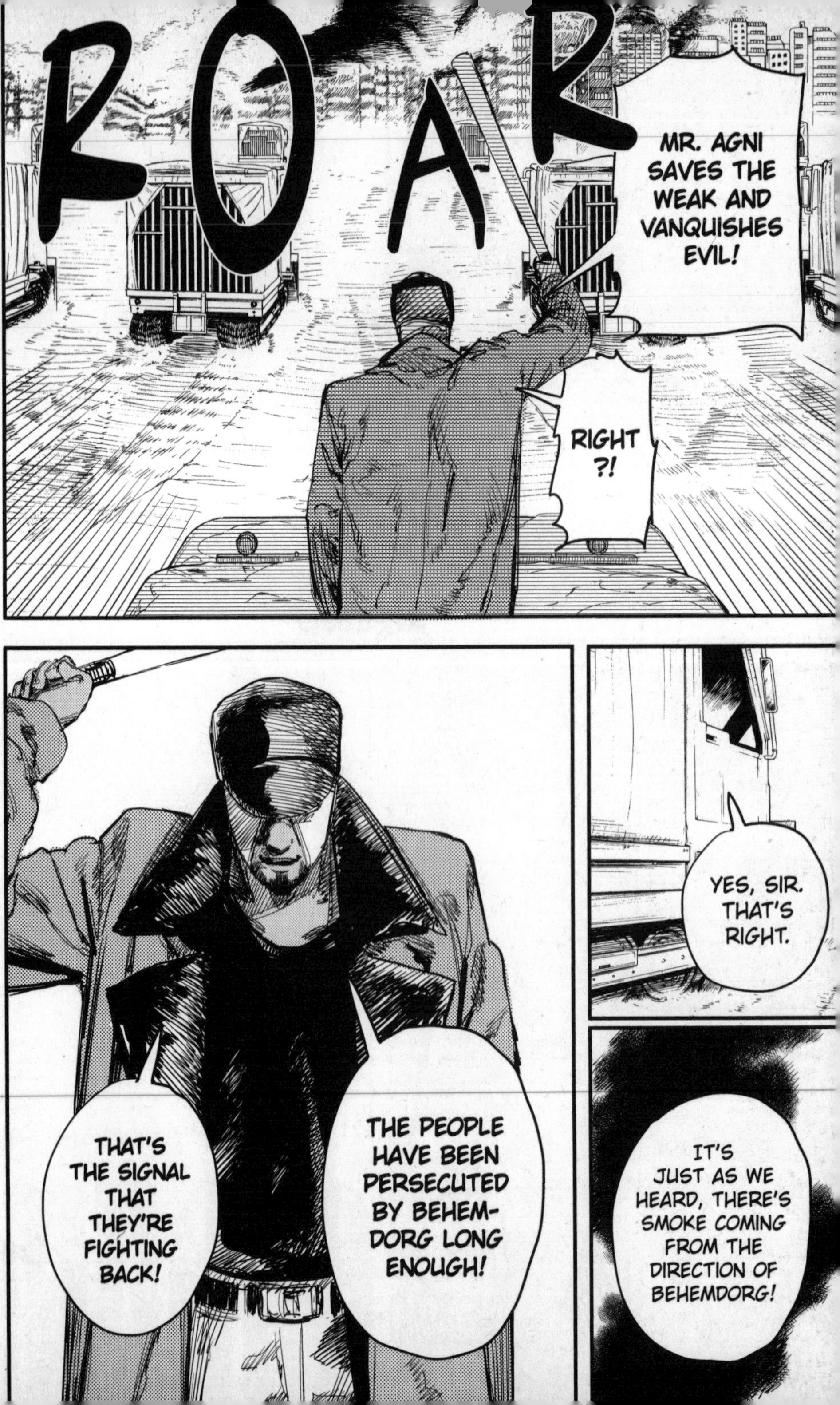
ROAR
MR. AGNI SAVES THE WEAK AND VANQUISHES EVIL!
RIGHT ?!
YES, SIR. THAT'S RIGHT.
IT'S JUST AS WE HEARD, THERE'S SMOKE COMING FROM THE DIRECTION OF BEHEMDORG!
THE PEOPLE HAVE BEEN PERSECUTED BY BEHEM-DORG LONG ENOUGH!
THAT'S THE SIGNAL THAT THEY'RE FIGHTING BACK!

COVER DESIGN

NOBUHIRA OKAMOTO

EDITOR

TSUCHIHARA KOBAYASHI

MAIN ASSISTANTS

YUKINOBU RYUU

YUUJI KARAI

YUUGO TAKAHASHI

RIRI HAMADA

AIMI URIO

CHAPTER 26

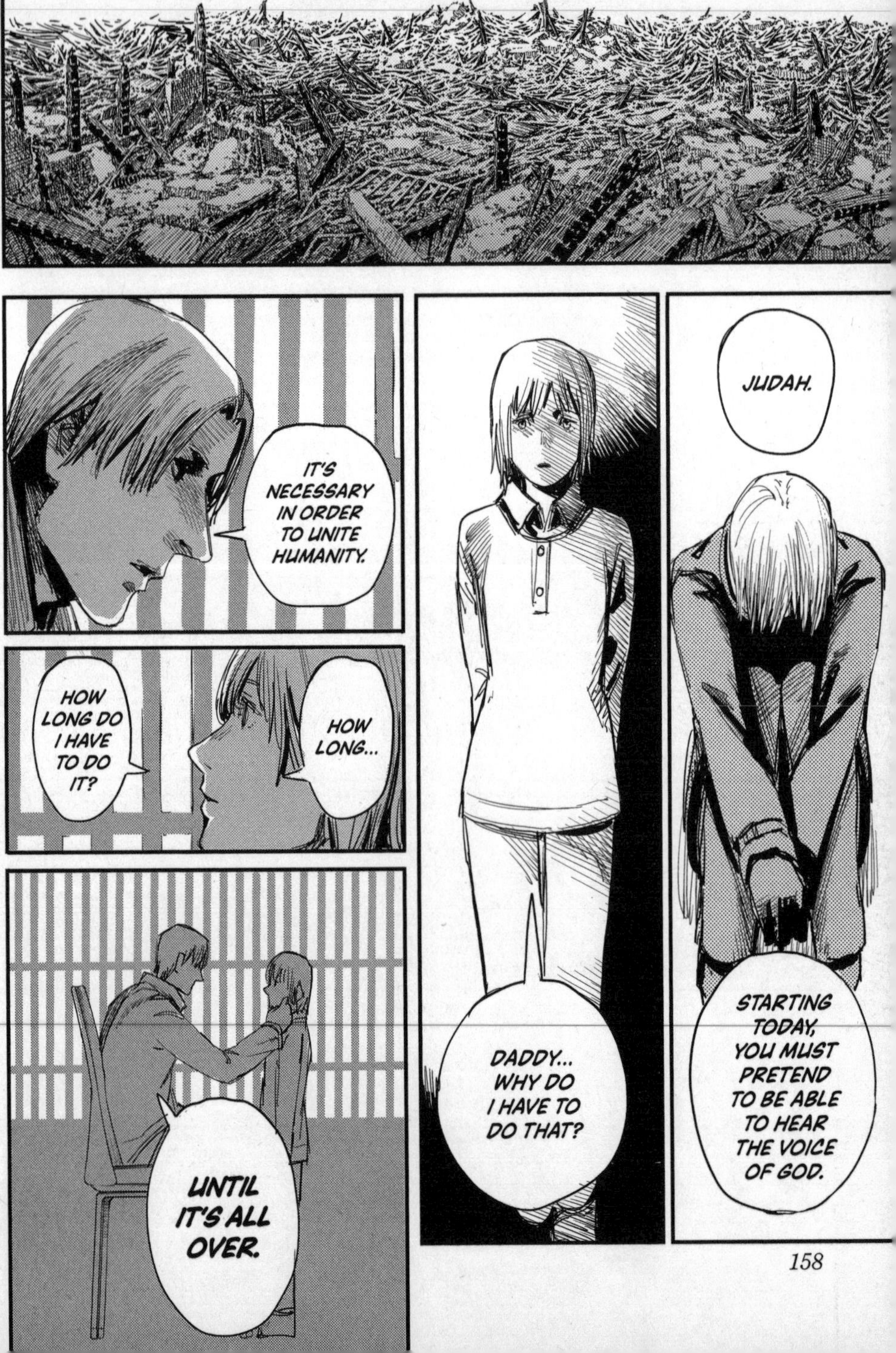
JUDAH.
STARTING TODAY, YOU MUST PRETEND TO BE ABLE TO HEAR THE VOICE OF GOD.
DADDY... WHY DO I HAVE TO DO THAT?
IT'S NECESSARY IN ORDER TO UNITE HUMANITY.
HOW LONG...
HOW LONG DO I HAVE TO DO IT?
UNTIL IT'S ALL OVER.

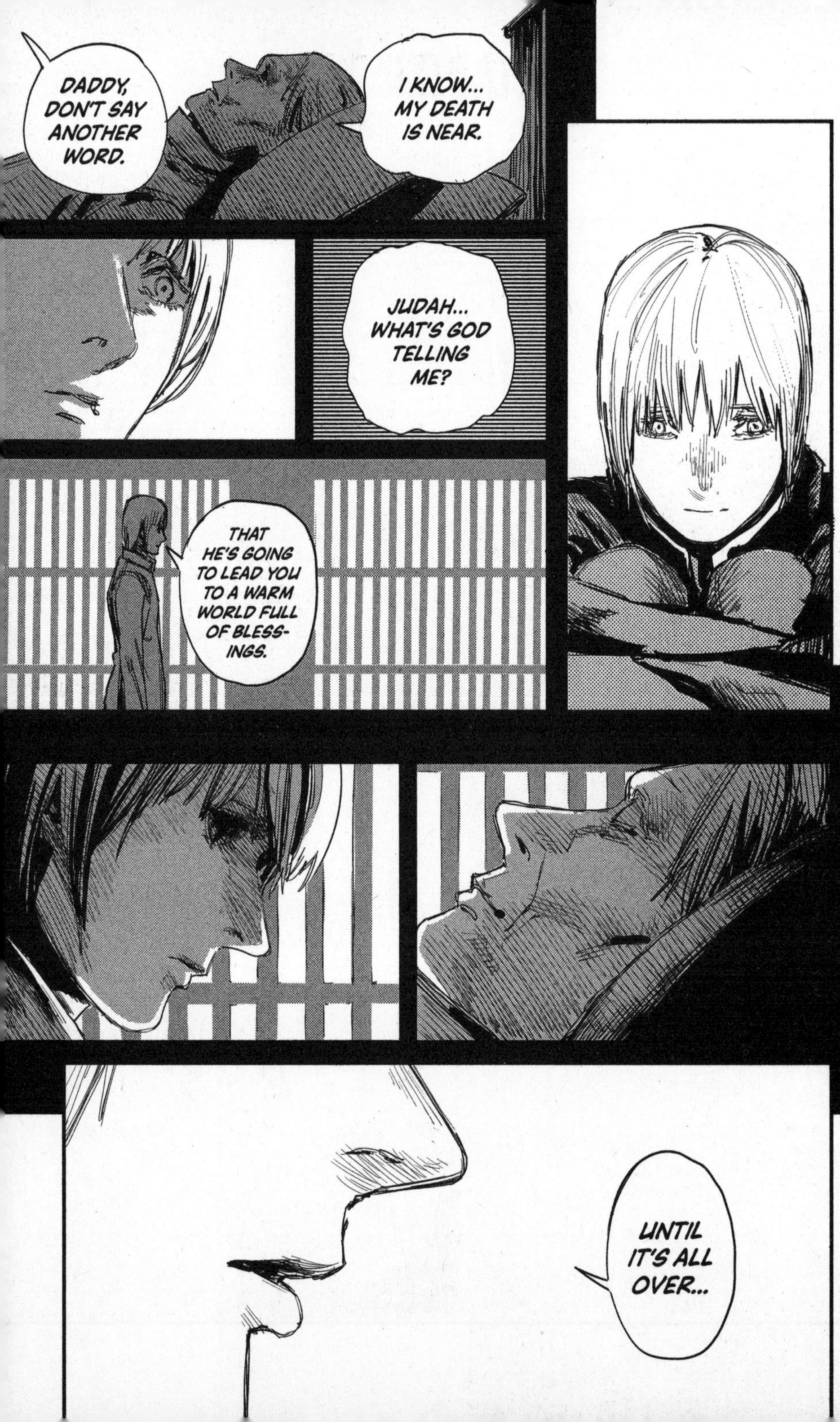
I KNOW... MY DEATH IS NEAR.
DADDY, DON'T SAY ANOTHER WORD.
JUDAH... WHAT'S GOD TELLING ME?
THAT HE'S GOING TO LEAD YOU TO A WARM WORLD FULL OF BLESS-INGS.
UNTIL IT'S ALL OVER...

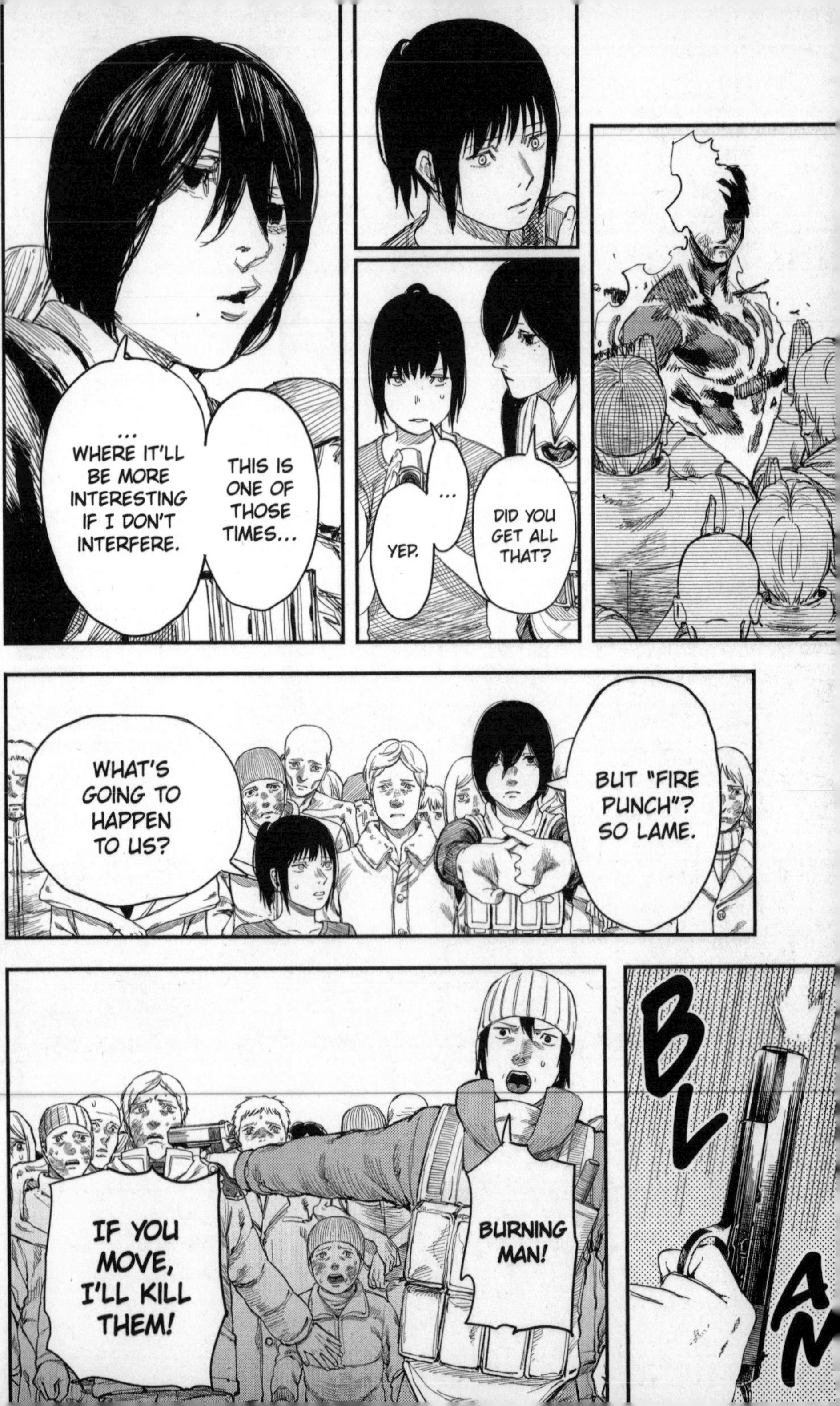
DID YOU GET ALL THAT?
...
YEP.
THIS IS ONE OF THOSE TIMES...
... WHERE IT'LL BE MORE INTERESTING IF I DON'T INTERFERE.
BUT "FIRE PUNCH"? SO LAME.
WHAT'S GOING TO HAPPEN TO US?
BLAM
BURNING MAN!
IF YOU MOVE, I'LL KILL THEM!

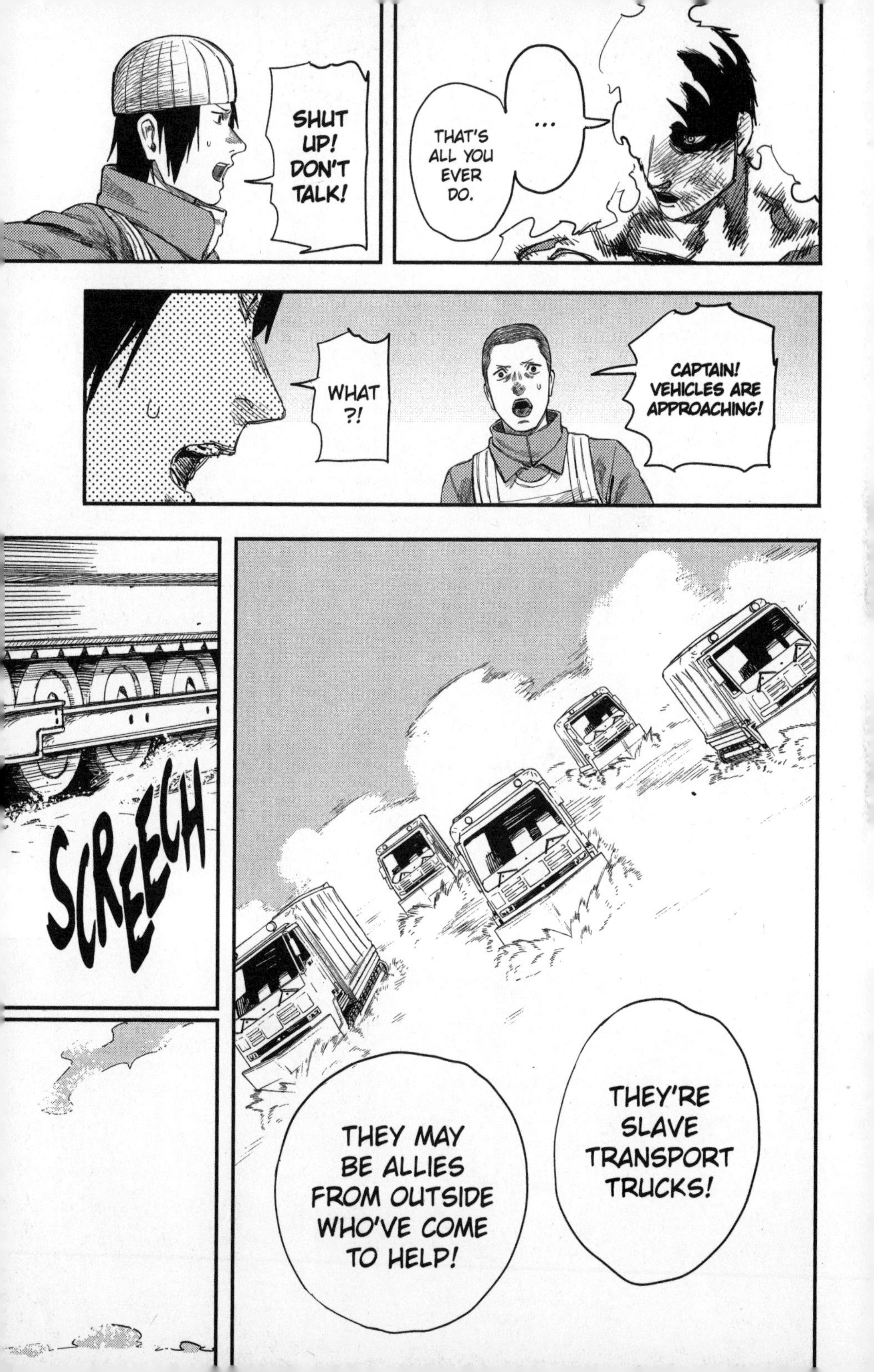
...
THAT'S ALL YOU EVER DO.
SHUT UP! DON'T TALK!
CAPTAIN! VEHICLES ARE APPROACHING!
WHAT?!
THEY'RE SLAVE TRANSPORT TRUCKS!
THEY MAY BE ALLIES FROM OUTSIDE WHO'VE COME TO HELP!
SCREECH

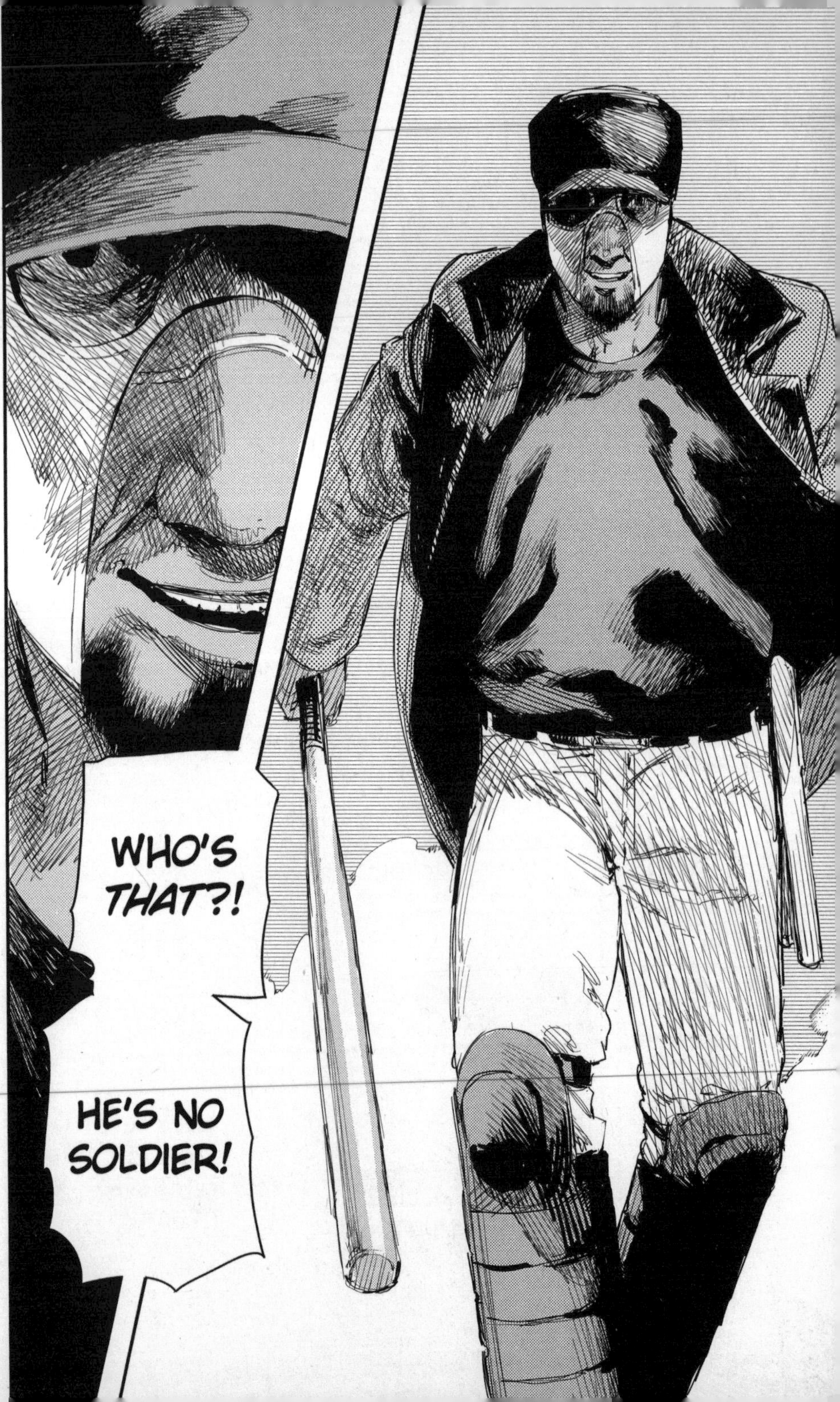
WHO'S THAT?!
HE'S NO SOLDIER!

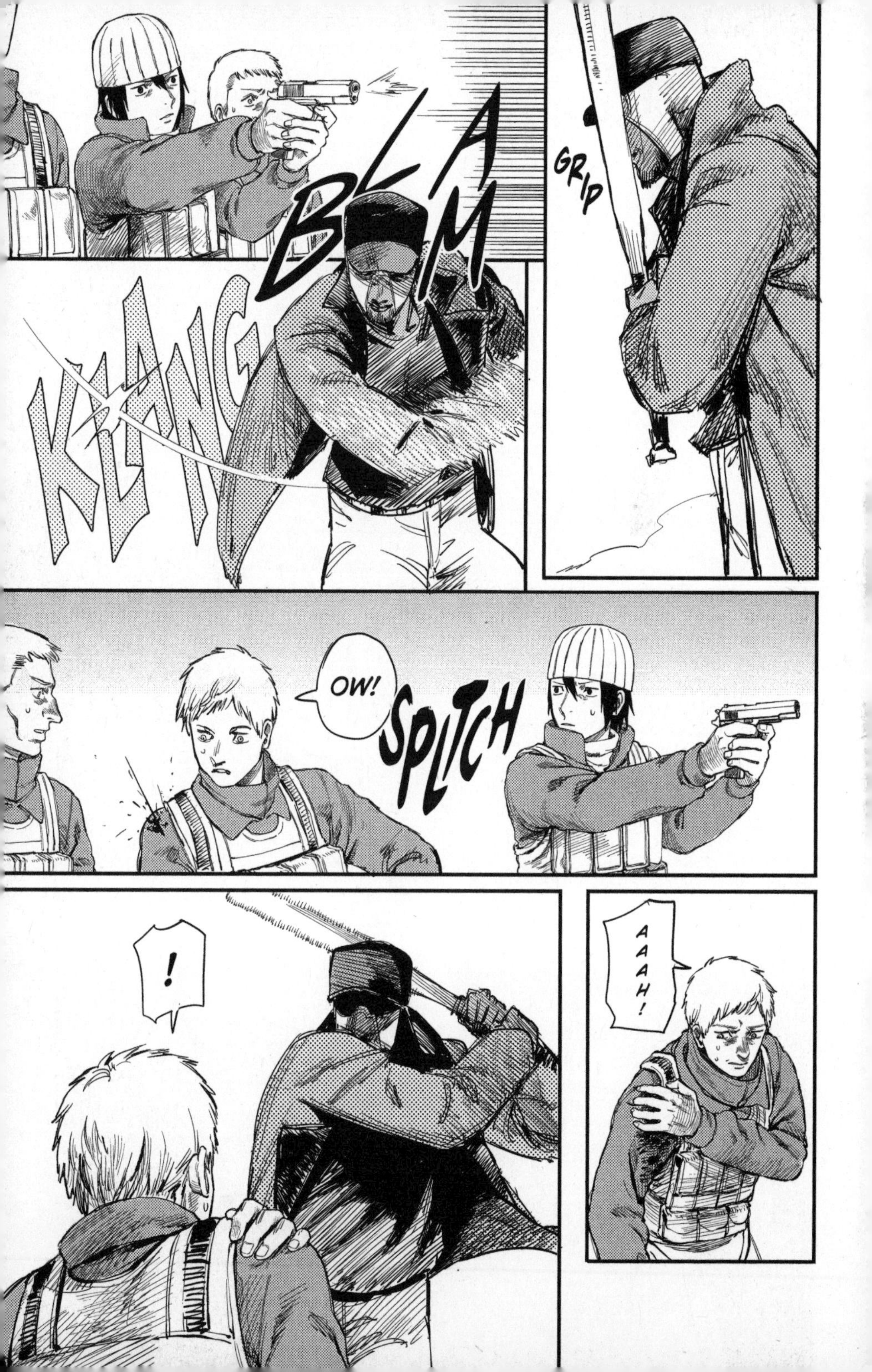
GRIP
BLAM
KLANG
SPLITCH
OW!
AAAH!
!

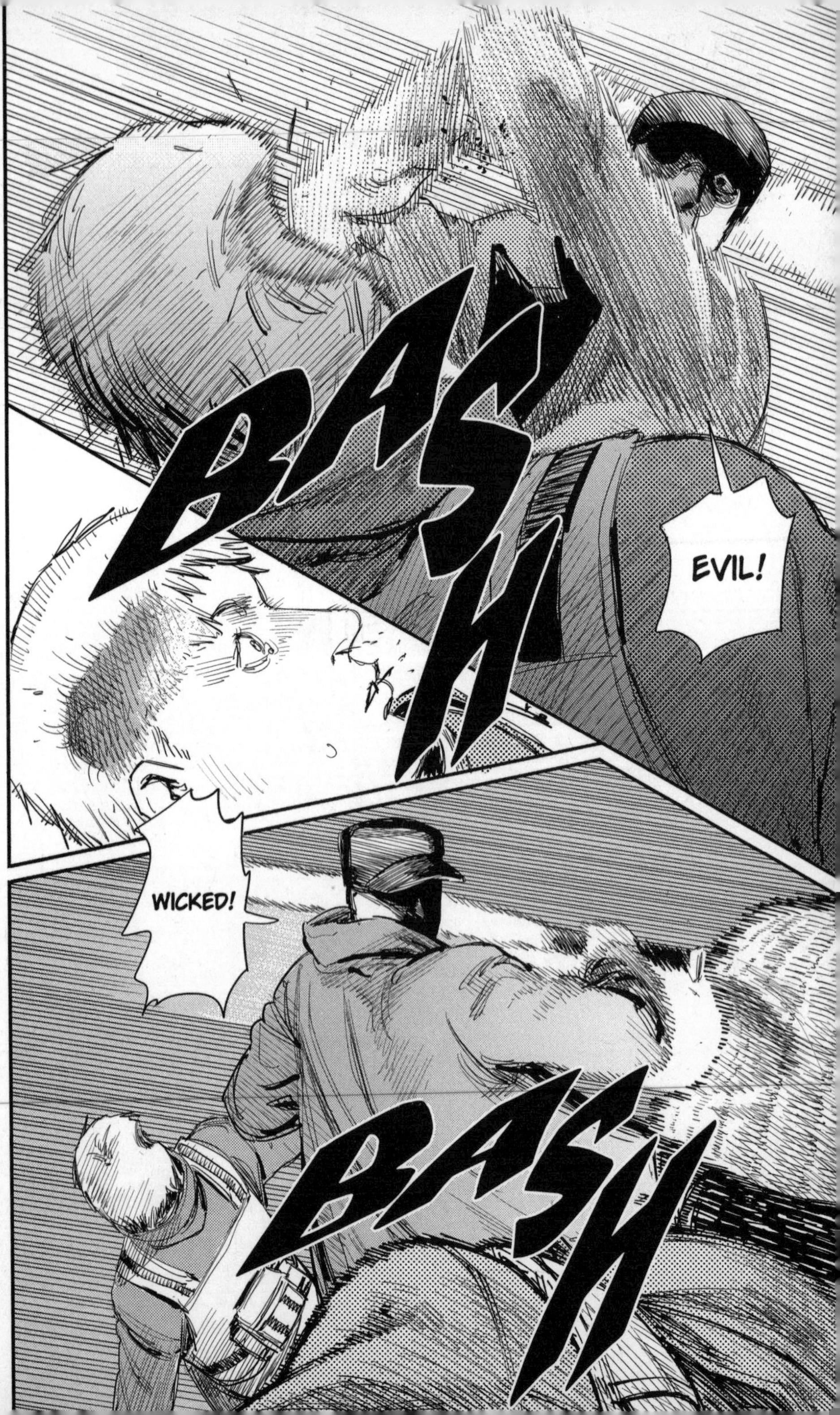
BASH
EVIL!
WICKED!
BASH

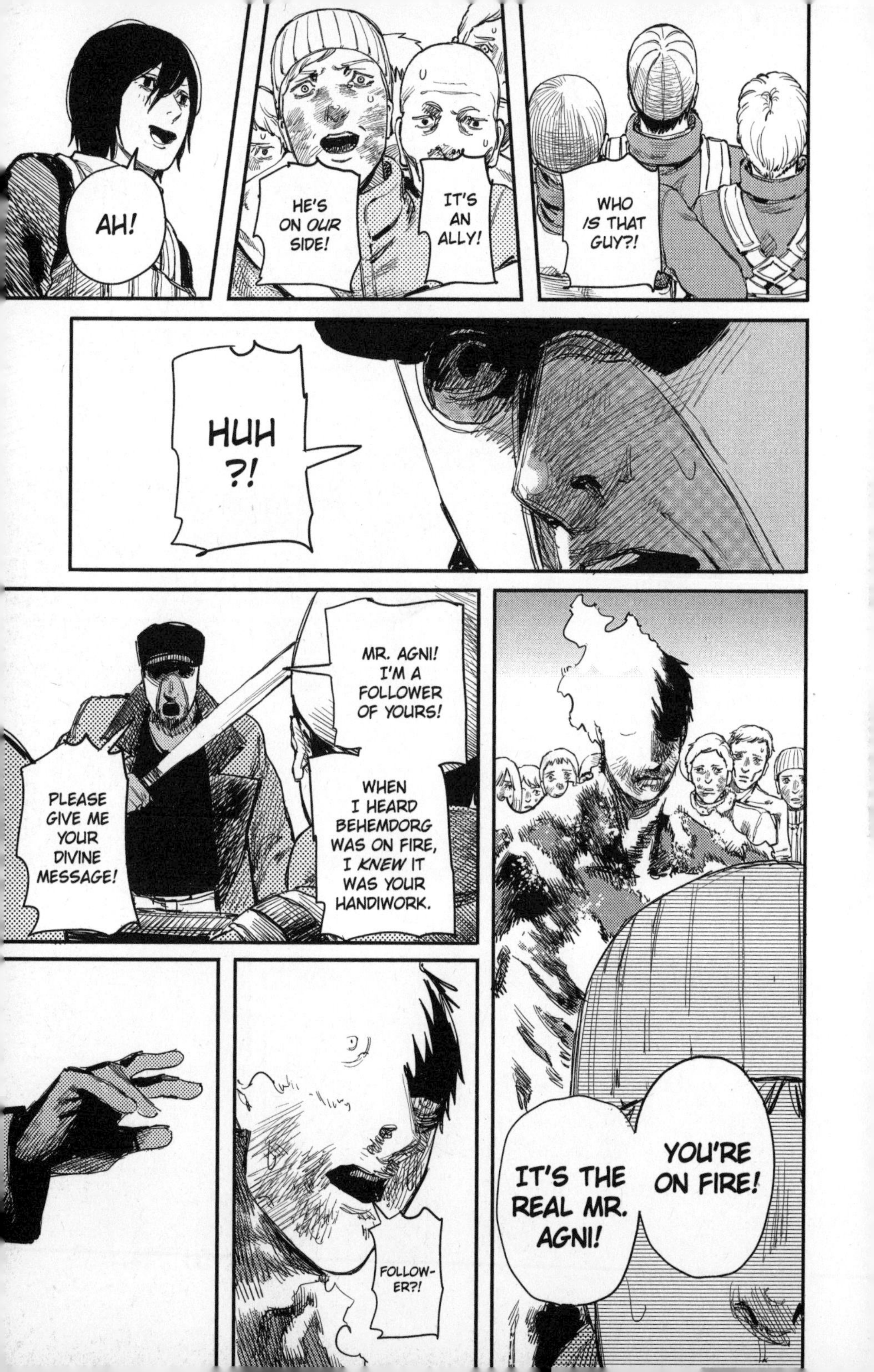
WHO IS THAT GUY?!
IT'S AN ALLY!
HE'S ON OUR SIDE!
AH!
HUH ?!
YOU'RE ON FIRE!
IT'S THE REAL MR. AGNI!
MR. AGNI! I'M A FOLLOWER OF YOURS!
WHEN I HEARD BEHEMDORG WAS ON FIRE, I KNEW IT WAS YOUR HANDIWORK.
PLEASE GIVE ME YOUR DIVINE MESSAGE!
FOLLOWER?!

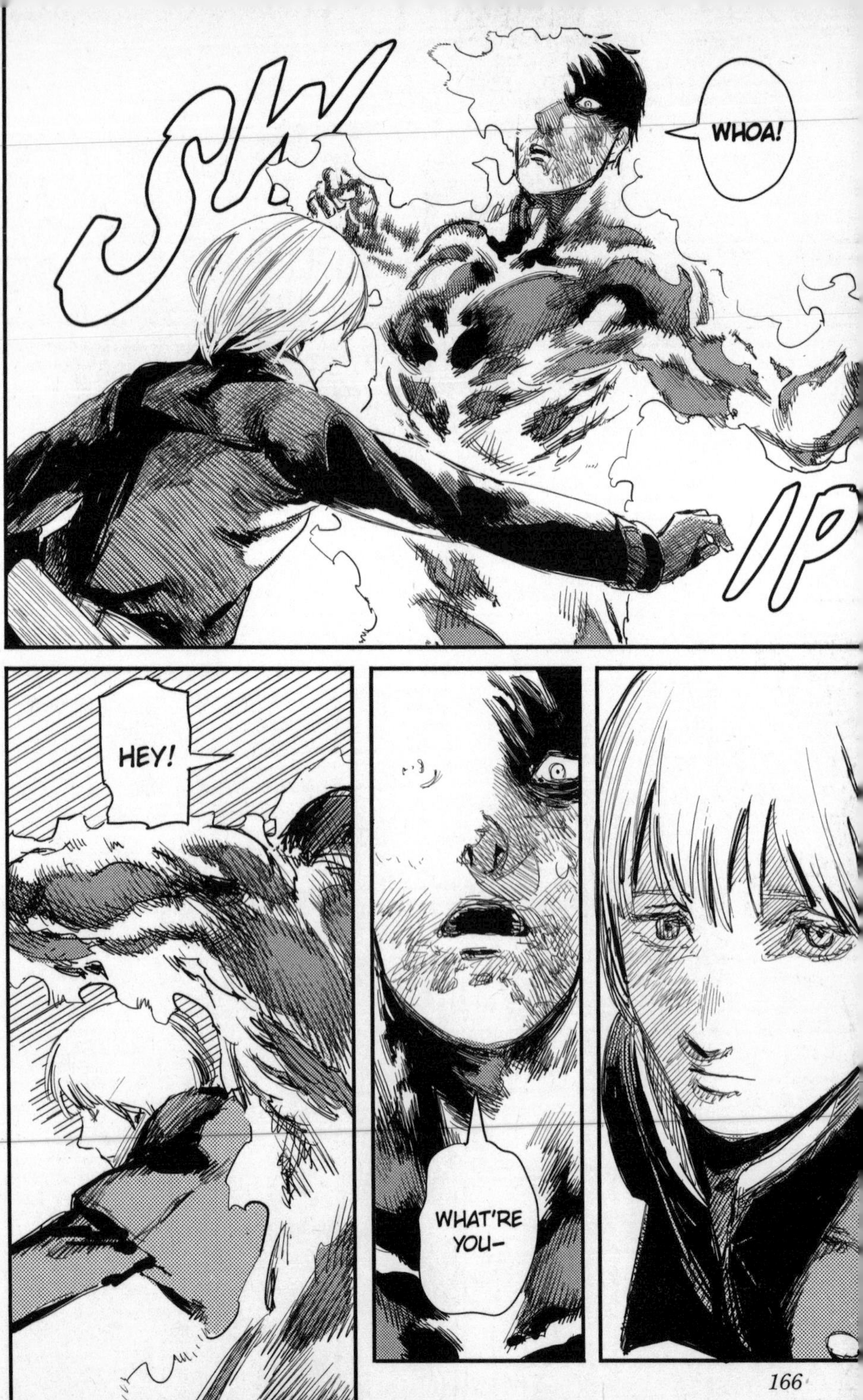
WHOA!
SW
IP
WHAT'RE YOU-
HEY!

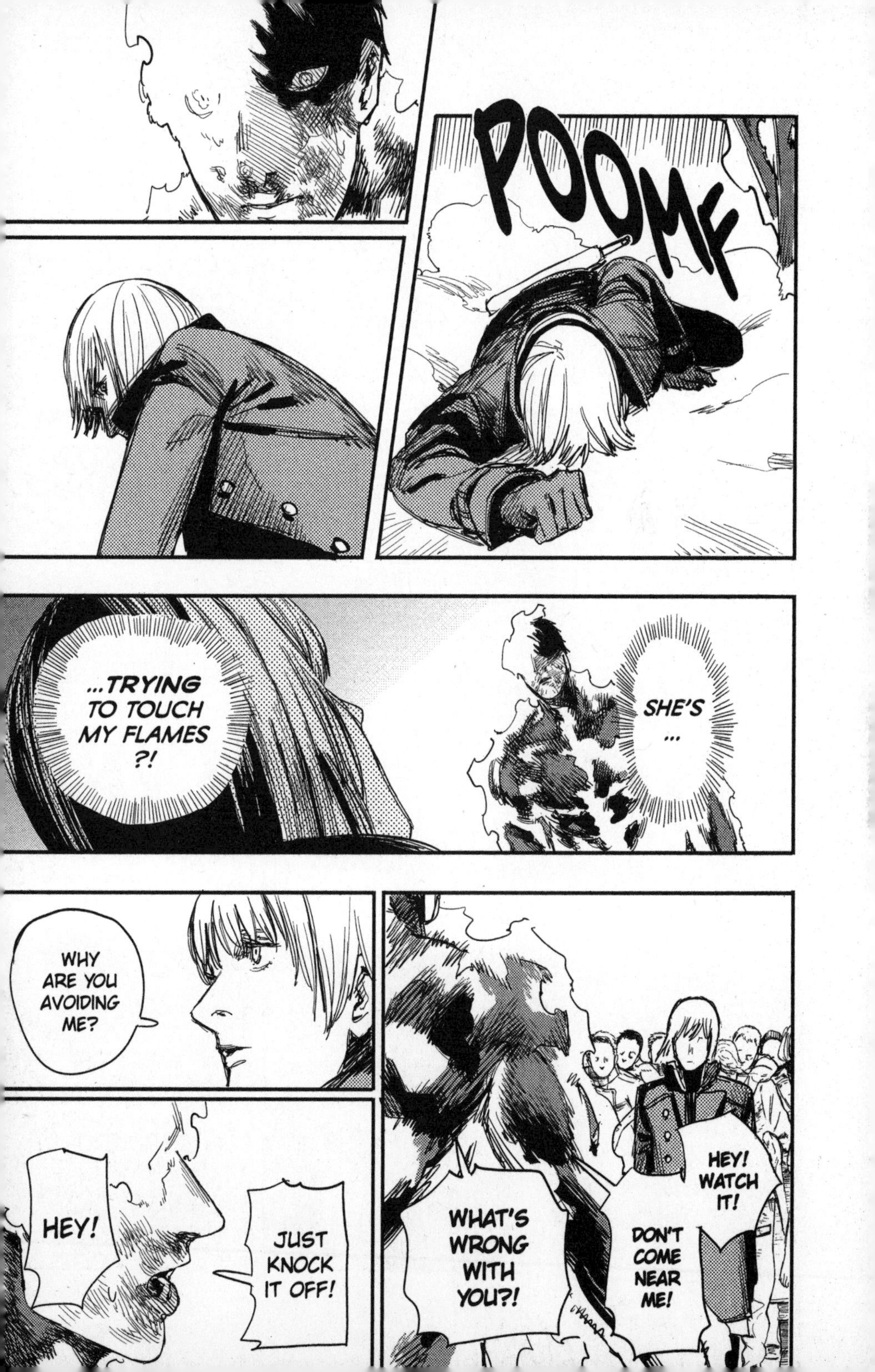
POOMF
SHE'S ...
...TRYING TO TOUCH MY FLAMES ?!
HEY! WATCH IT!
DON'T COME NEAR ME!
WHAT'S WRONG WITH YOU?!
WHY ARE YOU AVOIDING ME?
HEY!
JUST KNOCK IT OFF!

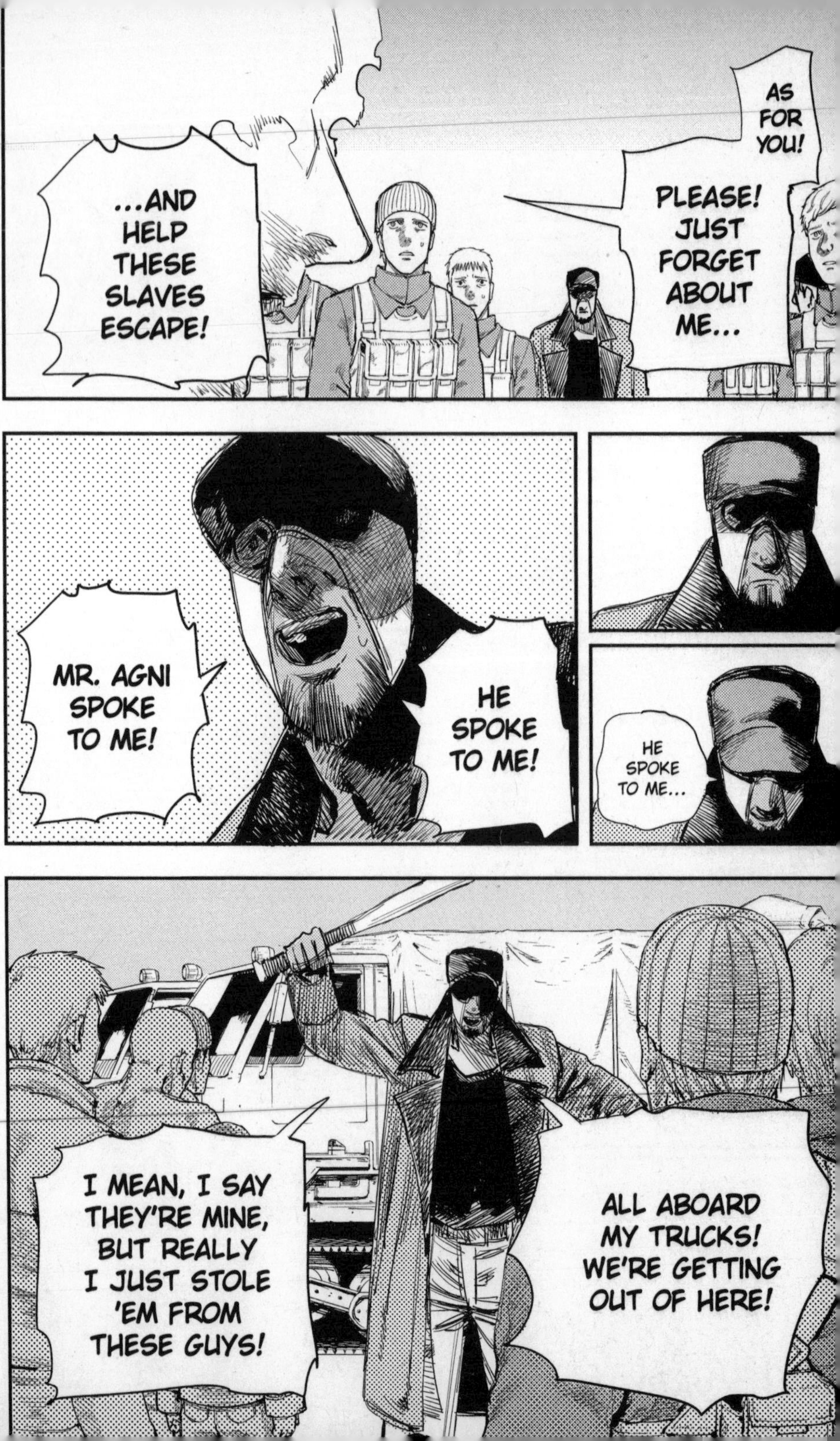
AS FOR YOU!
PLEASE! JUST FORGET ABOUT ME...
...AND HELP THESE SLAVES ESCAPE!
HE SPOKE TO ME...
HE SPOKE TO ME!
MR. AGNI SPOKE TO ME!
ALL ABOARD MY TRUCKS! WE'RE GETTING OUT OF HERE!
I MEAN, I SAY THEY'RE MINE, BUT REALLY I JUST STOLE 'EM FROM THESE GUYS!

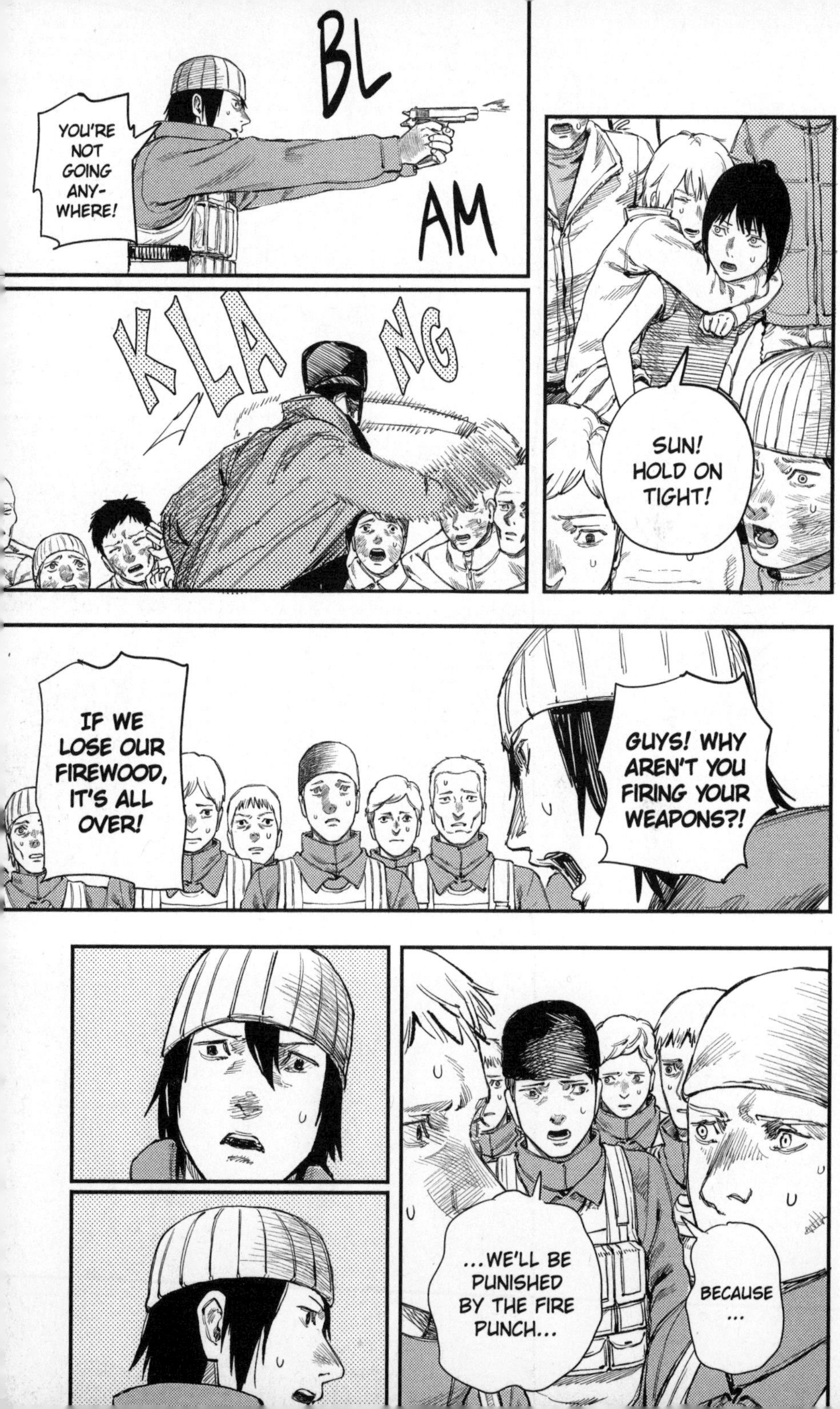
SUN! HOLD ON TIGHT!
YOU'RE NOT GOING ANY-WHERE!
BL
AM
KLA
NG
GUYS! WHY AREN'T YOU FIRING YOUR WEAPONS?!
IF WE LOSE OUR FIREWOOD, IT'S ALL OVER!
BECAUSE ...
...WE'LL BE PUNISHED BY THE FIRE PUNCH...

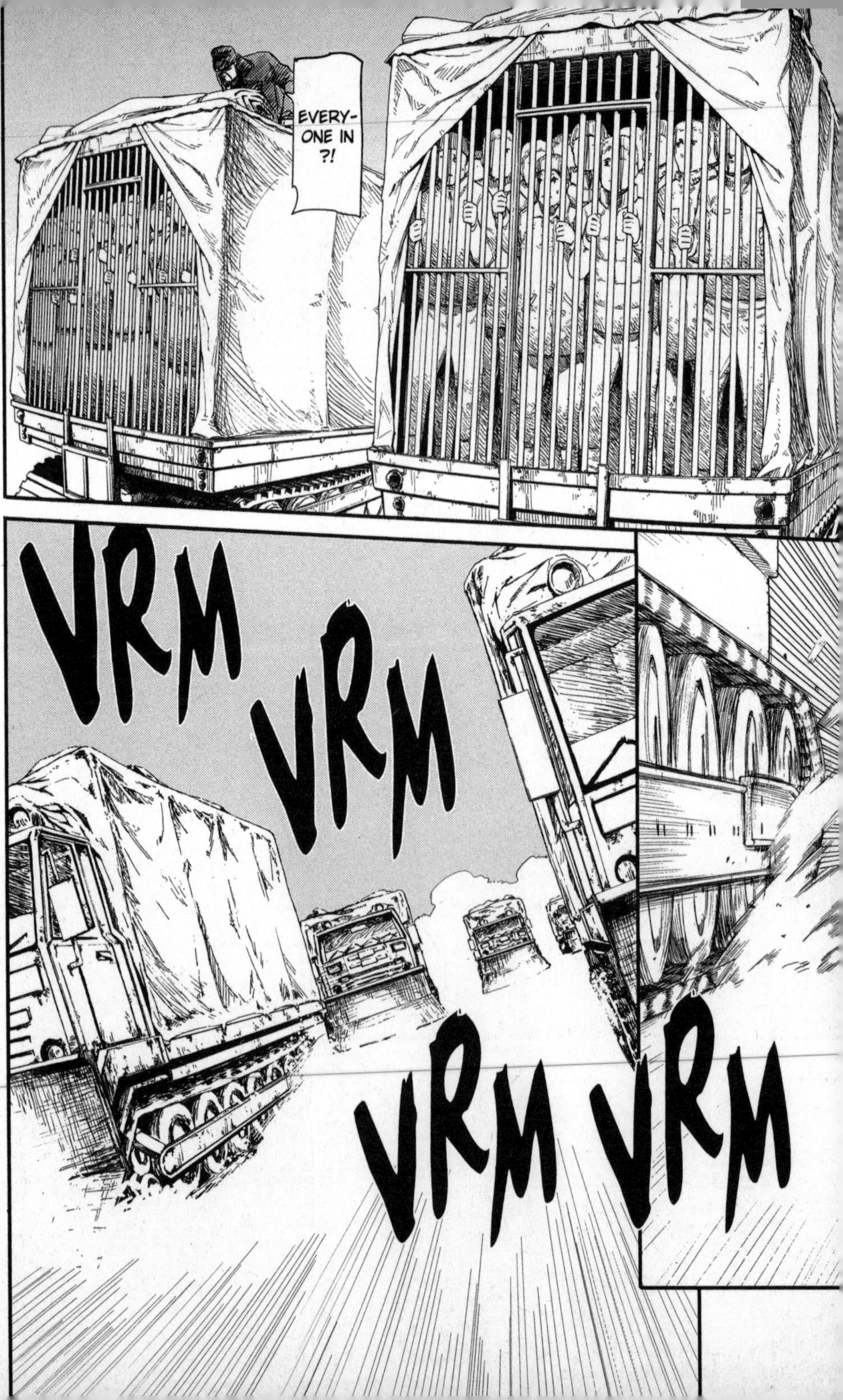
EVERY-
ONE IN
?!
VRM VRM
VRM VRM

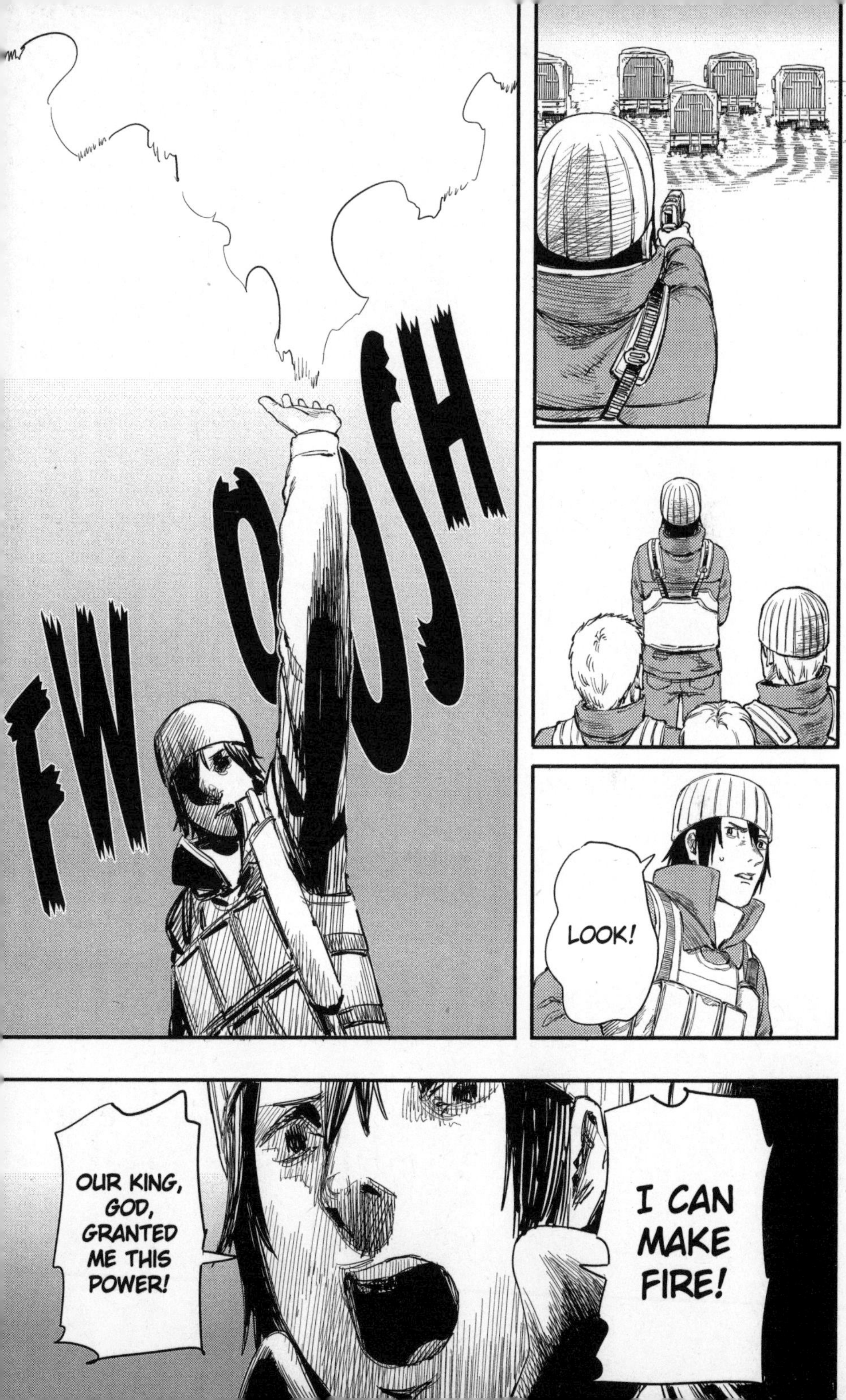
LOOK!
FWOOSH
I CAN MAKE FIRE!
OUR KING, GOD, GRANTED ME THIS POWER!

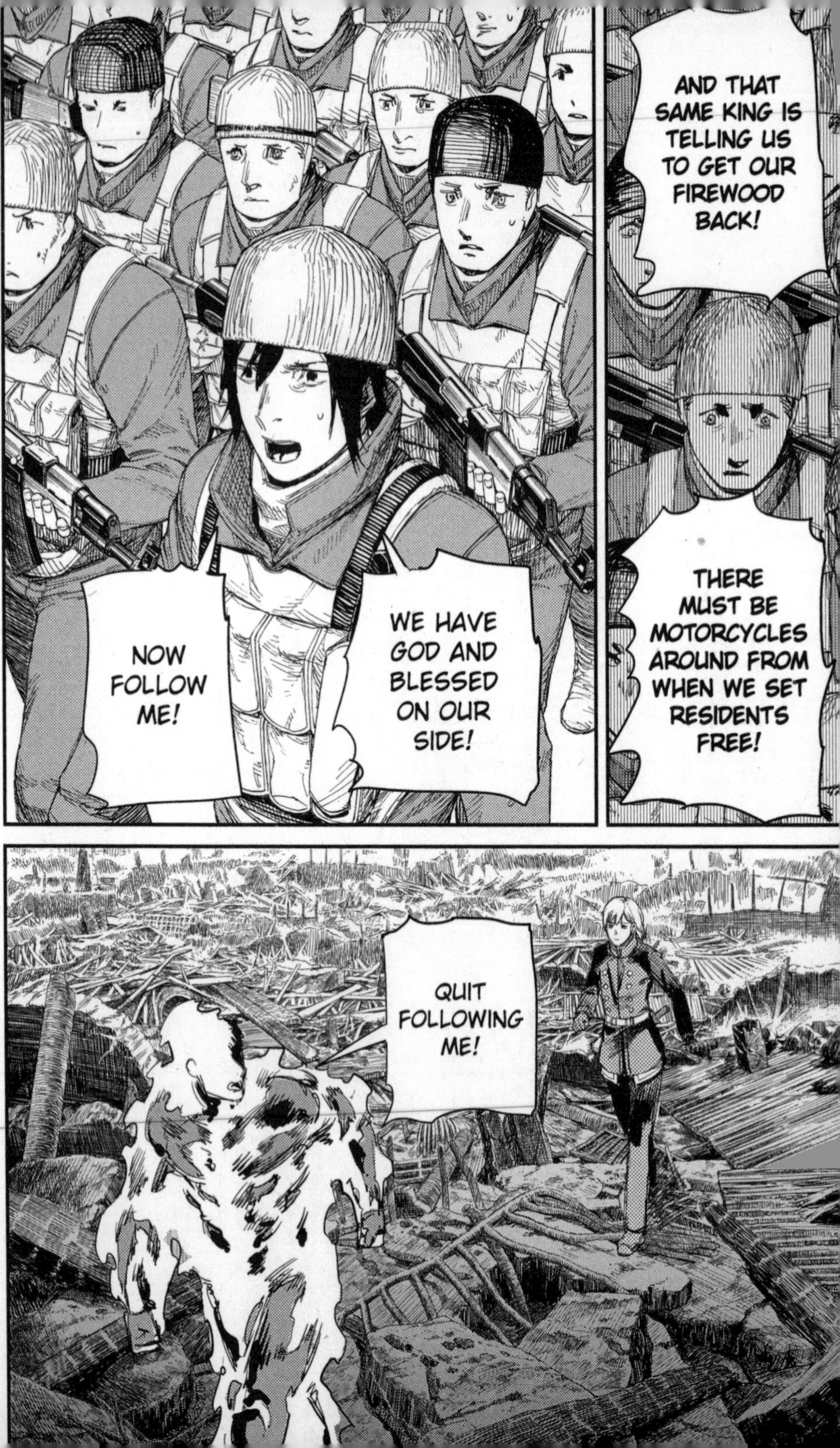
AND THAT SAME KING IS TELLING US TO GET OUR FIREWOOD BACK!
THERE MUST BE MOTORCYCLES AROUND FROM WHEN WE SET RESIDENTS FREE!
WE HAVE GOD AND BLESSED ON OUR SIDE!
NOW FOLLOW ME!
QUIT FOLLOWING ME!

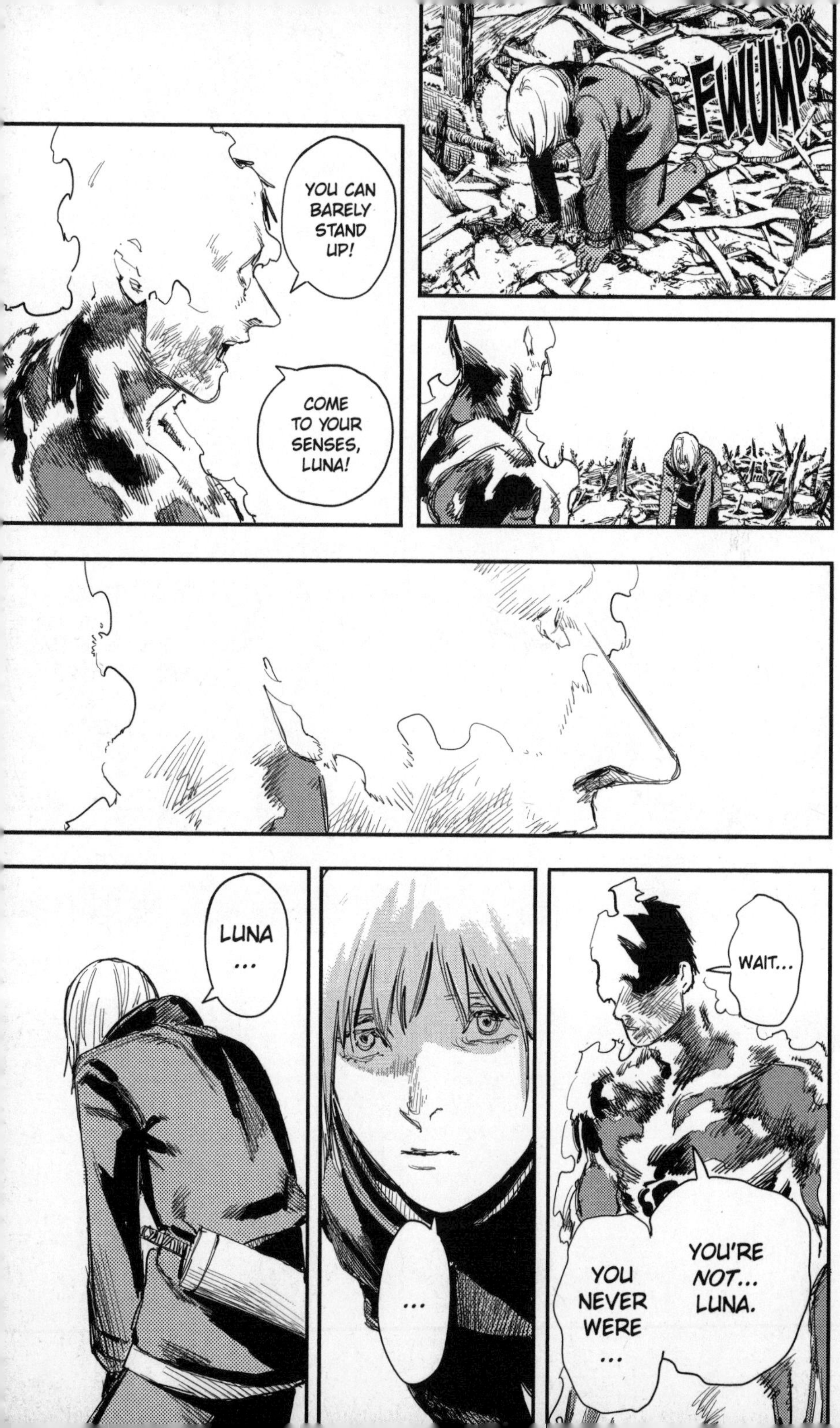
FWUMP
YOU CAN BARELY STAND UP!
COME TO YOUR SENSES, LUNA!
WAIT...
YOU'RE NOT... LUNA.
YOU NEVER WERE ...
...
LUNA ...

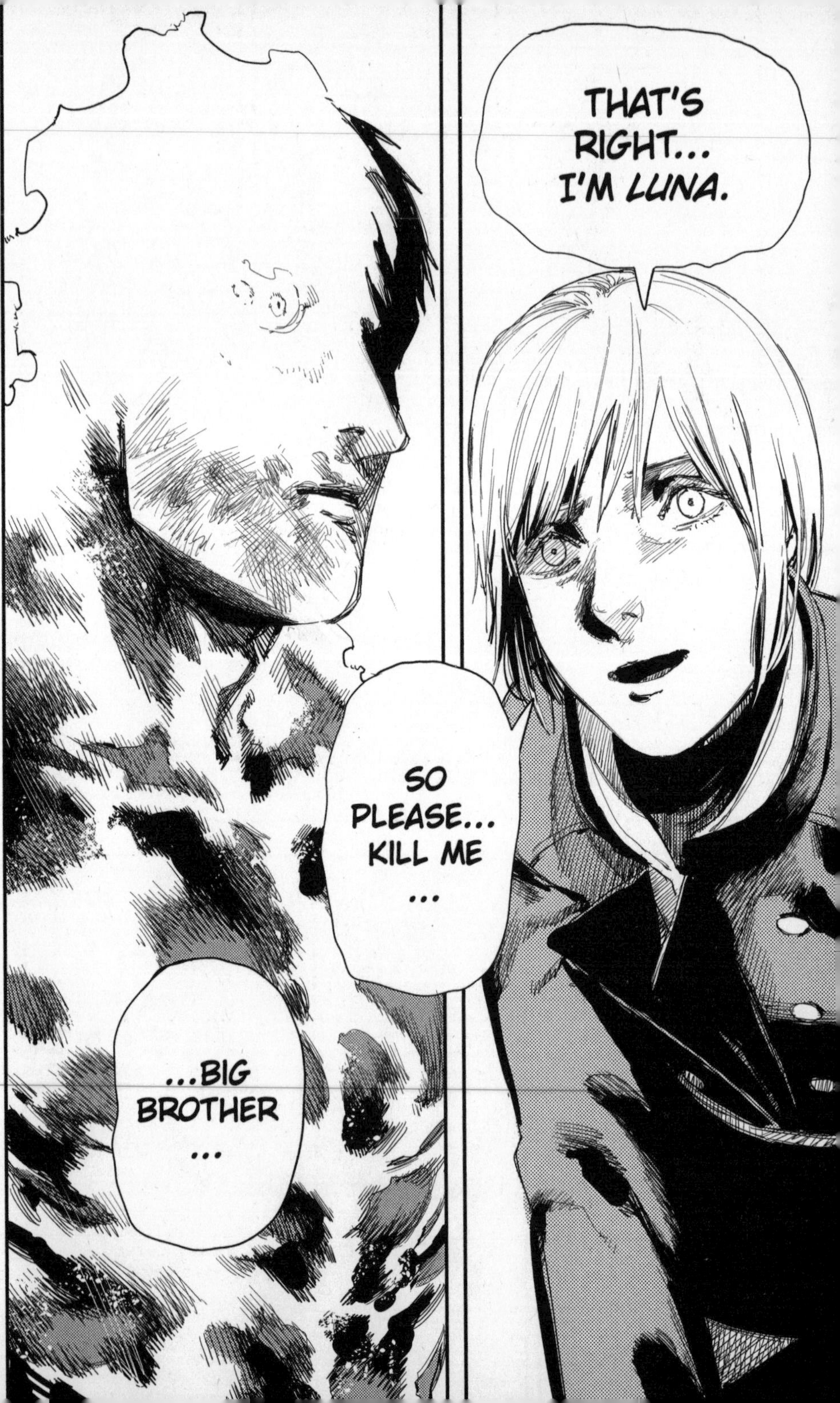
THAT'S RIGHT... I'M *LUNA.*
SO PLEASE... KILL ME ...
...BIG BROTHER ...

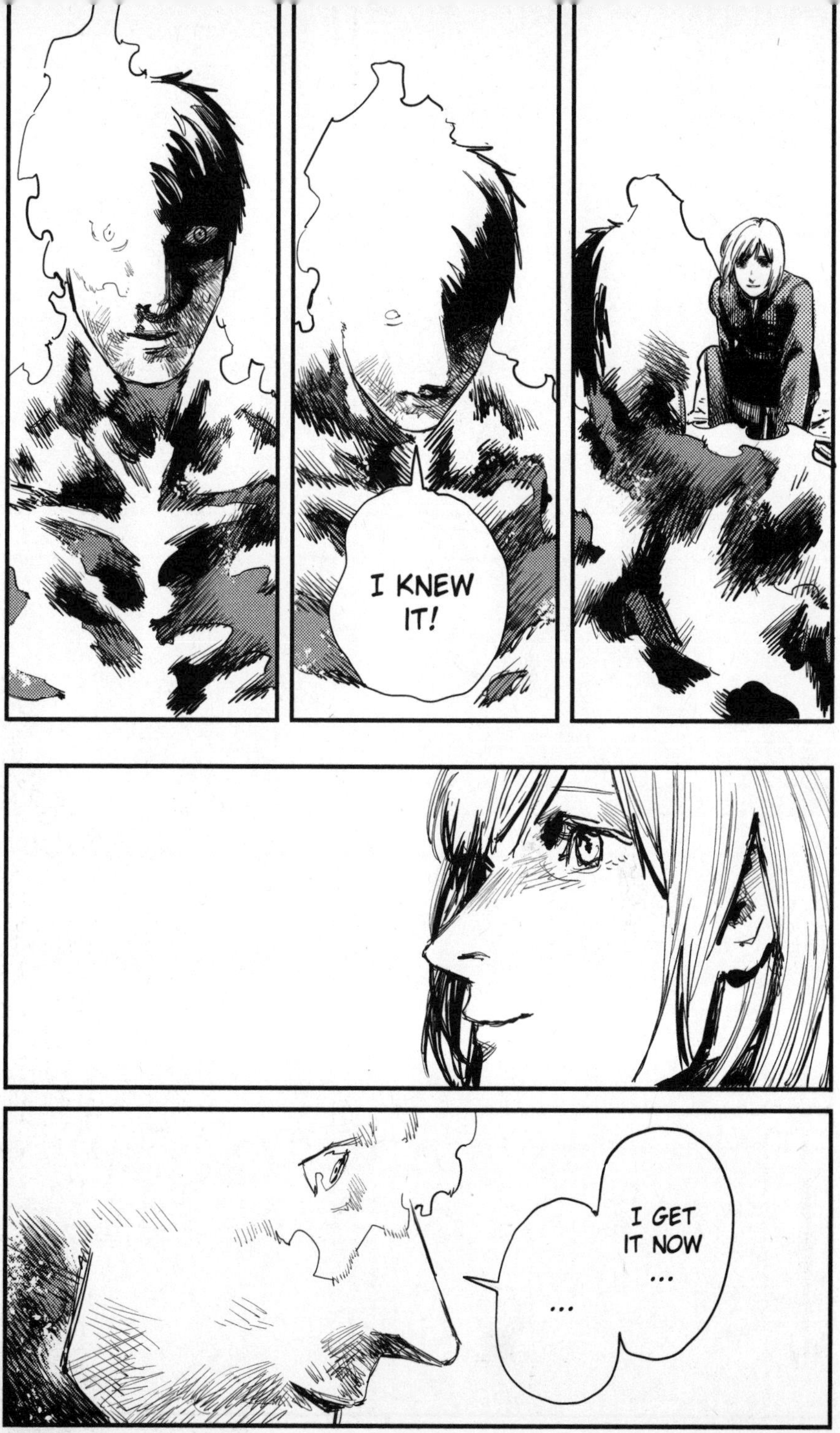
I KNEW IT!
I GET IT NOW ... ...

CHAPTER 27

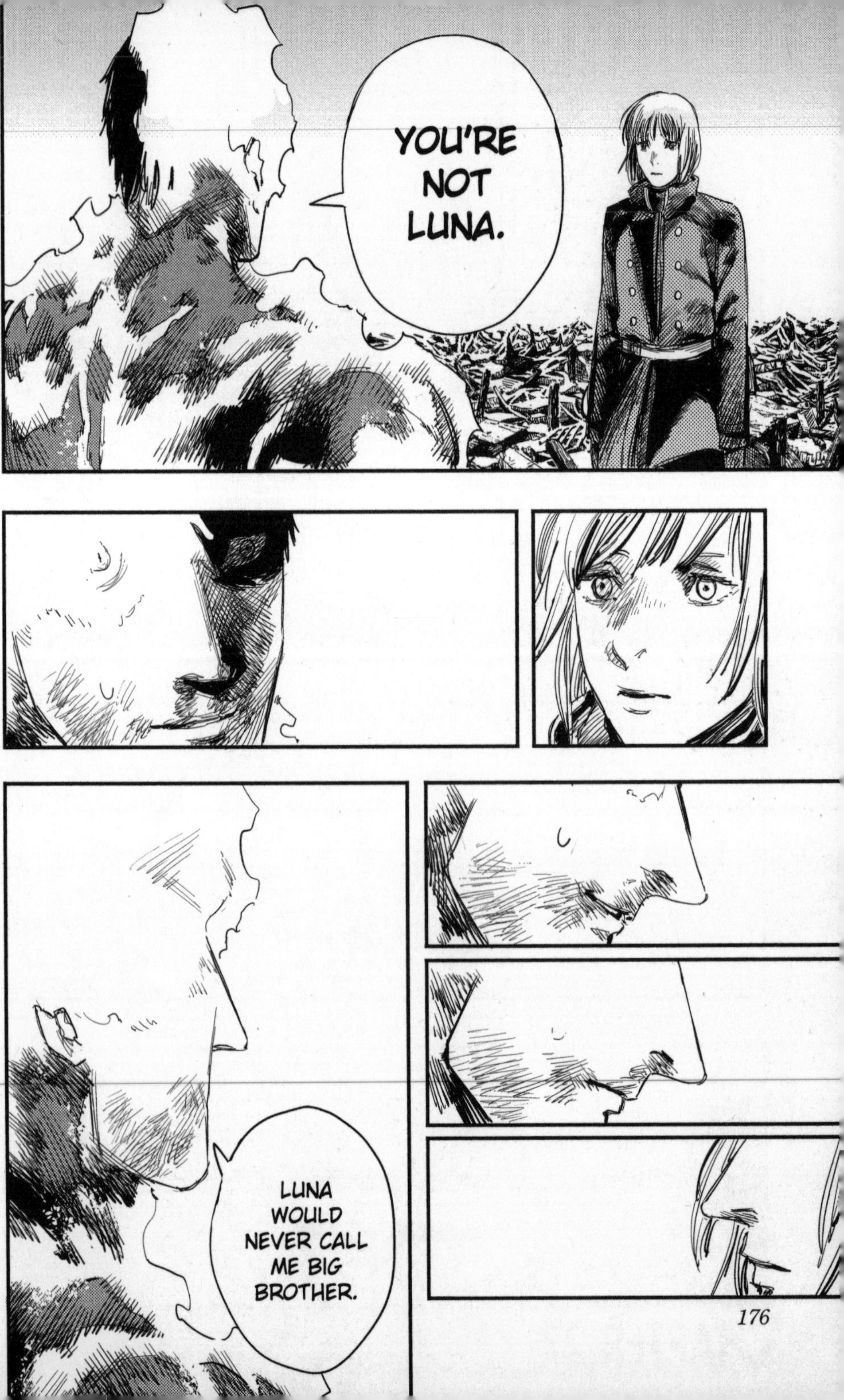
YOU'RE NOT LUNA.
LUNA WOULD NEVER CALL ME BIG BROTHER.

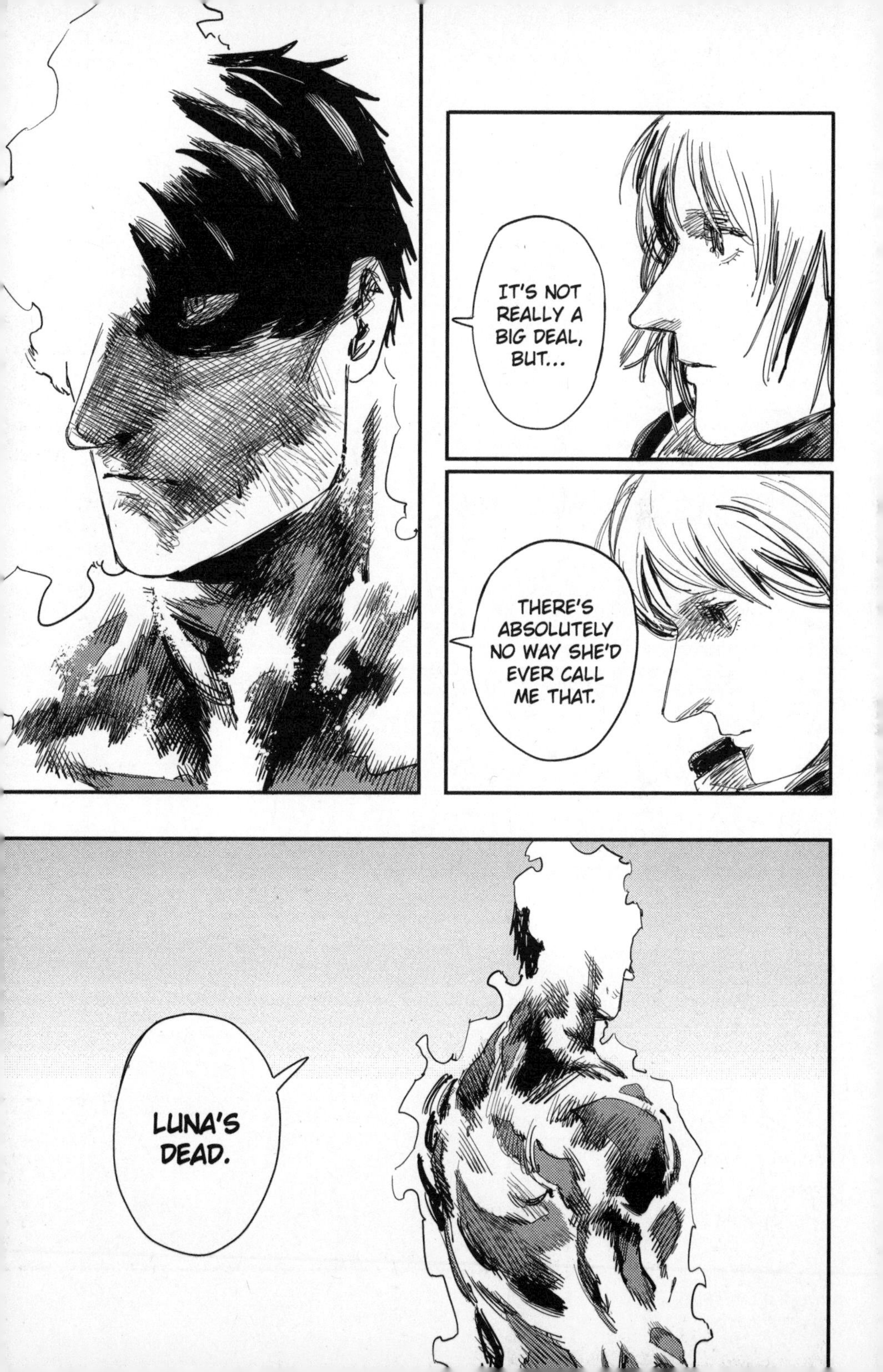
IT'S NOT REALLY A BIG DEAL, BUT...
THERE'S ABSOLUTELY NO WAY SHE'D EVER CALL ME THAT.
LUNA'S DEAD.

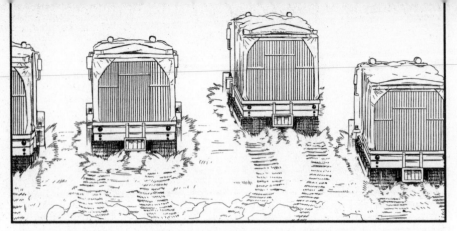

HFF...
I NEED
TO SIT.

SORRY
I'M SO
HEAVY.

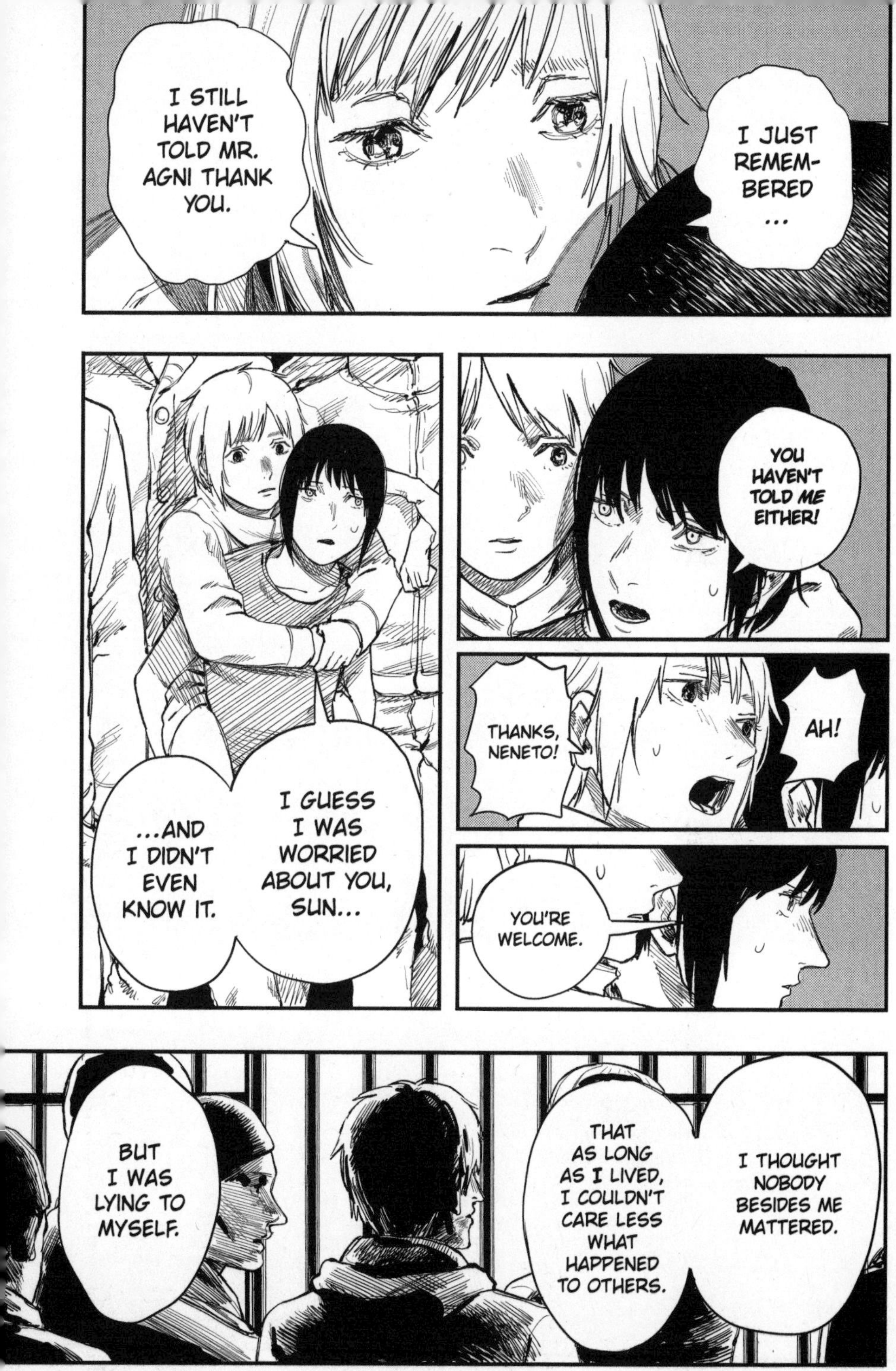
I JUST REMEMBERED...
I STILL HAVEN'T TOLD MR. AGNI THANK YOU.
YOU HAVEN'T TOLD *ME* EITHER!
AH!
THANKS, NENETO!
YOU'RE WELCOME.
I GUESS I WAS WORRIED ABOUT YOU, SUN...
...AND I DIDN'T EVEN KNOW IT.
I THOUGHT NOBODY BESIDES ME MATTERED.
THAT AS LONG AS I LIVED, I COULDN'T CARE LESS WHAT HAPPENED TO OTHERS.
BUT I WAS LYING TO MYSELF.

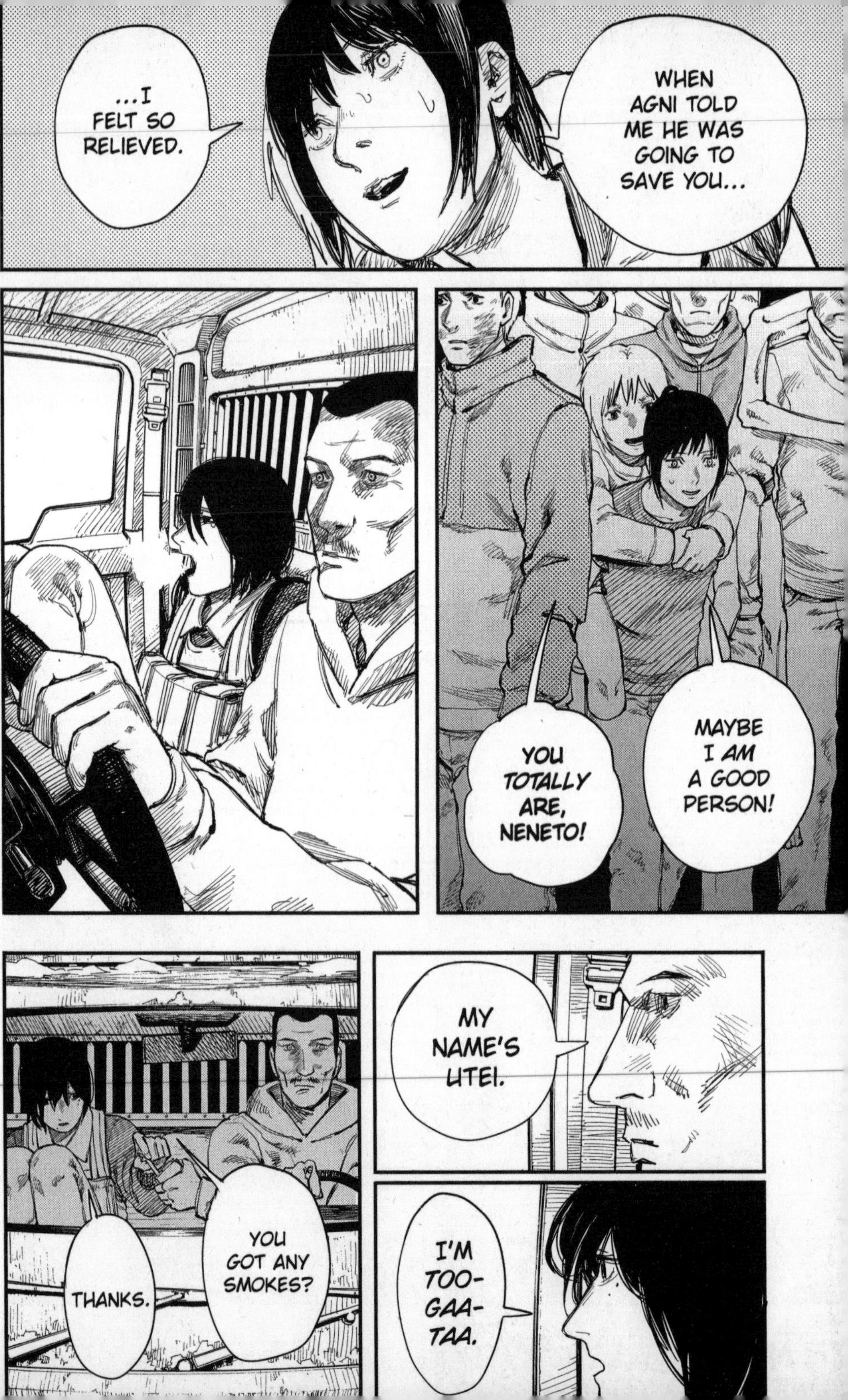
WHEN AGNI TOLD ME HE WAS GOING TO SAVE YOU...
...I FELT SO RELIEVED.
MAYBE I AM A GOOD PERSON!
YOU TOTALLY ARE, NENETO!
MY NAME'S UTEI.
I'M TOO-GAA-TAA.
YOU GOT ANY SMOKES?
THANKS.

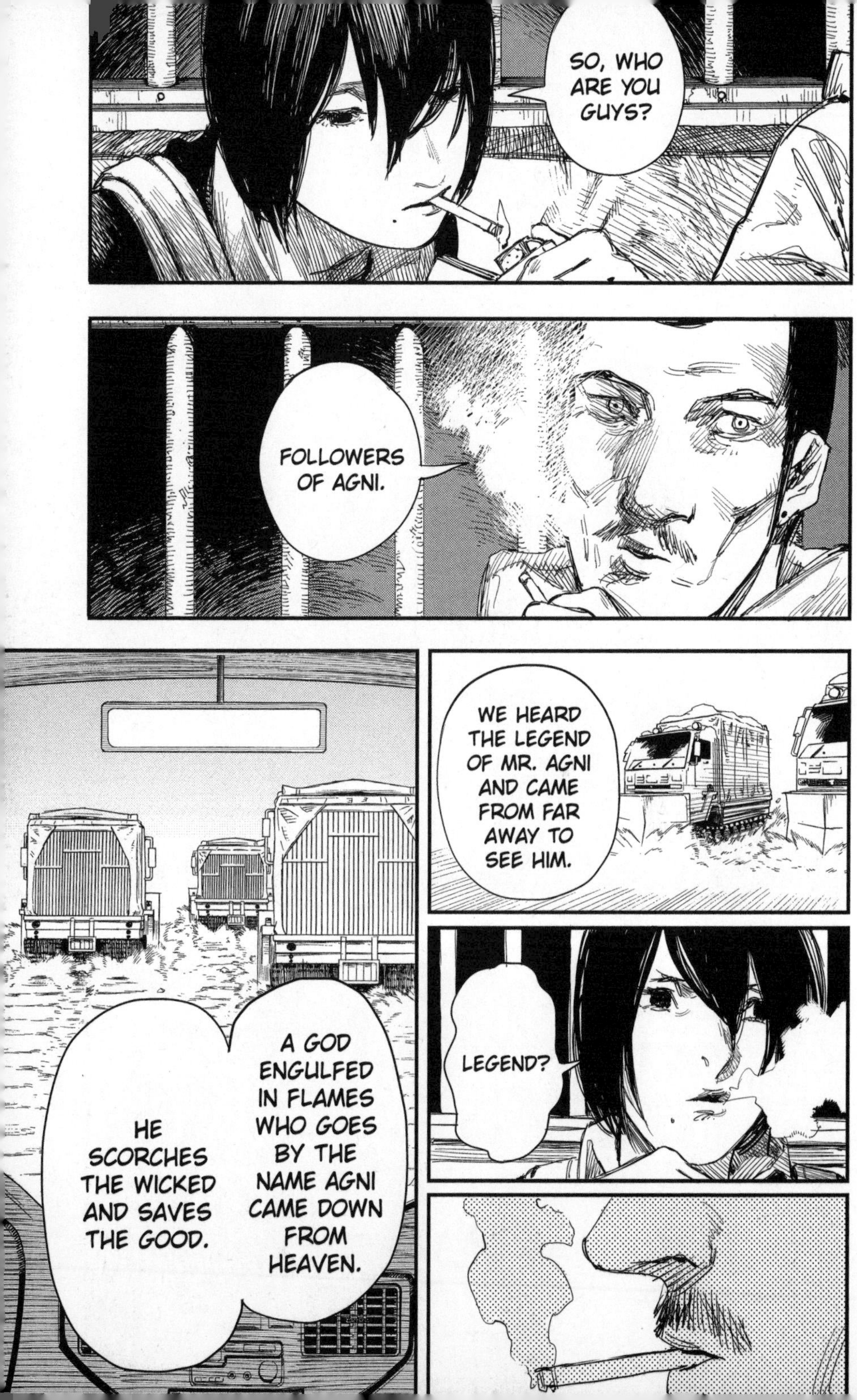
SO, WHO ARE YOU GUYS?
FOLLOWERS OF AGNI.
WE HEARD THE LEGEND OF MR. AGNI AND CAME FROM FAR AWAY TO SEE HIM.
LEGEND?
A GOD ENGULFED IN FLAMES WHO GOES BY THE NAME AGNI CAME DOWN FROM HEAVEN.
HE SCORCHES THE WICKED AND SAVES THE GOOD.

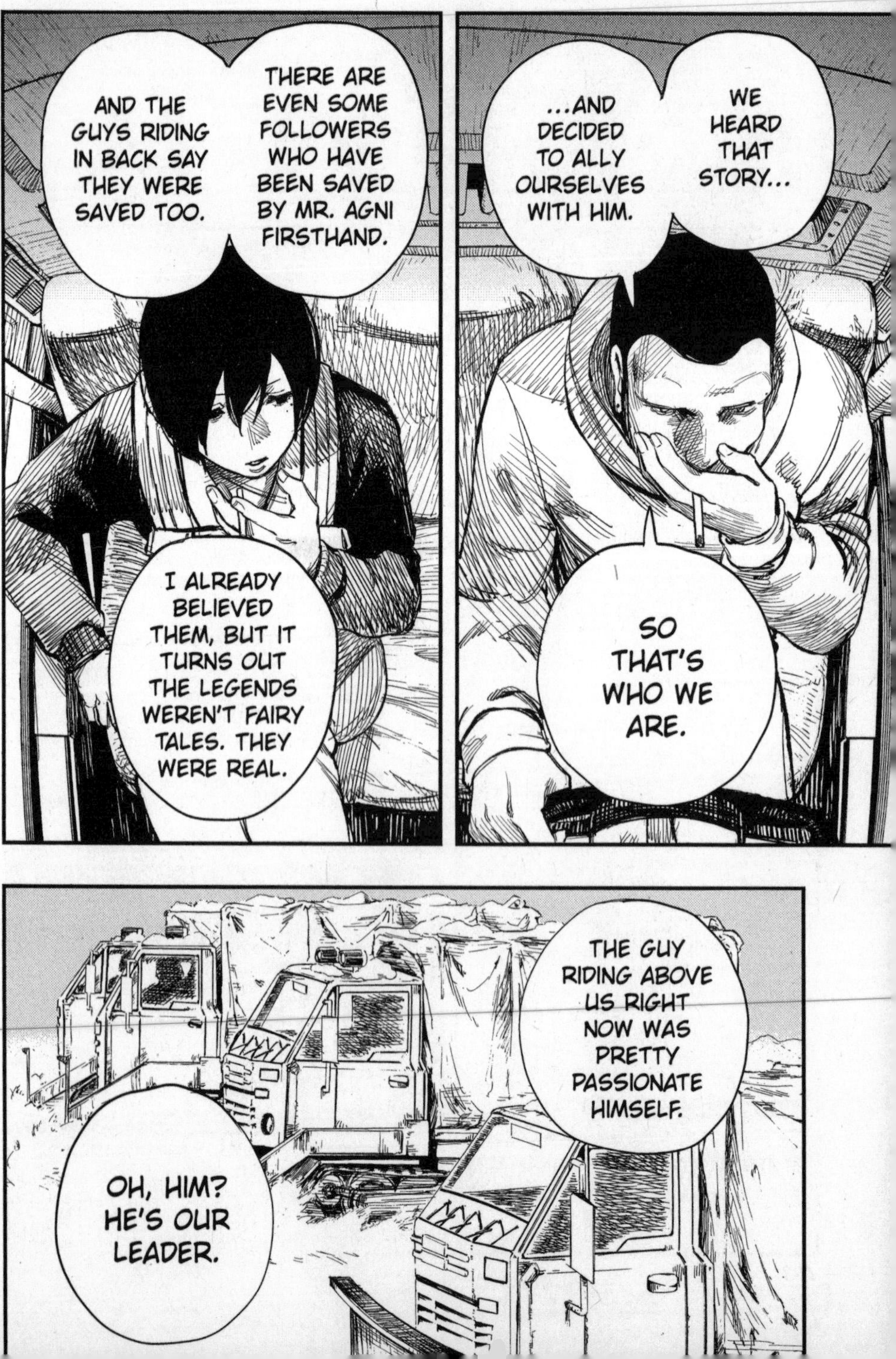
WE HEARD THAT STORY...
...AND DECIDED TO ALLY OURSELVES WITH HIM.
SO THAT'S WHO WE ARE.
THERE ARE EVEN SOME FOLLOWERS WHO HAVE BEEN SAVED BY MR. AGNI FIRSTHAND.
AND THE GUYS RIDING IN BACK SAY THEY WERE SAVED TOO.
I ALREADY BELIEVED THEM, BUT IT TURNS OUT THE LEGENDS WEREN'T FAIRY TALES. THEY WERE REAL.
THE GUY RIDING ABOVE US RIGHT NOW WAS PRETTY PASSIONATE HIMSELF.
OH, HIM? HE'S OUR LEADER.

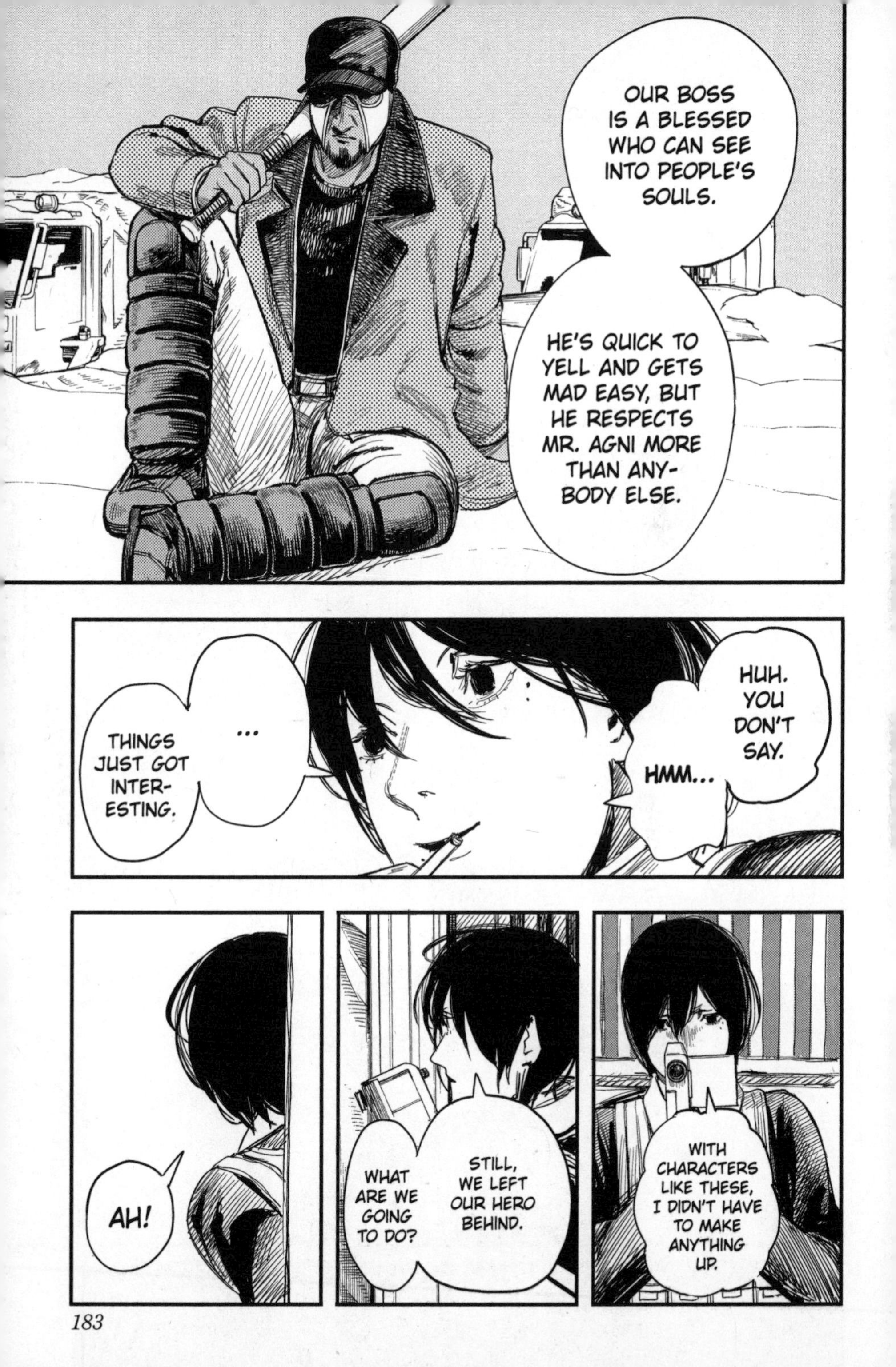
OUR BOSS IS A BLESSED WHO CAN SEE INTO PEOPLE'S SOULS.
HE'S QUICK TO YELL AND GETS MAD EASY, BUT HE RESPECTS MR. AGNI MORE THAN ANY-BODY ELSE.
HUH. YOU DON'T SAY.
HMM...
...
THINGS JUST GOT INTER-ESTING.
WITH CHARACTERS LIKE THESE, I DIDN'T HAVE TO MAKE ANYTHING UP.
STILL, WE LEFT OUR HERO BEHIND.
WHAT ARE WE GOING TO DO?
AH!

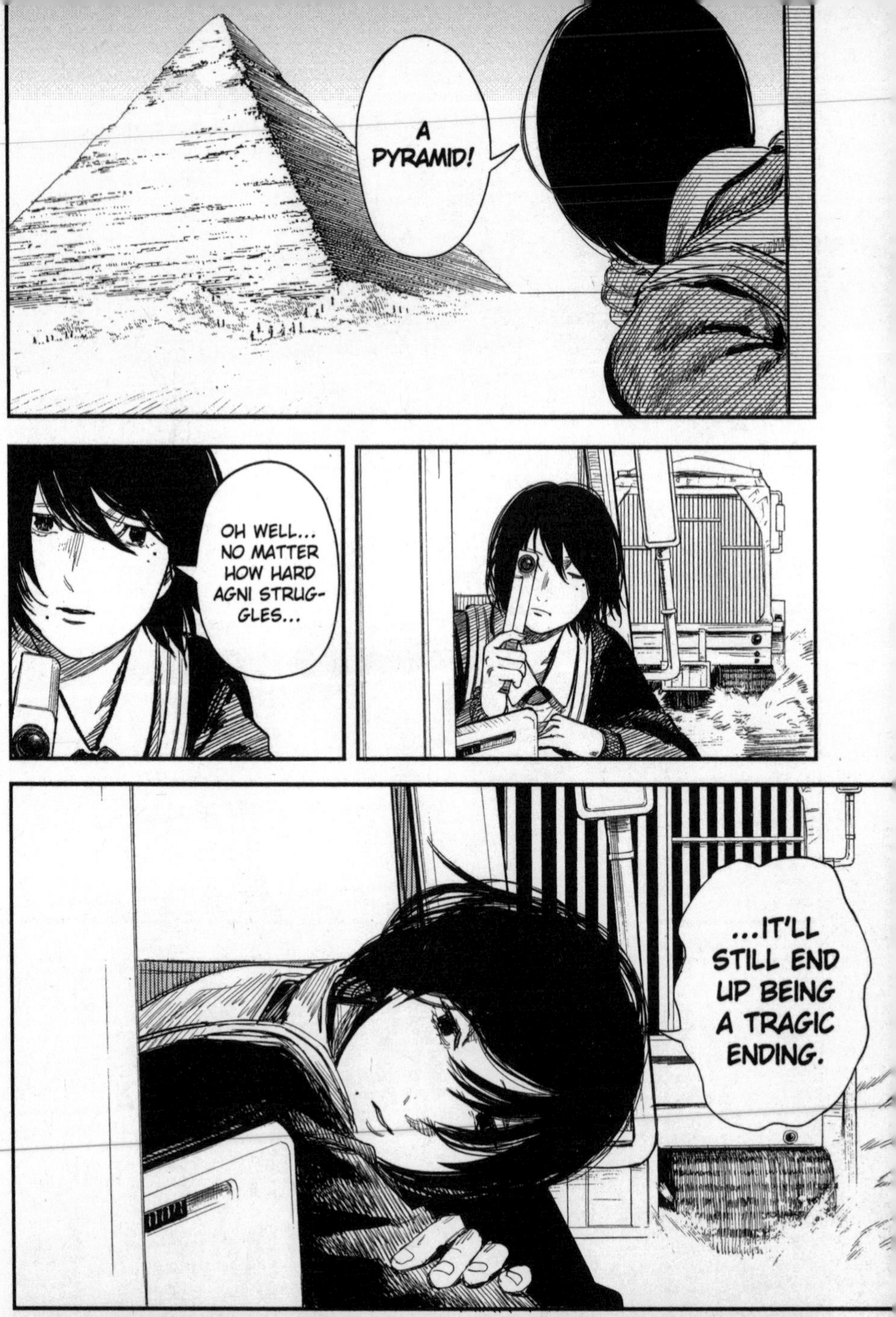
A PYRAMID!
OH WELL... NO MATTER HOW HARD AGNI STRUG-GLES...
...IT'LL STILL END UP BEING A TRAGIC ENDING.

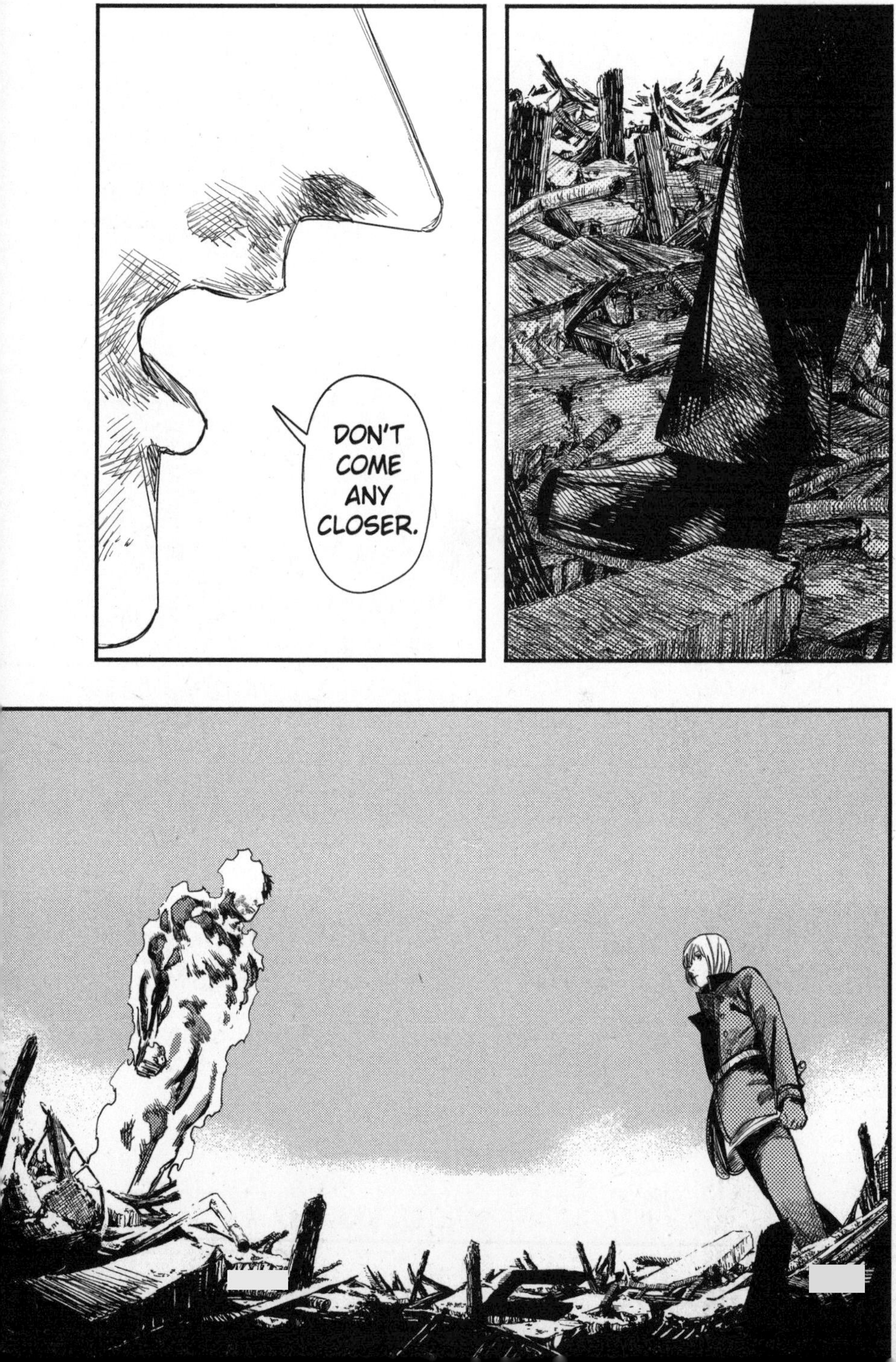
DON'T COME ANY CLOSER.

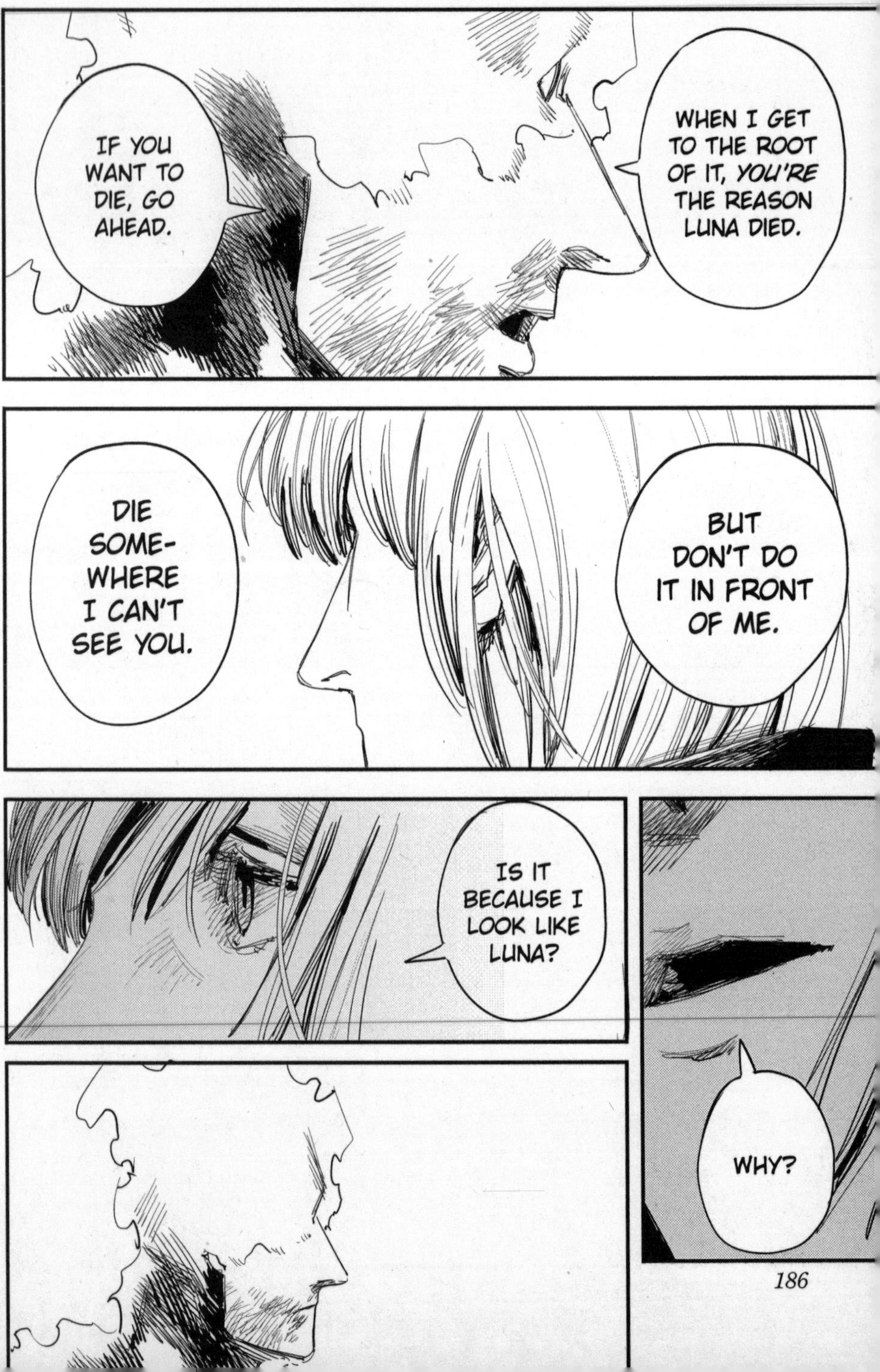
WHEN I GET TO THE ROOT OF IT, *YOU'RE* THE REASON LUNA DIED.
IF YOU WANT TO DIE, GO AHEAD.
BUT DON'T DO IT IN FRONT OF ME.
DIE SOMEWHERE I CAN'T SEE YOU.
WHY?
IS IT BECAUSE I LOOK LIKE LUNA?

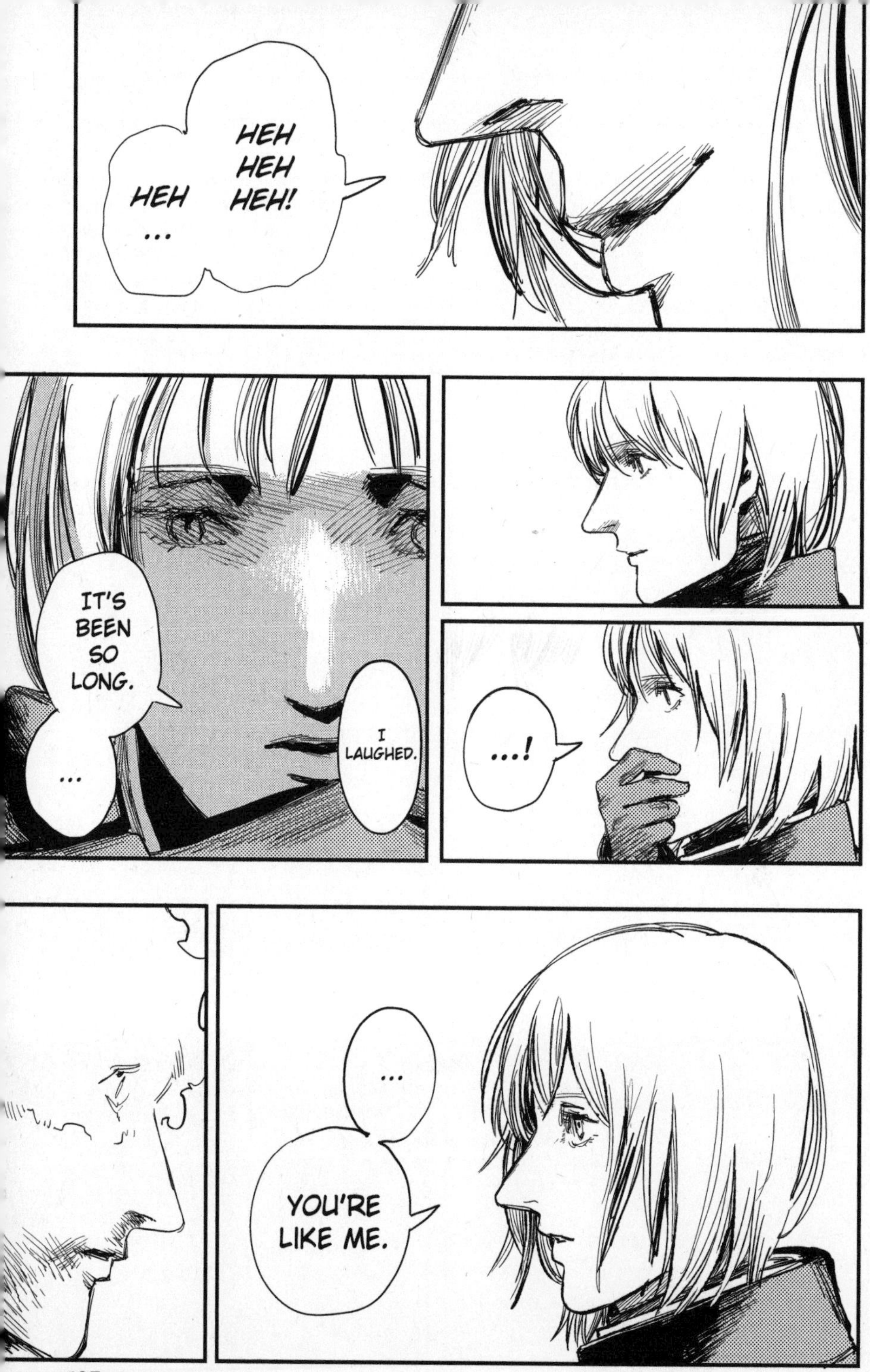
HEH HEH HEH!
HEH ...
...!
IT'S BEEN SO LONG.
...
I LAUGHED.
...
YOU'RE LIKE ME.

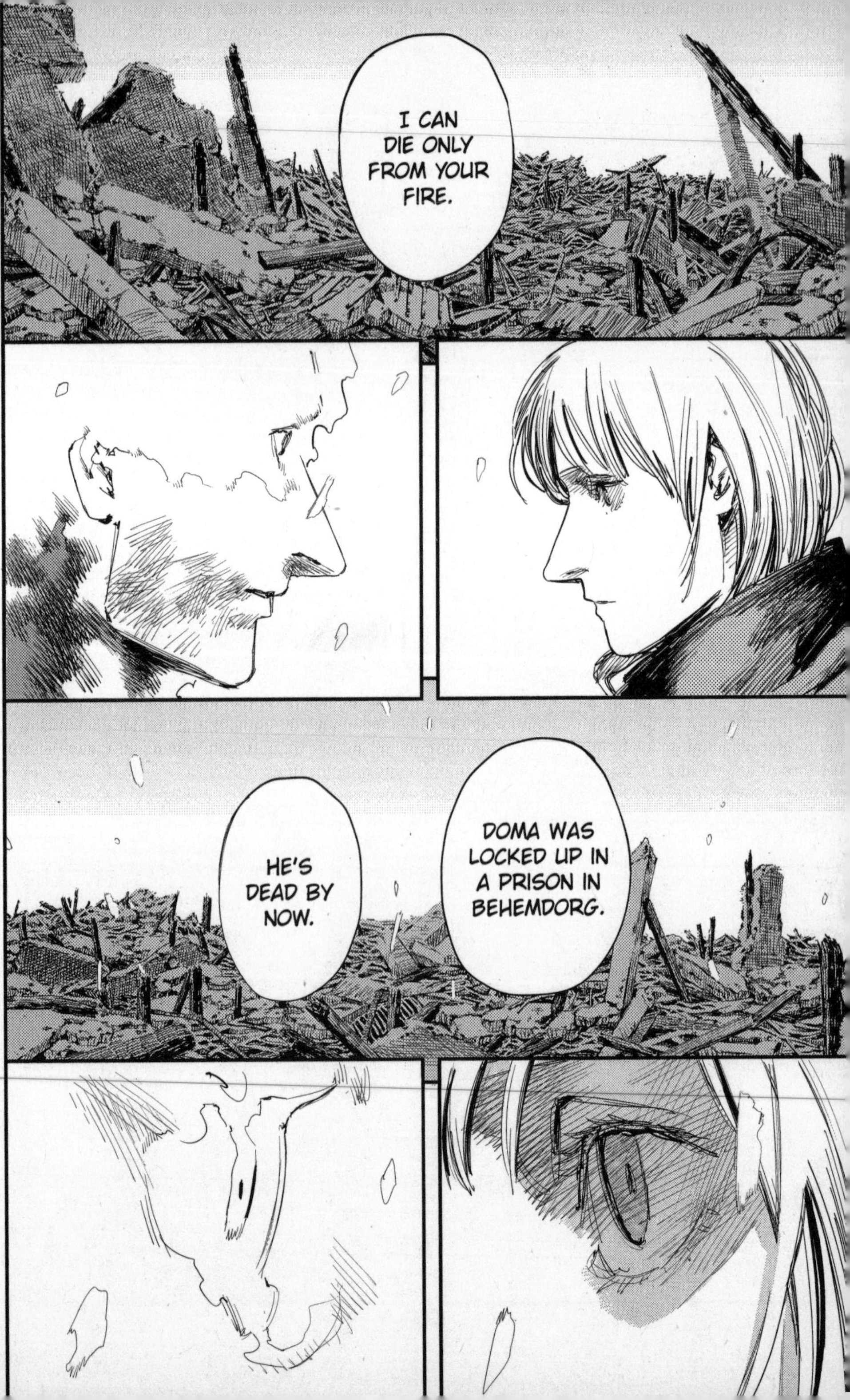
I CAN DIE ONLY FROM YOUR FIRE.
DOMA WAS LOCKED UP IN A PRISON IN BEHEMDORG.
HE'S DEAD BY NOW.

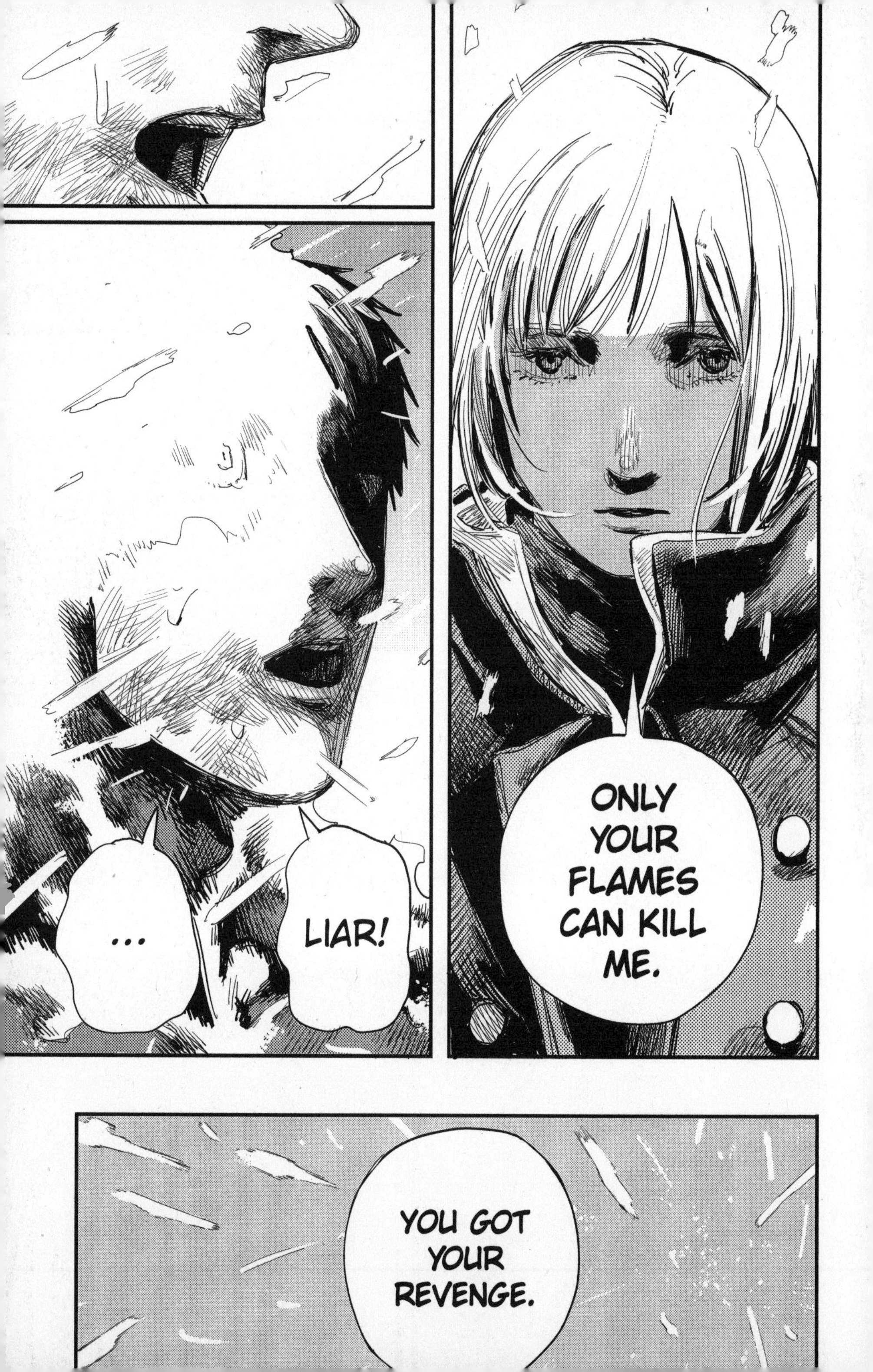
ONLY YOUR FLAMES CAN KILL ME.
LIAR!
...
YOU GOT YOUR REVENGE.

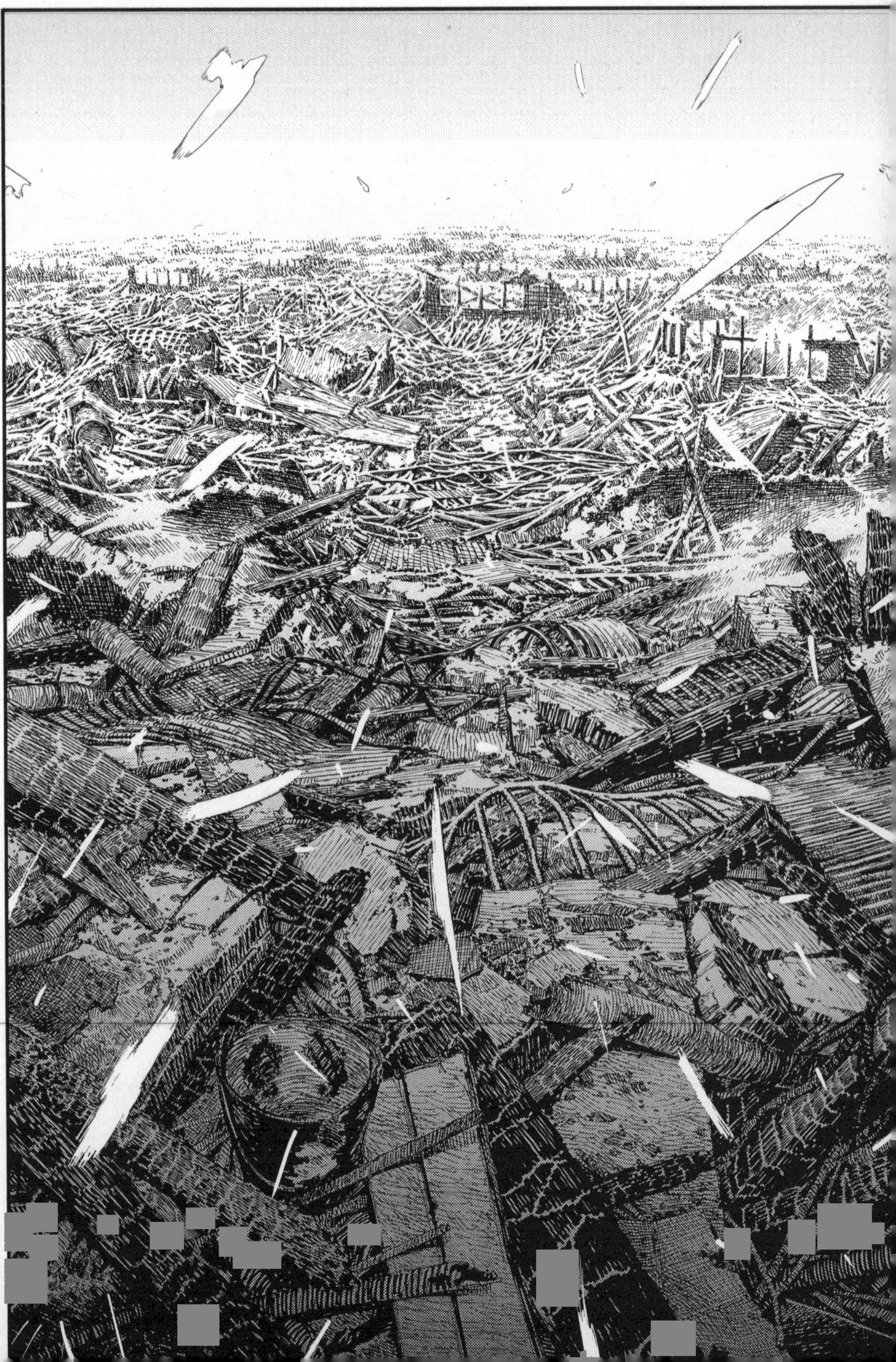

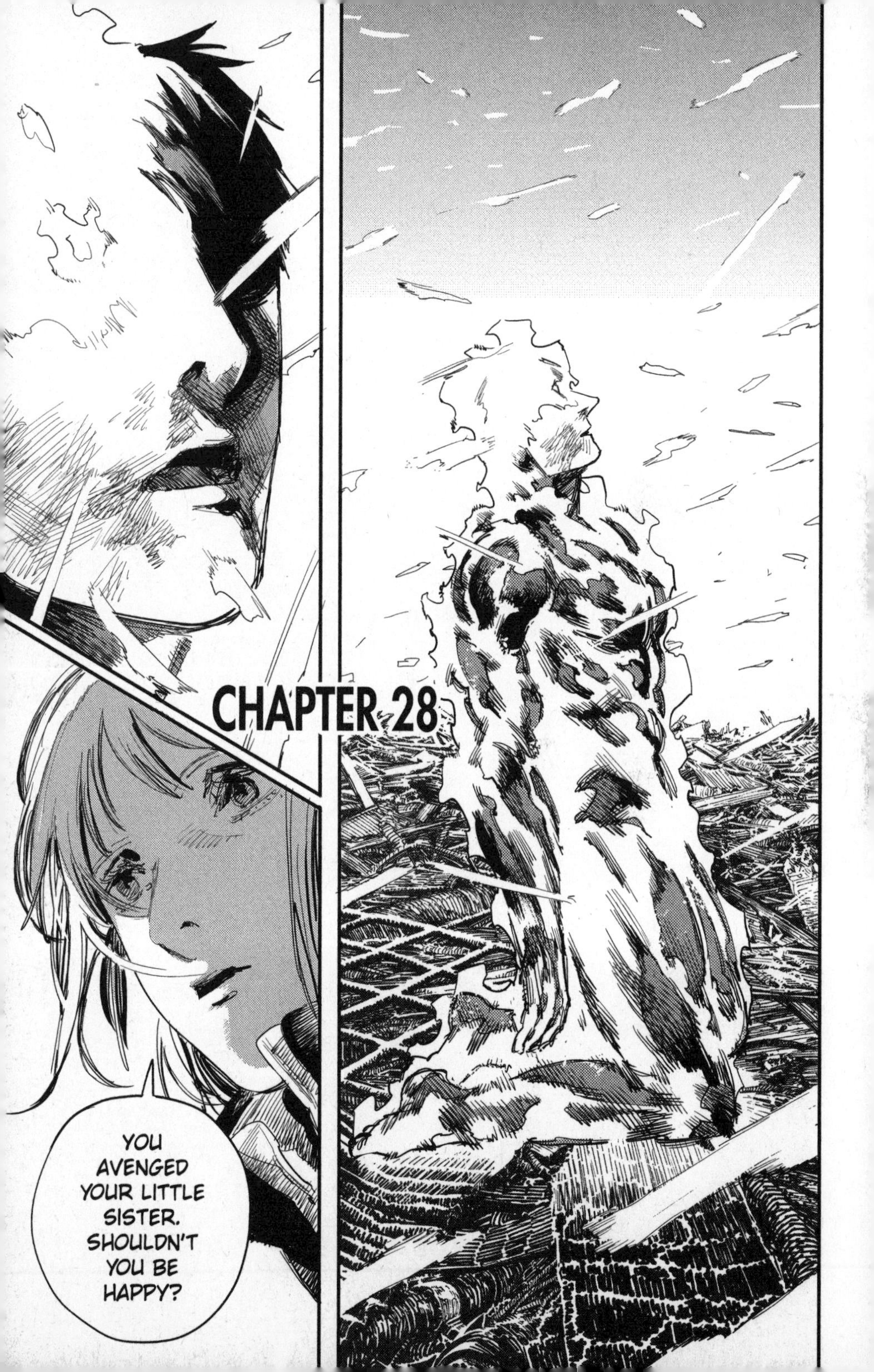
CHAPTER 28
YOU AVENGED YOUR LITTLE SISTER. SHOULDN'T YOU BE HAPPY?

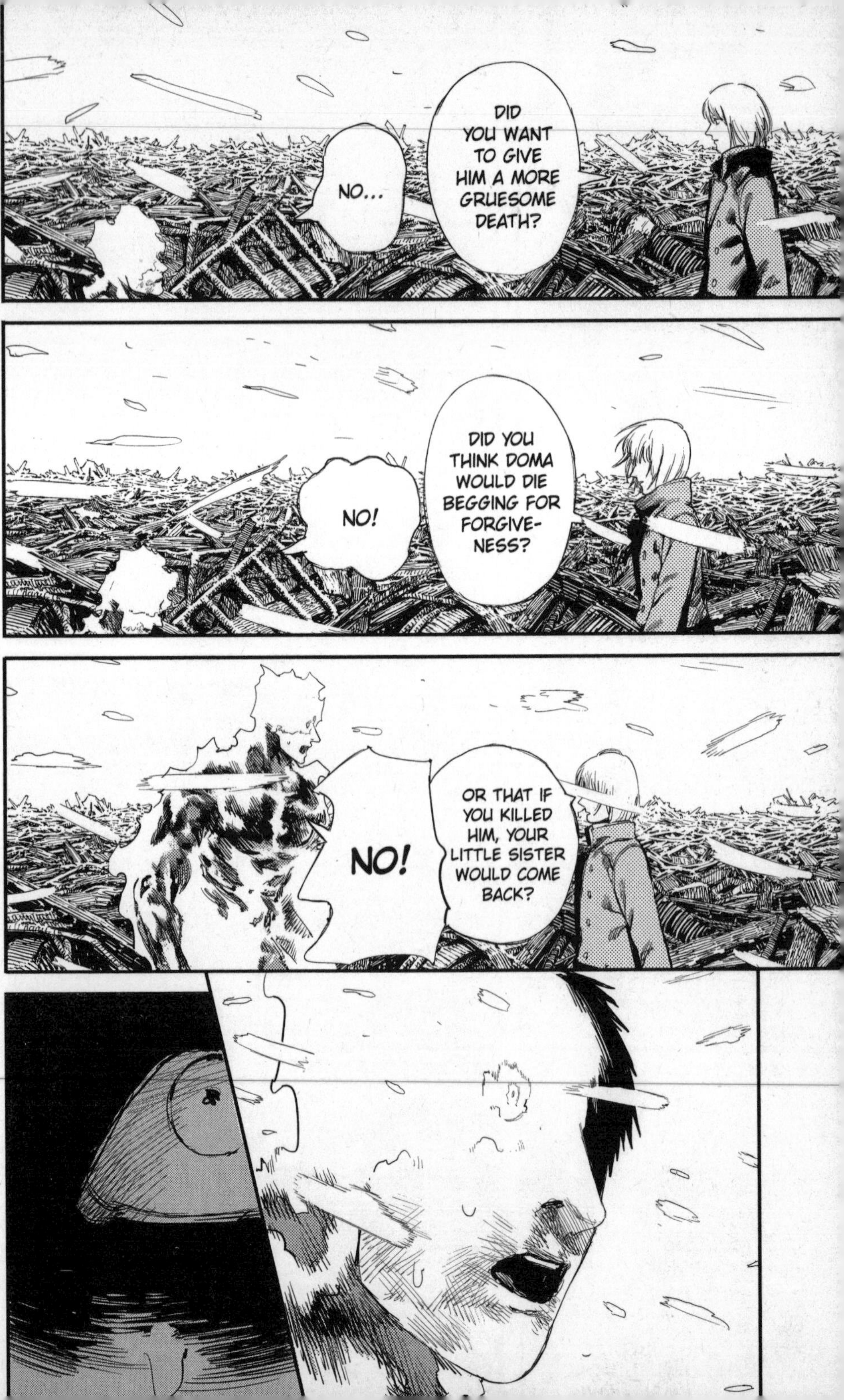
DID YOU WANT TO GIVE HIM A MORE GRUESOME DEATH?
NO...
DID YOU THINK DOMA WOULD DIE BEGGING FOR FORGIVE-NESS?
NO!
OR THAT IF YOU KILLED HIM, YOUR LITTLE SISTER WOULD COME BACK?
NO!

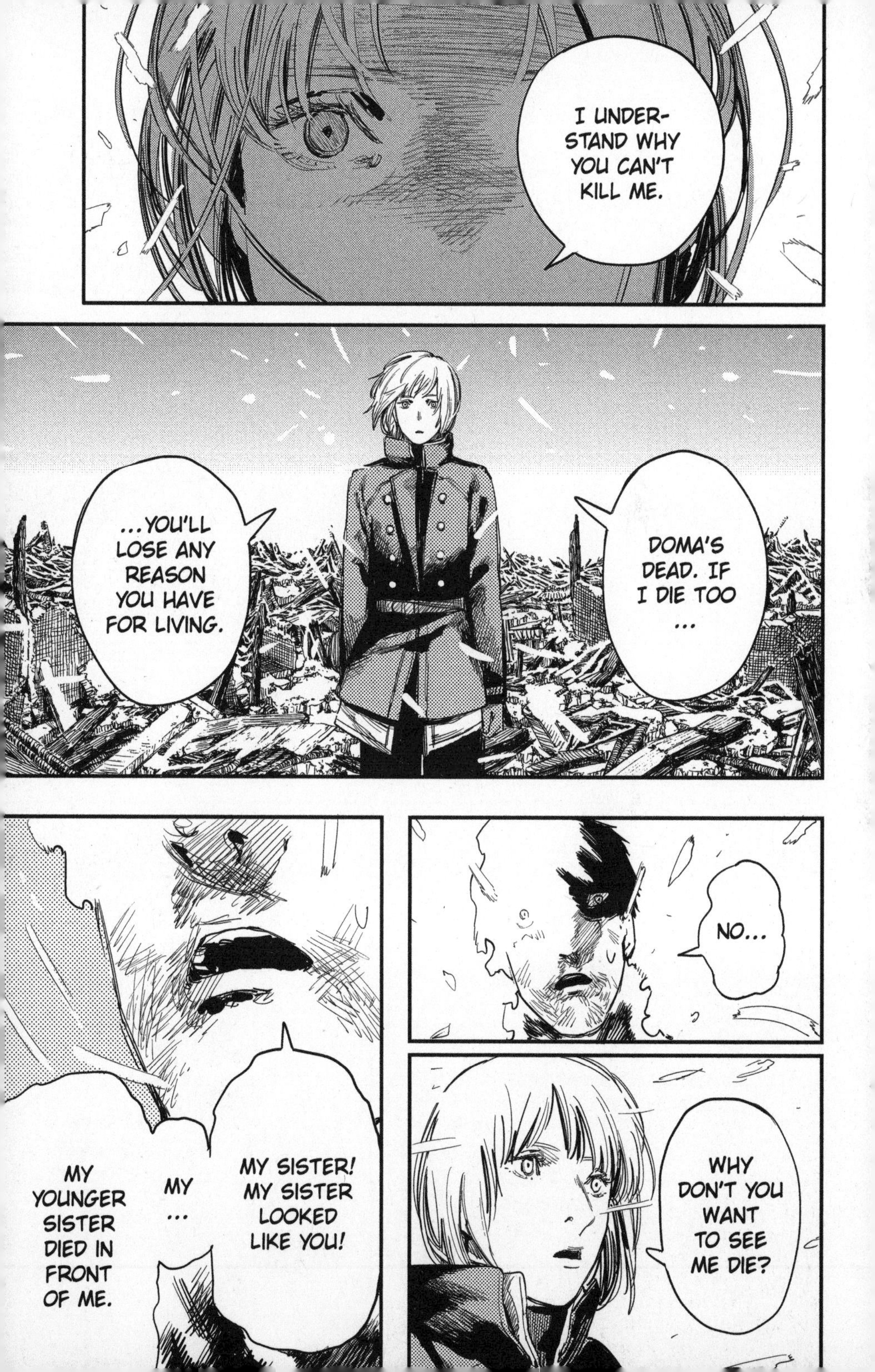
I UNDER-STAND WHY YOU CAN'T KILL ME.
DOMA'S DEAD. IF I DIE TOO ...
...YOU'LL LOSE ANY REASON YOU HAVE FOR LIVING.
NO...
WHY DON'T YOU WANT TO SEE ME DIE?
MY SISTER! MY SISTER LOOKED LIKE YOU!
MY ...
MY YOUNGER SISTER DIED IN FRONT OF ME.

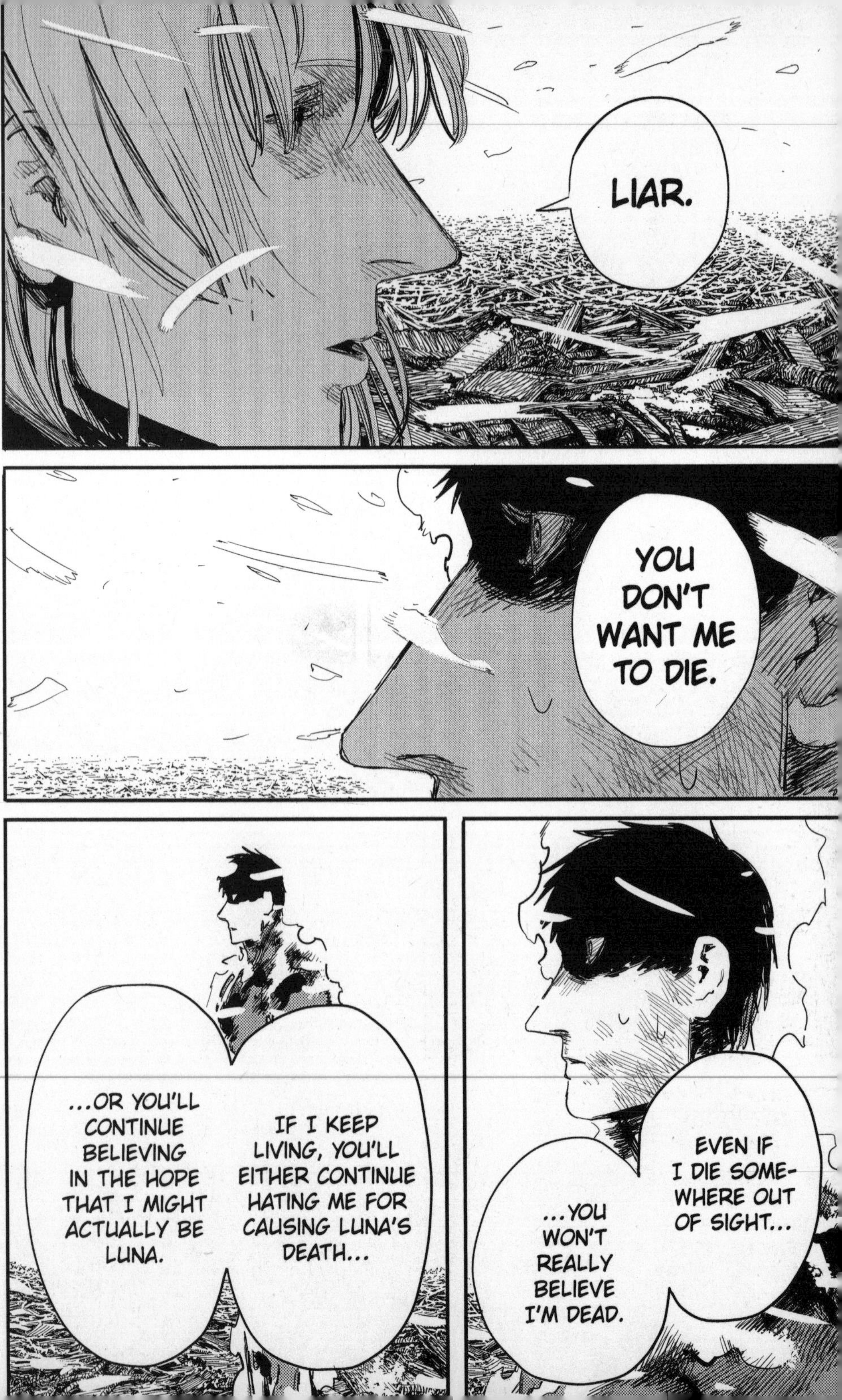
LIAR.
YOU DON'T WANT ME TO DIE.
EVEN IF I DIE SOME-WHERE OUT OF SIGHT...
...YOU WON'T REALLY BELIEVE I'M DEAD.
IF I KEEP LIVING, YOU'LL EITHER CONTINUE HATING ME FOR CAUSING LUNA'S DEATH...
...OR YOU'LL CONTINUE BELIEVING IN THE HOPE THAT I MIGHT ACTUALLY BE LUNA.

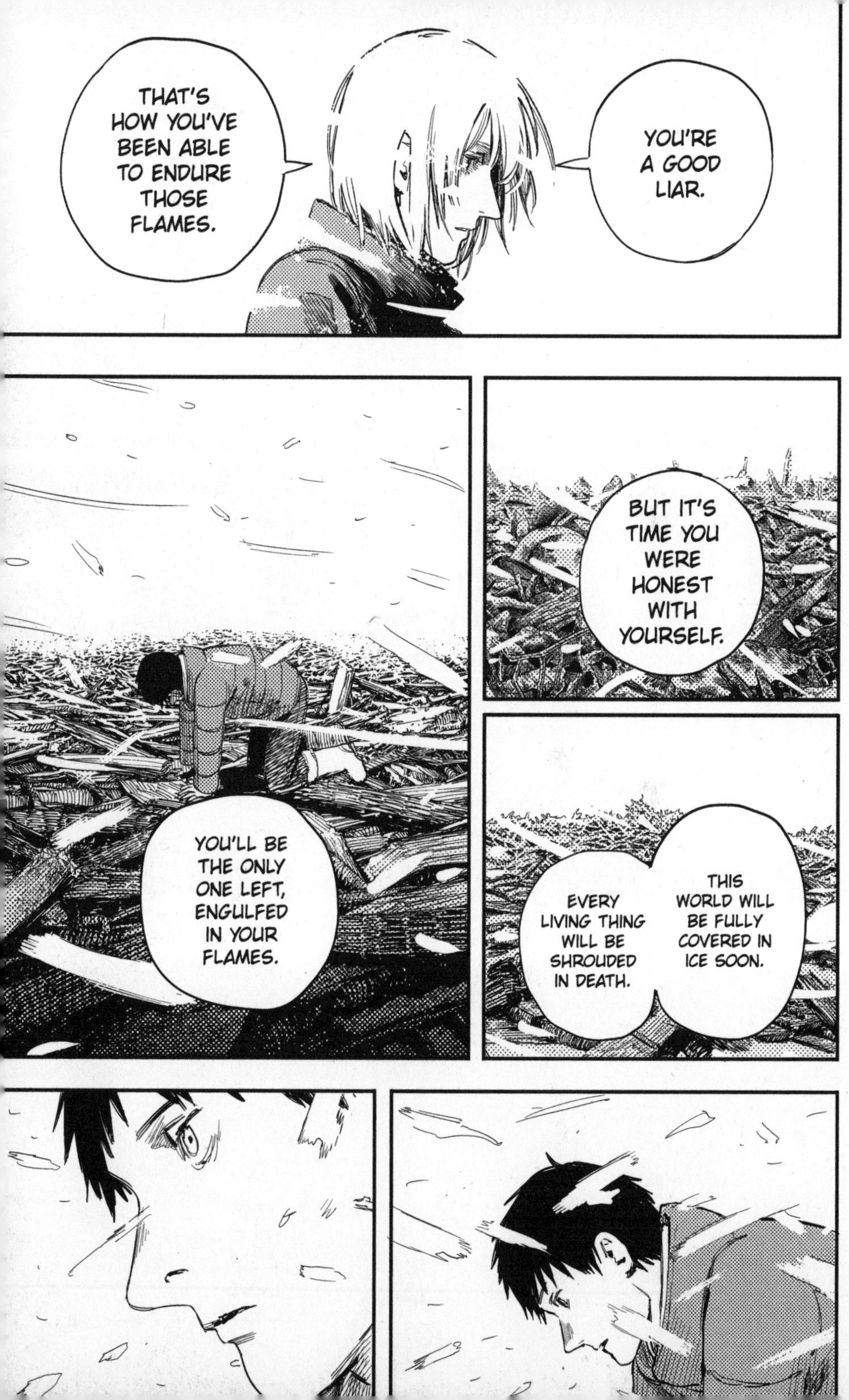
YOU'RE A GOOD LIAR.
THAT'S HOW YOU'VE BEEN ABLE TO ENDURE THOSE FLAMES.
BUT IT'S TIME YOU WERE HONEST WITH YOURSELF.
THIS WORLD WILL BE FULLY COVERED IN ICE SOON.
EVERY LIVING THING WILL BE SHROUDED IN DEATH.
YOU'LL BE THE ONLY ONE LEFT, ENGULFED IN YOUR FLAMES.

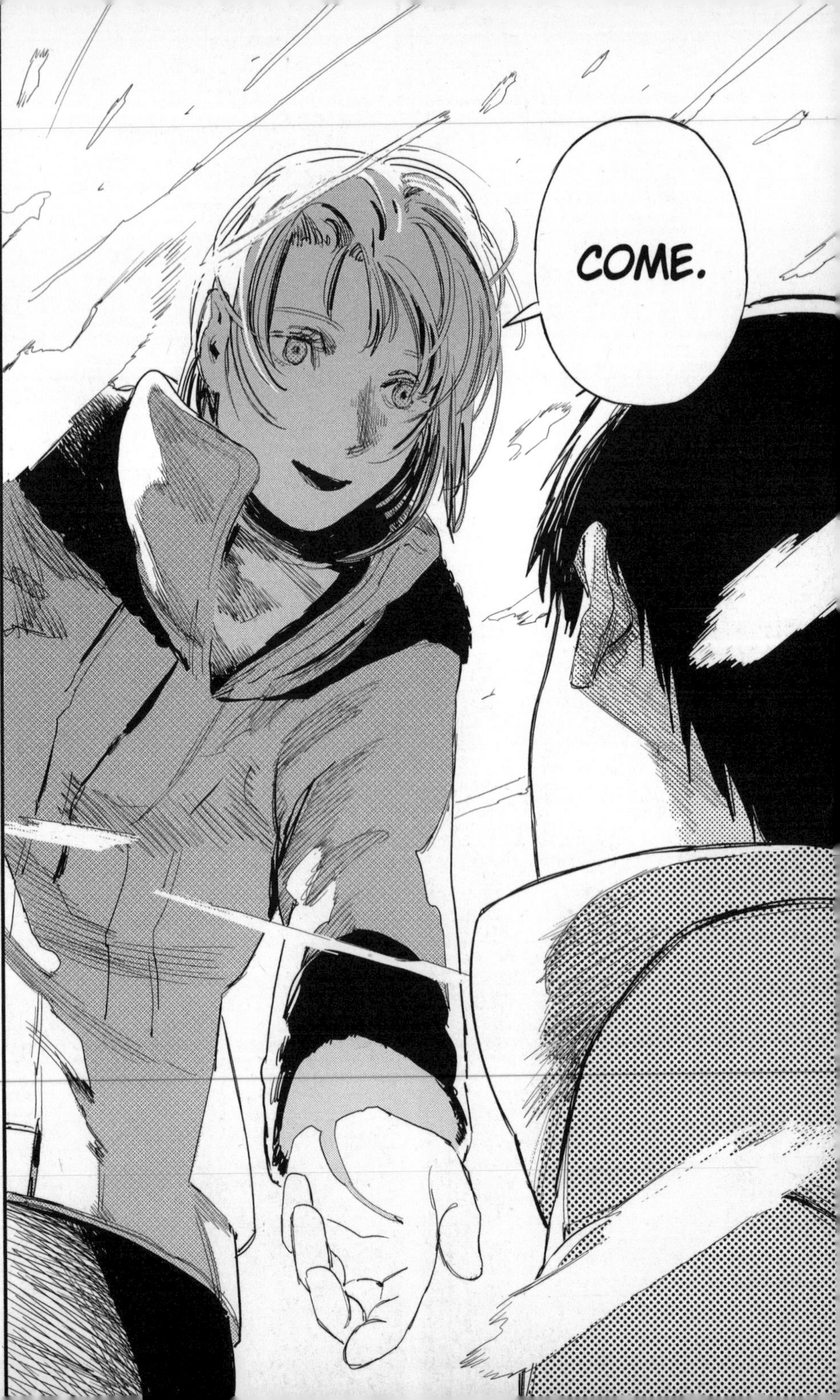
COME.

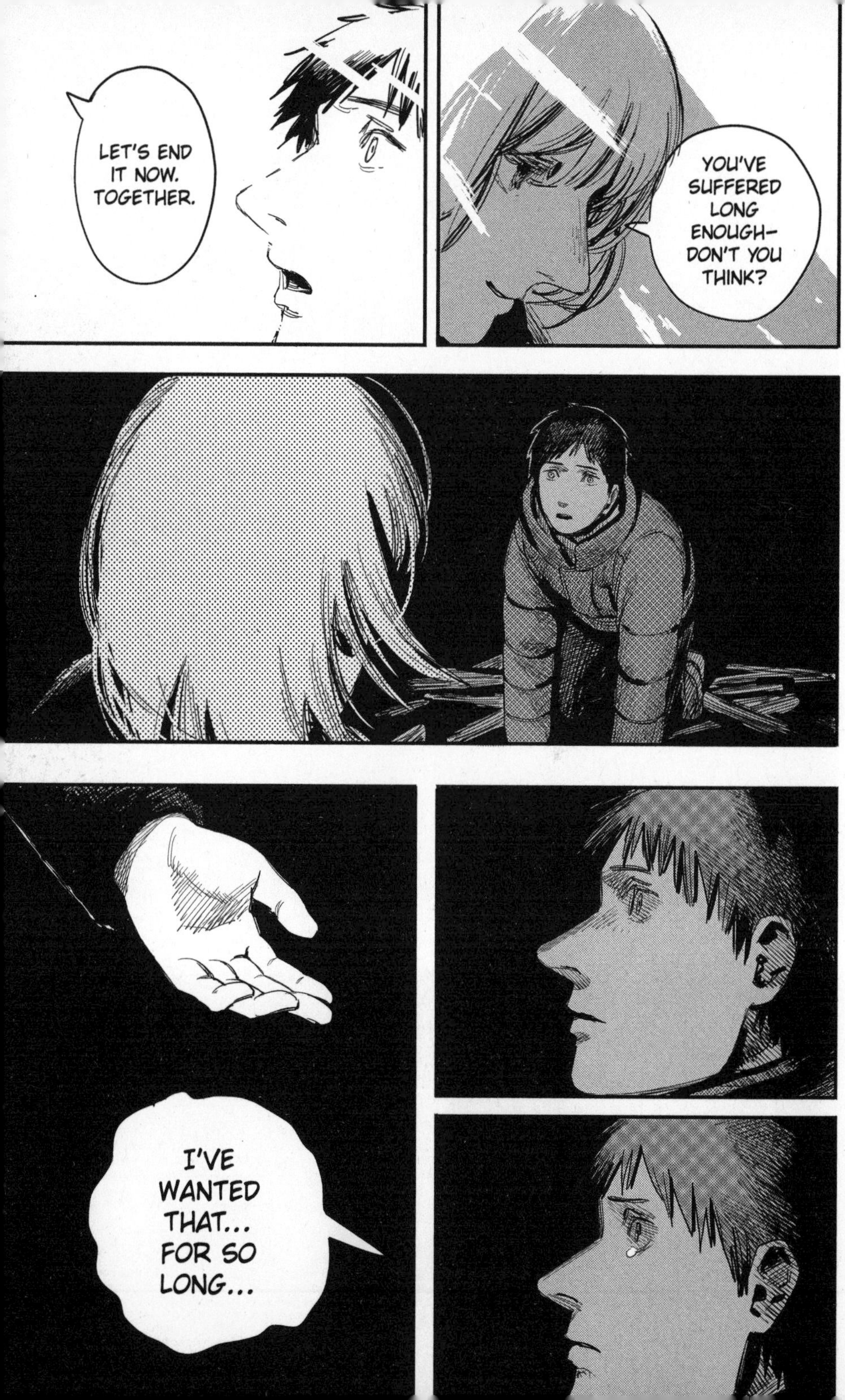
YOU'VE SUFFERED LONG ENOUGH-DON'T YOU THINK?
LET'S END IT NOW. TOGETHER.
I'VE WANTED THAT... FOR SO LONG...

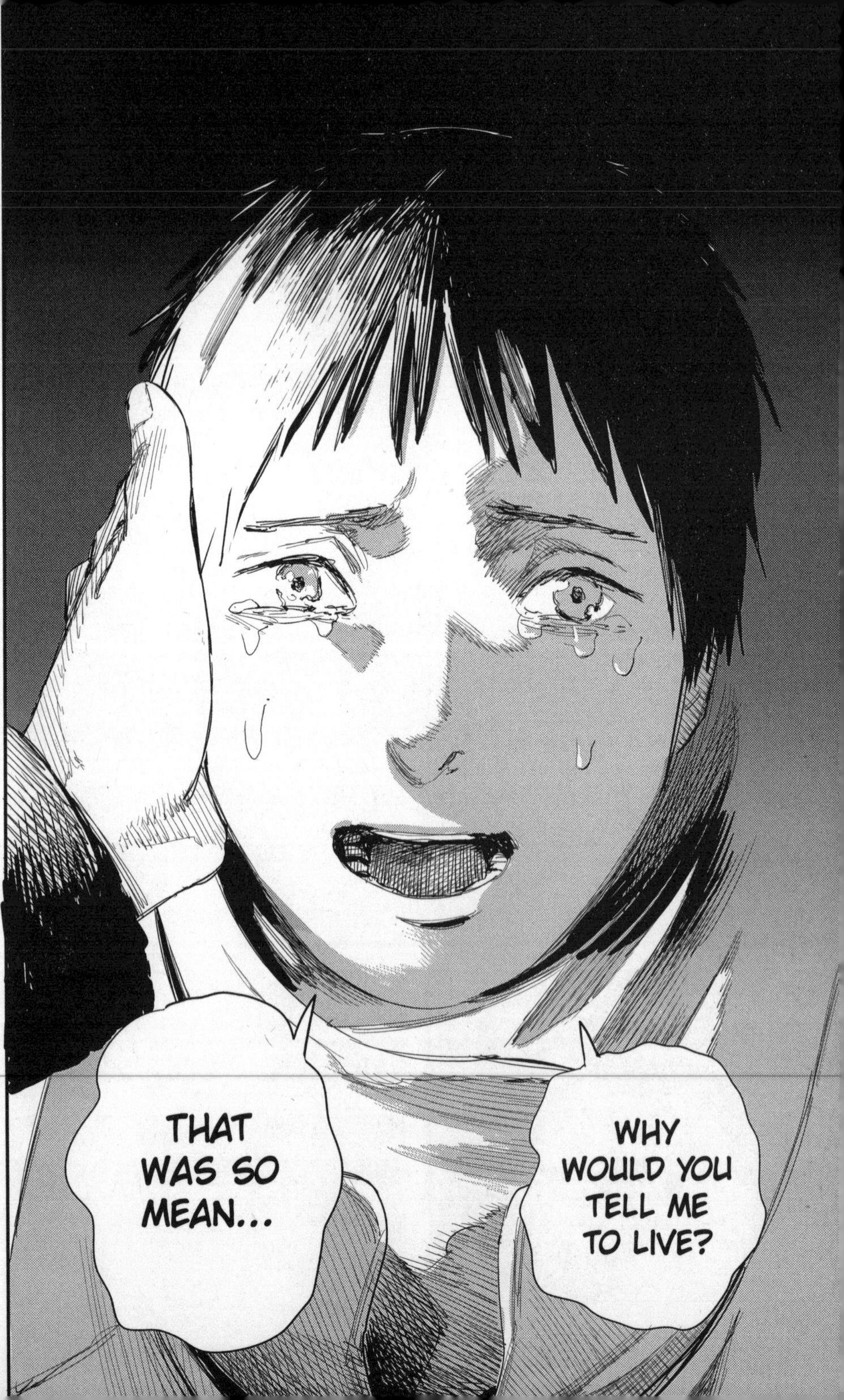
WHY WOULD YOU TELL ME TO LIVE?
THAT WAS SO MEAN...

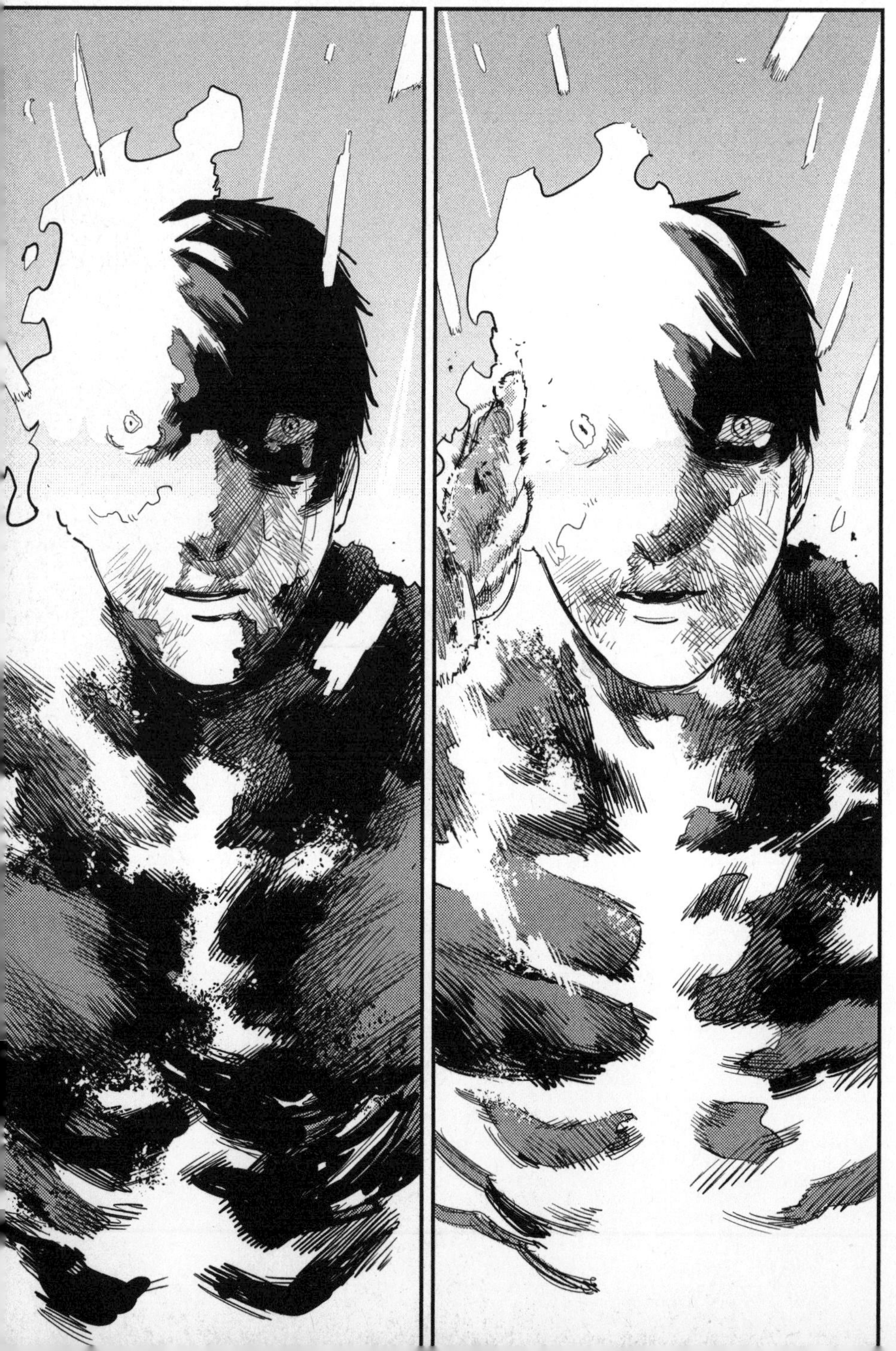

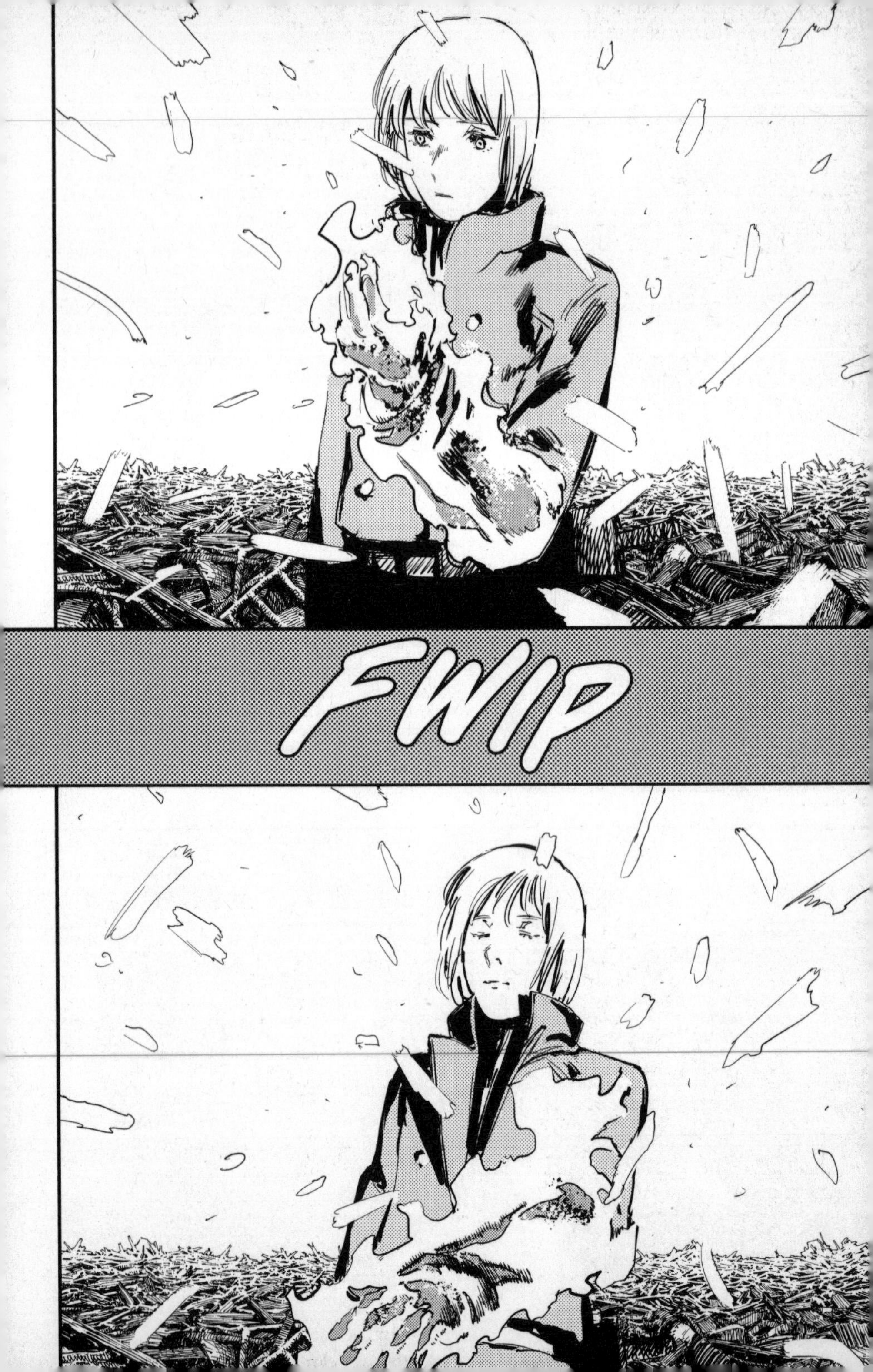
FWIP

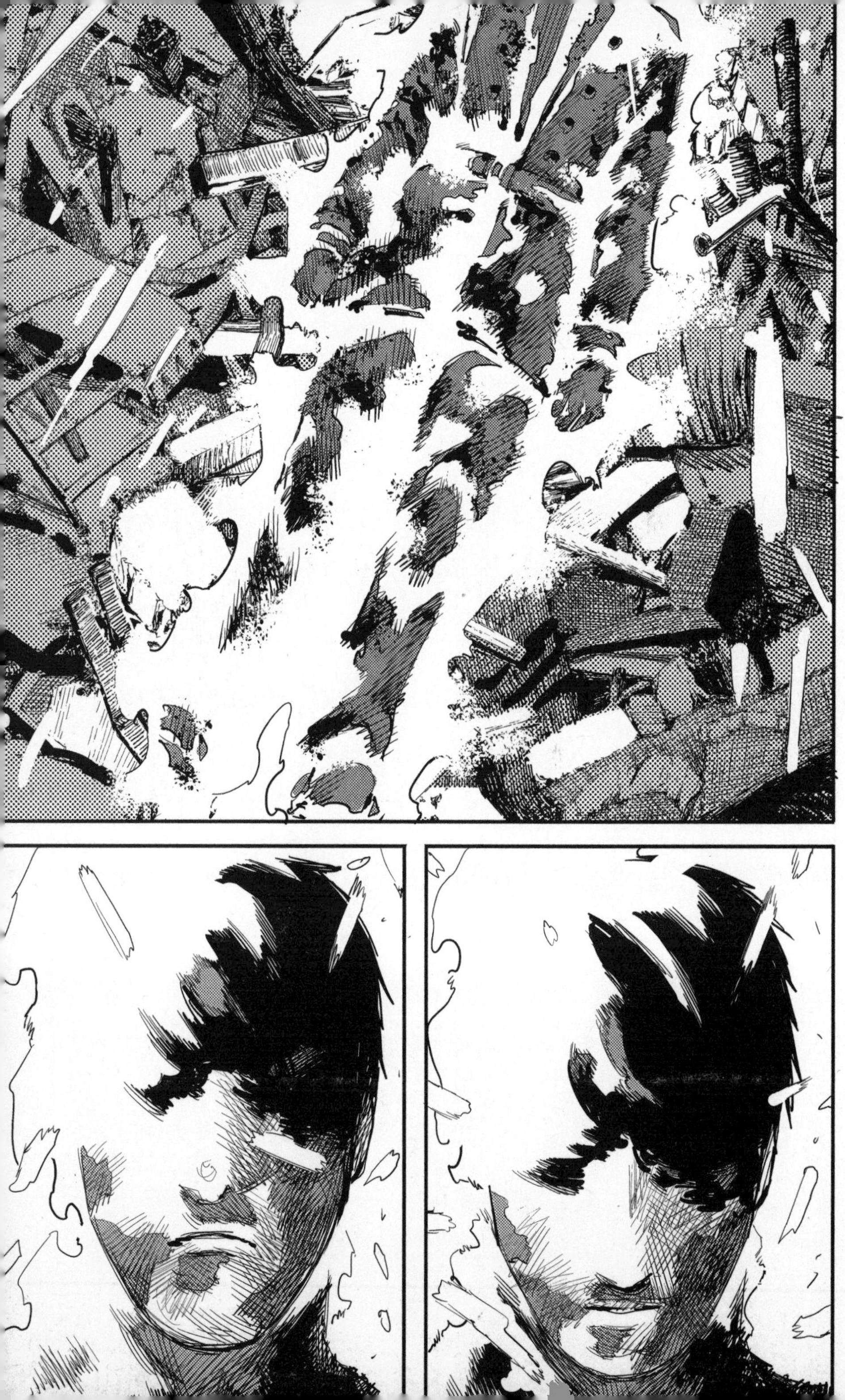

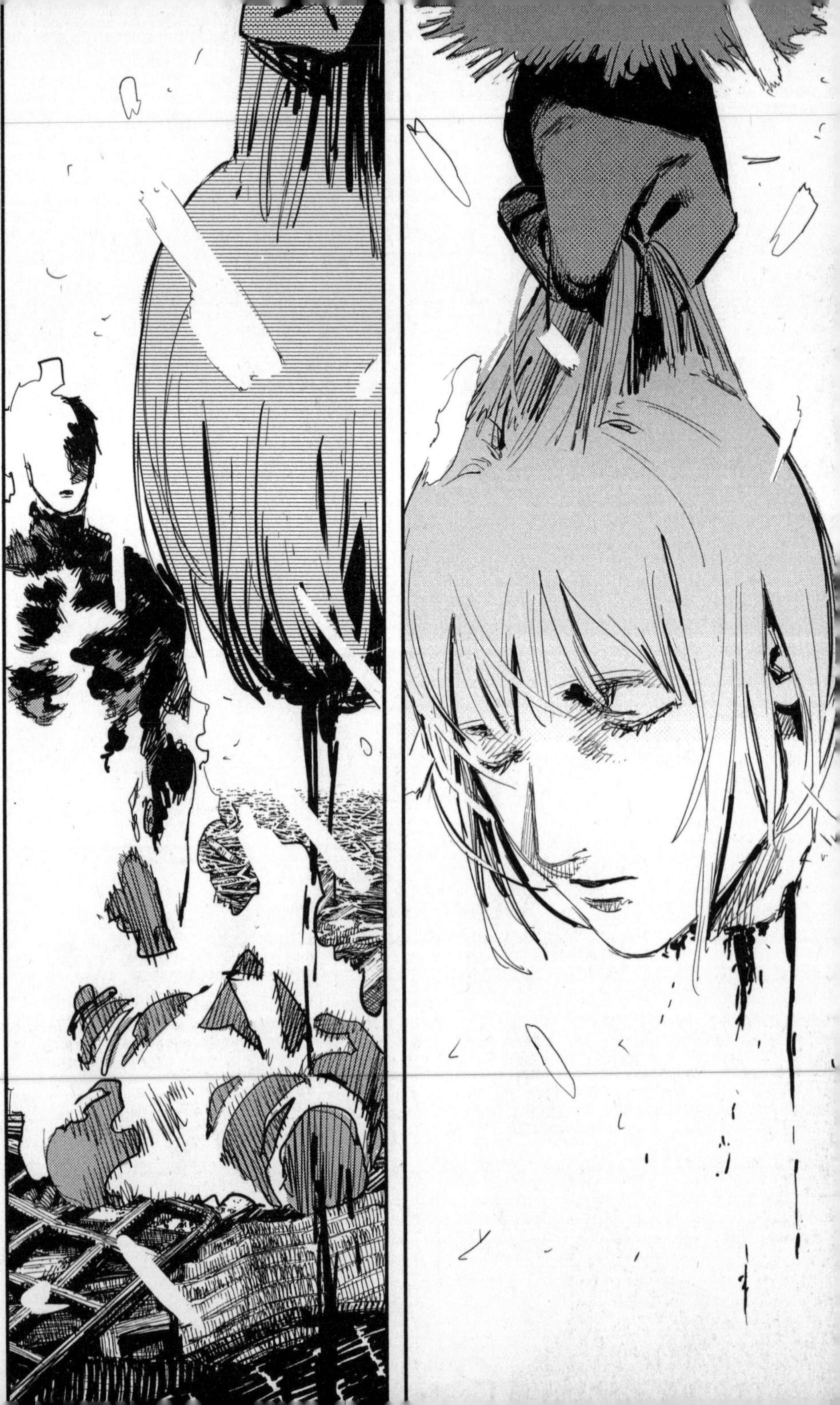

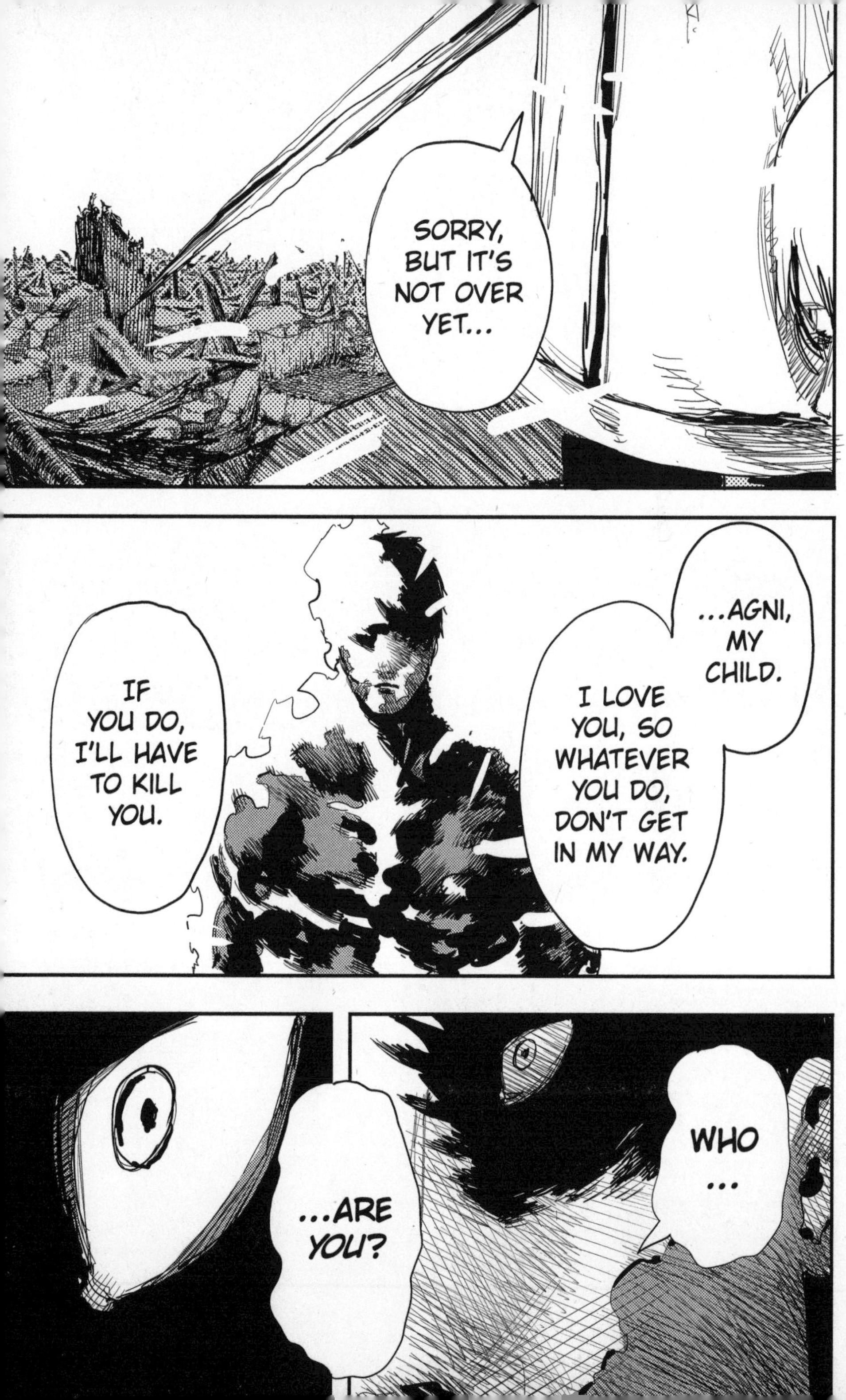
SORRY, BUT IT'S NOT OVER YET...
...AGNI, MY CHILD.
I LOVE YOU, SO WHATEVER YOU DO, DON'T GET IN MY WAY.
IF YOU DO, I'LL HAVE TO KILL YOU.
WHO...
...ARE YOU?

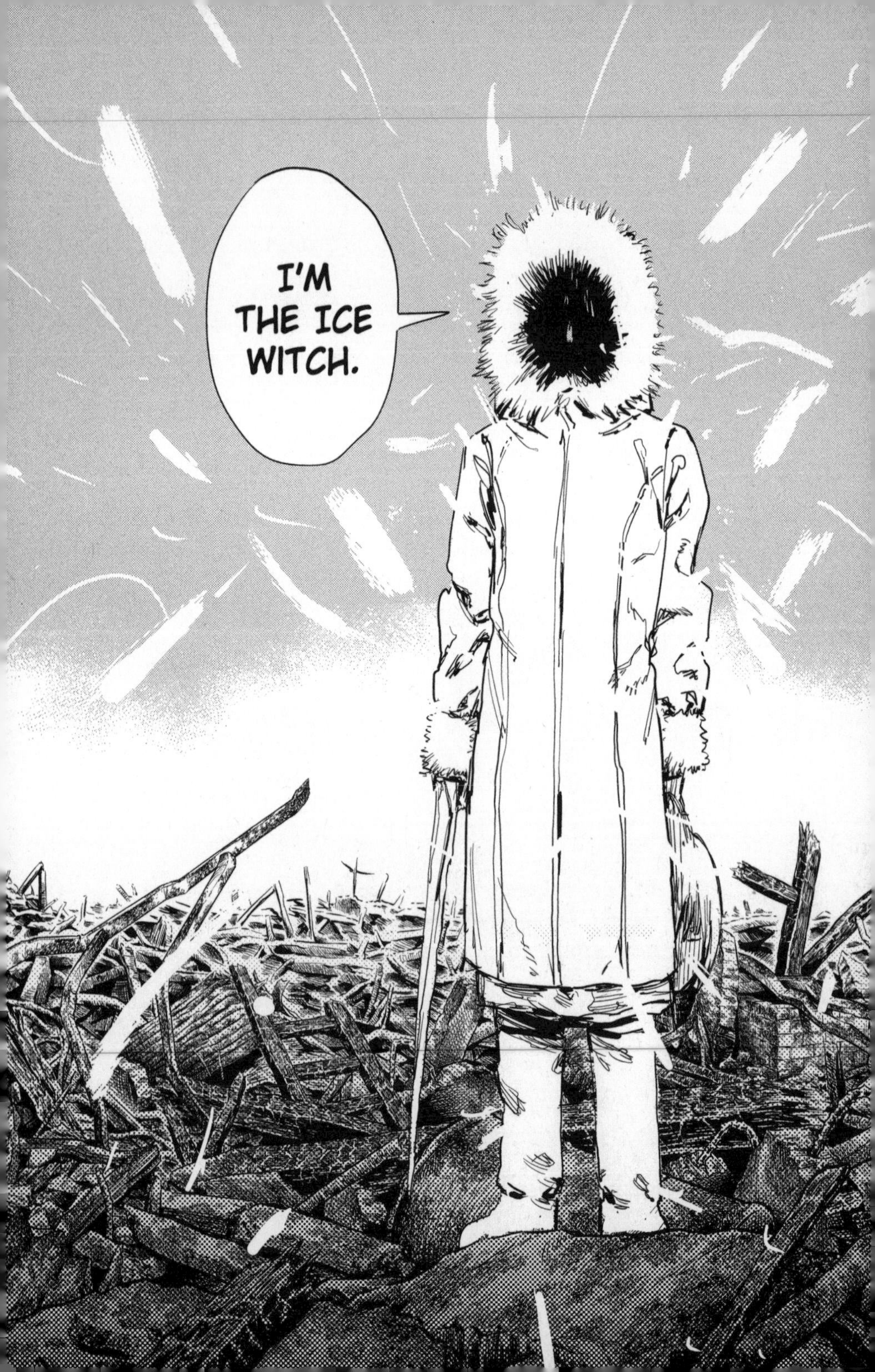
I'M THE ICE WITCH.

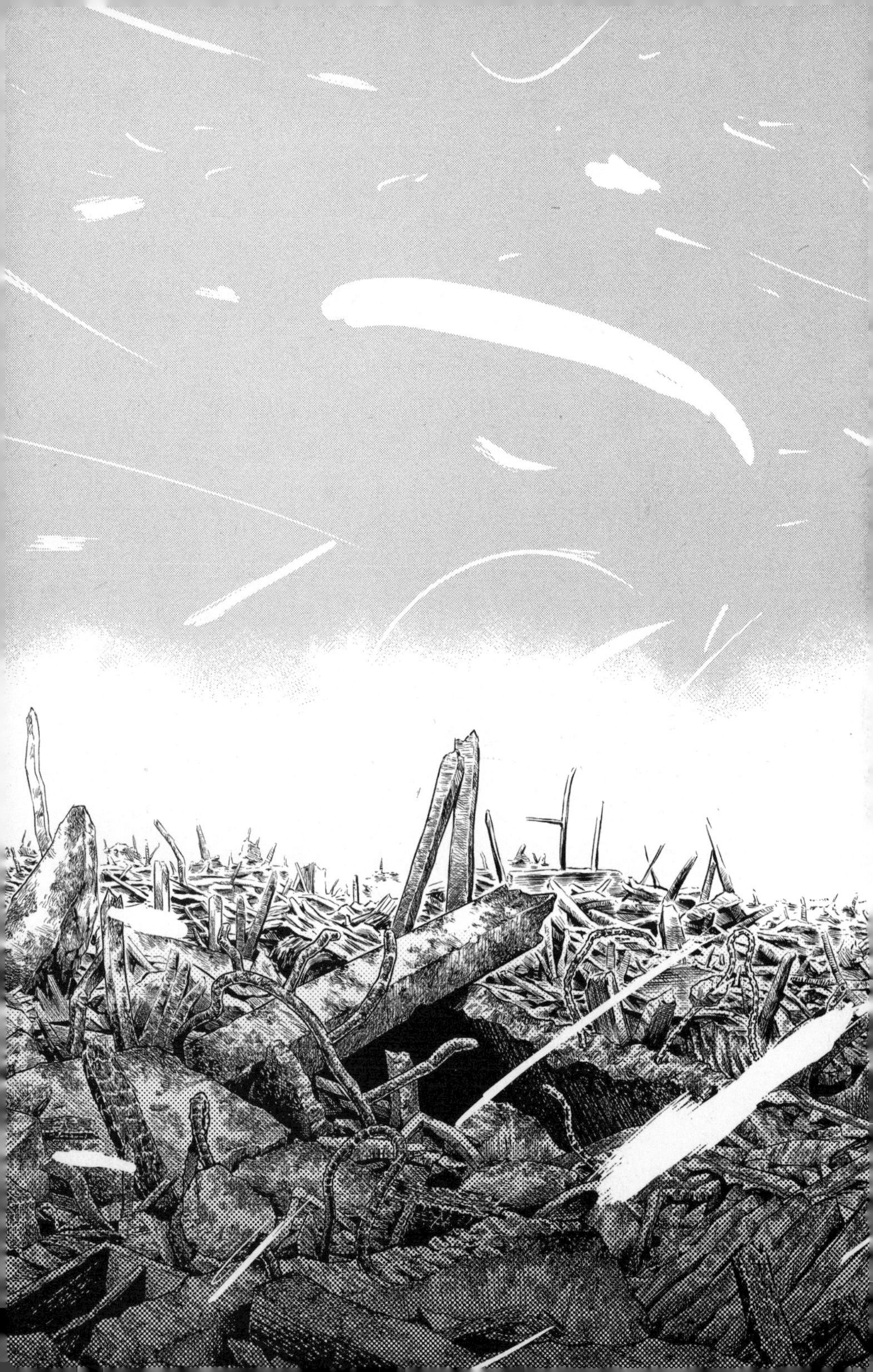

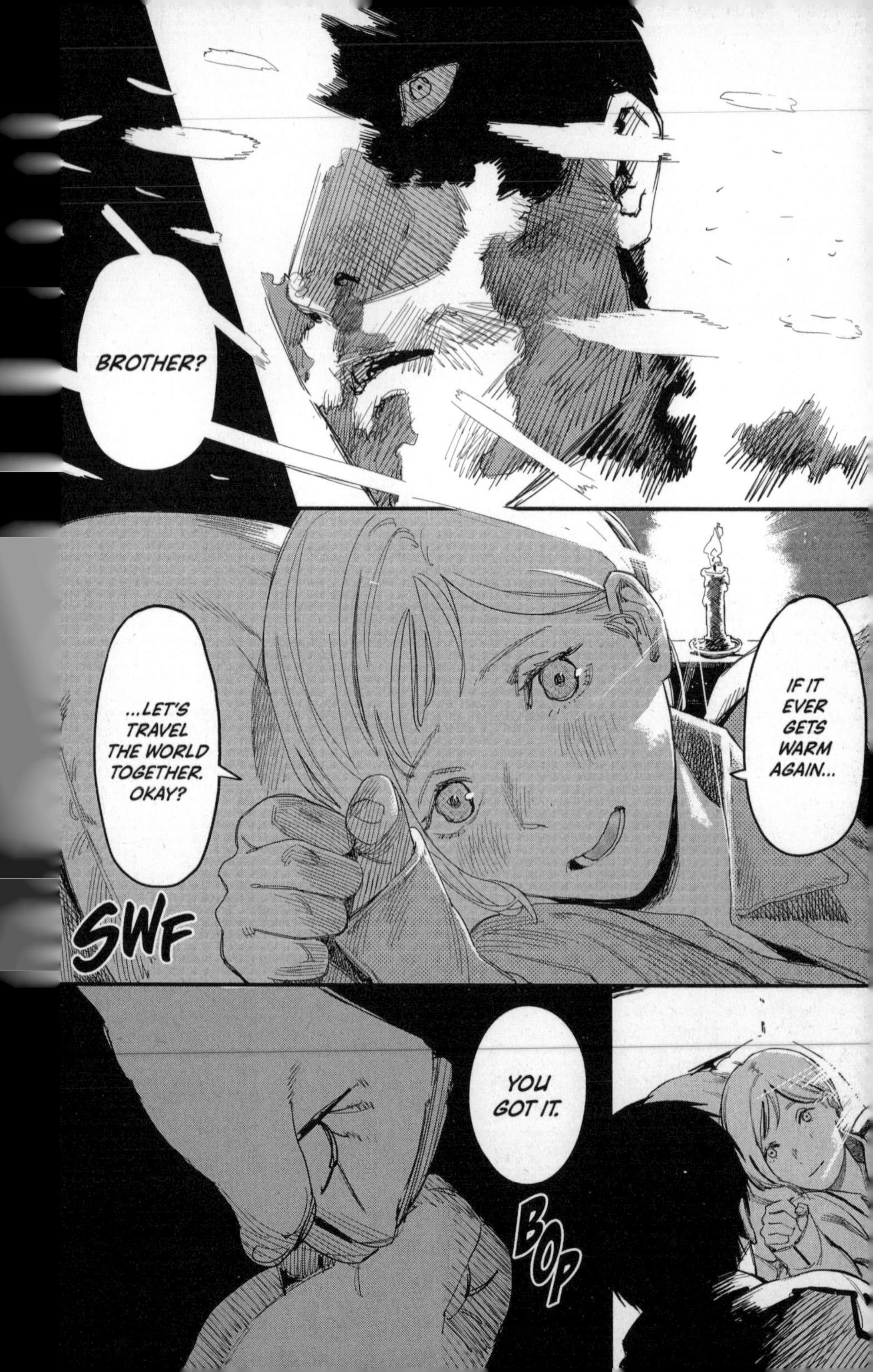
BROTHER?
IF IT EVER GETS WARM AGAIN...
...LET'S TRAVEL THE WORLD TOGETHER. OKAY?
SWF
YOU GOT IT.
BOP

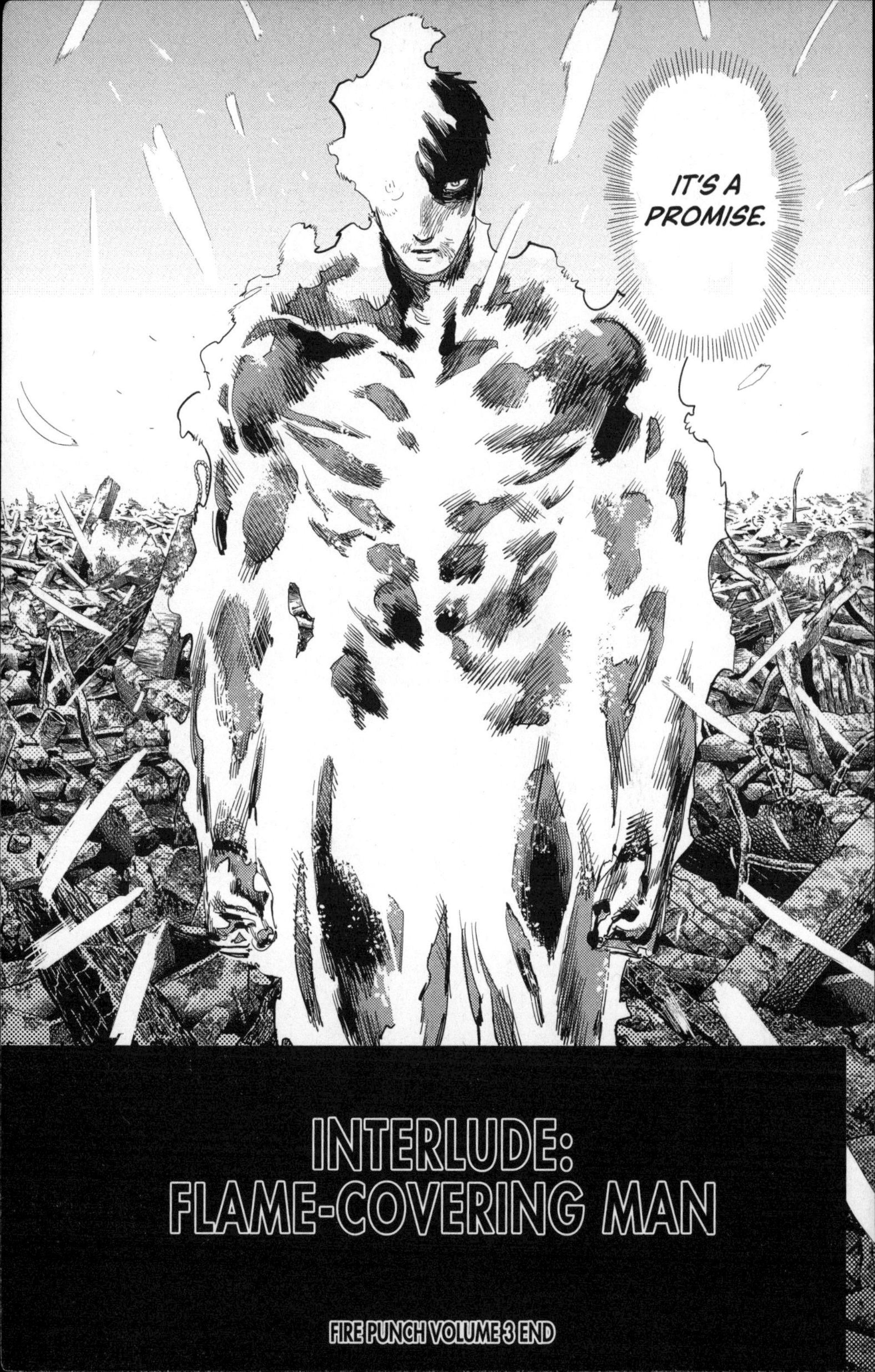
IT'S A PROMISE.

INTERLUDE: FLAME-COVERING MAN

FIRE PUNCH VOLUME 3 END

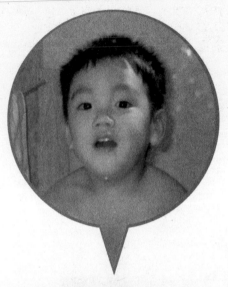

TATSUKI FUJIMOTO

My home has seven storehouses.

Tatsuki Fujimoto won Honorable Mention
in the November 2013 Shueisha Crown
Newcomers' Awards for his debut one-shot
story "Love Is Blind," which was published
in volume 13 of *Jump SQ.19*. Fujimoto's
follow-up series, *Fire Punch*, is the creator's
first English-language release.

FIRE PUNCH

Volume 3
VIZ Signature Edition

Story and Art by Tatsuki Fujimoto

Translation: Christine Dashiell
Touch-Up Art & Lettering: Snir Aharon
Design: Julian [JR] Robinson
Editor: Jennifer LeBlanc

FIRE PUNCH © 2016 by Tatsuki Fujimoto
All rights reserved.
First published in Japan in 2016 by SHUEISHA Inc., Tokyo.
English translation rights arranged by SHUEISHA Inc.

The stories, characters and incidents mentioned in
this publication are entirely fictional.

Printed in the U.S.A.

Published by VIZ Media, LLC
P.O. Box 77010
San Francisco, CA 94107

10 9 8 7 6 5 4 3 2 1
First printing, July 2018

PARENTAL ADVISORY
FIRE PUNCH is rated M for Mature. Contains
graphic violence and sexual situations, and is
recommended for mature readers.

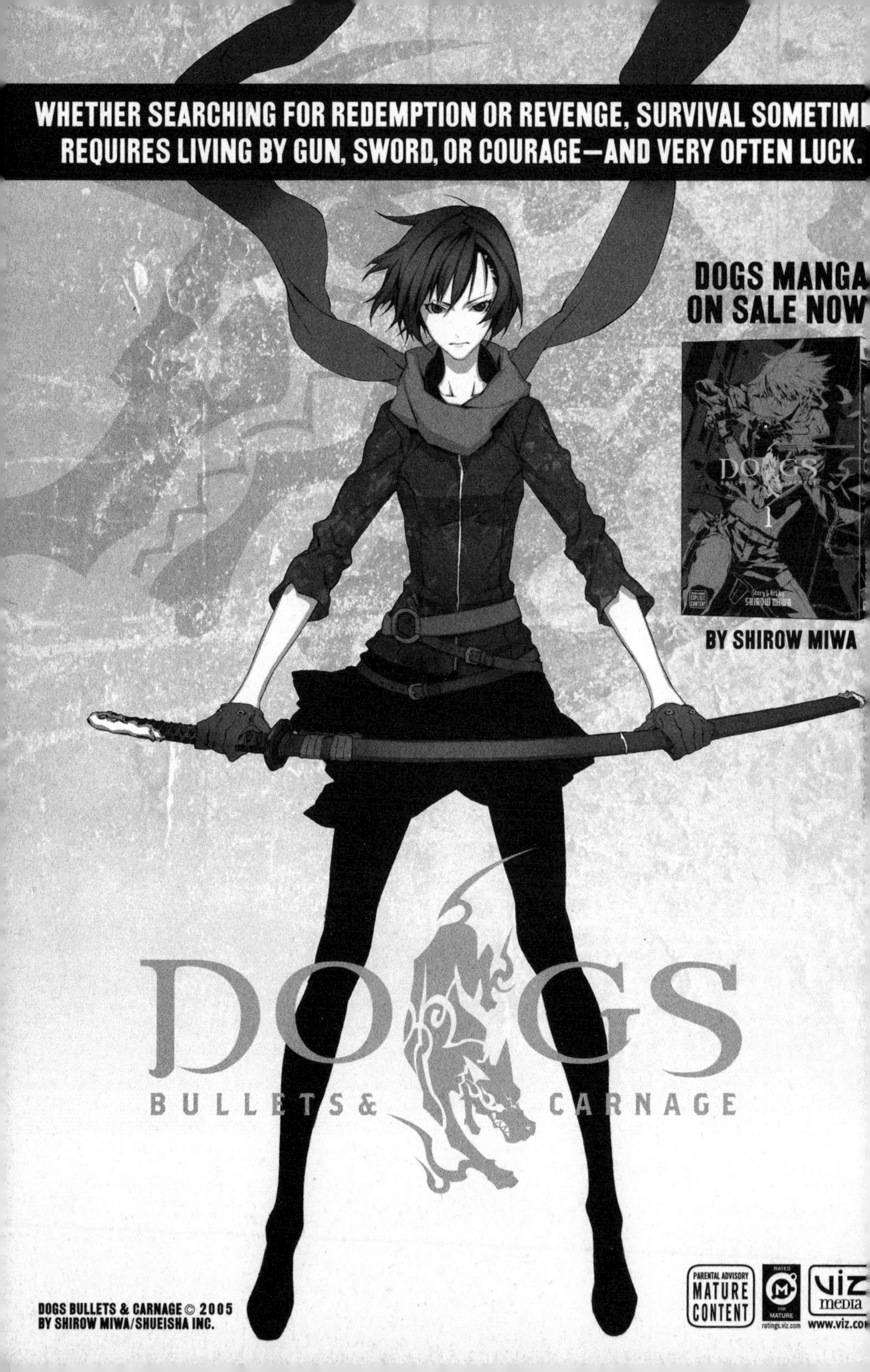
WHETHER SEARCHING FOR REDEMPTION OR REVENGE, SURVIVAL SOMETIM
REQUIRES LIVING BY GUN, SWORD, OR COURAGE—AND VERY OFTEN LUCK.
DOGS MANGA
ON SALE NOW
DOGS
1
BY SHIROW MIWA
DOGS
BULLETS & CARNAGE
DOGS BULLETS & CARNAGE © 2005
BY SHIROW MIWA/SHUEISHA INC.
PARENTAL ADVISORY
MATURE
CONTENT
RATED
M
FOR
MATURE
ratings.viz.com
viz
media
www.viz.co

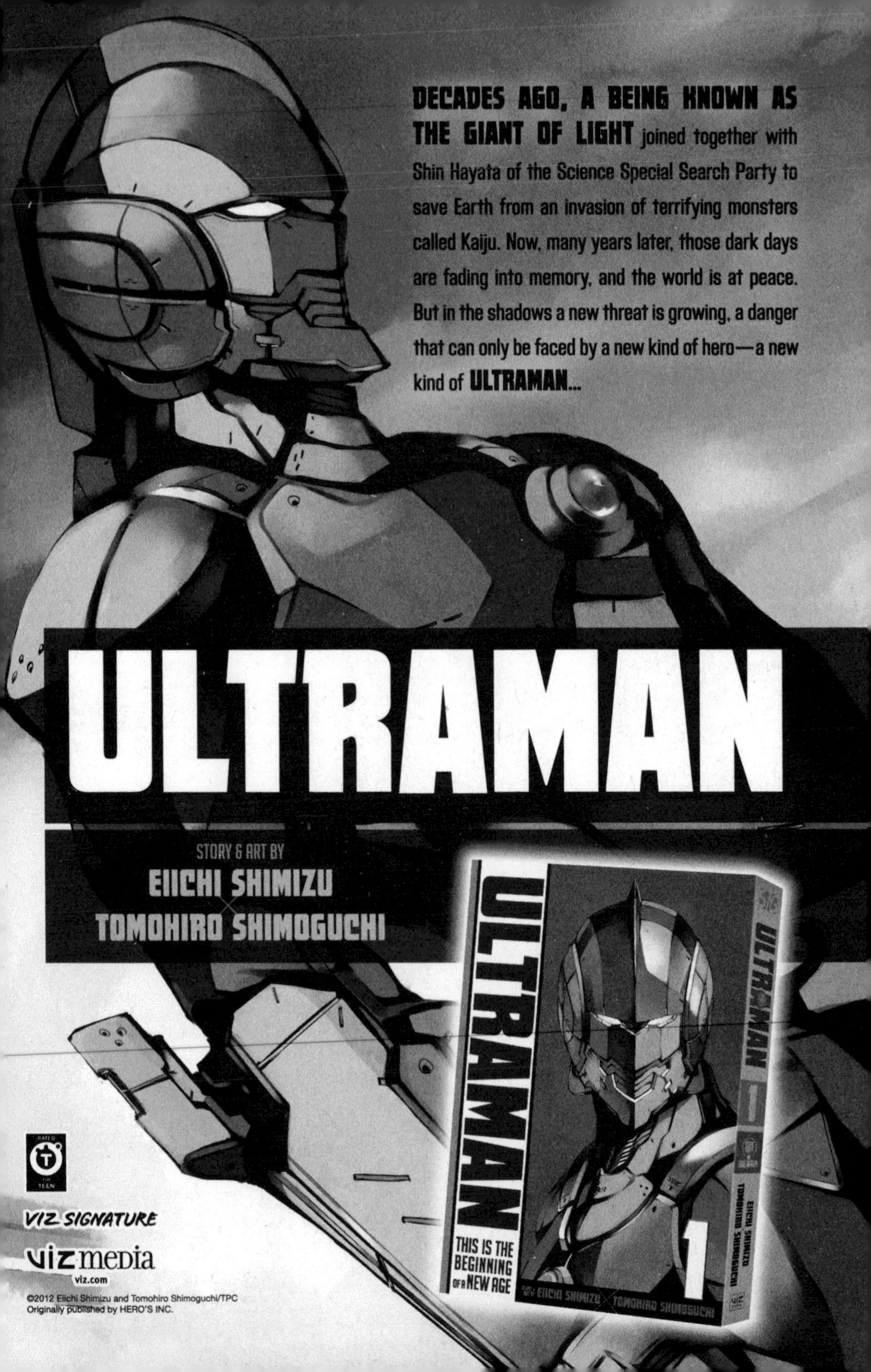
DECADES AGO, A BEING KNOWN AS THE GIANT OF LIGHT joined together with Shin Hayata of the Science Special Search Party to save Earth from an invasion of terrifying monsters called Kaiju. Now, many years later, those dark days are fading into memory, and the world is at peace. But in the shadows a new threat is growing, a danger that can only be faced by a new kind of hero—a new kind of ULTRAMAN...
ULTRAMAN
STORY & ART BY
EIICHI SHIMIZU × TOMOHIRO SHIMOGUCHI
ULTRAMAN
THIS IS THE BEGINNING OF A NEW AGE
1
EIICHI SHIMIZU × TOMOHIRO SHIMOGUCHI
RATED T FOR TEEN
VIZ SIGNATURE
viz media
viz.com
©2012 Eiichi Shimizu and Tomohiro Shimoguchi/TPC
Originally published by HERO'S INC.

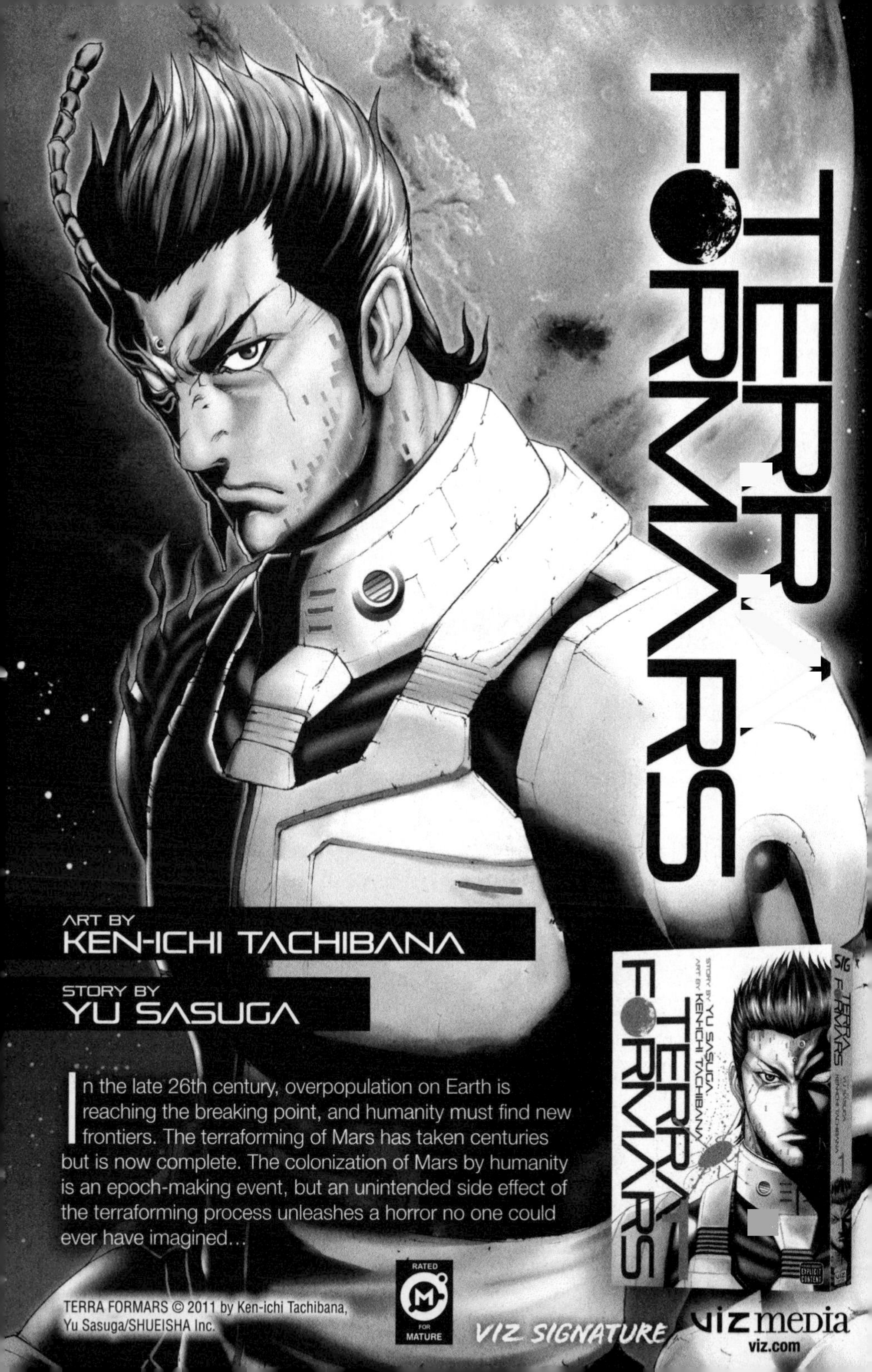
TERRA FORMARS
ART BY
KEN-ICHI TACHIBANA
STORY BY
YU SASUGA
In the late 26th century, overpopulation on Earth is reaching the breaking point, and humanity must find new frontiers. The terraforming of Mars has taken centuries but is now complete. The colonization of Mars by humanity is an epoch-making event, but an unintended side effect of the terraforming process unleashes a horror no one could ever have imagined…
STORY BY YU SASUGA
ART BY KEN-ICHI TACHIBANA
TERRA FORMARS
RATED M FOR MATURE
TERRA FORMARS © 2011 by Ken-ichi Tachibana, Yu Sasuga/SHUEISHA Inc.
VIZ SIGNATURE
viz media
viz.com

UZUMAKI

Story and Art by **JUNJI ITO**

SPIRALS... THIS TOWN IS CONTAMINATED WITH SPIRALS...

Kurouzu-cho, a small fogbound town on the coast of Japan, is cursed. According to Shuichi Saito, the withdrawn boyfriend of teenager Kirie Goshima, their town is haunted not by a person or being but by a pattern: uzumaki, the spiral, the hypnotic secret shape of the world. It manifests itself in everything from seashells and whirlpools in water to the spiral marks on people's bodies, the insane obsessions of Shuichi's father and the voice from the cochlea in our inner ear. As the madness spreads, the inhabitants of Kurouzu-cho are pulled ever deeper into a whirlpool from which there is no return!

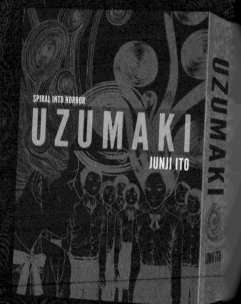

SPIRAL INTO HORROR

UZUMAKI
JUNJI ITO

UZUMAKI

JUNJI ITO

A masterpiece of horror manga, now available in a
DELUXE HARDCOVER EDITION!

GOODNIGHT PUNPUN

Story and Art by INIO ASANO

A dark coming-of-age tale
where slice-of-life slices back.

vizmedia
www.viz.com

VIZ SIGNATURE

OYASUMI PUNPUN © 2007 Inio ASANO/SHOGAKUKAN

Hey! You're Reading in the Wrong Direction!

This is the *end* of this graphic novel!

To properly enjoy this VIZ graphic novel, please turn it around and begin reading from *right to left*. Unlike English, Japanese is read right to left, so Japanese comics are read in reverse order from the way English comics are typically read.

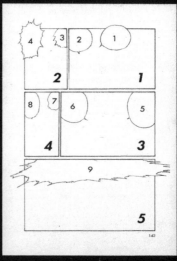

Follow the action this way

This book has been printed in the original Japanese format in order to preserve the orientation of the original artwork. Have fun with it!